THE PHILOSOPHY OF LEIBNIZ

Bust of Gottfried Wilhelm Leibniz by Johann Gottfried Schmidt (ca. 1788)

THE PHILOSOPHY OF LEIBNIZ

Metaphysics and Language

Benson Mates

OXFORD UNIVERSITY PRESS
New York   Oxford

Oxford University Press

Oxford   New York   Toronto
Delhi   Bombay   Calcutta   Madras   Karachi
Petaling Jaya   Singapore   Hong Kong   Tokyo
Nairobi   Dar es Salaam   Cape Town
Melbourne   Auckland

and associated companies in
Berlin   Ibadan

First published in 1986 by Oxford University Press, Inc.,
200 Madison Avenue, New York, New York 10016

First issued as an Oxford University Press paperback, 1989

Oxford is a registered trademark of Oxford University Press

Library of Congress Cataloging in Publication Data

Mates, Benson, 1919–
The Philosophy of Leibniz.

Bibliography: p.
Includes index.
1. Leibniz, Gottfried Wilhelm, Freiherr von, 1646–1716.
I. Title.
B2598.M279   1985   110′.92′4   85-7249
ISBN 0-19-503696-4
ISBN 0-19-505946-8 (PBK)

2 4 6 8 10 9 7 5 3

Printed in the United States of America

Acknowledgments

Like many other workers in the vineyard of Leibnizian studies, I am the beneficiary of the kindness and assistance of the scholars at the Leibniz Archive in Hanover and the Leibniz Research Center in Münster. They are unfailingly helpful to the visitor, even though their time is more than sufficiently occupied with editorial and other duties. In particular, I owe a debt of gratitude to Albert Heinekamp, Heinz-Jürgen Hess, Heinrich Schepers, Gerda Utermöhlen, and Wilhelm Totok for their advice and hospitality. To Professor Schepers I owe especial thanks for providing me with the items listed in the Bibliography as "Fasz. 1" and "Fasz. 2," as well as for photocopies of many of the manuscripts. And I am also most grateful to Fabrizio Mondadori, who sent me a photocopy of the rare Jagodinski edition of the *Elementa* (see Bibliography under "Jag"). I should add that I have learned a great deal—whether it shows or not—from the publications of all these scholars.

Many of my interpretive ideas have been stimulated by, if not borrowed outright from, the writings of G. H. R. Parkinson and Nicholas Rescher. Hans Burkhardt's excellent study (see Bibliography under "Burk") covers much of the same ground as this book; its reliability and thoroughness are such that I have to be relieved when, as in most instances, it agrees with what I say. As will be evident in the footnotes, there are many other authors to whom I am indebted for ideas and stimulation.

Two less obvious debts, which I share with most serious students of the subject, are to the *Leibniz Bibliographie* (originally edited by Kurt Müller and now brought up to 1980 in a revised edition by Professor Heinekamp) and to L. E. Loemker's classic series of English translations. Each of these works represents a huge amount of careful scholarship, and no doubt the latter, more than any other single factor, is responsible for the revival of Leibniz studies in England and America. Additional English translations by

G. H. R. Parkinson, Jonathan Bennett and Peter Remnant, H. T. Mason, and others are advancing these studies further.

For helpful criticism of portions of the book I owe thanks to many of my students, including especially Donald Rutherford and Ali Toraby-Moghadam. But most of all I am obliged to Robert Sleigh and Richard Epstein, who read the entire manuscript and offered very useful comments and suggestions.

The frontispiece, which pictures a bust of Leibniz by Johann Gottfried Schmidt, is from a photograph furnished by Professor Heinekamp and the Leibniz Archive.

Research for this book was greatly facilitated by grants from the American Council of Learned Societies and the National Science Foundation.

Berkeley, California   B. M.
November 1985

Contents

THE PHILOSOPHY OF LEIBNIZ

Introduction

1. In recent years there has been a remarkable rebirth of interest in the philosophy of Leibniz. This is due to several mutually reinforcing factors. Logicians and philosophers of logic have found that his views on some of the matters that concern them most, such as identity, truth, and necessity, were well thought out, systematic, and, when considered together with the reasons behind them, deeply intuitive. Philosophers of language have become aware that his writings are a mine of sophisticated and valuable ideas in that area. Metaphysicians, especially those of nominalistic bent, have been interested to see how this great mind attempted to cope with the obvious problems involved in nominalism and nominalistic reductions. And epistemologists and philosophers of science are finding that he discusses, in a very modern way, a wide variety of issues that are central to their interests, too.

Accelerating all of this have been the renewed progress of the great Berlin Academy edition of Leibniz's works and also the appearance of *Studia Leibnitiana*, a journal devoted principally to the intellectual history of his time. We owe these welcome developments primarily to the scholars of the Leibniz Archive (Hanover) and the Leibniz Research Center (Münster) in Germany. Besides their editorial work and the books and articles they themselves have contributed, these experts are providing very complete bibliographic information that is extremely helpful, even essential, to anyone doing serious work on the subject. They also organize congresses and symposia, at which the growing numbers of researchers in this field can exchange ideas and keep up with the latest developments. In short, their service has been, and will continue to be, indispensable for the success of these studies.

The aim of the present work is to add its bit to this Leibniz renaissance by offering a critical account of some of the fundamentals of his philosophy. Such criticism as is included will be, for the most part, internal, taking note of contradictions and other unwelcome consequences that seem to follow from his principles. (External criticism is rather out of place here, though I shall probably not be able to conceal from the reader that much of Leibniz's doctrine strikes me, as it did Russell, as a certainly interesting and perhaps heuristically useful fairy story.) Internal criticism is justifiable and even necessary, I think, because in pointing out what appear to be inconsistencies or other unacceptable results, I shall be not only informing the reader about the views of Leibniz but also giving evidence relevant to the acceptability of my interpretations. After all, the goal is to promote, by whatever means, the understanding of the doctrines in question.

Now, anyone who proposes to expound in summary fashion the philosophy of one of the classical figures has to deal with a number of problems, most of which are too obvious to require recital here. But the study of Leibniz brings with it some special difficulties of which the reader should be aware and which account for certain features of this book.

2. The first and foremost difficulty is that in setting forth the philosophy of Leibniz, one does not know where to begin. Some advice on this problem is found in a well-known passage in *Alice in Wonderland*:

> The White Rabbit put on his spectacles. "Where shall I begin, please your Majesty?" he asked.
> "Begin at the beginning," the King said, very gravely, "and go on till you come to the end: then stop."[1]

But unfortunately we cannot follow this good advice, for Leibniz's philosophy has no "beginning," that is, no unique, logically primitive set of axioms. Contrary to what many commentators seem to have supposed, he does not treat his philosophical principles as a deductive system in which certain propositions are to be accepted without proof and the rest are to be deduced from these. Instead, it is clear that he regards his doctrine simply as a network of important truths that have many interesting logical interrelationships. He deduces the various principles from one another in different orders and combinations. Often he gives alternative definitions of the same concept, sometimes even showing how to derive these from one another. It is obvious that he has no particular order of theorems and definitions in mind.[2]

Therefore, talk of "question begging" and "vicious circles" in proofs and definitions has no clear application to Leibnizian philosophy, since those terms acquire sense only in relation to some deductive system explicitly or implicitly indicated. Rather, as noted above, Leibniz's attitude is that of a kind of philosophical explorer, who reports what he finds to be the case and who notices that there are important logical interconnections among his discoveries. He himself puts the matter clearly enough when he says: "My

---

[1] The Complete Works of Lewis Carroll. New York, 1941, 126.
[2] In one text (LH IV vii B 2 57–58; Fasz. 1. # 40, 136), he states explicitly that it makes no difference which possible definition of a concept you choose, as long as you can deduce the others from it as theorems.

principles are such that they can hardly be torn apart from each other. He who knows one well knows them all."[3]

3. This same logical integration makes it futile to argue about whether Leibniz's metaphysics is derived from his logic or his logic from his metaphysics, an issue that has seemed of major importance to a number of commentators, including, preeminently, Russell and Louis Couturat. For, not to belabor the point, in Leibniz's philosophy "everything is connected with everything."

Indeed, the relation of his metaphysical principles to those the commentators call "logical" (but which in most cases are better classified as belonging to metalogic or the philosophy of logic rather than to logic itself) is so close that it is often difficult to tell them apart. This difficulty is increased by Leibniz's carelessness about matters of use and mention; we get the impression that frequently he doesn't care whether he is understood to be talking about sentences, propositions, or the corresponding states of affairs, or, again, about descriptions, concepts, or the individuals to which the descriptions, as expressing the concepts, refer. Consequently he often makes pronouncements that, taken in one way, would be metaphysical principles, and taken in another, would be logical.

For example, the "logical" claim that the complete individual concept of Alexander contains all of his "predicates" (properties) is, for Leibniz, practically interchangeable with the metaphysical claim that the soul of Alexander contains at all times traces of everything that has happened to him and even signs of everything that will happen to him. Or again, the metaphysical view that the universe of individual substances is like a great sea, in which the slightest motion anywhere produces some change everywhere else, is an almost indistinguishable counterpart of the "logical" claim that everything is related to everything and that every relation is "grounded in accidents of the relata"—that is, that all relations are internal.

In general, we probably ought to take Leibniz's word for it that from his point of view the "true metaphysic" hardly differs at all from the "true logic," since they both amount to natural theology.[4]

4. For the expositor, one practical effect of these interconnections is that any account of Leibniz's philosophy has to contain a certain amount of repetition. It is not possible simply to take up each topic in order, setting forth only what needs to be said about that topic in particular and then proceeding to the next. If, for instance, we attempted to include under the heading of Truth all Leibnizian doctrine relevant to truth, the result would amount to almost the whole story. Hence, some relatively arbitrary divisions must be drawn, and more repetition must be tolerated than would otherwise be acceptable. It will even be necessary, in a few instances, to employ some of Leibniz's technical terminology (for example, "purely extrinsic denomination") before we reach the sections in which we explicitly consider and define

---

[3] G II 412 (L 599).   [4] G IV 292.

those terms. With cross-references in the notes I have tried to compensate somewhat for the unsatisfactoriness of this.

I may mention in passing that Leibniz is sometimes regarded as "the logicians' philosopher," but to this a certain reservation needs to be added. Although it is certainly important to investigate the logical relationships among his various doctrines, and although "It follows that . . ." is no doubt the most frequently occurring phrase in the entire Leibnizian corpus, we must unfortunately grant that C. S. Peirce was right when he said that "the reasoning of Leibniz was *nearly*, if not quite, of the highest order."[5] When we get down to cases, we find that Leibniz's declarations about what follows from what in his system cannot be accepted uncritically; usually more than a few suppressed premises have to be added if the argument is to go through with anything approaching formal validity.

5. Another special problem confronting Leibniz scholarship is that in order to find out what he thought and said about any major topic, there are not one, two, or three places to look, but literally dozens of texts to take into account. During his lifetime he published only one philosophical book, the *Theodicy*, and a small number of philosophical articles. In 1765, nearly fifty years after his death, another book, the *New Essays*, was published from a manuscript that he had prepared but held back because of the death of Locke, on whose *Essay* it was a commentary. Neither of the books contains his best work; both are long and rambling accounts, hastily written, poorly organized, and seldom showing the sharpness and insights of which he was capable.

Leibniz's better work is contained in the great mass of letters, drafts, notes, and bits and pieces he left behind, most of which are preserved in the State Library of Lower Saxony, in Hanover, Germany. Portions of this material have been published by a number of editors, and the aforementioned Academy edition of the entire corpus has been under way, through two world wars and other vicissitudes, since the beginning of this century. But an equally large amount has not yet been edited, so that any exegete takes some risk that tomorrow a "coupon" or other item will be found in which Leibniz asserts the exact opposite of what, it has been concluded, "he must have thought" or "he would have said." The more serious problem, though, is simply that there are so many places to look, with so little useful indexing, that it is often a very onerous task to discover what he did say about any given matter.

We must keep in mind, of course, that most of this miscellaneous material, on which we have to rely so heavily, was not intended for publication. To any careful reader it soon becomes evident that Leibniz often wrote out philosophical ideas as a kind of dialogue with himself, to see where they would lead, and without making any commitment to accepting them as part of his considered system. Thus, such texts must be used with discretion by

---

[5] *The Nation* 68 (1899): 210.

anyone seeking to reconstruct that system. On the other hand, the availability of the manuscripts of these deliberative pieces sometimes provides unexpected rewards for the scholar; by observing what has been crossed out and what has been put in its place, he can occasionally get a deeper insight into what the author had in mind.

Still another problem is that in his letters Leibniz often adapts himself to the terminology of his correspondent and sometimes argues from premises that are the correspondent's and not necessarily his own. These texts, too, must be used with great care when we are seeking to understand his use of critical terms or hoping to discover his true doctrine on some point. Many of the drafts, notes, and even the *New Essays* present similar difficulties.

6. It has been fashionable, certainly since Jaeger's well-known work on Aristotle but also before that, to treat the pronouncements of all thinkers as exhibiting their intellectual "development" rather than as providing a "synchronic" picture of their thoughts.[6] This methodology is based on the obvious fact that people change their minds, so that if we indiscriminately lump together what they say at all the different periods of their lives, we shall almost certainly find incoherence and contradiction. It does seem to bring with it its own dangers, however; once the historian has concluded that a philosopher's thought (or that of a given historical period) developed in a certain way, there is a tendency to disregard or reinterpret evidence that doesn't fit the adopted hypothesis. (A good example of this, if one is needed, was the "reconstruction" of Aristotle's *Protrepticus* to support the thesis that Aristotle gradually developed from a Platonist into an Aristotelian.)[7]

A great deal of excellent work has been done in dating the thousands of items that constitute Leibniz's *Nachlass*. Most of the letters carry their own dates, of course, and sometimes what is said in a draft or memorandum will coincide almost verbatim with what appears in a letter. Watermarks give further clues, and there are several other kinds of supporting evidence.

When the materials are put in order as well as can be, it becomes obvious that Leibniz did change his mind on many topics, as would be expected. Indeed, he himself tells us about some of these changes, mostly having to do with his views on matters of physical science.

But on the fundamental points of his philosophy, his constancy over the years is little short of astonishing. For instance, from the first of his publications, at age seventeen, to the end of his life he never wavered in holding to the rather unusual and implausible doctrine that things are individuated by their "whole being"; that is, every property of a thing is essential to its identity.[8]

---

[6] W. Jaeger, *Aristoteles*, Berlin, 1923. Stein (1888), with his "*entwicklungsgeschichtliche Methode*," is an earlier example.

[7] See W. G. Rabinowitz, *Aristotle's Protrepticus and the Sources of its Reconstruction*. Berkeley and Los Angeles, 1957.

[8] Or, perhaps, that every accident of an individual is unique to that individual. He holds both (1) that A is the same as B if and only if A and B have the same properties (that is, fall under the same concepts), and, of course, (2) that A is the same as B if and only if A and B have every individual accident in common.

And in general, if one compares the doctrines of the *Discourse on Metaphysics* (1686) with those of the *Monadology* (1714), one sees that during his last thirty years there was almost no change in any of them. In fact, I have yet to find a single basic metaphysical principle on which he changed his mind over time; the few verifiable changes are on such relatively minor matters as, for example, whether minds occupy points in space.

Consequently, in this account of the elements of Leibniz's philosophy I have felt free, on the whole, to cite him without paying much attention to the date of the passage cited. None of the inconsistencies that I shall point out can be explained, so far as I can see, as indicating an independently confirmable change of mind. It is always possible, of course, that I am in error on this, and so the reader is hereby warned that my "synchronic" approach may be the source of apparent difficulties.

7. It was mentioned earlier that Leibniz often falls into what is today called "use-mention confusion." Usually, when we ask ourselves whether he is talking about language, thought, or the world, the answer seems to be "none and all of these."

This state of affairs is best understood, in my opinion, by reference to the concept of "definiteness of intention," introduced several years ago by the Norwegian philosopher Arne Naess.[9] Consider an example. We ask somebody, one of Naess's seafaring compatriots, say, if he agrees that a certain ship is "a ship of five thousand tons." Suppose that his reply is "yes." Then we ask him a series of questions designed to discover whether by "ton" in this context he means a unit of weight or a unit of volume; if the volume of displacement of water was meant, we inquire whether seawater or freshwater was intended, there being a difference in volume because of a difference in weight. And so on. Sooner or later, Naess observes, we shall reach the point where the subject must admit, if he is honest, that he intended neither A nor non-A. Either he was unaware that such a distinction was relevant to the sentence in question, or at any rate he was not attending to that distinction when he made the assertion. Roughly speaking, the farther we go down our list of questions before reaching this point, the more definiteness of intention we ascribe to the subject in his use of the given sentence.

This concept is obviously far from precise, but it is nonetheless useful, especially in interpreting the writings of authors who can no longer be interviewed. We often would very much like to know whether, in saying such and such, the author meant this or that. For example, we ask whether, in the *Categories*, Aristotle was classifying words or things. Part of what he says suggests the former interpretation, and part suggests the latter. Probably the truth is that the distinction was below his level of definiteness of intention when he wrote the text in question: he didn't mean words and he didn't mean things; he just wasn't attending to that distinction, though of course he was perfectly capable of drawing it if the matter had been raised.

---

[9] Naess (1952), 256ff.

I think that the same considerations apply to Leibniz. When he is thinking specifically about matters metaphysical, he is perfectly capable of distinguishing the individual substance Alexander from the complete individual concept of Alexander, and both of them from the name "Alexander." But he doesn't attend to these distinctions all the time, and on occasion he produces assertions relative to which they are below his level of definiteness of intention. In such instances there will be no completely satisfactory answer to the question whether he "really" means this or that; the best we can do is to interpret him in whichever way makes the most sense in relation to the general outlines of his system.

It must be added, however, that all of our interpretative generosity cannot save Leibniz from certain unwelcome consequences of the inherent incoherence of such notions as those of "proposition" and "concept." Carefulness about use and mention only serves to show up these problems more clearly, not to solve them.

8. As would be expected, this book's account of Leibniz's philosophy differs in many details from those given by other commentators, but there are two major differences that I wish to point out here.

The first of these results from giving due attention to Leibniz's distinction between "essential" and "existential" propositions. Any proposition 'A is B', he tells us, is equivalent to the corresponding proposition 'AB is an entity'. Thus, "Caesar is a Roman" is equivalent to "Caesar the Roman is an entity." But the word "entity" is ambiguous; it can mean the same as "possible thing" or it can mean the same as "actually existing thing." If it is taken in the former sense, the propositions concerned are called "essential"; if it is taken in the latter sense, they are "existential."

Clearly, the two kinds of propositions have different truth conditions. The essential proposition "Pegasus is a winged horse" is true, since Pegasus the winged horse is a possible thing; but the existential proposition expressed by the same words is false, for Pegasus the winged horse does not actually exist. In general, existential 'A is B' is false if 'A exists' is false, whereas this is not necessarily the case with essential 'A is B'.

This distinction gives us a way of reconciling some important Leibnizian texts that have seemed inconsistent with one another. Thus, sometimes he says that 'A is B' is true if and only if the concept B is included in the concept A, while elsewhere he says that 'A is B' is false if no actual entity falls under A. In particular, sometimes he indicates that all propositions of the form 'A is A' are necessary truths, while in other texts he proposes to represent truths of the form 'No A is B' as 'AB is not AB'. Expositors who have been impressed by one set of texts have tended to ignore or "interpret" away the others, and their opponents have done likewise, mutatis mutandis.[10] The above-mentioned distinction allows us to reconcile such apparent inconsistencies

---

[10] This comment, I am embarrassed to say, applies especially to Mates (1968), as well as to many of the replies it provoked.

by concluding that in some cases Leibniz is referring to essential propositions, while in other cases only existential propositions are being discussed.

The same distinction may throw some light on another puzzle. Leibniz says that even in a contingent truth of the form '*A* is *B*', the concept *B* is included in the concept *A*; but he also implies that a contingent truth is one that is true of the actual world but not of all possible worlds. So we are left to wonder how, when the concept *B* is included in the concept *A*, the proposition '*A* is *B*' can be false of some possible world. No help is provided by his famous doctrine that the difference between a necessary and a contingent truth is that in the former the opposite yields a contradiction in a finite number of steps, while in the latter the analysis goes on to infinity. The only way out seems to be to restrict the "possible-worlds" semantics to existential propositions and their combinations, and to regard the "length-of-analysis" distinction as applying only to propositions taken essentially. (Even this interpretation leaves a residue of difficulties, however, as will be explained in chapter 6.)

The second major difference between this account and its predecessors lies in the emphasis placed on what I believe to be the basic metaphysical scheme underlying Leibniz's philosophy. That scheme, in summary, is as follows. Reality consists exclusively of individual souls, including, of course, God, who is the creator, and ourselves, who are among the "creatures." Any created monad, at any time, is in some state or other, that is, has various "accidents." God, too, is in this or that state, but outside the temporal sequence. The accidents of substances are individual; Socrates and Plato are both wise, but the wisdom of Socrates is not the wisdom of Plato. Indeed, there is literally nothing "in common" to Socrates and Plato. What, then, about *wisdom*? The strict answer, according to Leibniz, is that neither this nor any other abstractum exists. Discourse about ideas or thoughts is, if properly understood, reducible to discourse about the dispositions of minds to think in certain ways.

Thus, although Leibniz's philosophy of language, considered prima facie, subscribes to the Aristotelian framework that contrasts language, thought, and the world, only the last of these three "realms" really exists. Statements appearing to be about concepts, propositions, attributes, relations, and other elements of the other two categories are only *compendia loquendi* for statements about the elements of the real world, namely, the monads.

I cannot claim that this interpretation is supported unambiguously by all of the relevant texts, and fluctuations in Leibniz's use of the crucial terminology ("substance," "accident," "attribute," "property," "concept," "subject," "predicate," to mention a few of the terms involved) makes a really definitive treatment practically impossible. But I do claim that the scheme as outlined fits most of what he says and makes sense of portions of his doctrine that are otherwise hard to understand. For example, it allows the interpretation of the principle of the Identity of Indiscernibles as asserting the nontrivial metaphysical "fact" that no two individuals are so alike as to fall under exactly the same concepts. To say that x is the same as y does not *mean* that x and y fall under the same concepts, but the principle guarantees that (fortunately for us) if x is different from y, then it is at least in principle possible for some mind to tell them apart.

One less weighty innovation that nevertheless deserves mention is the possible-worlds model described in chapter 4. That model serves to show that, contrary to what has often been claimed, there is nothing incoherent in Leibniz's doctrine that each monad "mirrors" the states of all the others, including their "mirrorings" of it.

9. A few words about the limitations of this study are in order here. In an interesting passage Leibniz says:

Philosophy has two parts, the theoretical or speculative, and the practical. Speculative philosophy is based on genuine Analysis, of which the mathematicians give examples, but which ought also to be applied to metaphysics and natural theology, in providing good definitions and solid axioms. Practical philosophy, on the other hand, is based on a genuine Topic or Dialectic, that is to say, on the art of estimating the degrees of proof. This is not yet found in the writings of logicians; only jurists have given examples, which should not be scorned and can serve as a beginning for constructing a science of proof, suitable for verifying historical facts and for giving the sense of texts.[11]

This book restricts itself to a part of what Leibniz describes as "speculative philosophy." I shall not consider his views on probability or his part in founding that science, and I shall not take up his various maxims concerning legal reasoning. But even within the domain of "speculative philosophy" I shall be omitting all consideration of his formal logical calculi and of his many attempts to formalize or arithmetize the theory of the syllogism. These have been dealt with satisfactorily by other authors, and I have nothing useful to add. Theological controversies, too, where they are not closely connected with more purely philosophical issues, have been ignored, even though Leibniz devoted a large part of the *Theodicy* to them.

On the other hand, I have given a relatively large amount of space to an account of Leibniz's life. To understand his thought processes, we should know a little about what kind of person he was. A full, reliable biography of this great man is long overdue.

10. To the catalog of complaints and excuses about special difficulties confronting the expositor of Leibniz, it is only fair to add something about what makes his philosophy so attractive to those of us who are drawn to it.

First of all, Leibniz was a true philosopher, a follower of Socrates, a seeker after clarity, truth, and wisdom. Like Socrates, he placed an especially high value on being clear about what we mean by what we say. (He would have been horrified by the obscurantism that appeared in some of the later German philosophy purporting to derive from his work.) His struggle for clarity is attested by the long lists of definitions that are found among his manuscripts. To have a deep understanding of what is said, he thought, is to

---

[11] A.2.1.434.

be able to define one's terms—that is, to be able to answer satisfactorily the question "What does that mean?" with respect to any and all components of one's discourse and, further, to be able to answer the same question again with respect to the components of those answers, and so on. He was trying, in his way, to bring into philosophy the clarity and precision of mathematics.

Second, Leibniz's writings are full of interesting ideas and suggestions. As Gottlob Frege said:

Leibniz, in his writings, spread out such an abundance of seminal thoughts that there is hardly another philosopher who can be compared with him in this respect. A portion of these ideas were worked out even in his own day, and with his collaboration; another portion were forgotten but were later rediscovered and further developed. This justifies the expectation that in his works there is still a great deal that now appears dead and buried but that will eventually enjoy its resurrection.[12]

The reader who delves into this mine of ideas is led on by tantalizing hints and suggestions. Often one doesn't quite understand what Leibniz had in mind, but one knows from experience that if one keeps on hunting through his work, it is probable that, sooner or later, an explanation will turn up.

Let me give one example of the kind of tantalizing statement to which I refer. Here, following some general metaphysical remarks, Leibniz is trying to refute the claim, made now and again by metaphysicians ever since Diodorus of Megara, that whatever is possible must happen somewhere at some time—past, present, or future. He argues as follows:

. . . nor are there [in the actual world] any bodies that are not at some definite distance from us. For if there were, it would not be possible to say whether they exist at this present moment or not, which is contrary to our first principle. From this it also follows that not all possibles exist.[13]

Obviously this passage suggests some sort of connection between the measurement of time and that of space, and there also seems to be an implication that possible-but-nonactual objects—for example, Pegasus—are "not at some definite distance from us." Further, we do not know to which "first principle" Leibniz is here referring. So the exact import of the passage is unclear. But there is every reason to believe that eventually a text will be found (if, unbeknownst to me, this has not already happened) that will provide an explanation. These kinds of challenge occur frequently in the Leibnizian writings, and without doubt they are part of what piques our curiosity and keeps up our interest.

Lastly, there are the features mentioned at the outset of this Introduction, namely, that many of the topics Leibniz discusses are right at the center of present-day philosophical activity, so that his works are a mine of ideas that can be applied to issues now in the limelight.

11. To conserve space in the notes, I cite Leibnizian texts and some of the

---

[12] Frege (1969), 9.
[13] Grua 263. See n. 20 to chap. 4.

better-known commentaries with the help of certain more or less standard abbreviations. These are indicated beside the respective entries in the Bibliography. The Academy edition is cited by series, volume, and page; for example, "A.2.1.145" refers to page 145 of volume 1 of series 2. If an English translation of a cited passage exists, reference to it is usually given immediately following the citation of the original. Because the pagination of the Remnant-Bennett translation of the *New Essays*[14] is identical with that of the Academy text, a single citation serves both purposes in that case.

Some brief texts are quoted in the notes; others are paraphrased (usually because a direct quotation would not fit the context grammatically). A direct quotation is indicated by quotation marks or placement as a block quotation unless the text is in Latin; absence of such treatment indicates paraphrase. Explanatory words inserted by me in quotations or paraphrases are enclosed in square brackets. Because of the relative inaccessibility of Leibniz's writings, I have quoted him much more frequently and generously than would otherwise be appropriate.

Finally, a postscript about my use of certain pronouns. The English language, like most other natural languages, is saturated with what in today's terminology are called "sexist" elements. I share the wish that these features, which increasingly grate upon the sensibilities of readers, could be eliminated. But the requisite changes in vocabulary and syntax seem to me overwhelming in number and almost impossible to accomplish without creating an entirely new language. (Incidentally, Leibniz's projected *lingua philosophica*, with its lack of inflection to indicate gender, number, case, person, tense, or mood, would have gone a long way in this direction.) As things are, I think that a more promising approach is to try to change our *philosophy* of language and not the language itself. Instead of attempting to redesign the tool, try to clarify the conditions and implications of its use.

From this point of view, I am retaining what I take to be a conventional use of the pronouns "he," "his," and "him," namely, that they (instead of the corresponding feminine forms) are employed when we are speaking of persons generally. Perhaps the experts can tell us whether the subjugation of women is part of the causal history of this convention and of many others like it. We should hardly be surprised if it were. At any rate, I shall here insist in Humpty-Dumpty fashion that, as used by me, the pronouns in statements like "If anyone loses his passport, he is in trouble," or "Each person is entitled to his own opinion," or "He who laughs last, laughs best" do not have any special reference to males. I wish to use these pronouns simply as bound variables. For many other languages, with respect to which the grammatical category of gender is less likely to be confused with the biological category of sex, the point is clearer.

---

[14] In letters to Bartholomew des Bosses (G II 433, 498) Leibniz says that the former's Latin translation of the *Theodicy* is elegant, skillful, and frequently better than the original. I think he would join me in saying the same of Remnant and Bennett's English translation of the *New Essays*.

I

Life and Works

Gottfried Wilhelm Leibniz is without doubt one of the most imposing figures in the history of Western thought.[1] Although he is known principally as a philosopher ("this is the best of all possible worlds") and as a mathematician (coinventor of the differential and integral calculus), the immense scope of his intellectual activity and attainments amply justifies his characterization as a polymath, polyhistor, or universal genius.

Leibniz's contributions to philosophy, mathematics, and most of the other areas in which he worked are all the more remarkable because they were made in his spare time, as it were. By profession he was a lawyer. During most of his life he earned his living by serving as a legal counselor and general factotum to a succession of princes; even the greater part of his voluminous historical research was occasioned and guided by his employers' desire to establish lines of inheritance to wealth or title. Despite such duties, and in addition to his studies in philosophy and mathematics, he managed to make significant contributions in the fields of theology, jurisprudence, political and economic history, philology, politics, technology, and architecture; he was also knowledgeable in physics, chemistry, astronomy, geology, archaeology, linguistics, and literature, and his correspondence and papers are full of

---

[1] For the biographical information in this chapter I have relied principally on the following works:

CHRONIK   K. Müller and G. Krönert, *Leben und Werk von Gottfried Wilhelm Leibniz: Eine Chronik*, Frankfurt: Klostermann, 1969.

GUHRAUER   G. Guhrauer, *Gottfried Wilhelm Freiherr von Leibniz: Eine Biographie*, 2 vols. Breslau, 1846. Reprinted Hildesheim: Olms, 1966.

FISCHER   K. Fischer, *Gottfried Wilhelm Leibniz: Leben, Werke und Lehre*, 5th ed. Heidelberg: Carl Winters, 1920.

TOTOK   W. Totok and C. Haase, eds. *Leibniz: Sein Leben, sein Wirken, seine Welt*, Hanover: Verlag für Literatur und Zeitgeschehen, 1966.

analyses and original ideas in such diverse areas as medicine and public health, numismatics, military science, cryptanalysis, genealogy.[2]

Leibniz's motto was: In the realm of spirit, seek clarity; in the material world, seek utility.[3] Accordingly, his theoretical writings are largely analytic; that is, they attempt to define concepts clearly and to draw out their implications. He was true to the second part of his motto, too: in practical affairs he seems to have asked himself, with respect to every situation and artifact with which he came in contact, how it could be improved. Thus in the enormous *Nachlass* we find, along with the most abstract metaphysical musings, ideas for everything from a power saw and a machine for catching fish to a way of keeping Venice from sinking further into the Adriatic, or from a design for better nails (with little ridges that would keep them from coming out of the boards so easily) to a scheme for a new religious order dedicated to public health (so that the impossibly great financial burden that really adequate health care for everyone would entail could be eased somewhat by enlisting a large number of medical auxiliaries who would be recompensed in part by promises of rewards in the hereafter).[4]

In short, Leibniz was a Renaissance man, perhaps one of the last. Yet with all this, he was apparently an unaffected, gentle, reasonably modest and agreeable fellow, who could associate comfortably with people from all stations and walks of life, a *Kinderfreund* who often had the neighbourhood children at his house (where, as we are told, he watched them play and eventually sent them home again with a *Zuckerbrot*).[5] In fact, the worst things that even Johann Georg Eckhart, his envious and backbiting assistant, could find to say about his personality were that he did not like to be contradicted and found it hard to admit that he was wrong, and that he was rather tight about money.[6] The former fault seems hardly worth mentioning, and the latter becomes more than understandable when one reads the numerous letters in which Leibniz has to beg his aristocratic employers to send him even the modest sums they had promised.

It should be mentioned parenthetically that there is very little evidence to support Russell's unfortunate charge that while Leibniz was one of the supreme intellects of all time, "as a human being he was not admirable."[7] Russell based this charge on his own erroneous conclusion—which, because

[2] A glance at the contents of LBr and LH will show the immense scope of Leibniz's interests.

[3] Fischer 31.

[4] For the religious order, see C 4. Many of the technical proposals are to be found in Gerland (1906); e.g., for the nails, saw, and fishing machine, see pp. 331–33. Other proposals were for a better way to make brandy and a new method of combating dysentery (K. Müller, in Totok 51).

[5] Guhrauer 2, 364. Op. cit., 347: Leibniz would never kill a fly, no matter how much it had incommoded him, "because it certainly would not be right to destroy an artificial machine of comparable complexity."

[6] Guhrauer 2, 337, 352–53. On not liking to be contradicted, cf. A.6.6.461.

[7] Russell (1945), 581. Elsewhere Russell charged that Leibniz's "utter lack of moral elevation . . . led him to publish by preference his worst writings, to ruin the consistency of his system for the sake of orthodoxy, and to mislead the world . . . as to the grounds of his metaphysical tenets." Russell (1903), in Frankfurt (1972), 365.

of the eminence of its author, has regrettably achieved wide currency among philosophers—that Leibniz had a public and a private philosophy: a public one, "designed to win the approbation of princes and princesses," in which the Deity plays a central role, and a private one, in which the origin of the world is explained without reference to God.[8] But a study of the relevant manuscripts, many of which have been edited since Russell wrote, leaves no room for doubt that Leibniz was a sincere believer; admittedly he was not much of a churchgoer, but he certainly was no atheist.[9] The "esoteric" philosophy, which Russell says was left unpublished in Leibniz's desk, turns out to be all of a piece with the exoteric doctrine he put before the public.[10]

We are told, however, that in Hanover Leibniz did have the reputation of a nonbeliever. "He went to church seldom or not at all," writes Eckhart, "and took Communion very infrequently. At least in the nineteen years I have known him I don't know of his doing it once. The clergymen often berated him publicly for this, but he stuck to his ways."[11] Consequently the common people called him in Plattdeutsch *"Loevenix,"* that is, *Glaubt nichts,* "believes nothing."[12] This opinion may have been reinforced by the report that Leibniz refused, even on his deathbed, to take Holy Communion.[13] But such rumors are irrelevant to the question of his sincerity, for at that time the general public in Hanover knew no more about his philosophical doctrines than they do now.[14]

1. The Early Years (1646–72)

Leibniz was born in Leipzig on 1 July, 1646, two years before the Peace of Westphalia, which brought an end to the terrible Thirty Years' War. His father, Friedrich Leibniz, was a professor of moral philosophy at the University of Leipzig; his mother, Catherina, was the daughter of a prominent jurist. Leibniz always supposed, judging by the surname, that his father's family was ultimately of Slavic origin.[15] But it is now known that the name was originally a place-name and as such shows nothing about the genealogy of the

---

[8] Here Russell has in mind a passage at G VII 194 (R 296), where Leibniz says, "Everything possible demands that it should exist, and hence will exist unless something else prevents it, which also demands that it should exist and is incompatible with the former; and hence it follows that that combination of things always exists by which the greatest possible number of things exists." But, as has often been noted, this passage does not rule out creation by God. I think that *exigit existere* is just another way of saying "would exist if nothing prevents," i.e., "has a claim to existence." As late as 1968, however, Russell had not changed his views on these matters. See O'Briant (1979), 220.

[9] In the preface to the *Theodicy* (G VI 25, H 49–50), Leibniz contrasts unfavorably the "outward expression of religion" with "consideration of the inner essence of [religious] theory."

[10] This is conclusively argued by Blumenfeld (1981).

[11] Guhrauer 2, 332.

[12] Op. cit., 333.

[13] Op. cit., 329. See p. 30.

[14] Unless I am mistaken, the average *Hannoveraner* today tends to associate the name "Leibniz" first of all with a kind of cookie, the so called *Leibniz-Keks.*

[15] Cf. *Vita Leibnitii a se ipso breviter delineata,* Guhrauer 2, Beilage, 52.

family, which had lived in the area around Leipzig since at least the middle of the fifteenth century.[16]

When Leibniz was only six years old, his father died, leaving him and his sister, Anna, to the care of the thirty-one-year-old widow.[17] She was his father's third wife, a pious woman who until her own death twelve years later conscientiously devoted herself to the upbringing of her children. Anna later married a clergyman, Simon Löffler, whose son by a previous marriage, Friedrich Löffler, eventually became Leibniz's only legal heir.

By the time Leibniz was four, his father had taught him to read, and although he entered school at the usual age of seven, most of his early education seems to have been achieved at home alone in the family library. There he taught himself Latin by reading the historian Livy, getting over the difficult passages, as he tells us, by looking at the woodcut pictures with which the books were illustrated. Two years later he took up the study of Greek. By that time he was fluent enough in Latin to commence his lifelong practice of composing poems in honor of holidays, weddings, retirements, and other suitable occasions. At about the same time he began intense study of Aristotelian syllogistic, which gave him such evident satisfaction that his mother and his teachers, who had previously worried lest he devote his life to the production of (presumably mediocre) Latin poetry, now became fearful that he would become intellectually bogged down in scholastic quibbles.

In 1661, at the age of fifteen, Leibniz entered the University of Leipzig, his modest financial resources augmented by a scholarship.[18] He attended lectures on philosophy and mathematics and on Greek, Latin, and Hebrew language and literature. Two years later, at seventeen, he produced his first publication, entitled *Disputatio metaphysica de principio individui* (Metaphysical disputation on the principle of individuation).[19] This was a baccalaureate dissertation written under the guidance of Jakob Thomasius, a professor of rhetoric with whom he kept up an interesting philosophical correspondence for a number of years thereafter. The *Disputatio*, though hard to read because of its scholastic style, is noteworthy for containing an idea that became the cornerstone of Leibniz's later philosophy—namely, that

---

[16] For several generations before Leibniz's father, the family had spelled its name Leubnitz. Leibniz's father and his half brother, Johann Friedrich, used Leibnütz, Leibnüz, and Leibnitz. Leibniz himself used Leibnütz until his mother died, then for a time Leibnüz, and after 1671 Leibniz. Correspondingly he shifted the Latin form from Leibnuzius and Leibnuezius to Leibnitius. Etymologically the name probably derives from the Slavic Lipnice, which refers to a certain kind of grass that grows in river bottoms; variants on this appear as names of rivers and places all over eastern Europe.

Leibniz is sometimes called Gottfried Wilhelm Freiherr von Leibniz, but although he occasionally employed this title himself, he was never officially raised to the peerage. Cf. K. Müller, in Totok 7–10. Cf. also W. Kabitz, in Fischer 709.

[17] Leibniz also had a half brother and a half sister, children of his father's first marriage.

From here on, unless there are notes to the contrary, I am following Guhrauer. It should be noted, however, that recent scholarship is tending to show that on many details Guhrauer is not very reliable. Cf. Wiedeburg (1969).

[18] Cf. Müller (1969), 226.

[19] A.6.1.3ff.

things are individuated by their "whole being" (*entitas tota*); that is, every property or accident of a thing is essential to its identity. Also in this essay he expressed himself in favor of nominalism as against realism, thus introducing another element that remained constant in his philosophy ever after.

In the next year, after a brief sojourn at the University of Jena, where he received instruction in mathematics from Erhard Weigel,[20] Leibniz returned to Leipzig and obtained the degree of master of philosophy. The dissertation was entitled *Specimen quaestionum philosophicarum ex jure collectarum* (Some philosophical issues found in the law),[21] which became his second publication. In it he emphasized the close connection between philosophy and jurisprudence. Shortly before he received the degree, and while he was still in his seventeenth year, his mother died—an event that was painful to him not only in the loss of a parent who had devoted herself single-mindedly to his welfare, but also because of a disagreeable inheritance controversy that arose between his aunt, on the one side, and his sister and himself, on the other.

Leibniz next turned to the serious study of law, obtaining his bachelor of laws degree at Leipzig in 1665. He then resolved to pursue the J.D. degree there, hoping that this would lead to a post in the law faculty. But academic politics intervened; after a great controversy, the point of which is not entirely clear,[22] a committee of faculty and students voted against admitting him to candidacy for the degree.[23] He therefore changed his plans. Leaving his native city, never to return except when in transit to other places, he went to the University of Altdorf, near Nuremberg. There he was accepted, and in short order he attained the degree. The doctoral dissertation, his public defense of which was a tour de force, was entitled *Disputatio inauguralis de casibus perplexis in jure.*[24]

The *casus perplexi* were juristic antinomies, that is, cases in which valid legal grounds exist for both of the opposing sides. The question is: on what basis, if any, should such cases be decided? Leibniz considers several possibilities: (1) The judge can refuse to make a decision; or (2) he can flip a coin; or (3) it can be left to his free discretion (his "common sense"), independently of law; or (4) it can be settled on the basis of general ethical principles of charity, equity, humanity, utility, and so forth, which are wider than the positive law. Leibniz concludes in favor of (4). He argues that positive law has force only by virtue of a contract that, in setting up the state and giving legislative power to the sovereign, limits the applicability of natural law. Where the positive law does not apply decisively, we must therefore fall back on natural law and try to make decisions in accord with it.

The faculty of Altdorf judged Leibniz's ability and promise so favorably that they immediately offered him a professorship. But he declined the offer,

---

[20] Cf. Fischer 40–41.

[21] A.6.1.69ff.

[22] Cf. A.6.1.xix.

[23] Later, he said that this was all for the best! (Fischer 44–45)

[24] A.6.1.231ff. Cf. Fischer 50. Also dating from 1666 is the *Dissertatio de arte combinatoria* (A.6.1.163ff.), the first part of which was his *Habilitationsschrift*.

saying that he was "headed in an entirely different direction." Nobody knows just what he meant by that remark. G. E. Guhrauer, his biographer, thinks it signifies that he believed his various schemes for reforming the sciences could not be furthered from within the confines of academe; but a less high-sounding explanation might be that he simply preferred to earn his living by practicing law instead of by teaching it.

At about this time Leibniz's remarkable qualities came to the attention of Baron Johann Christian von Boineburg, a celebrated diplomat who had served as first minister to the archbishop of Mainz, Elector Johann Philipp von Schönborn. (The elector of Mainz was the highest church dignitary in the Empire, and the primus of the electors.) Boineburg persuaded Leibniz to come to Frankfurt, where Boineburg lived, and for a time he supported Leibniz's studies. At his suggestion Leibniz brought out a two-hundred-page treatise entitled *Nova methodus discendae docendaeque jurisprudentiae* (A new method for learning and teaching jurisprudence),[25] prefacing it, also at Boineburg's suggestion, with a most flattering dedication to the "Eminentissimus" Prince Johann Philipp.

The *Nova methodus* is a thorough treatment of its subject, in the manner typical of Leibniz's youth. He begins with a section on learning in general, proceeding from a discussion of how animals and young children learn by what we should today call "positive and negative reinforcement," to a consideration of learning in adults. He stresses the importance of repetition and intensity of stimuli, quoting such dicta as Ovid's *Gutta cavat lapidem* (Drops of water will hollow out a stone), Aesop's *Testudo aquila celerior* (The tortoise is faster than the eagle), and the German proverb *Wer langsam geht, kommt auch nach* (The slowpoke gets there, too). In a second section he takes up matters specifically relevant to the teaching and learning of jurisprudence, ending with a detailed proposal for a two-year curriculum, which, he says, is obtained from the usual five-year course of study by eliminating the useless elements.

Whether Leibniz's proposals would be greeted with favor by present-day lawyers I have no idea, but apparently Boineburg and the elector were impressed. Together they offered him continued financial support, and so from that time until their deaths in 1672 the talented young man served the two in various capacities, including attorney, librarian, adviser on foreign affairs, and general handyman.

Leibniz's first major project in his new position was concerned with, of all things, the election of a king of Poland. In 1668 King John Casimir of Poland, under whom the country had suffered one calamity after another, voluntarily abdicated the throne. A large number of pretenders at once appeared, among whom the four candidates with the most support were Count Philipp Wilhelm von Neuburg, Prince Karl von Lothringen, Prince Jules de Condé, and the son of the czar of Moscow. Count von Neuburg asked Boineburg to go as his emissary to Warsaw, with the purpose of influencing the vote in the

---

[25] A.6.1.259ff.

Polish *sejm*. Against the advice of the elector, who favored Prince Karl, Boineburg agreed to do this; and he also offered to do some public relations work with the Poles to further Neuburg's chances for election. Young Leibniz was given the task of drawing up suitable campaign literature. All of this occurred in the fall of 1668; the *sejm* was scheduled to meet in the following spring. Leibniz worked "day and night the whole winter . . . without receiving any recompense whatever for it" and produced a remarkable 360-page treatise entitled *Specimen demonstrationum politicarum pro rege Polonorum eligendo* (Some political demonstrations concerning the election of a king of Poland),[26] using the pseudonym Georgius Ulicovius Lithuanus and purporting to be a Polish aristocrat.

The argument is in mathematico-deductive form, with propositions, proofs, corollaries, and conclusions. In the sixty propositions and their corollaries a number of criteria for the office (that the person selected should be just, prudent, a Catholic, of known ability, physically and mentally vigorous, patient, modest, not from a turbulent family, not a child, and so forth, and so on) are deduced from various plausible social and economic generalizations about Poland. Then, after obtaining three conclusions excluding the other principal candidates, Leibniz finally reaches the end result: *Conclusio IV: Neoburgicus utiliter eligetur*.

The outcome of all this effort was disappointing to the three associates. So much time was consumed in printing the large book that it did not reach Warsaw until after the election. In the meantime the Poles had rejected Neuburg and all the other foreigners, and, without the benefit of Leibniz's twenty-five proofs for his proposition 60, namely, "that the king should be from outside Poland and should not be a member of the Piast family," they chose instead the Piast Michael Wisniowiecki.

Although Leibniz's expectation that such a chain of deductions could really affect the outcome of the election seems a bit naive even in a twenty-two-year-old, the analytic power and philosophical content of the treatise were not insignificant and aroused the admiration of contemporary political scientists. In his later years Leibniz still valued this juvenile effort as showing how the form of mathematical reasoning, hitherto applied only in philosophy and law, could be used in political and diplomatic disputes.

On his return from Poland, Boineburg proposed that Leibniz next devote himself to the preparation of a new edition of a philosophical work published in 1553 by the Italian nominalist Marius Nizolius and entitled *De veris principiis et vera ratione philosophandi contra pseudophilosophos* (On the true principles and right way of philosophizing, against the pseudophilosophers). Leibniz complied, as usual dedicating the work, with a florid tribute, to his employer. It was published in 1670. Leibniz's prefatory dissertation[27] is philosophically interesting, mainly for its discussion of nomi-

---

[26] A.4.1.1ff. Cf. *Studia Leibnitiana* 1 (1969), 54ff., regarding the Polish translation of this work. Cf. also CL 562ff.

[27] G IV 127–76 (selections translated in L 121–130).

nalism. Although he recognizes some of the difficulties inherent in that doctrine, he is very strongly attracted to it himself. Thus, with reference to the nominalists' principle that entities should not be multiplied beyond necessity, he says: "From this principle they have deduced that everything in the world can be explained without any reference to universals and real forms. Nothing is truer than this opinion, and nothing is more worthy of a philosopher of our own time."[28]

And in many other passages, some of which we shall quote in later chapters, he expresses similar sentiments. He does, however, criticize Nizolius's overly simplistic attempt to identify universals with the aggregates or "herds" of objects falling under them; he points out that if "animal" denoted the aggregate of all animals, then "man is [an] animal" would mean "man is all animals taken together."[29] This preface deserves more careful study by philosophers of language than it has received up to now.

In the same year (1670) Leibniz began his correspondence with Henry Oldenburg, secretary of the Royal Society in London. With his first letter he enclosed a friendly and rather flattering letter for Thomas Hobbes, whose works he had been carefully studying and whose views on many topics he had made his own. Hobbes did not favor him with a reply, nor did he do so later when Leibniz wrote to him from Paris. The letters were not thrown away, however, and are preserved in the British Museum.[30]

Leibniz's next big project, the *Consilium Aegyptiacum* (Egyptian plan),[31] was begun in the fall of 1671. Louis XIV of France had been menacing his neighbors, particularly Holland. The bordering German states were fearful lest he should attack them as well.[32] Accordingly, Leibniz and Boineburg concocted a scheme for deflecting the French expansion to another direction: they would persuade Louis to attack Egypt instead. The elector was let in on the plan only later, but evidently he approved. Leibniz drew up numerous drafts of proposed memoranda; finally, as the political events were unfolding rapidly, he produced in great haste the document *Justa dissertatio*,[33] containing several hundred pages of arguments as to why Cairo and Constantinople should be the king's targets instead of Holland. Leibniz argues, for example, that the Egyptian expedition is "the greatest of the possible projects, and the easiest of the great ones," that it is risk-free and fits in so well with the king's goals that it looks almost preordained, that it would wrest from Holland the domination of the sea and of commerce, that it could be accomplished using only "superfluous" (that is, not otherwise employed) forces, and so on.

Through the king's foreign minister, Arnauld de Pomponne, Leibniz was invited to Paris to present this proposal in person, but by the time he arrived

---

[28] G IV 158 (L 128).

[29] G IV 160–61 (L 128–29). The point looks more convincing in Latin, where there is no indefinite article.

[30] G I 82–85. A more accurate version of the first letter is given at G VII 572–74 (L 105–7).

[31] A.4.1.215ff.   [32] See Klopp 2, 100ff.   [33] A.4.1.267ff.

there, England had already declared war on Holland, and France was about to follow suit. So the proposal needed drastic revision before it could be shown to anyone. This Leibniz never got around to doing; Paris had too many other attractions for him. Soon afterward both Boineburg and Schönborn died, the former quite unexpectedly; and that was essentially the end of the project. According to Guhrauer, the plan did eventually get to the king's council, where it was rejected with the comment that "holy wars went out of fashion with *Saint* Louis."[34] When, more than a hundred years later, Napoleon conducted his Egyptian expedition, certain people blamed Leibniz for planting the idea in his head. But the fact seems to be that Napoleon was unaware of the Leibnizian proposal until he received a copy of it after he took Hanover in 1803.[35]

2. Paris (1672–76)

Leibniz was delighted with Paris. He found it a very inexpensive place to live, with good room and board costing only about 25 sols per day.[36] But of course the intellectual attractions were what pleased him most. He reports that he spent much time in the libraries and that he saw Molière acting on the stage in one of his own plays.[37] What was most important for Leibniz's own development, however, was that he met the great mathematician Christian Huygens, who immediately recognized his extraordinary talent and set him seriously to work on mathematics. Leibniz also strove to perfect his calculating machine (first mentioned in June 1671), which was a significant advance over Pascal's, for whereas Pascal's would do only addition and subtraction in a direct way, Leibniz's would also do multiplication and division.[38] (In a letter of recommendation that he wrote for himself to Duke Johann Friedrich of Brunswick-Lüneburg, Leibniz boasted that his machine would even extract the square and cube roots, but unfortunately this was not true.)[39]

Sent to London in 1673 as an assistant in another diplomatic mission, Leibniz took his machine with him to exhibit it to the Royal Society. To his dismay, it was rather nastily criticized by Robert Hooke (of Hooke's Law). Hooke apparently was unable to appreciate the essential advantage of Leibniz's machine over his own device, which was a sort of mechanical slide rule that made use of a logarithmic scale. Other Englishmen were friendlier; Leibniz visited the famous chemist Robert Boyle and through him met the

[34] Guhrauer 1, 109. But see Wiedeburg (1969), who has examined the sources and has concluded (p. 217) that this remark was not directed to Leibniz's plan but to another.

[35] Guhrauer 1, 110–111.

[36] Chronik 33.

[37] Op. cit., 30. Molière died in the next year.

[38] Op. cit., 22, G III 196. Cf. G I 202, where he emphasizes its superiority to the slide rule.

[39] A.2.1.160; cf. Guhrauer 1, 113. I am grateful to Dr. Heinz-Jürgen Hess for pointing out to me that in 1671 there was no operable example of Leibniz's machine, and that the first model, built of wood in 1672, could not even accomplish division directly. The later models, made of brass, could indeed do the four basic operations directly, but to manage root extraction, the operator would have had to make use of series of which Leibniz was unaware before 1673.

mathematician John Pell, who gave him some useful instruction. He reports also that he bought all the books his modest purse would allow.

Returning to Paris, he immersed himself in mathematics. Although he received some offers of employment in Germany—among them a most flattering one from Duke Johann Friedrich, whose service he later entered—he managed to get permission from the successors of Boineburg and the elector to remain in Paris for a time, serving as tutor to Boineburg's son and doing various other tasks. There is an amusing letter in which he advises Boineburg's widow that her son has all the necessary abilities but simply will not apply himself.[40] Presumably the young man straightened himself out later, for he eventually held a number of important diplomatic posts.

Leibniz remained in Paris until 1676. This period was an extremely busy one for him. He continued his studies with Huygens; became acquainted with Nicolas de Malebranche, Antoine Arnauld, and the mathematician Walter Tschirnhaus; invented a special kind of clock that he exhibited to the French Academy of Sciences; became himself a member of that academy; and obtained a large number of mathematical results, culminating in 1676 in his discovery of the differential and integral calculus. The records show that also during 1676 he obtained access to Descartes's manuscripts, visited Spinoza, and made another trip to England, where he was allowed to see some of Newton's papers. It has been pointed out that not the least of the advantages of his stay in Paris was his achieving some fluency in French, for at that time almost all learned correspondence was conducted in Latin, French, or English, and only later did German come into use for such purposes.

Finally, in December of the same year, Leibniz agreed to go to Hanover to be librarian and adviser to the aforementioned Duke Johann Friedrich. He remained in that position for the rest of his life, under three successive dukes, the last of whom became George I of England. The contrast between Paris and Hanover—the former the intellectual center of Europe at the time and the latter a relatively insignificant town of about ten thousand souls[41]—must have seemed enormous to the brilliant young man, who was then reaching the height of his powers. But only later did Leibniz begin to complain about the intellectual isolation of his new home and to realize how much that isolation was costing him.[42]

3. In Hanover, under Three Princes

At first Leibniz was evidently pleased with his new position (though his letters do show that he had to keep asking the duke for a raise in salary). Early

---

[40] A.1.1.370–73.

[41] G. Scheel, in Totok 89.

[42] In 1696 he wrote from Hanover to Thomas Burnet (G III 175): "All my difficulties derive from the fact that I am not in a great city like Paris or London, which have a plethora of learned men from whom one can obtain instruction and assistance. For there is much that one cannot do by oneself. Here one finds hardly anyone with whom to talk; indeed, around here one is not regarded as a proper courtier if one speaks of learned matters, and without the Duchess (Sophie) one would discuss such things even less." Cf. Guhrauer 2, 278.

in 1678 he wrote to his friend Tschirnhaus, outlining some of the advantages that life in the court was providing: complete intellectual freedom, no bacchanalian or saturnalian disturbances, and practically no duties other than that of dressing reasonably well.[43] A few months later, however, he wrote to Herman Conring that he now had more duties, mostly legal.[44] In his "spare" time, of course, he was carrying on an immense correspondence with the learned world of his day; most of his papers in logic date from this period, as do his first plans to pump water out of the silver mines in the nearby Harz mountains.[45]

At the end of 1679 Duke Johann Friedrich died and was succeeded by his brother, Ernst August, who reigned until 1698. Leibniz wrote to Huygens:

> I have suffered a huge loss in the death of my lord the Duke, who, even apart from his princely qualities, was certainly one of the greatest men I have known. But his brother, the Duke of Osnabrück, who has taken up the reins of government and has already shown that in this House virtue and nobility are to be a certain extent hereditary, has given us grounds for some consolation over the loss, which could not be better made up than by such a successor.[46]

Soon, however, Ernst August put Leibniz to work on an incredibly time-consuming task that was to extend to the end of his life and that probably deprived Western philosophy of some great contributions.[47] This was the task of compiling a detailed history of the house of Brunswick-Lüneburg, from Otto the Child (768) down to the (then) present. The basic purpose, so far as one can make out, was to establish the legal claims of Ernst August to a connection with, and thereby an inheritance from, the famous and wealthy Italian house of Este. By the time of his death Leibniz had only reached the year 1005, and even the completed portion of the work was left to gather dust in the archives until it was finally published by Georg Heinrich Pertz in 1843.

To collect materials for this history, Leibniz spent the greater part of the years 1687–90 traveling in southern Germany, Austria, and Italy, visiting libraries, consulting other scholars, and examining records and manuscripts in monasteries and in private collections.[48] His route took him to Frankfurt, Munich, Vienna (where he remained for some nine months), Venice, Florence, Rome, and Naples, as well as to many smaller places along the way.[49]

[43] Chronik 51.

[44] Op. cit., 52–53.

[45] Water was normally pumped out of the Harz silver mines by means of waterwheels actuated by the streams on the surface. Thus, in drought years the mining was often brought to a stop by subterranean flooding. Leibniz drafted plans for a system of windmills that would pump water up from the pits into holding basins; on windless days the pumps were to be operated by releasing the accumulated water from these basins. But after six years of work on the plan, it was given up. Cf. K. Müller, in Totok 34–35.

[46] Chronik 60.

[47] Leibniz to Thomas Burnett, 30 October 1710 (G III 321): "If I were relieved of my historical tasks I would set myself to establishing the elements of general philosophy and natural theology, which comprise what is most important in that philosophy for both theory and practice."

[48] Chronik 83ff.

[49] Ernst August had approved only a trip to Modena, but Leibniz made a tour of it. Cf. K. Müller, in Totok 49.

In addition to exploring archives and making many valuable acquaintances in the learned world, he is said to have had certain experiences not essentially unlike those that befall the modern-day tourist. For example, Eckhart reports:

From Venice Leibniz went, as the only passenger in a small sailing vessel, along the coast and out to sea. A frightful storm came up. He has often told me how the seamen, believing that he did not understand their language, made plans in his presence to throw him overboard and divide up his possessions among themselves. He did not let on that he understood but instead took out a rosary that he happened to have with him and pretended to be praying. Upon this, one of the seamen announced that, inasmuch as the man was no heretic, he could not allow him to be killed. So Leibniz escaped with his life and was set ashore near Mesola.[50]

Leibniz was very well received in Rome. He was given unlimited access to the Vatican and Barberini libraries and was made a member of the Accademia Fisico-Matematica. He composed a votive poem for the health and safety of Pope Innocent XI, who was in his final illness, and upon the election of the new pope, Alexander VIII, he took up the pen again to write *Poenitentia gloriosa orbis Christiani carmen gratulatorium ad S.D.N. Alexandrum VIII Pontificem Maximum*. Perhaps partly in response to these gestures of goodwill, he was offered the position of custodian of the Vatican library, but on condition that he join the Catholic church—a condition he declined to meet.[51]

In December 1689 Leibniz reached Modena, the principal location of the Este family records and the ultimate destination of his trip. At Augsburg two years earlier he had found, by consulting the original manuscript of the *Historia de Guelfis principibus*, that in a crucial reference "Estense" had been miscopied by the editors as "Astense." And now in Modena, after working on various documents and records twelve hours a day for two solid months, he discovered what he was looking for: a complete account of "the true connection of the illustrious houses of Brunswick and Este."[52] From Modena he journeyed up the Po River to Ferrara and then to the abbey of Vangadizza. There he located the tombs of the old margraves of Este and managed to decipher the various identifying inscriptions, and in particular the epitaph of the Countess Kunigunde, whose son Welf IV (1070–1101) was the Bavarian nobleman who founded the Guelph dynasty.[53]

When Leibniz reported this crucial success to Hanover, he received by return mail, instead of congratulations, another assignment that was of quite a different nature and was in some ways even more difficult. The Duchess Sophie, his good friend at the court, asked him to arrange a marriage between

---

[50] Chronik 95; Guhrauer 2, 87–88. In "Murder considered as one of the fine arts," Thomas De Quincey recounts a similar story about Descartes. Cf. De Quincey (1897), vol. 13, 25–26. However, De Quincey is hardly a reliable source; cf. op. cit., vol. 5, 357n, where the "no two leaves are exactly alike" story (see p. 132) is transported to Kensington Gardens in London!

[51] Chronik 97; Guhrauer 2, 88, 93–94.

[52] Chronik 100.

[53] Guhrauer 2, 103; Chronik 101.

the Duke of Modena and one of the daughters of the late Johann Friedrich. A previous emissary, a Count Dragoni, had failed at the task—perhaps, as Sophie conjectures, because of his back trouble. "For," she wrote, "there is a close connection between one's back and the gland that M. Descartes talks about, and since the Count has a great deal of trouble with that part of himself, it is not surprising that he has done so poorly in negotiation."[54] Leibniz was more successful, though five years elapsed before Princess Charlotte Felicitas became the Duchess of Modena.

Two very important figures in Leibniz's life during this time were the just-mentioned Duchess Sophie, wife of Duke Ernst August, and her daughter Sophie Charlotte, later queen of Prussia.[55] These bright, talented, and energetic women provided some welcome relief from the general intellectual emptiness of the Hanoverian court. Duchess Sophie, whom Leibniz served for thirty-four years until her death in 1714, was a lively, good-humored lady who, as the first electress of Hanover and the mother of the first queen of Prussia and of the first Hanoverian king of England, played a significant role in the Europe of her time. She and Leibniz had frequent discussions on all manner of political, social, and philosophical topics, and when he was away from Hanover, they exchanged some three hundred letters.[56] She also saw to it that her daughter had the benefit of Leibniz's great learning.

Sophie Charlotte was an apt pupil, whose sharp mind helped Leibniz to clarify some of his own ideas. He tells us that his *Theodicy* was the outcome of their philosophical discussions, which in later years often took place during walks through the grounds of the Lietzenburg (Charlottenburg) palace in Berlin.[57] According to Frederick the Great, who was her grandson, "This princess had the genius of a great man and the knowledge of a savant; she did not deem it unworthy of a queen to admire a philosopher; the philosopher was Leibniz, and she bestowed her friendship on him with the thought that those to whom Heaven has given noble minds are the equivalent of kings."[58]

Something of Sophie Charlotte's nature, and of her regard for Leibniz, is suggested by what she is reported to have said on her deathbed: "Don't grieve for me, for I am about to satisfy my curiosity about things that even Leibniz was never able to explain—space, the infinite, being, and nothingness—and

[54] Guhrauer 2, 105.

[55] On this topic in general, see Fischer 243–92.

[56] Fischer 243.

[57] Chronik 179; Fischer 260–61; G VI 39ff. (H 63ff.). Like Leibniz in Hanover, Sophie Charlotte complains that in Berlin she has no one with whom to talk (Fischer 256).

A considerable portion of Leibniz's immense correspondence was with women. For a very interesting and informative account of this, see Utermöhlen (1980); she points out that Leibniz did not share the view, prevalent then and not unheard of in our own time, that in intellectual matters women are naturally inferior. Leibniz cites the Countess Anne Conway as one example, among others, of women with extraordinary philosophical "penetration," i.e., sharpness and depth (G III 336–37). And he chides the Countess Kielmannsegg: "It would be just as easy, Madame, for you and your friend to master geometry as it is for us, but you just don't want to take the trouble."

[58] Fischer 125.

for my husband, the king, I am about to provide a funeral-spectacle that will give him a new opportunity to display his pomposity and splendor!"[59]

For most of Leibniz's life, these women were his principal advocates at the courts in Hanover and Berlin. Sophie Charlotte's sudden death in 1705 devastated him;[60] it was such an obvious loss to him that he even received formal expressions of sympathy from the emissaries of foreign governments;[61] and when Duchess Sophie, whom he had served for so long, died in 1714, his ability to obtain support for anything other than continuing the Brunswick history came to an end.

To return to our narrative: Arriving back in Hanover in 1690, Leibniz accepted an appointment as librarian at nearby Wolfenbüttel, by Duke Anton of Brunswick-Wolfenbüttel. This was, of course, an addition to his duties at Hanover, which also included a librarianship, and he accepted the new position only because he could see that his historical researches were going to require his spending a considerable amount of time in the Wolfenbüttel library anyway.[62]

From this time on Leibniz remained in the vicinity of Hanover except for occasional sojourns, seldom of more than a few weeks' duration, in Berlin and Vienna. He continued to work on the history, though obviously with decreasing enthusiasm after the main question had been answered. (In 1691 he estimated that he could complete it in 1693 if he got sufficient support; as we noted earlier, however, at his death in 1716 he had reached only the year 1005.)[63] But in addition he administered the libraries and the mint, served as an adviser on legal and political questions, provided engineering and architectural advice, and did innumerable other jobs for his employers—all the while continuing to produce on the side the mass of philosophical, mathematical, theological, and other writing for which he is primarily known.

Under the circumstances, it is not surprising that his work was somewhat disorganized. Even as a young man in Paris he had written to his friend, the Hamburg jurist Vincent Placcius:

You will ask what I, who was so generous with promises, have since accomplished. The answer is: I have begun much, but carried out and completed nothing. . . . But I had to go to France . . . and have been occupied with everything other than jurisprudence . . . and have been studying mathematics, . . . , and so forth.[64]

Twenty years later the pattern is the same, and it was to remain the same for the rest of his life. Writing to the same friend in 1695, he says:

I cannot tell you how extraordinarily distracted and spread out [*zerstreut*] I am. I am trying to find various things in the archives; I look at old papers and hunt up unpublished documents. From these I hope to get some light on the history of Brunswick. I receive and answer a huge number of letters. At the same time, I have so many mathematical results, philosophical thoughts, and other literary innovations that

59 Ibid.
60 Chronik 195; G III 366–67.
61 Fischer 265

62 Chronik 105.
63 Op. cit., 107.
64 Op. cit., 43.

should not be left to disappear, that I often do not know where to begin .... Thanks to the help of a craftsman whom I have engaged, the calculator with which one can do multiplications up to twelve decimal places is finally ready. A year has gone by; I still have the craftsman with me in order to make more machines of this type, for they are in constant demand.[65]

Prominent among Leibniz's innumerable schemes for improving the world were his plans for reconciling the Protestants and the Catholics. Actually, his efforts in the direction of such a reunion had begun even at Mainz, where he joined in a project initiated by Boineburg and the elector. Perhaps impressed by the devastation of the Thirty Years' War, and in any event unable to see any really important doctrinal difference between the two churches, Leibniz never could understand why they should not get together. To illustrate this point, he used to tell the story of two English theologians and controversialists, the brothers John and William Rainhold, of whom he had heard on his trip to England.

Both brothers lived in the reign of Queen Elizabeth. John, who resided in the Spanish Netherlands, had become a Catholic; William, who lived in England, remained Protestant. In their letters they argued energetically about religious topics, each trying to draw the other over to his side, but in vain. Finally they set a time and place for a face-to-face debate, in order to convert one another. Both succeeded; both won; both lost. Each was persuaded by the other; each regretted that he had persuaded the other. So they switched religions and domiciles. John went to England in place of his brother; William remained in the Netherlands. And from then on, each defended his new belief with all possible sharpness.[66]

The treatise called *Systema theologicum*,[67] in which Leibniz examined the details of Catholic and Protestant creeds in order to show how their differences could be resolved, probably dates from 1686, just before he set out on the Italian trip. Later, at the urging of the Duchess Sophie, he entered into an extended correspondence about these matters with the French historian and theologian Paul Pellisson-Fontanier and with J. B. Bossuet, the bishop of Meaux. The latter, especially, hoped to convert Leibniz to Catholicism, and when it became obvious that this would not occur, the correspondence ceased. Leibniz also had a scheme for the union of the Reformed and Lutheran churches, but this met with no greater success than the other.

When Sophie Charlotte became queen of Prussia in 1701, the connection with Berlin increased the political importance of the house of Brunswick, and Leibniz had a new opportunity to realize some of his favorite projects. One such proposal was the institution of an academy at Berlin to promote science and culture, on the model of the French Academy in Paris. With the queen's help, the Berlin (Prussian) Academy of Sciences was founded on 11 July,

[65] Op. cit., 134; cf. G III 194.
[66] Guhrauer 2, 350.
[67] F 1 531–652.

1700, with Leibniz as its first president. He also pushed forward with plans to establish similar academies in Vienna and St. Petersburg.

These activities, and especially the travels they involved, did not endear him to the last of his three ducal employers, Georg Ludwig, who succeeded his father as duke of Brunswick-Lüneburg in 1698 and who in 1714 (without particularly wanting the honor) was crowned George I, king of England. George wished Leibniz to stay at home in Hanover and work on the history project, rather than gallivant around Europe on such missions as founding learned societies. Leibniz finally paid the penalty for his truancy when, also in 1714, George denied his request to be taken along to England as court historian. Instead he was ordered to remain in Hanover to complete the boring task on which he had labored for so many years.[68]

From his fiftieth year to the end of his life Leibniz suffered from gout. Eventually he began to walk with a limp, and by 1714, Eckhart reports, his feet, hands, and shoulders were affected to such an extent that he could no longer work in the uninterrupted way that was his custom. Later the gout was complicated by open sores on his right leg. Eckhart, as quoted by Guhrauer, conjectures that this new malady was brought on by Leibniz's own habits.

Normally he first went to bed at one or two in the morning. Often he just slept in his chair, and would be awake again and ready to go at six or seven in the morning. Sometimes he would remain several days in his chair. I believe that this is what led to his having an open sore on his right leg. This caused him difficulty in walking; he tried to remedy it, but only by putting blotting paper on it.

Later, to reduce the pain and to make the nerves insensitive he had a number of wooden clamps made, and these he screwed onto himself wherever he felt pain. I suspect that by doing this he so damaged his nerves that eventually he could no longer use his feet and had to stay in bed.[69]

To the end, Leibniz was skeptical of the medical profession, preferring to treat himself with various elixirs and potions that had been recommended to him by acquaintances.[70] The affected leg became progressively worse, and,

---

[68] W. Ohnsorge, in Totok 188: "On 30 November 1714 the King issued his Privy Council an official order in which he observed that Leibniz, after his absence in Vienna, had departed once again despite his promise of energetic work on the Guelph history. They were to remind him in the name of the King that as early as 1691 he had solemnly sworn to finish the work in a few years. Now more than twenty years had passed without any result. The King expects that until the end of the work Leibniz will desist from traveling and other distractions, 'in order that we and our house may finally have reliable information as to whether and when we can hope to enjoy the fruits of our long and patient wait.'"

[69] Guhrauer 2, 336.

[70] G VI 110 (131): "It is nature that cures us, rather than medicine." His skepticism is understandable when one reads his suggestions for needed improvements in the practice of medicine: blood tests and transfusions, autopsies, experimentation with animals and even with human beings if not dangerous to them, study of the spread of disease, regular measurement of the patient's temperature, regular physical examinations, routine recording of data about the course of the patient's illness, establishment of more medical schools, socialized medicine. Of professors of medicine he said: "They speak more to the ears than to the understanding" (E. Hochstetter, *Gottfried Wilhelm Leibniz 1646–1716*, in *Die Grossen Deutschen*, Berlin, 1956, vol. 2, 13); Hartmann and Krüger (1976); Steudel (1969).

confined to his bed, he was beset additionally by an attack of kidney stones. Not until the day before he died did he finally accept the services of a physician, who by then was able only to provide some relief from the pain. It is recorded that when, on his deathbed, he was asked by a servant whether he did not wish to take Holy Communion, he answered that they should leave him in peace, for he had done no harm to anyone and therefore had nothing to confess.[71] Then he requested pen and paper and began to write something, but finding that he could no longer read what he had written, he tore up the paper and lay back in the bed. Shortly thereafter he pulled his nightcap over his eyes, turned onto his side, and quietly breathed his last.

The funeral, it seems, was a scandal to Hanover and to Germany. Unlike Newton, whose casket was escorted by dukes, earls, and other dignitaries to its honored niche in Westminster Abbey, with a large segment of the London populace paying homage, Leibniz is said to have gone to his grave "more like a robber than what he really was, the ornament of his country." His mysterious friend, John Ker of Kersland, who happened to be passing through the city at the time, reported that although the entire court of Hanover had been invited to the funeral, no one attended except Eckhart and a few servants.[72]

Leibniz's remains were interred in the Neustädter Kirche, a Protestant church near the ducal palace. They were not destined to rest in peace.[73] For more than fifty years the grave was forgotten, and although in 1790 a large sandstone slab, with the inscription OSSA LEIBNITII, was installed, even at that time doubt was expressed whether it was placed over the right crypt. The doubts grew, especially since the relevant church documents had been lost, until finally, in 1902, the remains under the slab were exhumed and examined by an expert. Although no really decisive evidence was found (the casket, which had been described in some detail by Eckhart, was entirely decomposed), the expert, a Professor Dr. W. Krause, concluded that the skeleton was indeed that of Leibniz.[74] But there is more to the story. In World War II

---

[71] Guhrauer 2, 329.

[72] *The Memoirs of John Ker of Kersland*, London, 1726, 117: "I must confess, it afforded me matter of strange reflection, when I perceived the little regard that was paid to the ashes by the Hanoverians; for he was buried in a few days after his decease, more like a robber than what he really was, the ornament of his country." Ker of Kersland is sometimes described as a "Scottish nobleman," but the *Encyclopedia Britannica* (11th ed., s.v. Ker, John), in surprisingly animated language for an encyclopedia, calls him a "Scottish spy," a "knave," and a "man of the worst character," whose true name was Crawford but who assumed the name and arms of his wife's family, and who died in a debtor's prison. The *Britannica* article specifically casts doubt on the reliability of the *Memoirs*. It says that Ker sold the manuscript to Edmund Curll the bookseller, a fellow prisoner who was serving a five-month sentence for publishing obscene books, and that when Curll later published it, he was sentenced to the pillory at Charing Cross. Perhaps Ker's dubious reputation is what leads G. Scheel, in Totok 85, to write: "Die offenbar unausrottbare Legende, dass dem Sarge nur sein Gehilfe Eckhart gefolgt sei und dass die Beerdigung der eines Strassenräubers geglichen habe, sollte endlich aus der Literatur verschwinden." Cf. Guhrauer 2, 331.

[73] For the following, see Fischer 291–92; Müller (1968), 43–46; W. Kabitz in Fischer 774–75; Krause (1902); Graeven (1916), especially pp. 7ff.

[74] He noted, incidentally, that the cranial capacity (1,422 cc) was extremely small for a

the church received a direct hit in an aerial bombing attack, and Leibniz's slab was pulverized. It was later replaced by a marble one, which is what the visitor to the church now sees.

After Leibniz's death, his sole legal heir, Pastor Friedrich Simon Löffler, the stepson of his sister, Anna, arrived promptly in Hanover to claim his inheritance. Besides an extensive library and a large number of manuscripts, Leibniz had left the sum of 12,000 thalers.[75] Pastor Löffler was evidently very eager to realize the maximum amount of cash from the estate; he of course took the 12,000 thalers, and he later received an additional 5,210 florins that had been due Leibniz for services in Vienna.[76] He sold a valuable portrait of Leibniz to a secondhand dealer for 3 thalers, and apparently he would have put up the remainder of Leibniz's belongings for auction if George I had not intervened to seal the house and preserve the books and manuscripts for the state.[77]

By the latter part of the eighteenth century, the magnitude of Leibniz's genius began to be publicly recognized in Germany. Monuments were put up in several places. In Hanover, with funds subscribed by local citizens and some Göttingen professors, the so-called Leibniz-Tempel was erected. This is a classic round temple with a cupola supported by twelve Ionic columns, sheltering a white marble bust sculpted by the Irish sculptor Christopher Hewetson. On the frieze, in large gold letters, is the inscription GENIO LEIBNITII. Originally located a short distance from the building in which the royal library was housed from 1719 until the recent past, the temple was moved in 1935 to a park adjacent to the great garden at Herrenhausen.[78] Unfortunately, that park is also adjacent to the campus of the local university, which probably explains why the philosophical pilgrim today is likely to find the statue adorned with garish paint and embellished with the latest student slogans. There is a certain irony in this, for at heart Leibniz was a peacenik, if there ever was one.

We have a few descriptions of Leibniz's person, by himself and by others. According to these, he was a rather thin, balding man of ordinary stature, not at all striking in appearance or manner. There are many references to his plainness. Boineburg, in a letter of recommendation written to Paris in 1672, assures Pomponne that despite Leibniz's unprepossessing exterior, he is an

---

German (average 1,696 cc), which hardly accords with Eckhart's testimony that Leibniz had a large head (Guhrauer 2, 334).

[75] One would like to know what 12,000 thalers amounted to. If the tradition is believable, it must have been a considerable sum, for Löffler's wife is supposed to have fallen to the floor in a faint when her husband returned home with such booty. But perhaps the following facts are more relevant: (1) Leibniz's yearly salary in 1677 was 500 thalers, and later in his life it rose to about 1,000 thalers; (2) a thaler contained about 20 grams of silver. Of course, the question is much more complex than this might suggest, as there were many different kinds of thaler, containing varying amounts of silver at varying times, and Leibniz had other income and perquisites.

[76] K. Müller, in Totok 58.

[77] Chronik 262.

[78] G. Scheel in Totok 85–86.

immensely promising young man.[79] Leibniz himself, in a letter of 1673 to his friend Lichtenstern, regarding a possible court position in Denmark, says, "I feel myself burdened with a deficiency that counts for a great deal in this world, namely, that I lack polished manners and thereby often spoil the first impression of my person. Wherever people attach great weight to such things, which I do not, and wherever it is a question of 'socialize if you want to succeed,' there I am out of place."[80]

In another text, making the same point, he tells how he once went into a Paris bookshop to inquire about Simon Foucher's *Critique de la recherche de la vérité*. When he described the work as "metaphysical," the bookdealer and a bystander, who had sized him up as some sort of country bumpkin, decided to amuse themselves at his expense and began by asking him sarcastically whether he did not even know the difference between metaphysics and logic. By sheerest coincidence Foucher himself chanced to enter the shop just then and, immediately recognizing Leibniz, began to speak of him with an admiration and deference that left the scoffers agape. Their attitude toward Leibniz changed at once, of course; his every remark was now approved and applauded, and the compliments flowed profusely. Leibniz says that he had never before seen so clear a demonstration of how appearances and preconceptions can affect human reason.[81]

Leibniz once wrote a description of himself for a doctor friend.[82] "His temperament is not really sanguine nor peevish, nor phlegmatic or melancholy—though peevishness may appear to predominate. He is slender, of medium stature, with a pallid face, hands that are often cold, feet that, like his fingers, are too long and narrow in proportion to the rest of his body." "His voice is weak . . . and he has trouble pronouncing the sounds *G* and *K*." "He has a sweet tooth and puts sugar in his wine." "Strong perfumes delight him." The series of more or less disconnected facts continues: he is nearsighted, sleeps well, likes to work late at night rather than in the morning, has been sedentary since he was a boy, has always read a great deal and reflected on what he read, is an autodidact in most branches of knowledge, doesn't care very much for conversation though he greatly prefers it to games and exercises that involve bodily motion. It ends with the odd remark that "the animal spirits are too active in him, and for that reason I fear that one day, because of his continual studying and excessive meditation, his skinny body will perish of consumption or some other disease."

Many years later Eckhart and others added some further items. Leibniz walked somewhat stooped over, so that he did not look as tall as he was. He ate a great deal but drank very little, watering his wine to avoid heartburn. Never having cooked for himself, he simply ate whatever the innkeeper sent over and at whatever time his studies would permit. Each morning he would be driven to the Leineschloss from his rented rooms in the "Leibniz-House." He never settled permanently in Hanover, although, typically German, he

[79] Fischer 292.   [81] LH 339.
[80] Op. cit., 111.   [82] Guhrauer 2, Anmerkungen, 59ff., translated at 338ff.

had his little garden just outside the Aegidien gate, in which he grew tobacco and other exotica, and had silkworms feeding on mulberry trees.[83]

Leibniz remained a bachelor all his life. Once, in his fiftieth year, he was eager to get married. But the intended person asked for time to think it over, and meanwhile he lost the inclination. He sometimes said that he had always thought there was plenty of time, but one day he realized that now it was too late. People said that Leibniz followed the maxim that *Heiraten sei gut, doch müsse ein weiser Mann sein ganzes Leben darauf denken* (Marriage is a great thing; a wise man will consider it his whole life).[84] Perhaps this lifelong consideration is what emboldened him, a bachelor to offer the notorious "Wedding Present" advice to a bride.[85]

4. Works

The philosophical works for which Leibniz has chiefly been known were composed in the years between 1690 and 1716. Unfortunately, he never wrote out a full and systematic account of his views. Indeed, the one and only large philosophical work that he published during his lifetime was the *Theodicy*, in which, according to its subtitle, he proposed to explain and presumably to reconcile the goodness of God, the freedom of man, and the origin of evil. Concerning this book he wrote to Thomas Burnet:

> The greater part of the work was composed piece by piece, at a time when the late Queen of Prussia and I were having discussions of these matters in connection with Bayle's Dictionary and other writings, which were being widely read. In our conversations I generally answered the objections raised by Bayle and contrived to show that they are not so powerful as certain people who are not well disposed to religion would have us believe. Her Majesty frequently commanded me to set down my answers in writing, so that one could think them through more carefully. After the death of this great princess I gathered the pieces together, at the instigation of friends who had heard about them, and, with some additions, produced the book in question. It is a book of considerable size. As I have reflected upon this topic since my youth, I dare say that I have treated it thoroughly.[86]

The only other large philosophical work left by Leibniz is the *Nouveaux essais sur l'entendement humain*, a detailed commentary on Locke's *Essay*. This commentary, which has the form of a dialogue, was ready for publication by early 1704, but when Locke died in October of that year, Leibniz decided to withhold it, considering that one should not publish such a

---

83 Chronik 180.
84 Guhrauer 2, 363.
85 Guhrauer 2, Anmerkungen, 37ff.
86 G III 321; cf. Chronik 221.

critique when the author could no longer reply.[87] The *Nouveaux essais* finally appeared in 1765.

For the rest of what we know of the philosophy of Leibniz we have to rely on occasional journal articles and masses of letters, drafts, notes, and other bits and pieces. The *Nachlass* of manuscripts is enormous.[88] Leibniz carried on a very large correspondence, but besides this he was in the habit of "thinking on paper."[89] He wrote out philosophical ideas more as an investigator than as an advocate, and he seems never to have thrown away anything he had written. Accordingly, the *Nachlass* is a bewildering hoard of notes, drafts, and fragmentary statements, plus the manuscripts of pieces designed for publication and of letters actually sent (of which, in most cases, he kept copies). By far the greater part of this material, consisting of more than 57,000 items, is housed in the State Library of Lower Saxony, in Hanover. About 15,000 of these are letters, to more than 1,050 correspondents. From 1690 on Leibniz was exchanging letters with an average of 150 to 200 persons, and during one brief period the number of correspondents reached 650. Most of the correspondence is in Latin and French, with a lesser amount in German.

Plans to produce a complete edition of Leibniz's writings began in 1901, when the International Association of Academies assigned the task jointly to the Berlin Academy of Sciences and two French academies. By 1912 the formidable preliminary tasks were completed and the first volumes were almost ready. But World War I intervened, severely hampering the work. After the war, nationalism and chauvinism prevented a continuation of the collaboration between the French and the Germans, and the Berlin Academy decided to proceed alone. Under its auspices the first volumes appeared in 1923. The basic plan, developed by Professor Paul Ritter, envisaged seven series: I. General, political, and historical correspondence; II. Philosophical correspondence; III. Mathematical, scientific, and technical correspondence; IV. Political writings; V. Historical writings; VI. Philosophical writings; and

---

[87] G III 612 (L 656). In June 1704, when Locke was very ill, Lady Masham wrote to Leibniz: "Mr. Locke presents you his humble service and desires me to tell you he takes himself to be mightilie obliged to you for your great civilitie expressed to him; in which he finds you a master as well as in philosophy and everything else. His want of health, he says now, and the little remains he counts he has of life, has put an end to his enquiries into philosophical speculations. Though if he were still in the heat of that pursuit he could not be so ignorant of you or himself as to take upon him to be the instructor of a man of your knowne extraordinarie parts and merit . . ." (G III 351). Leibniz's judgment of Locke, in a letter to Nicholas Remond: "Mr. Locke had subtlety and skill and a kind of superficial metaphysics for which he was able to secure acclaim, but he was ignorant of the mathematical method" (G III 612). In a letter to Lady Masham, however, he calls Locke a "great man" and says that although not everybody can penetrate into his speculative system, everybody should conform to his practical philosophy (G III 367). Locke's judgment of Leibniz, in a letter to Molyneux: "You and I agree pretty well concerning the man; and this sort of fiddling makes me hardly avoid thinking that he is not that very great man that has been talked of him" (Locke's *Essay*, ed. A. C. Fraser, Oxford, 1894, vol. 1, xlv).

[88] The following comments on the *Nachlass* and the Academy edition are based on Schröter (1969) and Müller (1969). See also Hochstetter (1966).

[89] LH 338: "Often in the morning, when I am still in bed, so many thoughts come to me in a single hour that sometimes it takes me a whole day or more to write them out."

VII. Mathematical, scientific, and technical writings. Between the wars a few volumes were published, despite economic and political difficulties, but World War II brought the project almost to a standstill again. It is now going forward once more, thanks to the sustained efforts of three important research centers, in East Berlin and in Hanover and Münster in the German Federal Republic. A total of about sixty large volumes, ranging to more than eight hundred pages each, are planned; sixteen have appeared to date. In general, the material is being published in chronological order of composition, so that the early writings are already well covered but much of the later material, which contains most of what is interesting to philosophers, has not yet been reached. In the meantime, studies of Leibniz's philosophy have to be based primarily on C. I. Gerhardt's seven-volume edition of the *Philosophischen Schriften*, and on the older editions of J. E. Erdmann and Ludovicus Dutens.

II

The System in Outline

Reality, according to Leibniz, consists of an infinite number of individual substances, which he calls "monads," that is, "units."[1] One of these monads, God, exists by necessity, since the assumption that it exists is consistent and the assumption that it does not exist implies a contradiction. The infinitely numerous remaining monads are substances created by God; each of these exists, but no contradiction would follow from the assumption that it did not.

God's principal attributes are omniscience, omnipotence, and benevolence. In creating the actual world, he knew what all the possibilities were; he was able to create whatever he chose, and he wished to make the best possible choice. Accordingly, from the infinitely many possible worlds, any one of which could have been actualized (that is, from the infinitely many ways in which he could have created a world), he chose the best. Hence, this is the best of all possible worlds, in the sense that any change in it, when considered with all its necessary preconditions and consequences, would be a change for the worse.[2]

Lest it be supposed that such optimism is an obvious mistake, Leibniz reminds us that we human beings are inclined to underestimate the degree to which things are interconnected. In thinking of "improvements" that could be made in the actual world, we tend to overlook what the preconditions and consequences of such changes would have to be. Leibniz observes that "the wiser a man is, the fewer detached intentions he has, and the more

---

[1] In this initial summary I shall in the main forgo detailed citation of supporting texts. Most of the relevant passages will be found in the *Monadology* (G VI 607–23, L 643–52), the *Discourse on Metaphysics* (G IV 427–63, L 303–28), *The Principles of Nature and of Grace* (G VI 598–606, L 636–41), and the 6 February 1706 letter to the Duchess Sophie (G VII 565–70). There is also a summary in a letter to Arnauld (G II 135ff., M 170ff.)

[2] And not only that, but things are getting better and better all the time. LH IV vii B 2 37 (Fasz. 1, # 37, 129): "In nature, as in art, prior times are simpler and later are more perfect. For nature is the highest art."

the views and intentions he does have are comprehensive and inter-connected."[3]

Attempting to extrapolate this generalization to the limit—a move that, incidentally, is very characteristic of his thought—he argues (invalidly, of course) that an omniscient being would see in detail that everything is connected with everything else in such a way that the slightest change anywhere in the universe would involve a change in the whole. Thus, although it might be supposed that, for example, a world would be better than ours if it were like ours in practically all respects except that in it Judas did not betray Christ, such a supposition would rest on ignorance, probably complicated by defective reasoning. "What is deceptive in this subject," Leibniz says,

. . . is that one feels an inclination to believe that what is the best in the whole is also the best possible in each part. One reasons that way in geometry, when it is a question of maxima and minima. If the road from *A* to *B* that one proposes to take is the shortest possible, and if this road passes by *C*, then the road from *A* to *C*, part of the first, must also be the shortest possible. . . . But the part of the best whole is not of necessity the best that one could have made of that part. For the part of a beautiful thing is not always beautiful, since it can be extracted from the whole, or marked out within the whole, in an irregular manner.[4]

The monads, which constitute the actual world, are simple substances.[5] They have no parts, and consequently, according to Leibniz, they are characterized neither by extension, form, nor divisibility. Not being composite, they cannot begin or end gradually but must originate only through creation and be terminated only through annihilation.[6] From this, Leibniz seems to infer that each monad begins when the universe begins, and continues to exist until the universe comes to an end.[7] Leibniz also infers from the lack of compositeness that "no monad can be altered or changed in its inner being by any other created thing, since there is no possibility of transposition within it."[8] Yet every created being, including the created monads and aggregates of such, is subject to continuous change throughout the entire period of its existence; in other words, although the monad has no parts, it does go through a continuous series of states.

The states of a monad are called "perceptions," and the tendency to go from state to state is called "appetition." In its perceptions every monad "mirrors" every other monad; that is, the state of each monad at any given time "expresses" the states of all the others at that time—each monad is "a universe in miniature."[9]

Here the term "expression" is used in a rather abstract, technical sense, in

[3] G II 19; cf. G I 384. Baruzi (1905) (L 219): a truly wise person who is well informed will have nothing to find fault with (in the actual world).

[4] G VI 245–46 (H 260–61).

[5] Leibniz also sometimes applies the term "substance," in a secondary sense, to bodies. Cf. A.6.6.226 and chap. 11, sec. 2.

[6] G VI 152 (L 172).

[7] G II 99 (M 124–25), but cp. G II 370.

[8] G VI 607 (L 643). Cf. Baruzi (1905) (L 218), G II 116ff. (M 149ff.)

[9] G VII 566–67; G VI 616 (L 648); G II 457 (L 605); G IV 480 (L 457).

which it plays a central role in Leibniz's philosophy. It is carefully explained
in a number of texts, of which the following is typical:

> One thing is said to express another if it has properties that correspond to the
> properties of the thing expressed. ... There are various kinds of expression; for
> example, the model of a machine expresses the machine itself, the projective
> delineation on a plane expresses a solid, speech expresses thoughts and truths,
> characters express numbers, and an algebraic equation expresses a circle or some
> other figure. What is common to all these expressions is that we can pass from a con-
> sideration of the properties of the expression to a knowledge of the corresponding
> properties of the thing expressed. Hence it is clearly not necessary for that which
> expresses to be similar to the thing expressed, if only a certain analogy is maintained
> between the properties.[10]

It may at first seem that what Leibniz has in mind is some sort of structural
isomorphism between the expression and the thing expressed, as exists
between a circle and a projected ellipse or hyperbola, or between a map and
the terrain mapped, or between a musical composition and the pattern of
charges or indentations on a recording of it. But the relation is more general
than this, requiring only that from features of the expression it should be
possible to derive, by some sort of calculation based on a law, features of the
thing expressed, as in the case of the algebraic equation and the circle it
characterizes.[11] Still another example would be an encoded or enciphered
text and the plain text it represents.

Thus, in saying that at any given time the state of each monad expresses
the states of all the others, Leibniz is just asserting that, given a complete
knowledge of the state of any particular monad at any particular time, a sufficiently discerning mind could read off the state of any other monad at that
time.[12] Further, each state of a monad similarly reflects all past and future
states of that monad.[13] Consequently, if one knew completely the condition
of any single monad at any time, and if one had adequate logical powers, one
could determine the states of that and all other monads at all times.[14] This is
the sense in which "everything is connected with everything."

The idea that at every point in the space of monads there is at every given
time a vast multiplicity of events that reflect what is going on (or has been
going on) everywhere else may seem implausible. Russell offers an analogy:

> A photographic plate exposed to a portion of the night sky takes photographs of
> separate stars. Given similar photographic plates and atmospheric conditions, dif-
> ferent photographs of the same portion of the sky will be closely similar. There must,

---

[10] G VII 263 (L 207); cf. G II 112 (M 144), G I 383, C 15.

[11] G II 112 (M 144): "One thing expresses another (in my terminology) when there exists a
constant and fixed relationship between what can be said of one and of the other." However, in
support of the isomorphism interpretation, Leibniz says (at LH I xx 206) that whatever
expresses an organism must itself be an organism.

[12] C 15. Cf. Burk 162; Heinekamp (1976), 562.

[13] G III 66, G IV 433 (L 307–8).

[14] G IV 433–34 (L 307–8). For a full treatment of Leibnizian "expression," see Kulstad
(1977).

therefore, be some influence (I am using the vaguest word that I can think of) proceeding from the various stars to the various photographic plates. Physicists used to think that this influence consisted of waves, but now they think that it consists of little bundles of energy called photons. They know how fast a photon travels and in what manner it will, on occasion, deviate from a rectilinear path. When it hits a photographic plate, it is transformed into energy of a different kind. Since each separate star gets itself photographed, and since it can be photographed anywhere on a clear night where there is an unimpeded view of the sky, there must be something happening, at each place where it can be photographed, that is specially connected with it. It follows that the atmosphere at night contains everywhere as many separable events as there are stars that can be photographed there. [15]

It might also be pointed out that according to Newtonian mechanics, every body in the universe (that is, every object having mass) has a gravitational effect on every other body, regardless of their size and distance. (In this use of the term "body," any collection or aggregate of bodies, however spatially distributed it may be, itself constitutes a body.) To this, Leibniz adds the premise that "to all the movements of our body there correspond certain more or less confused perceptions or thoughts of our soul" and infers the conclusion that "the soul too will have some thought about all the movements of the universe."[16] Since every created monad has a body at every time, and the movements of that body correspond to the monad's changes of state, every change of state by any monad is registered by them all.

There is some reason, however, to believe that Leibniz's motivation in holding this thesis was derived more from logical than from quasi-physical considerations. He seems to think that, in general, if an object A has a property P at a given time and if at a later time it no longer has that property, then not only A but also every other object B in the universe will have changed; for B, which at the given time has the property 'coexists with A's having P',[17] will at the later time no longer have that property, and so it, too, will have changed. To be sure, this understanding of "change" departs a little from the ordinary, for if Theaetetus used to be shorter than Socrates but is now taller, we are accustomed to conclude only that at least one of them, and not necessarily both of them, has changed. But the problem of differentiating in a plausible way those properties of an individual that it can lose without changing, from those that it cannot, is no less difficult than the corresponding problem of distinguishing the essential from the accidental. Leibniz's inclination to regard every temporal alteration of properties as constituting a change is only the obvious counterpart of his inclination to regard every property of an individual as essential to its identity.

Although each monad "mirrors" all the others, there is no causal interaction among them—"they have no windows."[18] Instead, Leibniz postulates a

---

[15] Russell (1959), 18.

[16] G II 112–13 (M 144); cf. G VII 570.

[17] Or, more precisely, has the accidents that are the ground of the extrinsic denomination 'object coexistent with A's having P'.

[18] G VI 607 (L 643).

"preestablished harmony," much as would obtain between two perfectly synchronized clocks, so constructed that one strikes when the other shows the hour. The appearance of causation is there because of the constant conjunction of showings and strikings, but the states of each clock are the effects of antecedent states of that clock and are not caused by any states of the other.[19]

For most people this whole story, the "monadology," seems far removed from reality until it is realized that each of us has at least one monad readily available for inspection. Each of us—and here, of course, the reference is to the soul or mind, and not to the body—each of us *is* a monad.[20] Hence, some of the things Leibniz says about the monads—for example, that they have no extension, no form, no parts (where the possibility of independent existence is essential to the notion of "part")—begin to take on plausibility. On the other hand, the claim that each monad perceives or expresses all the others at every moment of time, and that it bears the traces of all that has ever happened to it, requires some explaining. And all of Leibniz's explanations have not sufficed to make his further claim, that the real world consists of nothing but monads, believable to many of his readers.[21]

Leibniz proposes to use the term "soul" for those monads whose perceptions are relatively distinct and are accompanied by memory. On this basis, animals have souls. "If a stick be shown to a dog, he remembers the pain which it has caused him, and he whines or runs away." In human beings, too, the sequence of perceptions is usually determined primarily by associations and memories. For most of us, our expectation that it will be daylight tomorrow is just an inductive result of what we have experienced up to the present time. For an astronomer, however, the same expectation is based on reason; this additional capacity is what distinguishes man from the other animals. Souls that are capable of reason and science, which "raise us to a knowledge of ourselves and of God," are called "spirits" or "minds." Leibniz adds:

> It is also by the knowledge of necessary truths, and by their abstractions, that we rise to *acts of reflection*, which make us think of that which calls itself "I," and to observe that this or that is within us: and it is thus that, in thinking of ourselves, we think of being, of substance, simple or composite, of the immaterial, and of God him-

---

[19] G IV 498 (L 459).

[20] A.6.6.85–86: The very concept of existence is derived from ourselves—we are the paradigm cases. Cf. A.6.6.129, G. VI 612 (L 646).

[21] Perhaps this is the place to mention an amusing but highly suspect story told by Christoph Mathaeus Pfaff, professor of theology at Tübingen, with whom Leibniz had some correspondence. In 1728 Pfaff published, in the *Acta eruditorum lipsiensis*, pp. 125–27, a notice in which he purports to quote Leibniz as saying, in response to Pfaff's criticism of the *Theodicy*, "You have grasped the matter accurately. And I am astonished that up to now nobody has perceived this game of mine. For it isn't necessary for philosophers always to be serious when, as you properly note, in devising hypotheses they are just testing their powers of thought." The point is supposed to be that even Leibniz regarded his philosophizing as a kind of joke, amusing but not serious.

self, conceiving that what is limited in us is in him without limits. And these reflective acts furnish the principal objects of our reasonings.[22]

As we have mentioned several times, every monad perceives everything in the universe; we ourselves are no exception to this. Most of our perceptions, however, are below the conscious level, and even our conscious perceptions, to which Leibniz applies the term "apperception," are more or less confused.[23] Further, even the relatively most clear and distinct apperceptions record (that is, express) only the structure, not the actual qualities of their objects.

Thus, when we take ourselves to be perceiving a material object, or body, what is really going on is that we are perceiving confusedly the elements of a monadic aggregate. Subliminally we do perceive each component monad separately, but since these many perceptions are approximately equally strong or equally capable of holding the attention of the soul, they are run together and perceived only confusedly.[24] Leibniz is fond of a simile in which the perception of a physical object is likened to that of the distant roar of the surf: the rushing, roaring noise, according to him, is a confused composite of innumerable small noises produced by the individual waves.[25] Or, similarly, our perception of a rainbow is a confused visual perception of a huge number of droplets of water; subliminally we see each one, but at the conscious level we are aware only of the arc of color. Thus, what we call "bodies," Leibniz holds, are really only *phenomena*. They are well-founded phenomena, however, for (unlike dreams, hallucinations, or other illusory experiences) they do relatively clearly represent the actual features of the aggregate of monads that are being confusedly perceived.[26]

It should be mentioned that, unfortunately, Leibniz also uses the term "substance" in a secondary sense to apply to bodies, and that "body" sometimes refers to the underlying monadic aggregate and sometimes to the perceived phenomenon.

Leibniz believed that all space is filled with bodies; there is no such thing as a perfect vacuum. (Whether in holding this he was thinking of the phenomena or of the underlying monadic aggregates is unclear.) Consequently, he inferred—though here is another conspicuous gap in his reasoning—that any movement of any single body requires some corresponding movement in every other body. Therefore, as he says,

Every body responds to all that happens in the universe, so that he who saw all could read in each one what is happening everywhere, and even what has happened and what

---

[22] G VI 612 (L646).
[23] A.6.6.115ff., 134, 177.
[24] C 10.
[25] G V 16 (NE 15); A.6.6.54, 403–4. Cf. G VI 534 (L 557).
[26] Sometimes—e.g., at C 13—the body is identified with the aggregate of monads that constitute the foundation of the phenomenon. Leibniz holds that everything in the physical world takes place according to the laws of mechanics (A.6.6.455).

will happen. He can discover in the present what is distant both as regards space and as regards time; *sumpnoia panta* [everything breathes together], as Hippocrates said.[27]

A living being, as Leibniz uses the term, consists of a body together with a single dominant monad that expresses with particular distinctness the other monads in the founding aggregate. If the dominant monad is a soul, the living being is an animal. As we have seen, since the body expresses all the universe through the interconnection of all matter in the plenum, and the soul expresses the body, the soul, too, expresses the whole universe via that ("its") body.[28]

Impressed by what the recently invented microscope had revealed about the existence of microorganisms and living cells,[29] Leibniz came to believe that living beings are "natural automata" that are composed of smaller living beings, which are composed of still smaller living beings, and so on, ad infinitum.

> Whence we see that there is a world of created things, of living beings, of animals, of entelechies, of souls, in the minutest particle of matter. . . . Every portion of matter may be conceived as like a garden full of plants and like a pond full of fish. But every branch of a plant, every member of an animal, and every drop of the fluids within it, is also such a garden or such a pond.[30]

This does not mean, Leibniz points out, that each soul has a monadic aggregate or body that is permanently attached to it. All bodies are in perpetual flux, like Heraclitus's river, so that the soul changes its body only gradually and by degrees, never all at once. What we call "birth" is merely a stage involving relatively rapid development and growth, and what we call "death" is just the opposite of this.[31] Thus, not only is there no real generation, but also there is no entire destruction or absolute death.

These principles provide Leibniz with a way of responding to the mind-body problem posed by Descartes. The soul follows its own laws, for its perceptions at any given moment are caused by its antecedent perceptions; and the body likewise follows its own laws, which Leibniz gratuitously assumes to be mechanical. But the two are fitted together in virtue of the preestablished harmony among all substances, which are all representations of the same universe.

Thus, the body does not act causally on the soul in the production of knowledge, nor the soul on the body in the production of motion. All ideas, which are dispositions of the soul to have certain kinds of perceptions, are innate although they may manifest themselves only on the occasion of sensory perception. The soul is not at birth a tabula rasa, as Locke had said, but more like an unworked block of marble with hidden veins that already

---

[27] G VI 617 (L 649); cf. A.6.6.54 and G VII 570.
[28] G VI 599 (L 637): Each soul is surrounded by an infinite number of monads forming its body.
[29] In this connection see Leibniz's eulogy of the microscope, in his *Meditation on the Common Concept of Justice*, in Riley (1972), 53.
[30] G VI 618 (L 650).
[31] G III 635 (L 658); GM III 553 (L 513); cf. GM III 575 (L 514), C 10, G II 126 (M 161).

outline the form that will be revealed by the sculptor.[32] Further, in answer to another question raised by Locke, the mind always thinks, for it is the very nature of a monad to be a percipient, active being. Dreamless sleep and unconsciousness generally are explained as periods in which all of one's perceptions are below the conscious level.

Although every monad expresses every other monad, only God perceives and conceives everything with perfect clarity. In each portion of the universe, God sees the whole universe. "He is infinitely more discerning than Pythagoras, who reckoned the height of Hercules from the size of his footprint."[33] God's conception of any individual involves everything that has happened, is happening, or will happen to that individual; it is the "complete individual concept" of that individual. For example, the complete individual concept of Adam involves, inter alia, that he was the first man, that Eve was his wife, and that he would have such and such progeny, including all of ourselves. Anyone of whom all this was not true would not have been Adam, but someone else. In other words, God, in deciding to create Adam, knew exactly what he was doing; he was considering *Adam*, as distinct from every other possible person, however similar, with whom we (with our limited powers) might confuse him.[34]

Leibniz, like some recent authors, notably W. V. Quine, could make no sense of essentialism, the doctrine that some attributes of an individual are essential and others are accidental.[35] From the beginning to the end of his intellectual career, as we have noted earlier, he considered that in this respect all of an individual's attributes are on a par; and since the alternative of taking all of them as accidental (which would require us to say, for example, that Adam could have had all the attributes of Bucephalus) was clearly unacceptable, he was driven to the other alternative of declaring them all equally essential.

Of course, at the Creation God considered not only the series of individuals he did create, but also infinitely many other series that were less good. As he considered these other series of possible individuals, his concepts were no more confused, of course, than when he thought of the individuals he actually created. In other words, he had before him, for each possible world, a set of complete individual concepts, determined in every respect. The concepts in any one series or possible world "reflect" one another; just as the concept of Adam involves that of Eve, so that Adam could not exist without Eve, so also the concept of Pegasus involves that of Bellerophon.

Now some things that in themselves are possible are not compossible. There could be a world in which there was no sin, and there can be (indeed,

---

[32] A.6.6.52.

[33] G VI 329.

[34] Cf. G VII 407, par. 66 (L 708).

[35] He does distinguish, however, between those attributes that a monad has throughout its existence, i.e., at all times, and those it has at some times and lacks at others; thus the attribute "rational" belongs to Alexander always, while the attribute "king" belonged to him for only a limited time. Cf. A.6.6.305.

is) a world in which there is forgiveness of sin, but there cannot be a world with both of these features; likewise, there could be a world in which there was no poverty, but such a world would exclude the exercise of charity, which in itself is possible (and also desirable). Even individual concepts can exclude one another in this way. For example, Adam's complete individual concept is not compossible with that of any nonexistent individual X; for if both Adam and X existed, they would stand in some relation to one another, and every relation is "grounded" in attributes of the relata, so that either the concept of Adam or that of X, or both, would have to contain attributes different from those it does contain—which is impossible.

According to Leibniz, everything "strives" for existence; that is, everything will exist unless prevented by the existence of something that is not compossible with it. Thus, the actual world is "maximal," in the sense that it contains everything that is compossible with what it contains. Since God's only reason for not creating something would be that he was going to create something else that was not compossible with it (for "to exist is better than not to exist"), we may infer that the other possible worlds are maximal in the same sense. And, since each complete individual concept reflects all the other individual concepts in its series, we see that no concept can belong to more than one possible world.

In short, the totality of complete individual concepts is partitioned by the equivalence relation of compossibility into mutually exclusive, jointly exhaustive sets of concepts; these, in effect, are Leibniz's possible worlds.

The distinction between the actual world and the various other possible worlds is associated with the division of true propositions into necessary and contingent. A necessary truth is a proposition true of all possible worlds; a contingent truth is a proposition true of the actual world but not of all possible worlds. However, Leibniz usually defines these terms in another way: a necessary truth is one the opposite of which implies a contradiction; a contingent truth is a truth that is not necessary.

There is a problem here, for Leibniz also holds that in every true affirmative proposition, whether singular or universal, necessary or contingent, the concept of the predicate is contained in the concept of the subject. This dictum refers primarily to propositions of the form 'A is B', with singular subject, and to propositions of the form 'Every A is B', with general subject. The problem is: how can the opposite of a true contingent proposition fail to imply a contradiction if its predicate concept is part of its subject concept? For example, if crossing the Rubicon is part of the very concept of Caesar—that is, part of what it is to *be* Caesar—how can "Caesar did not cross the Rubicon" fail to imply a contradiction?

Leibniz says that this bothered him for a long time before he hit upon the solution: "imply" means "yields in a finite number of steps," where a "step" is a substitution (of *definiens* for *definiendum*, or vice versa) made in accord with a definition.[36] In a contingent proposition, he says, it would take an infinite

[36] FC 179 (L 263–64).

number of steps to produce the contradiction, and hence only God can see in such a case how the predicate concept is contained in the concept of the subject.

But this "solution" would seem to explain at most how we mortals, who are unable to accomplish infinite analyses, might mistakenly suppose that such a proposition as "Caesar crossed the Rubicon" was contingent, that is, could have been false, while God would be aware that anyone who would not cross the Rubicon would not be Caesar.

Leibniz was more bothered by another, though related, apparent consequence of his scheme. His picture of a completely deterministic world, of which every single aspect, however minute, is the result of a perfectly knowledgeable choice by a completely benevolent God, leaves him with some explaining to do as concerns the existence of sin and of evil in general. His treatment of these matters, which form the principal topic of the *Theodicy*, is an acknowledged dialectical masterpiece—but whether it is a masterpiece of sophistry or of clearheaded philosophy is open to question.

Leibniz distinguishes three types of evil: metaphysical, physical, and moral. Metaphysical evil is mere imperfection, physical evil is identified with suffering, and moral evil is sin.[37] The existence of metaphysical evil is a consequence of the previously mentioned incompossibility of certain things or states of affairs that are possible in themselves; to create the best possible world, God had to leave out various features that, considered by themselves, were good. Metaphysical evil is the absence of these putative goods. As to whether God willed the existence of these goods (in which case their nonexistence calls his omnipotence into question) or willed their nonexistence (thus displaying a lack of benevolence), Leibniz distinguishes the "antecedent will" from the "consequent will." The antecedent will, he says, "is detailed and considers each good separately qua good"; the consequent will "is complete, final, and decisive, and results from the conflict of all the antecedent wills." Leibniz concludes: "God wills antecedently the good and consequently the best."[38]

As concerns moral evil, or sin, one might suppose that God, not Judas, was responsible for the betrayal of Christ, since God created that state of affairs. Indeed, one might even suppose that God thereby damaged not only Christ but also Judas by causing him to sin. Leibniz's answer is that God's choice was not whether Judas should sin, but rather whether Judas-who-was-going-to-sin (*Judas peccaturus*) should nevertheless exist; and since it is better to exist than not to exist, no injury was done to this individual by God's decision.[39] Further, God's decision was that Judas-who-was-freely-going-to-sin should exist, and hence Judas acted freely and cannot shift his responsibility over onto the Deity. In other words, God determined that Judas should sin freely.[40] The possibility of sinning is a necessary concomitant

[37] G VI 115 (H 136).
[38] G VI 115–16 (H 136–37).

[39] See chap. 5, sec. 5. Cf. Fasz. 2, 300–301.
[40] G II 52 (L 334); G VI 255 (H 270).

of freedom of action and therefore had to be included for the sake of this greater good.

Physical evil, consisting of "sorrows, sufferings, and miseries," is declared by Leibniz to be the result of moral evil. "It is true," he says, "that one often suffers through the evil actions of others; but when one has no part in the offense, one must look upon it as a certainty that these sufferings prepare us for a greater happiness."[41] But in general he seems to think that we deserve what we get, and that a world in which people reap their just rewards is better than one in which they do not.

It therefore appears that at bottom the source of all three types of evil is the same, namely, the impossibility of combining all the goods that are separately possible. To create the best combination, God had to leave out certain states of affairs that were in themselves desirable, and, worse, he had to include certain conditions that were in themselves undesirable.

Leibniz brings another distinction to bear on this topic. This is the distinction between absolute and hypothetical necessity. He applies the qualifier "absolute" to the kind of necessity we have described above, while a proposition P is called "hypothetically necessary" if it is not absolutely necessary and the hypothetical proposition 'If this world exists, then P' is absolutely necessary—or, what amounts to the same thing, if the conjunction 'This world exists, and not-P' is absolutely impossible.[42] On this basis it turns out that every contingent truth is hypothetically necessary. When Leibniz's opponents argue that his doctrine makes "Judas sinned" a necessary truth, thus exonerating Judas, Leibniz replies that the necessity here is only hypothetical, not absolute. And he adds that this sort of necessity "inclines, without [absolutely] necessitating."

So much for our preliminary sketch. Now let us get down to details.

---

[41] G VI 261 (H 276).
[42] See chap. 6, sec. 2.

III

Propositions and Concepts

Underlying Leibniz's entire logic, metaphysics, and philosophy of language is the traditional view that the essential role of language is to represent our thoughts about the extralinguistic world. This is surely the common person's view; the philosophical version of it goes back at least as far as Aristotle:

Spoken words are the symbols of mental experience, and written words are the symbols of spoken words. Just as all men have not the same writing, so all men have not the same speech sounds, but the mental experiences, which these directly symbolize, are the same for all, as also are those things of which our experiences are the images.[1]

1. The Three Regions

In accord with this outlook, Leibniz speaks of three distinct "realms," or "regions," namely, the real world, the region of thought and ideas, and language.[2] His terminology is by no means uniform, but on the whole we can see that the scheme is, in outline, as follows.

Reality, in the most fundamental sense of that term, is regarded as consisting exclusively of individual substances—the so-called monads.[3] Each of

---

[1] Aristotle, *De Interpretatione*, 16a3–5. Leibniz observes (C 497) that the example of Chinese characters shows that symbols can represent the thoughts directly, not via the sounds.

[2] A.6.6.301.

[3] G II 270 (L 537): "Indeed, considering the matter carefully, it may be said that there is nothing in the world except simple substances and, in them, perception and appetite. . . ." G II 119 (M 153): "Only indivisible substances and their different states are absolutely real." LH IV vii C 76r: "What is real [*res*] is either immutable, i.e., God, or mutable, i.e., a created being [*ens creatum*]. A created being is either a substance, which can perdure through change in itself, or an accident, which cannot." Leibniz here includes aggregates or "heaps" of substances as *res*. Cf. LH IV vii C 77r: "A substance, properly speaking, is either primitive [*primitiva*], namely, God, or derivative [*derivativa*], namely, a created thing [*creatura*]." On the other hand, "real" and its

47

these substances, at any given time, is, of course, in some condition or state (mode). Leibniz frequently uses the term "accident" in that connection, but he does not wish to hypostatize the accidents of substances as an additional type of entity in the real world.[4] In a secondary sense he sometimes applies the term "substance" to aggregates of monads, and especially to those aggregates that are the foundation of the appearances we call "bodies." The term *substantiata* ("substancelike things") is also employed to denote such collections.[5]

The region of *ideas* is inhabited, of course, by ideas. The most important subclass of ideas is that of *concepts*; in fact, when Leibniz is presenting his own metaphysics and not accommodating himself to the terminology of others (for example, to that of Locke), it seems that he uses the terms "idea" and "concept" interchangeably.[6] Propositions, attributes, relations, terms, and, in general, all abstracta are special cases of concepts.[7] These various categories are imperfectly distinguished from one another; in some instances they plainly overlap or perhaps even coincide.

Leibniz describes the region of ideas as an "intelligible world in the divine mind." Usually he seems to regard the minds of mortals not as containing their own species of less-perfect concepts but rather as grasping less perfectly

---

cognates are often used by Leibniz much more widely to refer to items in the region of ideas—e.g., so-called real ideas. Thus, G II 492 (L 609): Phenomena are *realia*.

It is thus necessary to distinguish several senses in which he uses the term "reality." In one sense it denotes what is real, i.e., the individual substances-with-accidents. In another sense it denotes a common feature of all real things; in this sense Leibniz says (G I 272): "Reality is conceivability." (*nihil aliud enim [est] realitas quam cogitatibilitas*.) There are still other senses of these terms in Leibniz; see Heinekamp (1968), 207ff.

⁴ G II 458 (L 606): The inherence of an accident in a subject is a state of the subject. Sometimes Leibniz calls accidents "qualities" or "modifications" of their substances. Cf. A.6.6.217, 228.

⁵ C 13, 438; A.6.6.213. LH IV vii C 76r: "A substantial being [*ens substantiale*] is either a substance, which cannot fail to perdure through its changes, or a *substantiatum*, which can perdure through some of its changes and is an *ens per aggregatum*, as, e.g., a wagon, a machine, a herd, a river."

⁶ Concerning ideas generally, see G VII 263–64 (L 207–18 and A.6.6.254ff. At G IV 452 (L 321) Leibniz says: "The expressions that are in the soul, whether conceived or not, can be called *ideas*, but those which are conceived or formed can be called *notions* or *concepts*." But elsewhere he does not stick to this distinction. Cf. A.6.2.488: A *Notio, Conceptus, Idea* is a thought [*cogitatio*] insofar as it is a thought of something.

⁷ Perhaps propositions are not even *special* cases. At C 381 (P 71) Leibniz says, "Every term, even an incomplex one, can be taken as a proposition as though 'true' were added; e.g., 'Man is true' or 'Man is an animal is true'." C 382 (P 71): "Just as any term can be conceived as a proposition, as we have explained, so also any proposition can be conceived as a term; thus, man's being an animal is true, is a proposition, is of such a kind, is a cause, is a reason, etc." For more on this, see n. 24 and cf. PLR 7n.

Usually "property" seems coextensive with "attribute" and even with "concept," but at G II 258 (L 533), A.6.6.63, and elsewhere, Leibniz uses it in a more restricted sense to refer to "perpetual" features of the subject, as distinct from temporary features (whether of the subject itself or of its properties), which he calls "modifications." In this use, "king" would represent a modification but not a property of Alexander the Great, while "man" would represent a property. This sense of the word "property" is the same as the special sense Leibniz sometimes gives to the expression "essential property."

the true concepts that are God's; perhaps, however, he would say that to have a deficient idea is to have a deficient grasp of a perfect idea.[8]

At any rate, he considers ideas to be what we should today call "dispositional properties" of the minds that have them; more precisely, to have an idea is to have a disposition to think in a certain way.[9] Thus, the region of ideas should not be thought of as a domain of entities somehow hovering above the real world of monads but possessing a different kind of "being." In many texts Leibniz emphatically denies that there really are such things as these; statements that appear to be about them, he tells us, are only *compendia loquendi* (abbreviated ways of talking) that replace more complex and lengthy statements about individual substances.[10]

The third region is that of *language*. Words—that is, marks and sounds—are phenomena or collections of similar phenomena, where phenomena, again, are explained as certain states (called "perceptions") of individual substances. Written discourse stands for oral discourse, which in turn represents the concepts, propositions, and other elements of thought about the real world of individuals.[11]

In sum, reality consists exclusively of individual substances or monads. One of these monads, God, exists eternally and unchanging, outside the temporal series. The remainder, including ourselves, exist through all time, continually undergoing changes that range all the way from the nearly imperceptible to the relatively drastic. Ideas, concepts, propositions, and so forth, are "in God's mind," but this does not mean that his mind is a kind of receptacle in which such entities reside or have some sort of shadowy existence. It means only that he "has" the ideas, which in turn means only that

---

[8] E 445 or D.2.222 (L 592): "Many of the Platonic doctrines are most beautiful—that there is an intelligible world in the divine mind, which I also usually call the region of ideas; and that the object of wisdom is the really real [*ta ontos onta*] or simple substances, which I call monads and which, once existing, endure always...." Cf. G VII 310. Other denizens of the region of ideas are truths or propositions (A.6.6.397); space, time, and motion (GM VI 247, L 445); possibles (G II 55, L 336); place, position, quantity, number, proportion (C 9); possible worlds (G IV 556, L 575, G VI 363). At G II 305 (L 488) the region of ideas is said to be in God himself.

As noted in the text, when Leibniz uses the term "idea," he seems usually to be talking about God's ideas. When he considers ours, he classifies them, first, into *clear* and *obscure*, where an idea is clear to the extent that it enables us to recognize objects as falling under it, and then into *distinct* and *confused*, where an idea is distinct to the extent that we can analyze it into its components. Our ideas of colors are clear but confused; our ideas of geometric figures are, to the extent that we are expert, clear and distinct. A maximally distinct idea is called *adequate*. G IV 422–23 (L 291–92); G IV 449–50 (L 319–19).

The dispute whether all ideas are innate or not is a dispute *de nomine* (G III 307).

[9] G VII 263 (L 207). A.6.6.118: Ideas are distinguished from thoughts; the latter, always accompanied by sensation, are actual; the former are dispositional. A.6.6.87: Truths are not thoughts but are rather dispositions to think; there are truths that have never been thought. Cf. also G IV 451–52.

[10] Grua 547.G V 491: confusion of the ideal and the actual gives rise to problems, e.g., the labyrinth of the continuum.

[11] A.6.6.444 (in a speech by Philalethes, not challenged by Theophilus). However, we can learn to refer written signs directly to things, without going through sounds as intermediaries; cf. n. 1 above. Sometimes thought itself uses words instead of the concepts they represent, especially when the concept is very complex. G IV 423 (L 292).

he has the capacity or disposition to think in certain ways. Thus, by including one very special individual in his nominalistic ontology, Leibniz achieves some of the advantages ordinarily thought to flow from Platonism. Finally, by means of language, the constituent signs of which are phenomena founded on certain monad states, we manage to record and communicate our thoughts, which are themselves monad states. In the last analysis, therefore, there is only one realm; everything is reducible to the states of monads.

Such is the basic scheme, and we shall do well to keep it in mind as we strive to understand the intricacies of Leibnizian doctrine.[12]

That task is complicated, however, by the fact that Leibniz's use of the relevant terminology is not at all uniform, and also, even more troublesome, by the fact that he is very careless about the distinctions involved. Thus, like many modern authors, he often confuses propositions with sentences, ascribing to the former various features that properly belong to the latter. More generally, he amalgamates concepts of all kinds with the linguistic expressions that are supposed to represent them. This sometimes prevents us from knowing exactly what he means to say on important topics, and occasionally it even leads to outright contradiction.[13] He also does not always attend properly to the distinction between concepts and the individuals falling under them. Thus, for example, when he speaks of the "subject" of a proposition, he may be referring to a word or to the subject concept of the proposition or to the individual or individuals that fall under that concept.[14]

These kinds of confusion can give rise to philosophical afflictions much more serious than mere ambiguities and superficial contradictions. Thus, the confusion of propositions with sentences has led Russell and some other expositors of Leibniz to spill a great deal of ink over the essentially non-sensical question, "Is every proposition of subject-predicate form?" (The corresponding question about sentences has a relatively clear sense, and I suppose that its answer is "no"; but up to now nobody has given a coherent and plausible criterion for determining the "form" of a proposition, that is, of the meaning of a sentence, as contrasted with the sentence itself.)

Leibniz himself, by confusing concepts with the linguistic expressions that represent them, gets into a hopeless tangle about the individuation of

---

[12] Cf. Burk 333.

[13] Thus, in the paper entitled *Specimen calculi universalis* (C 243, P 39) he contradicts himself within the space of a few lines while explaining what a term is: "For us, every simple term is a name. . . . By "term" I understand, not a name, but a concept, i.e., that which is signified by a name; you could also call it a notion, an idea."

One is reminded of Aristotle's account of nouns and verbs; "A noun [*onoma*] is a spoken sound significant by convention, without time . . .; a verb [*hrema*] is what additionally signifies time ; when uttered by themselves, verbs are nouns (*De Interpretatione* 16a19–b19). Perhaps great philosophers are entitled to a few such lapses, especially in writings not intended for publication.

[14] C 403: "For an individual substance is a subject that is not in [*non inest*] any other subject." LH IV vii C 70r: A substance is a complete term, i.e., one involving everything that is said of whatever *it* is said of. Cf. PLR 6–7; Parkinson says that Leibniz is not to be blamed for these ambiguities, as he inherited them from the Scholastics and Aristotle.

concepts. For, as we shall see, one of his fundamental principles implies that if the propositions 'All A is B' and 'All B is A' are true, the concepts A and B must contain one another and hence (presumably) must be identical. But Leibniz denies this result; he explicitly mentions several pairs of concepts—for example, the concept Triangle and the concept Trilateral—of which he says that the concepts differ although both of the respective universal generalizations hold. These and related difficulties, which go to the heart of his metaphysics and philosophy of language, will be considered more thoroughly in the appropriate places below.

Of course, in ascribing such confusions to Leibniz I do not mean to suggest that he was incapable of distinguishing, for example, the word "Adam," the complete individual concept of Adam, and Adam himself—far from it.[15] The difficulties arise only from the fact that in crucial texts he fails to attend rigorously to his own distinctions.

The reader will appreciate that Leibniz's carelessness about these distinctions creates problems for would-be expositors. As philosophers who are interested in the tenability of his doctrines, we cannot be content with merely paraphrasing his actual words, preserving all their vagueness and ambiguity. Even to do a responsible job of expounding his views, we need to understand his pronouncements at least well enough to permit reasoning with them. For in choosing among the various possible interpretations of an author's dicta, one has to consider logical relationships. Ceteris paribus, an interpretation is preferable if it preserves consistency and relevance. Unfortunately, use of this canon inevitably involves doing some "reconstruction" and ascribing to Leibniz various relatively unambiguous and precisely formulated tenets concerning which, in truth, the most that can be claimed is that he probably would have assented to them if his attention had been drawn explicitly to their connection with some of his distinctions and doctrines.

2. Notation

To those who suspect that metaphysics in general arises from use-mention confusion, it will come as no surprise that it is very difficult to set forth metaphysical doctrines while using quotation marks consistently and correctly. I have not solved this problem completely satisfactorily, but I have done my best.

In what follows, the primary use of double quotation marks and displayed

---

[15] Cf., e.g, the "Dialogue on the Connection between Things and Words," G VII 190–94 (L 182–85), the topic of which is precisely the relation of words, thoughts, and things.

It may be appropriate to give, for the record, a clear example of the kind of use-mention confusion that so often mars his reasoning. At G II 370 (L 597) he purports to be showing that "even an infinity of points gathered into one will not make extension," but he in fact does show, of his point B, not that it is an "infinity of points gathered into one," but only that it can be described in an infinite number of ways, as "the vertex of triangle BCD," "the vertex of triangle BDE," "the vertex of triangle BEF," etc.

lines will be to form designations of linguistic expressions, as contrasted with propositions and concepts. We say, for example, that "Caesar crossed the Rubicon" is a sentence, beginning with the word "Caesar." But sometimes such phrases as, for example,

> the proposition, "Caesar crossed the Rubicon"

or

> the proposition that Caesar crossed the Rubicon

will be used as elliptical for the corresponding phrase

> the proposition expressed by the sentence, "Caesar crossed the Rubicon,"

and in like manner we shall use, for example,

> the concept, "rational animal"

or

> the concept Rational Animal

for

> the concept expressed by the phrase, "rational animal."

When variables are involved, single quotation marks will be used correspondingly as quasi quotes.[16] Strictly speaking, the values of such variables as "A," "B," "C," will be certain kinds of linguistic expressions, though in many cases it will appear that they are concepts. For example, if we write

> For any concepts A, B, the essential proposition 'A is B' is true if and only if B is included in A,

this is to be taken as short for

> For any (appropriate) expressions A, B, the sentence 'A is B', interpreted essentially, is true if and only if the concept expressed by B is included in the concept expressed by A.

These conventions are unsatisfactory in several respects, and if I had a better way of preserving some measure of use-mention clarity while remaining reasonably close to Leibniz's own formulations, the reader may be sure that I would have followed it.

3. Propositions

Leibnizian definitions of the word "proposition" amply illustrate the difficulties just mentioned. The following is a typical example.

---

[16] Quine (1947), 33ff.

A *proposition* is that which says, as regards two terms or two attributes of things, that one, called the predicate, is contained in the other, called the subject, in such a way that the predicate must apply to everything to which the subject applies. This is said either (1) absolutely or (2) conditionally, that is, as a consequent of another proposition, called the antecedent. Thus every proposition says either that the predicate is contained in the subject or that the consequent is contained in the antecedent.[17]

The sense of this quotation will become somewhat clearer subsequently.

Leibniz's notion of attribute, or property, is such that the same attribute may belong to a thing at different times or may belong to the thing at one time and not at another. For instance, in 1674 Leibniz himself had the attribute "in Paris"; in 1670 he lacked that attribute. There is some question as to whether Leibniz meant to express this sort of fact by means of propositions or properties of propositions. One can say that the proposition "Leibniz is in Paris" was true in 1674 but false in 1670, or that the proposition "In 1674 Leibniz was in Paris" is true and the proposition "In 1670 Leibniz was in Paris" is false. In the latter, the temporal references, "in 1674" and "in 1670," may be considered to modify the copula "is," and the attribute is "in Paris." There are texts in which Leibniz endorses both of these interpretations simultaneously, saying that the copula always connotes a time and that the same proposition can be true at one time and false at another.[18] For reasons that will become clear later, we shall adopt the latter way of handling the matter, in which the time modifies the copula. Leibniz himself, however, does not seem to consider the distinction important, and indeed, when no metaphysical point about propositions and attributes is at stake, such sentences as "'Leibniz is in Paris' was true in 1674" are apparently completely interchangeable with their counterparts, as "In 1674 Leibniz was in Paris."

One possibility that must be rejected is that of building the time reference into the predicate, as if we were to understand "Leibniz is in Paris in 1674" as asserting that Leibniz has (timelessly) the attribute "is in Paris in 1674." For it turns out that such a notion of attribute cannot be fitted into his other doctrines.

Associated with this matter is Leibniz's view that it is impossible for a proposition about an object to change in truth value unless there is an actual change in the object.[19] This point is especially important in connection with his understanding of relational propositions. Thus he holds that when "Socrates is taller than Theaetetus" changes from true to false, there must be a change in Socrates as well as in Theaetetus; and when X's wife dies, so that 'X is a widower' becomes true, there must be change in X, even if X is far away in India and completely unaware of what has happened. But Leibniz frequently ignores the time parameter and writes as though, in the proposition 'A is B', either the attribute B is (timelessly) contained in A or it isn't. Usually, but not

---

[17] G VII 43–44. Cf. C 51, 321, 397 (# 195), 498, and Burk 128. Leibniz uses *propositio* and *enunciatio* interchangeably; cf. C 260.

[18] LH IV vii B 3 (Fasz. 2, 353–54).

[19] LH IV vii C 107–8 (Fasz. 2, 413).

always, we can see how to expand his metalogical statements so as to incorporate the necessary references to time.[20]

The propositions ordinarily considered most basic by Leibniz are those expressed by simple sentences of the form "*A* is *B*," possibly supplemented by the quantifiers "some," "no," or "all."[21] He seems to think—because of his nominalistic metaphysics, as I conjecture—that whatever can be said at all can be expressed in such propositions. For if the world consists of nothing but individual substances-with-accidents, then it would seem that the totality of propositions expressed by sentences of the form "*A* is *B*" (with singular subjects) would describe everything that is the case, and all other descriptive propositions should somehow be reducible to these basic types.

Propositions expressed by sentences of the forms just mentioned are also called "propositions *tertii adjecti*." For any proposition of *tertii adjecti* form there are, according to Leibniz, equivalent propositions of the types called *secundi adjecti* and *primi adjecti*.[22] Corresponding to the *tertii adjecti* proposition '*A* is *B*' (Latin, '*A est B*') are the *secundi adjecti* proposition '*AB* is' ('*AB est*') or '*AB* is an entity' ('*AB est ens*') and the *primi adjecti* proposition '*A*'s being *B* is (the case)' ('*A esse B*, *est*'). Leibniz offers no explanation of this terminology. He appears to hold that in each case there are three equivalent propositions and not just three "forms" of a single proposition. But this is not entirely clear, and each interpretation is supported by some texts.

Some examples may clarify matters. Corresponding to the proposition "Caesar is a Roman," which is *tertii adjecti*, we have the proposition *secundi adjecti* "Caesar the Roman is an entity" and the proposition *primi adjecti* "Caesar's being a Roman is the case."

Leibniz gives *secundi adjecti* versions or equivalents for the other types of categoricals, as follows. 'Every *A* is *B*' is equivalent to '*A* not-*B* is not an entity', 'Some *A* is *B*' is equivalent to '*AB* is an entity', 'No *A* is *B*' to '*AB* is not an entity', and 'Not every *A* is *B*' to '*A* not-*B* is an entity'.[23]

The propositions *primi adjecti* are very infrequently mentioned. A related transformation figures in the reduction of conditional propositions 'If *A* is *B*, then *C* is *D*' to the corresponding categoricals '*A*'s being *B* is *C*'s being *D*'. It appears that Leibniz regards '*A*'s being *B*', ('*A esse B*') as expressing a proposition that is either the same as, or equivalent to, that expressed by '*A* is *B*', and hence that he regards propositions as concepts.[24]

---

[20] Ibid.

[21] C 49 (P 17). S 474: "*Propositio simplex*: *A* is *B*, where *A* is called the subject, *B* the predicate, 'is' the copula."

[22] See C 391–92 (P 80–81) for "*est*" *secundi* and *tertii adjecti*, and G II 472 for "*est*" *primi adjecti*. For a discussion of the senses of these terms, see P xlv, n. 1. Cf. also C 232 and Burk 131–32.

[23] At G VII 212 (P 116), written after 1690, Leibniz calls these transformations "my old analysis." He does not reject them but notes that 'No *A* is *B*' could also be transformed to '*AB* ≠ *AB ens*' and 'Some *A* is *B*' to '*AB* = *AB ens*'.

[24] C 389 (P 78), C 262. Cf. LH IV vii C 73–74 (Fasz. 2, # 103, 403): "If *A* contains *B*, then *C* contains *D*" can be formulated as "*A*'s containing *B* contains *C*'s containing *D*."

C 260: "And when I say that *A* is *B*, and *A* and *B* are propositions, I mean that *B* follows

Propositions of the form '*A* is *B*' can in principle have singular or general subjects. Most of the examples given by Leibniz have singular subjects, as in "Caius is wise" (*Caius est sapiens*), but occasionally he mentions propositions like "The pious are happy" (*pius est felix*). These are Aristotle's "indefinite" propositions, and I have not been able to see clearly how the Leibnizian *secundi adjecti* and *primi adjecti* transformations make sense with respect to them, nor am I able to work out satisfactory (Leibnizian) truth criteria in their case. Accordingly, henceforward I shall consider only such propositions '*A* is *B*' as have singular subjects. In fact, for reasons that will become apparent later, I shall have to make a further restriction, requiring that the subject concept *A* in such propositions be what Leibniz calls a "complete individual concept." Thus,

Caesar is a Roman

and

Caesar the Roman is an existent thing

will be considered propositions of the form "*A* is *B*," but

Man is mortal

and

The victor of Pharsalus is a Roman

will not.

Simple propositions are also classified as *essential* or *existential*. This is connected with the fact that the word *ens* (entity), which occurs in sentences expressing propositions *secundi adjecti*, is, according to Leibniz, ambiguous: in one sense it is equivalent to *existens* (an actually existing thing), while in the other sense it denotes whatever is abstractly possible. There is a corresponding ambiguity of *est* (is) in the sentences expressing propositions *tertii adjecti*. Thus, '*A* is *B*' can be equivalent to '*AB* is an existent thing' or to '*AB* is an abstractly possible thing'.[25] The difference will be clearest in a case like

---

from *A*." (In the same paragraph, however, he appears to give a counterexample to the proposed reduction of conditionals to categoricals. He says that although "God is just" follows from "God is wise," the wisdom of God is not the justice of God.)

As concerns the question whether '*A esse B*' expresses a proposition, compare the above quotation from C 260 with the statement at C 232: "Every categorical proposition can be conceived as a terminus complexus to which is added either '*est*' or '*non est*' *secundi adjecti*; thus 'Every man is rational' can be thought of as '[*A*] nonrational man is not [*non est*]'." At G II 472 it is explained that a proposition is a *terminus complexus* (a term that is assertoric), while a concept is a *terminus incomplexus*, and that every *terminus complexus* can also be transformed into a *terminus incomplexus* plus "*est*" *primi adjecti*; thus "Man is rational" becomes "Man's being rational, is [the case]."

[25] C 392 (P 81). At G VII 319 (L 363), however, *ens* is explained as a term wider than *existens* (and thus not as sometimes just meaning the same as *existens*). This fits in with the definitions (at A.6.2.487 and elsewhere) of *ens* as "what can be distinctly conceived" and of *existens* as "what can be distinctly—i.e., accompanied by distinct concepts—sensed or perceived."

"Pegasus is a winged horse," the *secundi adjecti* form of which is "Pegasus the winged horse is an entity." If *ens* is taken in the first sense, the propositions expressed will be existential and false, for Pegasus does not exist. But if it is taken in the other sense, they express true essential propositions to the effect that the winged horse Pegasus is a possible existent.

In a somewhat different form, the same distinction is found in Aristotle, who says (*Metaphysics*, 1017b1–10) that we apply "seeing thing" both to that which actually sees and to that which potentially sees, and similarly with "intelligent" and "tranquil." Here the ambiguity is transferred from the single word *ens* to all the nouns and adjectives of the language. Ockham, citing this Aristotelian text, nevertheless draws the distinction in Leibniz's way: *Similiter dividitur "ens" in ens in potentia et in ens in actu.*[26]

At any rate, this fundamental ambiguity, which Leibniz thought he detected in the most elementary components of our discourse, allows us to reconcile a number of apparently incompatible assertions that occur in his writings on logic and the philosophy of language. For example, in some places he indicates that all propositions of the form '*A* is *A*' are true and even necessary; elsewhere he offers '*AB* is not *AB*' as equivalent to 'No *A* is *B*'.[27] And sometimes he says that '*A* is *B*' is false if *A* does not denote an existent thing, while elsewhere he sets '*A* is *B*' equivalent to 'If something is *A*, then it is *B*'.[28] These and many other seeming inconsistencies may be resolved if we are free to interpret some of his assertions as concerning essential propositions and others as concerning those that are existential.

Leibniz himself uses the two senses of *ens* to clarify the traditional dispute over the so-called existential import of categoricals. In one text he examines the question whether 'Some *B* is *A*' follows from 'Every *A* is *B*'. Considering the particular case of "Every laugher is a man," he writes:

> Every laugher is a man: that is, laugher and laugher-man are equivalent. But a laugher is an entity, by hypothesis; therefore a laugher-man is an entity; therefore a man-laugher is an entity, that is, some man is a laugher. Here, in the proposition "A man-laugher is an entity," "entity" must be taken in the same way as in the proposition "A laugher is an entity." If "entity" is taken to refer to possibility, that is, as meaning that there is a laugher in the region of ideas, then "Some man is a laugher" must not be understood as other than "A man-laugher is an entity," namely, as possible, that is, in the region of ideas. But if "A laugher is an entity" is taken to refer to what really exists, "A man-laugher is an entity" can also be taken to refer to this, and it will be true that

---

And at A.6.6.486 Leibniz writes as though "Every man is an animal" means both that the extension of "animal" includes that of "man" and that the intension of "animal" is included in that of "man." This would seem to imply that the copula *est* and, correspondingly, the term *ens* have simultaneously both meanings. At any rate, Burk 346 and Kauppi (1960), 215–16, are clearly mistaken in supposing that *ens* never has the sense of *existens*.

[26] Ockham, *Summa Logicae: Pars Prima*, ed. P. Boehner, St. Bonaventure, N.Y. 1951, chap. 38.

[27] C 393 (P 82).

[28] Ibid.

some man actually laughs.... The words of our language, then, are ambiguous, but the ambiguity is removed by our analysis.[29]

This passage, when read in its context, in effect directs our attention to the following sequence:

(1) *Omne A est B*	(Every *A* is *B*)	hypothesis
(2) *A = AB*	(*A = AB*)	(1)
(3) *A est ens*	(An *A* is an entity)	hypothesis
(4) *AB est ens*	(An *AB* is an entity)	(2), (3)
(5) *BA est ens*	(A *BA* is an entity)	(4)
(6) *Quoddam B est A*	(Some *B* is *A*)	(5)

It purports to show that on the assumption that some actual or possible entity falls under the concept *A*, 'Some *B* is *A*' follows from 'Every *A* is *B*'; if an actual entity is assumed to fall under *A*, 'Some *B* is *A*' will assert the existence of an actual entity *AB* (and 'Every *A* is *B*' will have existential import), while if only a mere possible is assumed to fall under *A*, then 'Some *B* is *A*' will assert only that *AB* is a possible thing (and 'Every *A* is *B* will have only what might be called "essential import").[30]

It appears, therefore, that the essential interpretation of an elementary *tertii adjecti* sentence may be obtained by transfrorming it into *secundi adjecti* form and then taking *ens* as referring to purely possibles, while the existential interpretation is obtained by taking *ens* as meaning the same as *existens*.[31] It should also be mentioned here that for Leibniz the word *ens* is always equivalent to *possibile* ("possible"), and that therefore the latter term also has two senses, according as absolute or hypothetical possibility (which we shall discuss later) is meant.[32]

---

[29] G VII 214 (P 118); cf. G VII 213 (P 117). Couturat (CL 359) thinks that Leibniz's point in this passage is that 'laugher" (and, mutatis mutandis, all other general terms) is ambiguous, sometimes referring to those who are actually laughing and sometimes to those who have the capacity to laugh. But Leibniz clearly assigns the ambiguity to *ens*. Note G VII 300 (L 226): All *A* is *B*; some *A* is *A*; therefore, some *A* is *B*.

[30] Burkhardt (1974), 63–64, 66, concludes from this passage and others that Leibniz does not accept existential import for universal or particular propositions. As I read it, the passage states quite the contrary.

[31] C 375 (P 65): "What is to be said about the propositions '*A* is an existent' or '*A* exists'? Thus, if I say of an existing thing, '*A* is *B*', it is the same as if I were to say '*AB* is an existent'; e.g., 'Peter is a denier', i.e., 'Peter the denier is an existent'." C 392 (P 81): "The particular affirmative proposition 'Some *A* is *B*', transformed into a proposition *secundi adjecti*, will be '*AB* is', i.e., '*AB* is a *res*', either possible or actual depending on whether the proposition is essential or existential." I suspect that often, as here, *res* equals *ens* and thus shares its ambiguity.

Fitch (1979), 35, citing C 392–93, # 150ff., thinks that "is not a *res*" means "is impossible," where the impossibility is absolute, not hypothetical. This interpretation would have Leibniz holding that if 'No *A* is *B*' is true, then it is absolutely necessary. Cf. nn. 32 and 36 to chap. 5.

[32] At C 271, after analyzing "No just person is forsaken" first as "A forsaken just person is not existent" and then as "An existent forsaken just person is a *non-ens* or *impossibile*," Leibniz adds the crucial explicative comment, "namely, hypothetical impossibility, postulating existence or the series of things." As we shall see later, in the Leibnizian metaphysics, whatever is hypothetically possible either has been, is now, or will be the case, i.e., is part of the actual world. That *ens* equals *possibile* is stated in many places, e.g., C 360 (P 51), 259, 271, 376, 392; Grua 325,

4. Concepts

In accord with standard scholastic doctrine as found, for example, in Ockham,[33] Leibniz considers that the terms of propositions are concepts.[34] That is, the proposition represented by a sentence '*A* is *B*' contains as components (called the "subject term" and the "predicate term," respectively) concepts represented by *A* and *B*.[35] Since propositions themselves are concepts, they can appear as subject or predicate in other propositions; thus, as mentioned earlier, the conditional proposition 'If *A* is *B*, then *C* is *D*' is analyzed as '*A*'s being *B* is *C*'s being *D*'.

Leibniz says that concepts are formed by abstraction from things.[36] As we have noted, however, it is also clear that when he speaks about concepts, he is usually referring to God's concepts, not ours; these could not have been obtained by such abstraction.[37] The point has some importance, bearing as it does on the question whether all simple attributes—and hence all components of all possible concepts—are exemplified in the actual world.[38]

Signs are said to "represent" concepts and to "express" the things that fall under those concepts.[39] In an ideal language, we are told, "the expression of a given thing [*res*] is to be composed of the expressions of those things the ideas of which compose the idea of the given thing.'[40] (This, presumably, applies to the canonical or written-out expressions; to make his notation manageable, Leibniz clearly expects to introduce abbreviations.[41]) Here again, however, his use of terminology is not uniform: sometimes he speaks of signs as being "of" concepts, and of concepts as "representing" things.[42] But usually the context makes fairly clear what is meant.

Concepts are simple (primitive) or complex (derivative), with the com-

---

326. Cf. Jag 8: "The concept *impossible* is twofold, viz., that which does not have essence, and that which does not have existence, i.e., which neither has been, is now, or will be the case. . . ." Regarding the idea of existence as a component of other ideas, see A.6.6.265.

[33] See Ockham, *Philosophical Writings*, ed. P. Boehner. London, 1957, xxviiff.

[34] C 361 (P 52), 364 (P 54 n. 2), A.6.6.357, G IV 422 (L 291), 433 (L 307).

[35] G IV 422 (L 291): Propositions contain concepts. At G III 224, "notions," "concepts," and "terms" are offered as synonyms.

[36] G II 182 (L 518). Thus they are *entia rationis*, not real. At C 512 (PM 6) Leibniz defines "clear," "distinct," and "adequate," as applied to concepts.

[37] G II 131 (M 238): "Can it be denied that everything (whether genus, species, or individual) has a complete notion, according to which it is conceived by God, who conceives everything perfectly? . . ."

[38] At G II 45 (M 49) Leibniz says that he "does not deny . . . that we conceive of possibilities only through the ideas which exist in [i.e., characterize] the things that God has created," and at G II 55 (M 61) he endorses this view as "very solid."

[39] We may use '*x* falls under the concept *y*' as equivalent to '*y* is a concept (or the concept) of *x*'. Leibniz uses '*y* is said of *x*' as equivalent to these (Fasz. 2, 411). For "the individuals falling under the concept" Leibniz uses *singularia sub notione comprehensi* (G VII 240, P 136, L 375). Cf. Burk 167.

[40] LH 80–81.

[41] C 326.

[42] G IV 422 (L 291).

plex ones resulting from simpler ones by operations we may call "negation" (or "complementation") and "product formation."[43] Thus, the concept Wise Man is the product of the concepts Wise and Man, and the concept Non-divisible is the negative of the concept Divisible. Since the concept Gold (*aurum*) is the concept Heaviest Metal (*metallum ponderosissimum*), it contains as a part the concept Metal (*metallum*) "in the nominative case," as Leibniz says with typical use-mention confusion.[44]

As concerns simple concepts, Leibniz argues that there *must* be such concepts:

> There must be simple terms, for if we do not conceive of anything per se, we don't conceive of anything at all. It would be as though we should respond to a questioner always using words that he does not understand, and, when he asks for an explication of these, by again using others that he doesn't understand, so that if I keep on in this way he won't understand anything.[45]

However, Leibniz never favors us with a list of the simple concepts. What is sometimes cited as such turns out to be only a list of "simpler" terms by which others are to be defined.[46] In a 1677 letter to Arnold Eckhard he does give *existence* as a *notio incomplexa sive irresolubilis*.[47] But some of the other things said in that same text are so odd—for example, that *cogitabilitas* is a component of every *qualitas cogitabilis*—that it is difficult to know how seriously to take the whole piece.

The operation of product formation appears to be commutative, associative, and idempotent.[48] As concerns negation, Leibniz does not indicate whether it is to be applied only to simple concepts or more generally. Neither

---

[43] C 512–13. At C 86 Leibniz proposes to construct a characteristic number for each positive or negative concept (term) "by multiplying together all the characteristic numbers of those positive or negative concepts out of which the given concept is composed." At S 472, however, he says that he prefers always to work with positive terms "by transferring the negation into the copula, thus getting free of many perplexities"; he has in mind the replacement of '*A est non B*' by '*A non est B*'. The "perplexities" are gotten rid of because a term containing no negative components is supposed to be always possible (S 480). At A.6.6.276, however, Leibniz says that he does not see why there should not be "privative," i.e., negative, ideas; cf. A.6.6.130.

Frege (1969), 13, notes that this type of composition doesn't work in the natural languages. His examples are *Berggipfel* and *Baumriese*, but better examples occur with adjectives—e.g., "pretty little" in Quine's "pretty little girls' school."

[44] C 51 (P 19).

[45] LH IV vii B 2 57r, quoted in Schepers (1966), P. 543, n. 11. The same point is made at A.2.1.497; cf. G VI 612 (L 646).

C 429ff.: If a concept *A* is "conceived through" a different concept *B*, then it must also be conceived through still another concept *C* as well, for it *A* were conceived only through *B*, *A* and *B* would be identical. Note also the implied synonymy of '*A* is conceived through *B*' and '*A* involves *B*'. For the definition of "involve," see Grua 535. Finally, note the curious claim that infinitely many things can be formed by the combination of a few; one wonders what sort of "combination" he has in mind here.

[46] Fasz. 2, 329ff. Cf. Grua 542.

[47] LBr 227, 34; Fasz. 2, 427.

[48] C 421, 394, 258, G VII 293. There is a problem about commutativity. As we shall see, Leibniz defines '*A* = *B*' as '*A* is *B* and *B* is *A*'. The equivalent *secundi adjecti* propositions for '*A* is *B*' and '*B* is *A*' are '*AB* is an entity' and '*BA* is an entity'. Therefore, if in general $AB = BA$, we have '*A* is *B*' always equivalent to '*A* = *B*'.

alternative fits in well with the rest of his doctrine. The first appears to rule out various types of concepts, for example, disjunctions of simples, and the second allows for concepts that are not reducible to conjunctions made up of simples and their negations, that is, that are not analyzable into such components.[49]

Leibniz comments that for the most part the analysis of complex concepts into primitive components that are conceived through themselves does not appear to be within the power of human beings, but that as regards the analysis of truths, we are in better shape: many such propositions can be proved absolutely by reduction to indemonstrable primitive truths. "Therefore," he recommends, "let us apply ourselves with maximum effort to this."[50]

In one very puzzling text Leibniz says that a primitive concept must be a concept of a thing that is conceived through itself, and that there is only one such thing, namely, God.

> But we can have no derivative concepts except by means of primitive concepts, so that in things there can be nothing except through the influx of God, and in the mind no thought except through the idea of God—though we do not have a sufficiently distinct understanding either of how the nature of things emanates from God nor their ideas from the idea of God. . . .[51]

He seems here to be confusing two quite different theses, namely, (1) that every primitive concept is a component of the idea of God and (2) that the idea of God is a component of every concept.

The "containment" relation among concepts is characterized by Leibniz in two ways. A concept A is said to be contained in a concept B, and B is said to involve A, if and only if it is impossible for there to be an object falling under B but not under A.[52] Alternatively, a concept A is said to be contained

---

[49] Cf. CL 334; G VII 261; Kauppi (1960), 150–51; Burk 102–3; Schneider (1974), 79. In one passage (LH IV vii C 17r; Fasz. 2, 380) Leibniz seems to contemplate a disjunctive concept, at least when it occurs as the predicate, as in "every conic section is a parabola, a hyperbola, or an ellipse."

[50] G II 227 (L 525): "Primitive concepts lie concealed in derivative ones but are hard to distinguish in them." Cf. G IV 425 (L 293); G VII 83ff.; C 431, 513, 514; G I 392. G V 15: Primitive (simple) ideas are nothing else than the attributes of God. Burk 172 suggests that Jungius was the source of Leibniz's idea that there are simple, unanalyzable concepts.

[51] C 513 (PM 8). Compare the following passage (A.2.1.497), which I also do not know what to make of:

> *Protonoemata secundum quid* and *protonoemata simpliciter* are rightly distinguished. . . . Certainly all things that are not explained by definition but have to be shown by example or have to be sensed in order to be known, as, e.g., heat, cold, and colors, are *protonoemata secundum nos*; however, they can be resolved, for they have their causes. I have often given thought to *protonoemata simpliciter*, i.e., those which are conceived through themselves . . . where the question[s] can be raised, first, whether there really are any *protonoemata*, or whether there is division *in infinitum* . . . and then, assuming that there are some (for it seems that nothing at all can be conceived if nothing is conceived per se), whether there is one only or many. If there is only one, how can so many composite concepts come from it? If there are many, they will have certain things in common, e.g., possibility; also, they will have certain relations among themselves, else they will not be able to come together to make composite concepts. Therefore, in what way are these concepts simple?

Cf. C 430: "If nothing is conceived per se, nothing at all is conceived."

[52] Grua 535; for "involve," see G VII 206.

in a concept B if and only if all the components of A are components of B.[53] It is not at once obvious whether these two characterizations are equivalent and, in particular, whether on the basis of the first one it holds generally that if A is contained in B and B is contained in A, then A and B are identical. If it does so hold, there is the unwelcome consequence, noted earlier, that there are no two distinct concepts that apply necessarily (or even contingently, assuming the Predicate-in-Subject principle) to the very same things—a result that Leibniz explicitly rejects, citing examples like the concepts Triangle and Trilateral.

Elsewhere Leibniz explains more generally what he means by the words "in" and "part":

> We say that an entity *is in* [*inesse*] or is an *ingredient* of something, if, when we posit the latter, we must also be understood, by this very fact and immediately, without the necessity of any inference, to have posited the former as well. Thus, when we posit any finite line, we also posit its end points as belonging to it.
>
> An entity which is in something and is also homogeneous to it is called a *part*, and that which it is in is called a *whole*: or a part is a homogeneous ingredient of a whole.[54]

Thus, he says, the parts of lines are not points, but other lines, although, in his use, points are "in" lines. On this definition it would appear that the component concepts of a complex concept are parts of it, assuming that all concepts are to be considered "homogeneous." At any rate, bearing in mind that attributes are concepts, we see that every concept is supposed to contain or involve all the attributes an object must have in order to fall under that concept.

The containment of concepts in other concepts is obviously (though, no doubt, in most cases unconsciously) a projection of the containment relations among the corresponding linguistic expressions. Just as the phrase "rational animal" contains the words "rational" and "animal," so also the concept Rational Animal is to contain the concept Rational and the concept Animal.

Not surprisingly, this sometimes leads to difficulties. Consider the true sentence,

Paris is the lover of Helen.

According to Leibniz's Predicate-in-Subject principle, which we shall discuss in detail in chapter 5, the concept Lover of Helen must be contained in the (complete individual) concept of Paris. But on the above criterion, the concept of Helen would have to be contained in the concept Lover of Helen, and hence, presumably, in the concept of Paris, which would seem to be absurd. This sort of difficulty may be what led to Leibniz's various attempts to eliminate all the oblique cases (in Latin) in favor of the nominative; maybe the containment isomorphism between concepts and their expressions is

---

[53] A.6.1.198: One concept contains another if all the primitive concepts in the latter are in the former. Cf. C 51 (P 19).

[54] GM VII 19 (L 667–68). But see Schmidt (1971), where five different Leibnizian definitions of the part-whole relation are given.

plausible, if at all, only when all components of the expressions are in the nominative case.

Observe also that if the aforementioned projection is accepted in full generality, we shall have concepts "occurring" more than once in other concepts, and hence the relation between concepts and their components will no longer be that of whole to part. Consider, for example, the concept expressed by the phrase

the apple given to Adam and eaten by him.

This concept would consist of the complete individual concept of Adam, together with the concept expressed by the form

the apple given to x and eaten by x,

or, equally well, of the same complete individual concept together with the concept expressed by the form

the apple given to Adam and eaten by x,

or, again equally well, of the same complete concept together with the concept expressed by

the apple given to x and eaten by Adam.

But, as was somewhere pointed out by Frege, a whole and any part of that whole uniquely determine the remainder. Therefore, the relation of concept to component cannot be that of whole to part. The upshot seems to be that the components of a complex concept cannot be taken to be simply the concepts expressed by the components of its expression, at least if the language permits expressions like those given above. In general, "reading off" the structure of thought from the structure of its expression in language would have to be a much more complicated matter than is usually and naively supposed.

Concepts obviously differ from one another in generality. A number of cases are worth distinguishing. If, for the moment, we may speak of "possible objects," we may say that both actual and nonactual-but-possible individuals (for example, Bucephalus and Pegasus) fall under the concept Horse. Only nonactual-but-possible individuals fall under the concept Hippogriff. In each possible world one individual at most will fall under the concept First Man (for example, Adam in the actual world, Deucalion in some other possible world, and nobody in a world containing no human beings); nevertheless, this type of concept does not completely determine an individual, for many different possible people could have been the first man.[55]

But some concepts do completely determine an actual or possible individual, distinguishing it in one respect or another from every other possible individual; such concepts are called by Leibniz "complete individual concepts." Thus, a complete individual concept contains every attribute of every

---

[55] G II 42 (M 45), 44 (M 48).

individual that can fall under it; it resolves every question that could be raised about such an individual—that is, it determines exactly one possible individual.[56] Another formulation, which would avoid the confusing notion of "possible individual" but which is heir to the difficulty mentioned in paragraph 8 of the Introduction, would be this: a complete individual concept is a concept that contains, for every simple attribute, either that attribute or its negation, but not both.[57] Both definitions, as we shall see later, would need amending in another respect; strictly speaking, a Leibnizian complete individual concept should not be thought of as a set of attributes but as a series of such sets, with the series ordered by time or some other relation as a parameter.

We may note also that sometimes Leibniz characterizes the complete concept of an individual, for example, Adam, as composed not of all the properties of that individual but of a core of "basic" (presumably simple) properties from which all of the others follow.[58]

In a well-known passage the concept King is contrasted with the complete individual concept of Alexander the Great:

Thus the quality of King which belonged to Alexander the Great, if we abstract it from its subject, it is not determined enough to define an individual, for it does not include the other qualities of the same subject or everything which the concept of this prince includes. God . . . in seeing the individual notion or *haecceitas* of Alexander, sees in it at the same time the basis and the reason for all the predicates which can truly be affirmed of him, for example, that he will conquer Darius and Porus, even knowing a priori (and not by experience) what we can know only through history—whether he died a natural death or by poison. Thus when we consider the connection of things, it can be said that there are at all times in the soul of Alexander traces of all that has

---

[56] G VII 311: "In the perfect concept of each individual substance is contained all its predicates, both necessary and contingent, past, present, and future. . . ." Ibid.: "In the perfect concept of an individual substance in a pure estate of possibility, considered by God, everything is contained that would happen to him if he existed, indeed, the whole series of things of which he is a part." Cf. Grua 540: To say that *x* is perfectly understood by *y* is to say that *y* can distinguish *x* from everything else. LH IV vii 7 C 103–4 (Fasz. 1, # 58, 186; also S 475): "If term *A* involves all terms *B*, *C*, *D*, etc., that can be said of the same thing [*res*], term *A* expresses a singular substance; i.e., the concept of a singular substance is a complete term, containing everything that can be said of that substance." At LH IV vii B 2 47–48 (Fasz. 1, # 39, 133), Leibniz contrasts general concepts like Learned and Divine with complete concepts like those of Alexander and Caesar. In the former, he says, from the fact that the concepts are different, it does not follow that the same thing cannot fall under both; but for the complete concepts it does follow. In connection with all of this cf. also S 478ff.; G II 20, 46, 131 (M 15, 51, 73); Grua 539, 542ff.; G IV 433; C 403; LH IV vii B iii 19–20.

G VII 390 (L 696): In actualizing an individual concept, God does not change it. This seems to imply that a concept of Existence is not part of the complete individual concept of Alexander the Great or of any other existent being; Leibniz says as much at C 23.

[57] LH IV vii C 107–8 (Fasz. 2, # 106): There can be as many singular substances as there are different combinations of all the compatible attributes.

Following LH IV vii C 103v, we would have still another characteristic of a complete individual concept: a concept that cannot be the predicate term in a true proposition unless that proposition is reciprocal, as in, e.g., "Peter is the apostle who denied Christ" and "The apostle who denied Christ is Peter."

[58] G II 44 (M 47–48).

happened to him and marks of all that will happen to him, and even traces of all that happens in the universe, though it belongs only to God to know them all.[59]

Similarly:

Let us take an example. Since Julius Caesar is to become perpetual dictator and master of the republic and will destroy the liberty of the Romans, this action is contained in his concept, for we have assumed that it is the nature of such a perfect concept of a subject to include everything, so that this predicate is included in it—*ut possit inesse subjecto.*[60]

A concept that does not contain every attribute of every individual that could fall under it is called by Leibniz the concept of an accident (or sometimes a genus or species); an example would be the concept King mentioned in the quotation above.[61]

"The concept of a species," Leibniz says, "contains only necessary or eternal truths, whereas the concept of an individual contains *sub ratione possibilitatis* what exists." He illustrates this by comparing the general concept of Sphere, which contains only those properties essential to all spheres, with that of the sphere that was placed on Archimedes' tomb. The latter concept contains not only the essential properties of the sphere but in addition those relating to the material of which it is made, its size, the place and time of its existence, and so on.[63] There is, however, some lack of clarity in Leibniz's use of "complete" in this connection. In one passage he declares that "everything (whether genus, species, or individual) has a complete concept which includes everything that can be said of the thing." But is "said of the thing" used in the same sense as applied to individuals, species, or genera? What can be said of the genus Animal? Presumably that it is a set and an abstract entity, that it includes the species Man, that it is denumerable. I think it doubtful that Leibniz had predicates like these in mind.[63]

In the case of complete individual concepts it is especially clear that Leibniz is referring to God's concepts, not ours, since he routinely speaks of *the* concept of Adam, *the* concept of Caesar, *the* concept of Alexander, and so on.[64]

---

[59] G IV 433 (L 307–8), S 475–76. A.6.6.66: "Whenever we find some quality in a subject, we ought to believe that if we understood the nature of both the subject and the quality, we would conceive how the quality could arise from it."

[60] G IV 437 (L 310). Cf. G IV 557 (L 576), where similar things are said about *bodies*. Maher (1980), in an admirably lucid paper, unfortunately bases his proposed account of Leibnizian contingency on the thesis that "contingent properties in general are not in the individual concepts of the substances which have them" (p. 240); this flies in the face of the present quotation about Caesar's concept and in that of many other Leibnizian pronouncements to similar effect.

[61] G IV 433 (L 307). At G II 49n (L 348 n. 2) Leibniz distinguishes the "complete concept" (*notio completa*) from the "full concept" (*notio plena*). He says that they coincide for individual substances, but for an abstraction like heat (*calor*) there is only the full concept, which contains whatever can be predicated *necessarily* of what falls under it.

[62] G II 39 (M 41–42).

[63] G II 131 (M 73). Cf. also G II 49n (L 348 n.2), where "full" concepts are distinguished in such a way as to imply that there could be a full but not complete concept of Sphere.

[64] LH IV vii C 109–10 (Fasz. 1, # 59, 191): "Thus in the concept of the apostle Peter God conceives everything which ever happened or will happen to this Peter."

An often neglected but extremely important distinction is that between concepts and the accidents of the substances falling under them.[65] Since properties (or attributes) are concepts, this, of course, implies also a distinction between them and the accidents. As has been adequately shown by Kenneth Clatterbaugh, Leibniz considers the accidents of any individual substance to be themselves individual, that is, to belong to that substance only.[66] Thus Milo and Ajax (not Leibniz's example) both fall under the concept Strong, but the strength of Milo is not identical with the strength of Ajax.[67] That is, that condition of Milo by virtue of which he falls under the concept Strong is peculiar to Milo; there would be no such condition if Milo did not exist, and no condition of anyone else could literally be identified with it. Concepts, on the other hand, are not generally individual in the same sense; only the complete concept of an individual substance is an *infima species* applying to that individual alone.[68] Unfortunately, I have to warn again that Leibniz is characteristically careless about this terminology; sometimes it seems that he simply uses all the terms "property," "attribute," "quality," and "accident" interchangeably.

By virtue of its accidents a given substance will fall under various concepts, of varying degrees of generality. If wisdom is one of the cardinal virtues, then the same accidents that place Socrates under the concept Wise will also place him under the concept Virtuous. And the same accidents that place him under the concept Man will also place him under the concept Animal. Thus there is a kind of partial ordering of the concepts under which a given individual falls. The ordering relation is not, as might be thought, simply that of concept inclusion. It seems, rather, more adequately (if less precisely) characterized in terms of the word "because": the concept expressed by A precedes the concept expressed by B in this ordering if and only if 'Because x is an A' is in general a satisfactory answer (if true) to the question 'Why is x a B?' The accidents of an individual are, as it were, limits to the ordered series of concepts under which the individual falls, but they are not themselves in the series. More about this when we consider the principle of the Identity of Indiscernibles.

We see also that by virtue of different sets of accidents a given individual

---

[65] Accidents are in the substances; concepts are in the mind. Thus, at A.6.2.588: "An accident is a mode of a substance whereby it can be thought [about]." A.6.6.221: Locke confuses ideas with qualities (= accidents). LH IV vii C 85r: If Titius is virtuous and later the same Titius is not virtuous, then a change is said to have taken place in Titius, and the *ens* which made Titius virtuous, viz., his virtue, ceases to be. G II 458 (L 606): As an individual substance undergoes changes, its modifications (accidents) come into being and cease to be (*nasci et interire*).

[66] Clatterbaugh (1973). Cf. G VII 401 (L 703–4). G II 253 (R 206): Although no accident belongs to more than one substance, no two substances lack a common predicate (property, attribute).

[67] Individual accidents are denoted by phrases of the form 'the ϕ of x', e.g., "the birth of Jesus Christ," "the royal power of Alphonso." Cf. A.6.6.328; LH IV vii C 111–14 (Fasz. 2, # 107, 417).

[68] At G II 131 (M 73–74), where Leibniz appears to *identify* individuals with *infimae species*, the context shows that he is talking about individual concepts, not the individuals themselves.

substance, at a given time, can fall under contrary concepts. For example, Agamemnon, who is both courageous and selfish, falls thereby under both the concepts Praiseworthy and Blameworthy; we say that qua courageous he is praiseworthy, and qua selfish, blameworthy. In general, to say that an individual I, qua A, is B, is to say that in relation to I the aforementioned partial ordering holds between A and B.

Needless to say, not all elements of the interpretation I am propounding in these pages are accepted by all expositors of Leibniz. For instance, some authors, notably Hidé Ishiguro, have ascribed to him the view that proper names like "Zeus" and "Pegasus," which do not denote individuals in the actual world, do not represent complete individual concepts. She says:

> Leibniz, however, seemed to take a different, alternative view: namely, that *only* the individuals in this world can be logically treated as individuals and have corresponding individual concepts, and that "Pegasus" or "Zeus" expresses only a general concept.[69]

Leibniz makes it very plain that there are infinitely many unactualized complete individual concepts. Indeed, his account of Creation includes that "amongst an infinite number of possible concepts [that is, concepts of possible individuals] God chose that of Adam."[70] In another passage he says:

> God, who decrees nothing without exact knowledge, has known perfectly, even before he decrees that there should exist this Peter who later denied Christ, what would happen to Peter if he were to exist; or *what is the same thing* [emphasis added], he has in his intellect a perfect concept or idea of possible Peter, a concept that contains all the truths concerning Peter. . . .[71]

Perhaps Profesor Ishiguro does not mean to deny this, but only to assert that for Leibniz no proper name expresses such an unactualized complete individual concept. Since, however, Leibniz rejects the idea that the name "Adam" expresses a concept instantiated by many "possible Adams," of which the "actual Adam would be only one, it is hard to see why he would give different treatment to names like "King Arthur," "Amadis of Gaul," or "Dietrich von Bern," which occur in accounts of situations that he regards as belonging to possible-but-nonactual worlds.[72]

---

[69] Ishiguro (1972), 134.

[70] G II 40.

[71] Grua 311.

[72] FC 178–79 (L 263). Note that at LH IV vii C 111–14 (Fasz. 2, # 107, 417), Leibniz describes the complete individual concept of a substance as virtually containing all that *de ipso possunt intelligi.* Perhaps in favor of Professor Ishiguro's interpretation, on the other hand, is a passage at LH IV vii C 85–86 (Fasz. 1, # 55, 174–75), where Leibniz concedes it possible, thorough metempsychosis, for the same person who formerly was Appius to now be Valerius; but he says that even if this holds for terms like "Appius," it won't hold for "I" or "you"—i.e., it is impossible that the same individual who is now you should later exist and not be you.

Professor Ishiguro explains further that

the concept of Alexander the Great is a full individual concept even if we do not know the full details of all that is true of Alexander, since we know *whom* it is of and hence that every predicate that is true of him is a component of the concept, and that nothing else is. The concept of Pegasus is not fully determined in this sense.[73]

She also says that we can "get at" the *haecceitas* ("thisness") of individuals in the actual world but not of things that exist in other possible worlds. Although Leibniz was not fond of the term *haecceitas*, which he scorned as part of the jargon of the Scholastic "philosophasters," observing that in any case it ought to have been *hoccitas* or *hoccimonia*,[74] in the Alexander passage quoted above he does seem to identify Alexander's complete individual concept with his *haecceitas*. But *we* are hardly in a better position to "get at" the complete individual concept of Alexander than to "get at" the concept of Pegasus; only God knows everything that would be true of these individuals if they existed, and he had to have such knowledge in order to carry out a Leibniz-style creation.

One other point of controversy concerns whether or not Leibniz meant to allow what we might call "inconsistent concepts," that is, such as contain as components some concept and its negation—for example, what might be represented by the phrase "black nonblack dog." There are texts supporting both possibilities. In the fragment entitled "Introduction to the Arcane Encyclopedia," where concepts are discussed at some length, we find a marginal note that reads: "A concept is either suitable [*aptus*] or unsuitable [*ineptus*]. A suitable concept is one that is established to be possible, or not to imply a contradiction."[75] This suggests that some concepts are inconsistent, that is, do involve contradiction. Also, the *secundi adjecti* form of 'No *A* is *B*' is '*AB* is not an entity', which, if true when taken essentially, would seem to have an absolutely impossible concept as subject.[76]

On the other hand, in the paper entitled "Meditations on Knowledge, Truth, and Ideas" we are told that there is no idea of the impossible: "At first glance we may seem to have an idea of the most rapid motion, for we understand perfectly what we are saying. But we cannot have any idea of the impossible."[77]

---

[73] Ishiguro (1972), 135. Concerning "full" concepts, see n. 61.

[74] A.6.2.411, 413. He himself does use *haecceitas* in the *Dissertatio de principio individui*, G IV 15ff., and at G IV 433 and elsewhere.

[75] C 513. Cf. G VII 293ff. and A.6.6.253ff. Mollat (1893), 7: "For there are concepts that imply a contradiction and answer to nothing definite." At G VII 224 (L 244–45, P. 43), in commenting on the theorem 'If *A* is *B* and *C* is *D* and *E* is *F*, then *ACE* is *BDF*', Leibniz says, "It makes no difference if the terms sometimes combined in this way are inconsistent. Thus a circle is nonangled; a square is a quadrangle; therefore, a square circle is a nonangled quadrangle."

[76] C 393.

[77] G IV 424 (L 293). G IV 450 (L 319): "Now it is obvious that we have no idea of a concept when it is impossible." At G II 573 (L 662) the possible is equated with the perfectly conceivable. And at G II 558 the possible is equated with the intelligible. At C 386 (P75) false terms (i.e., concepts under which no individual falls) are distinguished from impossible terms. At Jag 6–8 it is emphasized that we, as contrasted with God, can have ideas corresponding to the component

And sometimes we find this definition: "A concept [*notio, conceptus*] is what does not imply a contradiction, or does not involve the impossible."[78] This point of view would fit in with the fact that for every concept A, the proposition 'A is A', as an essential proposition, is a necessary truth and is equivalent to 'AA is an entity', where, of course, *ens* is equivalent to *possibile*. However, in the very paper in which we are told that there is no idea of the impossible, Leibniz goes on to say: "Thus the difference between a true idea and a false idea also becomes clear. An idea is true when the concept is possible; it is false when it implies a contradiction."[79] If there is a way of reconciling these various texts, it has eluded me up to now.

The matter had some importance for Leibniz because, as he points out in a letter to Thomas Burnet, if we follow Hobbes and Locke in making the truth of propositions depend on "the agreement or disagreement of ideas," we shall be faced with the difficulty that in the case of "chimerical" or impossible ideas, which embrace contradictions, there will be agreement and disagreement at the same time.[80] This is related, of course, to his frequently repeated observation, included also in the same letter, that a satisfactory real definition must be accompanied by a demonstration of the consistency of the *definiens*, whether a priori, by giving "requisites," or a posteriori, by experience, "because what actually exists cannot fail to be possible."[81]

---

characters in a complex character (like "that than which nothing greater can be conceived" or "the fastest motion" or "the number of all numbers") without having an idea corresponding to the whole expression. G VI 252 (H 267): "The objects of the understanding cannot go beyond the possible, which in a sense is alone intelligible.'

[78] LH IV vii C 101 (Fasz. 1, # 57, 180).

[79] Cf. A.6.6.397–98.

[80] G III 257; cf. G IV 424.

[81] G VII 214: In all (categorical) propositions it is tacitly assumed that the ingredient term is an *ens*. G VII 310: ". . . also, we only think ideas of things insofar as we intuit their possibility [*ideas quoque rerum non cogitamus nisi quatenus earum possibilitatem intuemur*]." C 397 (# 195) seems to imply that some false propositions contain impossible concepts. Perhaps the explanation is contained in C 393 (# 154) (P 82): "But if someone prefers signs to be used in such a way that $AB = AB$, whether AB is a *res* or not, and that in the case in which AB is not a *res B* and not-B can coincide—viz. *per impossibile*—I do not object. This will have as a consequence the need to distinguish between a term and a *res* or *ens*." On this entire matter, cf. CL 349ff.

IV

Possible Worlds

One of the most influential of Leibniz's contributions to philosophy is his doctrine of possible worlds. Indeed, what might be described as "The Story of Creation according to Leibniz" has had, in its way, the kind of influence on recent philosophizing that the more official story of Genesis has had on theology. Portions of it have even been set to music and sung with baritone, chorus, and orchestra, before a meeting of a learned society—a degree of recognition not often enjoyed by even the most famous philosophers.[1] We shall rehearse it once more.

1. Possible Worlds as Sets of Concepts

The actual world, which does exist, is only one of infinitely many possible worlds that could have existed.[2] It is the best of the possible worlds, in the sense that any change in it, when considered with all its necessary pre-conditions and consequences, would be a change for the worse; and that, of course, is why God chose it instead of one of the other possibilities.[3]

---

[1] Cf. *Der Internationale Leibniz-Kongress in Hannover*, ed. R. Schneider and W. Totok, Hanover, 1968, 67ff.

[2] From the "Metaphysical Discussion with Fardells" (1690), printed by Stein (1888), 322–25: "From an infinite number of possibilities God chose one world-series, consisting of an infinite number of substances, each of which exhibits an infinite number of actions."

[3] G VI 252, 362ff., 106–8 (H 267–68, 370ff., 127–29); Grua 305; A.2.1.117; G III 400; G VII 306 (L 489). There are nonactual possible worlds in which there is no sin (G VI 108, G III 33), or there are no people (Grua 342), or everybody is saved (Grua 341), or the pious are damned while the impious are saved (Grua 271), or bodies have no inertia (G II 170, L 517), or, in general, different natural laws hold (Jag 116, C 18). Cf. also G III 572ff., G VII 194ff., 302ff., G VI 362ff. Further discussion and references will be found in L. J. Russell (1969), 161–75, and Schneider (1974), 195.

To us mortals, with our limitations of knowledge and understanding, the obvious evils in the world may make it seem very far from the best. It is hard to see anything good about wars, pogroms, disease, poverty, or any of the other abominations with which mankind is afflicted. But, says Leibniz, although evils as such are worse than nothing, in combination with other things they can sometimes serve to improve the overall effect, like shadows in pictures or dissonances in music.[4]

We know but a very small part of an eternity stretching out beyond all measure. How tiny is the memory of the few thousand years that history imparts to us! Yet from such slight experience we venture to judge about the immeasurable and the eternal; as if men born and reared in prison or in the underground salt mines of Sarmatia should think that there is no other light in the world but the wretched torch which is scarcely sufficient to guide their steps. If we look at a very beautiful picture but cover up all of it but a tiny spot, what more will appear in it, no matter how closely we study it, than a confused mixture of colors without beauty and without art. Yet when the covering is removed and the whole painting is viewed from a position that suits it, we come to understand that what seemed to be a thoughtless smear on the canvas has really been done with the highest artistry by the creator of the work.[5]

Leibniz says that there must have been a best world—there can have been no tie for first place—else God would have created nothing, for he does nothing without a reason.[6] "Best," in this connection, is variously explained as "containing the most essence"[7] or as "achieving maximum effect with minimum outlay" (of space and time) or as "most perfect, that is, simplest in its laws and richest in phenomena."[8] (It is by no means clear, even within Leibnizian doctrine, that these conditions, whatever they may mean, are equivalent to one another.)

At the Creation, we are told, God made a choice between different possible systems, not between different ways of producing the same sys-

---

[4] GM III/2 574, G III 33. Grua 271: Just as the musician does not will dissonances per se but only to make the melody more perfect than it would be without them, so also God only wills sins as requisite to the complete perfection of the world.

Leibniz's arguments along these lines are ridiculed by Schopenhauer in vol. 2, bk. 4, chap. 46, of *Die Welt als Wille und Vorstellung*: ". . . the only merit I can grant [to the *Theodicy*] is that it gave occasion to the immortal *Candide* of the great Voltaire; whereby, indeed, Leibniz's often repeated and lame excuse for the evils of this world, namely, that the bad sometimes brings about the good, got an unplanned confirmation." Schopenhauer credits Hume with having discovered the "secret source" of the best-of-all-possible-worlds doctrine, viz., *heuchelnde Smeichelei*— hypocritical toadying to religion.

For his part, Schopenhauer offers a proof that this is the *worst* of all possible worlds. This world is constructed in just the way needed for continued existence, he says; if it were any worse—e.g., if the perturbations in the planetary orbits were any greater than they are—it would fall apart and cease to exist. Hence, any worse world could not continue to exist; therefore, this is the worst of all possible worlds.

[5] G VII 306 (L 489). Sarmatia is an ancient region of southern Russia.

[6] G II 424–25, E 448 (W 483), G VI 107, 232, 364 (H 128, 249, 372–73).

[7] G VII 303 (L 487). David Blumenfeld, citing this passage, has pointed out (1981, 78) that when Leibniz speaks in this connection of "the greatest number of things," the context shows that he probably means "the greatest number of types of things." Cf. Grua 286 and Jag 28. A.6.6.293: Essence is fundamentally nothing but the possibility of the thing under consideration.

[8] G IV 430–31 (L 305–6), G VI 603 (L 639), G VI 241.

tem.[9] This is a crucial point that differentiates Leibniz's conception of possible worlds from that of most recent writers. For him, no two possible worlds contain the same elements; if Peter had not denied Christ, he would not have been Peter. The main reason God had for choosing this world, rather than some other, was the presence in it of Jesus Christ, "its most noble element."[10]

The possible in no way depends on the actual. "You say," Leibniz writes to the cleric Isaac Jaquelot,

that the majority of modern theologians found God's decrees on his foreknowledge. But since the objects of that foreknowledge depend again on him, it comes down in the end to his choice of the best from among all the possibles, which is independent of a foreknowledge of what will actually take place.[11]

The actual world is described as "a chain of states or a series of things,"[12] It consists of everything—past, present, and future.

By "actual world" I mean the whole series and the whole collection of all existent things, lest one might say that several worlds exist at different times and different places. For the whole collection must needs be reckoned all together as one world. . . .[13]

God created the actual world in such a way that, except for miracles, it "unfolds" according to certain relatively simple natural laws, which men, by arduous scientific activity, may in some measure discover.[14] In relation to these laws of nature, which are true only because God has chosen to create a particular world like this one, there is a special sense of "possible," according to which a state of affairs is possible if its occurrence is compatible with the laws. In this sense of "possible," Leibniz believes that every event that is possible either has already happened, is now taking place, or will occur sometime in the future. But he emphasizes repeatedly that this "hypothetical" sense of the term is not to be confused with its "absolute" sense; in the latter, much that does not happen in the actual world is nevertheless entirely

[9] G II 182, G VI 148 (H 168). G III 573 (L 662): "There are many possible universes, each collection of compossibles making up one of them." G VI 252 (H 267): [There are] an infinity of possible sequences of the universe, each of which contains an infinity of creatures. . . . The divine wisdom distributes all the possibles it had already contemplated separately, into so many universal systems which it further compares the one with the other. G III 30: "Further, God had knowledge of possible things, not only as separate, but as coordinated in innumerable possible worlds, from which, by his most wise decision, he chose one."

At C 13 (PM 174), however, Leibniz, in a veiled reference to the principle of Sufficient Reason, speaks of a reason "why the [a?] world should exist in such and such a way, and should not have been produced in any other no less possible form." If this means that literally the *same* world could have existed in some other form, we have an inconsistency that I do not know how to explain.

[10] G III 35.

[11] G III 472.

[12] G VII 303 (L 487).

[13] G VI 107 (H 128). O. Saame, in his edition of the *Confessio Philosophi*, 152 n. 55, points out that the term "series of things" [*series rerum*], which Leibniz uses again and again, does not refer only to the temporal sequences but also to the general ordering of the elements of the world. He cites G II 263: "I do not say that a series is a succession, but that a succession is a series."

[14] G IV 431 (L 306), G VI 241, C 19–20.

possible, for the actual world is but one of infinitely many possible worlds and the number of unrealized possibilities is therefore very great indeed. Leibniz was well acquainted with the doctrine of the ancient Megarian logician Diodorus Cronus ("the possible is that which either is, was, or will be true"), and in several places he states that Diodorus's mistake was simply that of confusing hypothetical possibility with absolute.[15]

On occasion Leibniz gives reasons, such as they are, for his claim that the actual world is but one of many possibles. He says that certain things that are individually possible or possible per se are not jointly possible, and that consequently not everything possible can be actual.[16] Also, "God would have no choice or freedom if there were but one course possible."[17] Further, if we believe that everything possible is actual, we shall have to believe that all fanciful stories or novels, though they may be inconsistent with one another and with the facts, are realized together somewhere in the same universe—which is absurd.[18] And the possible-equals-actual hypothesis "would obliterate all the beauty of the universe," presumably because the actual world would no longer be better than any other—let alone the best.[19] Finally, there is the tantalizing statement we noticed earlier:

... nor are there [in the actual world] any bodies that are not at some definite distance from us. For if there were, it would not be possible to say whether they exist at this present moment or not, which is contrary to our first principle. From this it also follows that not all possibles exist.[20]

The distinction between the actual and the nonactual possible worlds is associated in Leibniz's philosophy, and in much current philosophizing, with the distinction between necessary and contingent truths. Statements true of all possible worlds are called "necessary" or "eternal" or "metaphysical" truths; those true of the actual world but not of all possible worlds are "contingent" or "factual."[21] As examples of the former category Leibniz mentions

[15] G II 442 (L 602), G III 572ff. (L 661ff.), G VI 442. For more on hypothetical necessity and possibility, see chap. 6, sec. 2.

[16] Grua 305, G VI 236, S 480.

[17] G VI 258, Grua 288, G II 55 (L 336). G IV 274: God cannot do the impossible.

[18] Grua 305, 325, FC 178–79, G II 55 (L 336), G III 572 (L 661), G VI 217 (H 235), G II 181, G III 558, A.2.1.299, Fasz. 2, 238. In this connection Leibniz often alludes to *L'Astrée*, a five-volume romance by Honoré d'Urfé (G III 572; cf. G VI 108). In connection with the doctrinal point mentioned in chap. 8, n. 5, it is amusing to remark that although this immensely long and boring fantasy contains relatively few occurrences of proper names of actual individuals, it does contain a few, e.g., that of Attila the Hun.

[19] FC 178–79 (L 263).

[20] Grua 263. Maybe the argument was something like this. If a body exists at all, it must be possible in principle to determine, from our perceptions, whether it exists at any given time. To make such a determination, we need to know, inter alia, its distance from us. But some possible bodies—e.g., Pegasus—are not supposed to be at any particular distance from us. Therefore some possible bodies do not exist.

A similar passage is found in LH IV vi 12F 14 (Fasz. 1, # 25, 73): "If there existed another series outside of ours, it would not be possible to say whether something in it existed simultaneously with something in ours, or not; therefore, it would not be possible to say whether it existed now, or not. Which is impossible. For necessarily it does or it doesn't exist now. *Mira ratiocinatio.*"

[21] C 18. Cf. R 32.

the truths of logic, arithmetic, and geometry; for the latter category he gives singular statements like "Caesar crossed the Rubicon" and generalizations like "A body tends to continue with the same velocity if nothing impedes."[22] Insofar as I am aware, Leibniz never defines a necessary truth as a proposition true of all possible worlds; as definitions he gives, instead, various versions of "a necessary truth is a proposition the opposite of which implies a contradiction."[23] The relation between the two criteria here implied will be discussed in chapter 6 below.

As indicated in the passage quoted earlier, Leibniz says that the actual world is the collection of all existent things—past, present, and future; he says also that the other possible worlds are, in a similar way, collections of *possible things*.[24] But it is worth noting that talk of possible things, although it permeates the Leibnizian writings, is, if taken literally, productive of paradox and quite foreign in spirit to his metaphysical outlook.[25] For, as we have mentioned before and shall consider at length in chapter 10, Leibniz was a nominalist, denying the reality of all abstract entities. Nothing that is not an individual substance really exists; meaningful statements that appear to be about concepts and other abstract entities must be *compendia loquendi* for statements about one or more actual individuals.

Most of Leibniz's references to possible objects can be rephrased in terms of individual concepts and hence will give way ultimately to statements about individuals.[26] This is not to say that it would make sense, in Leibnizian terms, to assert that a possible object *is* an individual concept; presumably the individual concept of Pegasus is not a possible horse; it is not by chance that concepts, like wishes, are not horses. The necessary rephrasings will be somewhat more complex. For example, the statement "at least one possible man is free of sin," seems replaceable, in Leibnizian contexts, by the statement, "there is a complete individual concept that contains the attribute of manhood but not that of sinning," which is itself perhaps equivalent to "God could have created a man not liable to sin." Similar maneuvers will accomplish the elimination of most of the other references to possible objects. In view of this, it would seem to be in the interest of clarity and economy to identify possible worlds with collections of individual concepts and not with collections of possible indviduals; and the actual world will then be that possible world containing only concepts for which there are corresponding individuals.[27]

---

[22] Grua 287–88. Cf. C 18, G IV 438 (L 310–11).

[23] C 17, 186; S 480; Grua 268, 289. In this definition he follows Bayle (G VI 217).

[24] G III 573 (L 662). He must be talking about *states* of monads, and not about the monads themselves, which exist through all time.

[25] Thus, it would be absurd to take literally Leibniz's often-repeated principle that all the possibles "strive for existence" (see, e.g., G VII 195). In the context of his philosophy this obviously means nothing more than that everything compossible with what exists, exists—i.e., if God could create x, then he would do so unless the creation of other things prevents it. Cf. Wilson (1971), 613.

[26] See chap. 10, sec. 2.

[27] Kalinowski (1983), 342, takes exception to identifying possible worlds with sets of individual concepts instead of with sets of possible individuals. At G II 54–55 (M 61–62), where

To say that there is an individual "corresponding" to a given individual concept is simply to say that there is an individual falling under (or "having") the series of complex attributes or states that constitute the concept in question, where to fall under a complex concept is to fall under all of its components. The complete individual concept of Adam thus consists of the series of states that Adam goes through; it involves "everything that has ever happened to him and everything that will happen to him, as, for example, that he will have such and such a progeny."[28]

Now, although Adam's concept is a structure built up out of Adam's attributes (and a time parameter), the complete individual concept of Pegasus cannot be satisfactorily described as similarly built up out of Pegasus's attributes, for, as will be explained more fully below, Pegasus has no attributes (since he does not exist).[29] Instead, we have to say something like the following: the complete individual concept of Pegasus consists of the series of states that Pegasus would go through if he existed. Of course, this characterization is not without its own problems, involving, as it does, an apparent quantification or abstraction into an oblique context.

As noted in the preceding chapter,[30] some commentators have suggested that, for Leibniz, nondenoting proper names like "Pegasus" or "Zeus" do not represent complete individual concepts but rather are, in effect, abbreviations for descriptions representing concepts that are general, not individual. For example, the proper name "Pegasus" might be short for "the winged horse ridden by Bellerophon," a description that Professor Ishiguro regards as representing a general concept under which many different possible individuals could fall.[31] I have said earlier that I see no reason to interpret Leibniz in this way, but we may note that in the present connection the issue is of minimal importance. For, whether or not Leibniz intended names like "Pegasus" and "Zeus" to represent complete individual concepts that are unactualized, he clearly held that there are infinitely many such concepts and that God's creation of any of the other possible worlds would have consisted in his creating individuals corresponding to some subset of these.[32]

Leibniz comes close to discussing the matter explicitly, he says that nonactual possible substances "have no other reality than that which they have in the Divine understanding" and in that sense are "figments of the imagination." He adds, "In order to call something possible, it is enough for me that one can form a concept of it, even though it should only exist in the Divine understanding, which is, so to speak, the domain of possible realities." However, I do not suggest that Leibniz ever said expressly that a possible world is a set of concepts.

[28] G II 12, 42, 131 (M 4–5, 45, 73); G IV 437 (L 310–11); S 475, 477.

[29] See chapter 5, sec. 3.

[30] Page 66.

[31] Ishiguro (1972), 135.

[32] There is, however, the following argument against letting nondenoting proper names represent general concepts. Suppose that a world containing Pegasus had been actualized; i.e., suppose that Pegasus had existed. Then, for every simple property P, either Pegasus would fall under P or he would fall under its complement $\bar{P}$, so that either the proposition

Pegasus is P

or the proposition

Pegasus is $\bar{P}$

Note also that a complete individual concept "completely determines" the corresponding individual. This is especially clear when Leibniz agrees with Arnauld that, strictly speaking, there cannot be several possible Adams.

> We must, therefore, not conceive of a vague Adam or of a person to whom certain attributes of Adam appertain, when we try to determine if all human events follow from the presupposition that he exists, but we must attribute to him a concept so complete that all which can be attributed to him may be derived from this.[33]

In other words, not only is there in fact at most one individual having the attributes included in this concept, but, speaking loosely again, no two possible individuals have all these attributes.

Also of some importance in this connection is Leibniz's point that the concept of an object is not changed when the object is created, or else God would not have succeeded in creating the very object he decided on in his deliberations.[34] So actualized concepts are not to be differentiated from the nonactualized ones by the presence of a simple or complex property called "existence."

The next point to observe is that Leibniz does not consider that every collection of complete individual concepts constitutes a possible world; the concepts in question must be *compossible* and the collection must be *maximal.*[35]

A pair of individual concepts, *A* and *B*, are compossible if no contradiction follows from the supposition that there are corresponding individuals for both of them—that is, if the statements '*A* exists' and '*B* exists' are consistent with one another.[36] On this basis one might suppose that, just as we can easily find three distinct statements *P*, *Q*, and *R* such that although *P* is

---

would be true. Thus, for every simple property *P*, either *P* would be included in the concept of Pegasus, or *P̄* would be so included; i.e., the concept of Pegasus would be a complete individual concept. So, if Pegasus had existed, the concept of Pegasus would have been a complete individual concept. But whether a concept is individual or general cannot plausibly be made to depend on what happens to exist. Otherwise, God could not create something according to plan, because the act of creation would change the plan; or, to shift from theology to semantics, the meanings of sentences would depend on their truth value, which is equally unacceptable.

At G VI 363, where Huggard (H 371) has Leibniz speaking of "several Sextuses" that resemble the "true Sextus," Leibniz's phrase is *des Sextus approchans*, i.e., "some approximations to Sextus." This makes it clear that in his subsequent references to "a Sextus" he is not, as some have thought, seriously using the proper name "Sextus" as a general term.

[33] G II 42 (M 45–46). Cf. G IV 433: ". . . the nature of an individual substance or of a complete being is to have a concept so complete as to suffice for understanding and deducing all the predicates of the subject to which that concept is applied."

[34] G VI 131, 255 (H 151, 270). Cf. Grua 303.

[35] G III 572–73 (L 661–62). At G III 573 (L 662), however, Leibniz does say that every collection of compossibles makes a possible world, seemingly ignoring that his doctrines require the collection to be maximal.

[36] Grua 325: "The compossible is that which, with another, does not imply a contradiction." Poser (1969), 62, quotes LH IV vii B 3 17v: "Incompossibile *A* ipsi *B* si posita propositione *A* existit, sequitur *B* non existit. Et eo casu etiam *B* incompossibile est ipsi *A*." Cf. Grua 289; C 360, 375ff., 529–30; A.6.6.265, 307; G III 572.

Hacking (1982), 193; "Rescher and Mates cannot be right about compossibility. Leibniz never says what they would like him to say. He regularly explains possibility as freedom from

consistent with Q and with R, yet Q and R are inconsistent with one another, so also we could expect to find three different individual concepts such that the first was compossible with the second and with the third, but the second was not compossible with the third. Our expectation would be mistaken, however. It is blocked by the Leibnizian doctrine that in the actual world and in every other possible world, each concept "mirrors" or "expresses" all the other individual concepts in that world.[37] Each individual of the actual world is related to all the others, and every relation is "grounded" in accidents of the substances related; the same would be true of any other possible world.[38]

Commentators have wondered how the existence of one individual could preclude that of another, especially since Leibniz denies the reality of relations.[39] It is not surprising that they are puzzled, for Leibniz himself says, "It is as yet unknown to men, whence arises the incompossibility of diverse things, or how it can happen that diverse essences are opposed to each other, seeing that all purely positive terms seem to be compatible inter se."[40]

At any rate, the "mirroring" principle clearly implies that concepts belonging to different possible worlds must be incompossible. It may be illustrated with Adam and Eve. Adam would not have been the same person if he had not been the husband of Eve, nor would Eve have been the same person

---

contradiction, but never goes on to give the same explanation for compossibility." With this compare the Leibnizian statements quoted above, especially that from Grua 325.

It might be thought that in taking compossibility as a *binary* relation Leibniz was overlooking the fact that a set of concepts might be pairwise satisfiable without being satisfiable as a whole. E.g., the set of three concepts—*Divisible by 2, Divisible by 3, Power of a Prime*—has this property. But in Leibnizian complete individual concepts this cannot happen, since the special features of Leibnizian "mirroring" guarantee that compossibility is a transitive relation.

[37] G II 40, 112 (M 43, 143–44); G III 465; G IV 434, 440; G VI 107, 329 (H 128, 341–42); G VII 263; C 15, 19. G VII 316–17: This is the nature of every individual substance: that the series of its operations expresses the whole universe. G VII 313: Changes and states of each substance express perfectly the changes and states of every other. From the "Metaphysical Discussion with Fardella," printed by Stein (1888), 323: "Thus each thing is connected with the whole universe in such a way, and one state of one thing is so involved with the particular states of other things, that in any one state of any one thing God clearly sees the universe implied and encoded (*veluti implicatum et inscriptum*)." See also C 521, G VII 311.

At G III 545 Leibniz implies, if I understand him correctly, that each monad of the actual world mirrors not only the whole actual world but also, via God, all other possible worlds. Further, G II 40 (M 43) implies that every possible monad expresses the laws (and hence, presumably, the other possible monads) of its own possible world.

Gregory Fitch (1979, 30) considers Leibniz's notion of mirroring too obscure to support the weight I am putting on it. I hope that the model to be given in section 3 below will allay such misgivings. There can be no doubt that Leibniz regarded the "mirroring" principle as absolutely central to his philosophy. Indeed, at G II 253 he goes so far as to assert that his whole philosophy follows from it. For historical information on the metaphor, see Nieraad (1970), 56–60.

[38] G II 486, G VI 107 (H 128), C 9. Cf. also C 521.

[39] E.g., Rescher (1979), 54ff.

[40] G VII 195 (R 296). Cf. the proof of the existence of God, shown to Spinoza in 1677, G VII 261ff. Here he makes it clear that by saying that all simple qualities are "compatible with each other" he means that they can all belong to the same subject. In the passage quoted in the text, however, I do not understand Leibniz's reason ("seeing that . . ."), for he now seems to be running together the two questions: (1) whether an individual's having an attribute P can exclude its having an attribute Q, and (2) whether one individual's having P can exclude another from having Q.

if she had not been the wife of Adam; thus, neither Adam nor Eve could have existed without the other.[41] Adam's concept also involves those of all his progeny, including those of Cain, Abel, Seth, and even ourselves. If Adam had not existed, none of us would have existed, and, what is perhaps more surprising, if any of us had not existed, Adam would not have existed. In short, if two individual concepts belong to a single possible world, then they are present together or absent together in every possible world.[42] Thus the relation of compossibility is transitive. Add to this the assumption that each individual concept is in itself capable of realization,[43] that is, is compossible with itself, and the obvious fact that the relation of compossibility between individual concepts is symmetrical, and one sees that this relation is an equivalence relation that partitions the totality of individual concepts into a set of mutually exclusive and jointly exhaustive equivalence classes.[44]

We are also told by Leibniz that the actual world is maximal, in the sense that it contains everything compossible with what it contains, and there is no reason no doubt that this holds of the other possible worlds as well.[45] Indeed, it follows from the mirroring principle mentioned above. If God could have created a world containing Bellerophon and his winged horse, Pegasus, the concept of Bellerophon must involve that of Pegasus and vice versa; hence it would be impossible to create Bellerophon (as contrasted with other possible

---

[41] Grua 358. It is very significant that at G II 42 (M 45) Leibniz indicates that to conceive Adam *sub ratione generalitatis*, we must not mention "Eve, Eden, or other circumstances which complete his individuality." At G VII 312, however, he seems to say that each individual in the world would still go its way "even if all the others were supposed nonexistent."

D'Agostino (1981), considering what he calls "Mates's equivocal solution of this problem," i.e., Leibniz's problem of "whence arises the incompossibility of diverse things," produces a discussion (pp. 92ff.) that is irrelevant to the issue because it confuses the two questions mentioned in n. 40. I may add that the views he ascribes to me (p. 93), and especially the purported direct quote, in no way resemble anything I have ever written. It must be a case of mistaken identity.

[42] G II 40–41 (M 43–44).

[43] G II 573.

[44] G VI 148, 252, 362 (H 168, 267, 370–71). Note that although no individual concept belongs to more than one possible world, for any hypothesis (e.g., that there was a siege of Keilah) there is a possible world "which differs from ours only in all that is connected with this hypothesis, and the idea of this possible world represents that which would happen in that case" (G VI 125, H 145–46; cf. Grua 342).

At G VI 362–63 (H 370–71), Jupiter does the partitioning into equivalence classes. Cf. also G II 182.

[45] G VII 194 (R 296): "Everything possible demands that it should exist, and hence will exist unless something else prevents it, which also demands that it should exist and is incompatible with the former." G III 572 (L 661): If the novel *l'Astrée* is compossible with the actual world, it is true. G VII 304 (L 448): "For just as all possibilities tend with equal right to existence in proportion to their reality, so all heavy objects tend to descend with equal right in proportion to their weight. And just as, in the latter case, the motion is produced which involves the greatest possible descent of these weights, so in the former a world is produced in which a maximum production of possible things takes place." The physical reference here is to the fact that a chain will hang in the form of a catenary. Cf. A.6.6.307.

At G VII 195 Leibniz makes an inference that I hope someone will be able to explain. He says that since a true proposition is one that is identical or can be deduced from identicals with the help of definitions, *it follows that* the real definition of Existence is this: from among the things that otherwise would exist, that exists which is maximally perfect or which involves the most essence.

individuals in varying degrees similar to him) without creating Pegasus, and vice versa. Therefore, every possible world containing the concept of Bellerophon must contain that of Pegasus and also every other complete individual concept that is compossible with the two of them.

In sum, the possible worlds are just the equivalence classes of complete individual concepts with respect to the relation of compossibility. There are infinitely many such worlds, we are told, and each world contains infinitely many concepts; every individual concept belongs to exactly one world.[46] Since Adam exists, there is no nonactual possible world W such that Adam would have existed if God had created W.

In view of certain controversies in the literature it is also worth pointing out that the possible worlds must clearly be restricted to collections of concepts of *created* or *to-be-created* individual substances.[47] God himself stands outside the actual world, which he created, and also outside all of the other possible worlds he considered in so doing.[48] I believe further that not only does Leibniz deny reality, that is, existence in the actual world, to all abstract entities (such as numbers, geometric figures, Platonic Ideas), but that he would not reckon any concepts of these as belonging to other possible worlds. It is not a contingent fact that these things do not exist; such questions as "What if, in addition to individuals, there had existed sets of individuals?" would not, for him, even make sense.

2. Puzzles about Mirroring

We have seen that the state of any monad at any time is supposed to mirror or express the states of all the other monads at that time, as well as its own past and future states.[49] Since the relation of mirroring or expressing is obviously transitive, this implies that the state of any monad at any time mirrors all states of all monads at all times. Further, if a state of monad A mirrors a state of monad B, monad A (in its state) is said to *perceive* monad B (in *its* state). It follows that every monad at every time is perceiving the whole universe of monads, in all past, present, and future states. Further, a monad's perceptions are *identified* with its states or the components of its states; if monad A has the same perceptions as monad B, A and B are identical.

Several well-known commentators, including H. Lotze, W. Windelband, E. Cassirer, H. Heimsoeth, and H. W. B. Joseph, have argued that these features of the monadology involve Leibniz in some sort of quasi-logical para-

---

[46] Grua 305, G III 573, G VI 252 (H 267); negative evidence at C 360. This was first pointed out by Nicholas Rescher (1967, 17). At G VI 363, as we have noticed, it is clear that the various "Sextuses" are *not* the same individual.

[47] See Wilson (1979). Thus, such questions as whether God could create a world of which he was a member, or a world of which he was not a member, as considered, e.g., in Burch (1979), are irrelevant to the Leibnizian scheme of possible worlds.

[48] G VII 566.

[49] See n. 37.

dox. Lotze, for example, has difficulty with the simile of a multiplicity of mirrors, each of them reflecting nothing but the others. He writes:

> Perception . . . is the general activity of all monads; but *what* do they perceive? You will hardly find an answer to this in Leibniz; the monads, each of them from its own point of view, mirror the universe, but the universe itself consists only of other monads. . . . Therefore, what each monad can reflect is only the way in which it itself is reflected in others and these are reflected in one another; there would be *no independent state of affairs or content in the universe* to serve as grist for this process of reflection.[50]

Windelband, in a similar vein, argues that if the properties of monad *A* are nothing more than its perceptions of monads, *B, C, D, . . .* , and those of monad *B* are nothing more than its perceptions of monads *A, C, D, . . .* , "then there is no real content in this system of mutually perceiving substances." Elsewhere, somewhat inconsistently, he concludes that since the monads do not differ from one another in the content of their perceptions, which in all cases is the universe, they can differ only in the degrees of clarity with which they express that universe.[51]

Cassirer, referring to the Lotze passage quoted above, agrees that it points to a serious "logical difficulty," but he says that Lotze has erred in supposing that the monads themselves are the objects of monadic perception, whereas, according to him, those objects are only *phenomena*.[52] He fails to notice, however, that Leibniz says unambiguously that the states of monads mirror the states of monads.

According to Heimsoeth's version of the problem:

> The whole world of substances resolves itself into a system of correspondences, in which there are no corresponding contents. Each monad is nothing but the expression of the others, which themselves are only expressions. Everything becomes function or relation, while indeed all relation is explained as something "merely ideal" or "merely mental," which can gain reality only insofar as it is grounded in individual substances as relata.[53]

Joseph, too, argues that Leibniz's "whole theory [that every monad expresses the universe from its own point of view] breaks down" because, according to him, it involves a "fundamental confusion." He notes that the successive states of any monad *A* are a factor determining what any other monad *B* perceives, while in turn the monad *B*'s perceptions, that is, its states, are a factor determining what *A* perceives; and thus, he claims, the states of *A* are both "logically prior" and "logically posterior" to those of *B*. It is plain that he regards this as a severe difficulty. He concludes: "We cannot

[50] Lotze (1868), 13–14.
[51] Windelband (1935), 356; cf. Mahnke (1925), 196–97.
[52] Cassirer (1902), 467–68.
[53] Heimsoeth (1912), 280n.

make the universe they express the universe of monads that express it . . . this leads to an infinite regress."[54]

Still another version of the same objection asserts that Leibniz's doctrine of mirroring should have led him to the Spinozistic conclusion that there is only one substance. For, it is said, if the attributes of monads are their perceptions, and if at all times every monad is perceiving the same thing, namely, the universe of monads, then by the Identity of Indiscernibles there is at most one monad.[55]

3. A Numerical Model of the Possible Worlds

So far as I know, Russell was the first to offer a numerical model in support of the claim that the relation of expression is possible between every pair of monads and between every monad and the whole system of monads.[56] The model to be described here is constructed on a basis somewhat different from his, and it is more fully worked out.

Like most models, this one will succeed in representing only some of the properties of the structure in question. The features of the Leibnizian scheme that we do seek to depict are the following:

1. The number of possible worlds is infinite.
2. The number of complete individual concepts in each possible world is also infinite.
3. Every complete individual concept belongs to exactly one possible world.
4. In the actual world, every individual goes through a continuous series of distinct states, a different one for each moment of time.
5. In the actual world, the state of any individual at any time mirrors the states of all other individuals at that time.
6. In the actual world, the state of any individual at any time completely determines and is determined by its states at all other times.
7. In the actual world, the state of any individual at any time is different from the states of all other individuals at all other times.

We shall suppose that a possible state of a possible individual is a composite "complete" property, in which each simple property P or its complement

[54] Joseph (1949), 144, 146, 158. More recent commentators are similarly puzzled. Cf. e.g., Levin (1980), who finds (p. 228) that "failure to resolve the circularity in the description of monads is what makes Leibniz's theory incoherent."

[55] Oddly enough, Russell himself seems to have accepted this line of argument. Russell (1959, 56–57), quoting a 1909 paper, says, "If the axiom of internal relations ('Every relation is grounded in the natures of the related terms') is true, it follows that there is no diversity, and that there is only one thing." He explains, "Nothing quite true of A can be said about A short of taking account of the whole universe; and then what is said about A will be the same as what would be said about anything else, since the natures of different things must, like those of Leibniz's monads, all express the same system of relations."

[56] Russell (1972), 397. Cf. also Russell, viii.

$\bar{P}$, but not both, is a factor.[57] According to (4) above, the states of any monad in the actual world form a continuous (temporal) series; we assume that the possible states of any possible individual also form some such series. Thus, every complete individual concept, whether or not there is a corresponding individual, will be considered to consist of a continuous series of "complete" properties of the aforementioned type. We shall represent each such concept by a segment of the ascending series of real numbers equal to or greater than 1, with each number in such a segment representing one of the successive states.[58]

Accordingly, let the ascending series of real numbers r such that $1 \leqslant r < 1\frac{1}{2}$ represent the successive states of monad 1 in world 1 (the actual world). Let the ascending series of real numbers r such that $2 \leqslant r < 2\frac{1}{2}$ represent the successive states of monad 2 in world 1. Generalizing, let the ascending series of real numbers r such that $p \leqslant r < p + \frac{1}{2}$ represent the successive states of the pth monad in world 1.

The states of the first monad of the second world are to be represented by the ascending series of real numbers r such that $1\frac{1}{2} \leqslant r < 1\frac{3}{4}$. The states of the pth monad in world 2 are to be represented by the ascending series of real numbers r such that $p + \frac{1}{2} \leqslant r < p + \frac{3}{4}$. In general, the states of the pth monad in the nth world are to be represented by the ascending series of real numbers r such that

$$p + \left(1 - \frac{1}{2^{n-1}}\right) \leqslant r < p + \left(1 - \frac{1}{2^n}\right).$$

To associate possible monad states with these real numbers, we proceed as follows. We suppose that the set of simple properties is denumerable, and we let

$$P_1, P_2, P_3, \ldots, P_n, \ldots,$$

be some enumeration of them. Now, given a real number $r \geqslant 1$, we consider the nonterminating binary expansion E_r of its reciprocal $1/r$. Then, according as the ith digit in E_r is 1 or 0, we let the simple property P_i or its complement $\bar{P}_i$ be a component of the monad state associated with r. Thus, for

---

[57] A.6.2.499 defines "state" as "an aggregate of contingent predicates." For "privative" concepts, see A.6.6.130, 276.

[58] In the myth at the end of the *Theodicy*, G VI 362ff. (H 370ff.), Theodorus is being shown what would happen to "a Sextus"—more accurately, to one of the Sextus approximations—in a nonactual possible world. There is a number on the forehead of this individual; Theodorus is instructed to look up the corresponding section in the book describing that possible world, and to "put your finger on any line you please," i.e., to select a time. There he will see, says Athena, in effect the full detail of the state indicated by that line, i.e., "a portion of the life of that Sextus." Our model assigns an ascending series of real numbers to each individual concept. We could let the least (i.e, the first) number in the series be the number "on its forehead." As we shall see, given this number and the number of a time, the state of the possible monad is determined.

example, for the number $5\frac{9}{11}$ we have the nonterminating binary expansion of its reciprocal, $\frac{11}{64}$, namely,

$$.001010111\ldots,$$

so that the monad state associated with $5\frac{9}{11}$ will be

$$\bar{P}_1\bar{P}_2 P_3 \bar{P}_4 P_5 \bar{P}_6 P_7 P_8 P_9\ldots,$$

which is a state of monad 5 of possible world 3.

For world 1, the actual world, we define time by means of the states of monad 1; that is, we use monad 1 as our clock.[59] To accomplish this, we must set up a one-to-one correspondence between times and those states. If a state of the "clock" monad is represented by the number r, we define the time of that state as $(r-1)/(3-2r)$ years after the Creation.[60] For example, the state represented by the number $1\frac{1}{4}$ occurs exactly $\frac{1}{2}$ year after the Creation, and the state represented by the number $1\frac{10}{21}$ occurs exactly 10 years after the Creation. We define states of different monads in the actual world as simultaneous if and only if their associated numbers differ at most by an integer.[61] For example, to say that a given state of a given monad in the actual world occurs exactly 10 years after the beginning is to say that it is simultaneous with the state of the clock monad corresponding to the number $1\frac{10}{21}$. Thus, the state of monad 5 at that time would be the state associated with $5\frac{10}{21}$, that is, the state

$$\bar{P}_1\bar{P}_2 P_3 \bar{P}_4 P_5 P_6 P_7 \bar{P}_8 P_9 \bar{P}_{10} P_{11} P_{12}\ldots,$$

since the binary expansion of $\frac{21}{115}$ is about $.001011101011$.

That the model represents the seven features mentioned earlier in this section is quite obvious. Given the state of any actual monad at any time, a sufficiently discerning mind will easily deduce the state of any other monad at that time. For if r is the number of a state of the qth monad, then the simultaneous state of the pth monad $(p > q)$ will be numbered $r + p - q$; thus, given the state of the qth monad, the calculator computes its associated real number r, adds $p - q$, and determines the state associated with the result. Further, if t is any time (measured in years after the Creation), the state of the pth actual monad at that time is represented by the number $p + t/(2t + 1)$. Thus, if Adam is monad 2 of the actual world, his state 20 years after the Creation is represented by the number $2\frac{20}{41}$ and consists (so far as my finite mind can calculate) of the complex property

$$\bar{P}_1 P_2 P_3 \bar{P}_4 \bar{P}_5 P_6 P_7 \bar{P}_8 P_9 P_{10} P_{11}\ldots,$$

---

[59] Grua 270: Before the world began, there *was* no time.

[60] On whether there was a first instant, see G III 581–82 (L 664).

[61] If we wish to define a "time" for the pth world, we can use any one of its monads as a clock and proceed analogously, letting states be simultaneous if their associated numbers differ at most by an integer.

which we read off from the binary expansion .01100110111 ... of the reciprocal of that number. Since a sufficiently discerning mind can calculate the state of any individual at any time, it is trivially the case that, given that individual's state at any time, this mind can determine what it must be at any other time.

We have taken no account of the different "degrees of clarity" with which the various monads of the actual world are said to perceive one another.[62] Perhaps a partial representation of this could be built into our model along the following lines. Let $n(A)$, $n(B)$, and $n(C)$ be the numbers of states of monads A, B, and C, respectively. Then, in these states, A perceives C more clearly than B does, if and only if the absolute value of $n(C) - n(A)$ is less than the absolute value of $n(C) - n(B)$. Thus, although each monad will perceive all states of all others, no two monads will perceive with the same degree of clarity. On this scheme, however, each monad will perceive all of its own past and future states more clearly than it perceives any state of any other monad, and, among its own states, it will perceive all of the near past and future more clearly than any of the more distant past and future. Obviously this does not quite fit Leibniz's intentions.

The model also does not adequately reflect what Leibniz says about the relation of temporal priority. He defines a state S of a given monad as prior to a state S' of that monad if S "involves a reason for" S'. Thus, he says, "my earlier state involves a reason for the existence of my later state." He adds: "And since my prior state, because of the connection among all things, involves the prior state of other things as well, it also involves the reason for the later state of those other things and thus is prior to them."[63] But in this model, although we have represented the "involve" relation, the later states of a monad determine the earlier states just as clearly as the earlier determine the later.

Perhaps someone can find a way of remedying these and other deficiencies in our scheme. Nevertheless, even as it stands, the model suffices to show that there is no inconsistency in the mirroring aspect of Leibniz's monadology.

---

[62] Leibniz says that monads cannot equally well express everything: "otherwise there would be no distinction between souls" G II 90 (M 113).

[63] GM VII 18 (L 666).

V

Truth

Leibniz has a very special, and philosophically notorious, way of understanding what it means to say that a proposition is *true*.

1. The Predicate-in-Subject Principle

His best-known and most important dictum on this subject goes as follows:

> An affirmation is true if its predicate is in its subject; thus, in every true affirmative proposition, necessary or contingent, universal or singular, the concept of the predicate is somehow contained in the concept of the subject, in such a way that anyone who understood the two concepts as God understands them would *eo ipso* perceive that the predicate is in the subject.[1]

Clearly, this assertion concerns only simple propositions of the forms '*A* is *B*' and 'Every *A* is *B*'. (Strictly speaking, the form pertains to the representing sentence, of course, and not to the proposition represented.) Complex propositions, such as conjunctions, disjunctions, and conditionals, are

---

[1] C 16–17; cf. C 402. Another typical statement (S 474): "A simple proposition is true if the predicate is contained in the subject; i.e., if by resolving the terms *A* and *B* (which is done by substituting other equipollent and more analyzed terms) it appears that the value or concept of the predicate is contained in the concept of the subject."

Other references, many from PLR 62 n. 5, are G II 43; G VII 300, 309, C 11, 51, 55, 85, 272, 388, 401ff., 518ff.; Grua 304, 305, 536; FC 179. At GM VII 261, C 518–19, S 474, and elsewhere, Leibniz ascribes the Predicate-in-Subject principle to Aristotle: "... in the Prior Analytics [Aristotle] wrote that the predicate [of a true proposition] is contained in [*inesse*] the subject—better, the concept of the predicate is in the concept of the subject—while, conversely, the individuals of the subject are included in the individuals of the predicate." A.6.6.396–97: Truth is a feature of propositions, not of sentences nor of inscriptions. At A.6.6.269 truth as applied to ideas is defined, and at A.6.6.398 it is reduced to that of propositions.

At G VI 300, "*A* is *B*," "*B* is truly predicated of *A*," "*B* is in *A*," and "the concept *B* is somehow contained in the concept *A*" are given as alternative formulations.

excluded prima facie, as are all negative propositions and all particular affirmative propositions.[2] For the simple affirmative propositions of singular or universal form, however, Leibniz seems to regard the assertion as completely self-evident; he repeats it in many places, often relying on the context to supply the qualifications explicitly indicated in the passage just quoted.[3]

This dictum, which may be called "the Predicate-in-Subject principle,"[4] is closely related to various other Leibnizian doctrines, including the doctrine concerning complete individual concepts. Leibniz explains:

> In saying that the individual concept of Adam involves all that will ever happen to him, I mean nothing else than what all philosophers mean when they say that the predicate is in the subject of a true proposition.[5]

And he adds:

> It is true that the consequences of so clear a thesis are paradoxical, but that is the fault of the philosophers, who do not follow out sufficiently far these perfectly clear notions.[6]

Thus, the completeness of individual concepts is considered by Leibniz to be a consequence of the Predicate-in-Subject principle as applied to singular propositions. Further, from this principle concerning the truth of propositions he infers the metaphysical claim that every individual substance, or monad, is causally independent of every other:

> In consulting the notion which I have of every true proposition, I find that every predicate, necessary or contingent, past, present, or future, is comprised in the notion of the subject, and I ask no more. . . . The proposition in question is of great importance, and deserves to be well established, for it follows that every soul is a world apart,

---

[2] Leibniz sometimes includes propositions expressed by sentences of the form 'Some *A* is *B*', but in his treatment of these he clearly confuses the question of whether the concept *B* is included in the concept *A* with the question whether the concept *B* is included in some concept that includes *A*. Thus, in considering, at C 51 (P 19), the proposition "Some metal is gold," he grants that the concept Metal does not contain the concept Gold, but he says that "some metal, with some addition or specification (e.g., 'that which makes up the greater part of a Hungarian ducat') is of such a nature as to involve the nature of gold." I do not think that he means that the concept "Metal that makes up the greater part of a Hungarian ducat" contains the concept Gold as a part, but rather that some metal, e.g., that metal which in fact makes up the greater part of a Hungarian ducat, is such that *its* concept contains the concept Gold.

[3] Generally Leibniz regards a proposition as false if and only if it is not true, as, e.g., at C 393 (P 82), but at C 364 (P 54 n. 2) he says that propositions containing impossible terms are neither true nor false.

[4] Broad (1975), 6ff.) uses the rather unfortunate phrase "predicate-in-notion principle." Cf. Broad (1949).

[5] G II 43 (R 216). Compare S 475–6: "Given that there is somebody who is Strong, Brash, Learned, a King, General of an army, Victor in the battle of Arbela, and the rest of what is ascribed in this way to Alexander the Great, God, intuiting the individual essence of Alexander the Great, will see a complete concept in which all of these are contained virtually, or from which they all follow. King does not follow from Strong, nor Victor from General, but from the concept of Alexander follow King, Strong, Victor, and General; and that there is such a concept is manifest from the previously given definition of true proposition. For when we say 'Alexander is strong' we mean only that Strong is contained in the concept of Alexander, and similarly as concerns the rest of Alexander's predicates."

[6] G II 43 (R 216).

independent of everything else except God; that it is not only immortal and so to speak incapable of being affected, but that it keeps in its substance traces of all that happens to it. It follows also in what consists the intercourse of substances, and particularly the union of soul and body. . . . Each substance expresses the whole sequence of the universe according to the view or respect which is proper to it, whence it happens that they agree perfectly together.[7]

It has generally been assumed that Leibniz considers Predicate-in-Subject containment to be both a necessary and a sufficient condition for the truth of the propositions in question. In earlier papers I have argued that it was only necessary; other scholars, including most notably Theo Meijering, have presented strong evidence for the more usual view.[8] It now seems to me that this issue is resolvable via the ambiguity of *ens* and *est*: if '*A* is *B*' and 'Every *A* is *B*' are essential propositions, the criterion is both necessary and sufficient, but if they are existential, it is necessary only or sufficient only.[9]

Thus consider, for example, a singular affirmative essential proposition '*A* is *B*'. This is equivalent to '*AB* is an entity' or '*AB* is absolutely possible'. (The distinction between the absolute and the hypothetical types of possibility and necessity will be discussed in chapter 6.) And, where *A* is a complete individual concept, the absolute possibility of *AB* is equivalent, for Leibniz, to *B*'s being included in *A*. Accordingly, "Pegasus is a winged horse," as an essential proposition, would seem to be true despite the non-existence of Pegasus, and the same holds for essential "Pegasus is Pegasus" and all other propositions of that form.[10]

Likewise, the universal affirmative essential proposition 'Every *A* is *B*' is equivalent, as we have seen, to 'An *A* that is not a *B* is absolutely impossible'. This too holds, according to Leibniz, if and only if the concept *A* involves or contains the concept *B*. An example would be "Every man is liable to sin"; taken essentially this amounts to the same as "A man not liable to sin is absolutely impossible,", and hence it is false.[11] Essential "Every man is an

---

[7] G II 46 (R 205). At first reading, Leibniz's claim that the Predicate-in-Subject principle implies that there is no causal interaction among created souls seems preposterous. I think that his willingness to make such an inference is a symptom of his general confusion of reasons and causes. He is following a tradition in which *causa* equals Greek *aitia*, where *X* is the *aitia* of *Y*'s being in such and such a condition if *X* is prominently mentioned in an appropriate answer to a question of why *Y* is in that condition. For Leibniz, God is the ultimate *aitia* for any created monad's being in any given condition; e.g., the deep answer to "Why did Caesar cross the Rubicon?" is "God chose to create Ceasar-who-was-going-to-cross-the-Rubicon," i.e., "God chose to create this sort of individual rather than some other." See chap. 9, sec. 2.

[8] Meijering (1978).

[9] This presupposes, however, that the subject of the sentence expresses a consistent concept. For there are, according to Leibniz, false sentences of the form "*AB* is *A*." E.g., he plainly regards the sentence "The necessary body is necessary" as false because it is impossible that there be a necessary body. (G III 433).

[10] At C 378 # 83 (P 67) he extends this to such essential propositions as "Man is an animal," which I am not considering to be strictly of the form "*A* is *B*." He says that this essential proposition is true, for the concept Man is the same as the concept Man-Animal and hence contains the concept Animal.

[11] Cf. C 392 # 144 (P 81), and note that according to G II 108 there are nonactual possible worlds in which there are people but no sin.

animal," on the other hand, is true, for it is absolutely impossible that there should be a man who is not an animal.[12]

But the corresponding existential propositions, as we shall see below, behave differently. In their case Leibniz clearly does not regard the inclusion of predicate in subject as a sufficient, nor perhaps even as a necessary, condition for truth.

2. Containment

As we saw in chapter 3, the containment relation among concepts is characterized by Leibniz in two ways: (1) The concept A is contained in (or is included in) the concept B, and B involves A, if and only if it is absolutely impossible for there to be an object falling under B but not under A. (2) The concept A is contained in B if and only if all the simple components of A are components of B. It is clear that Leibniz regards the two characterizations as equivalent. Thus, the concept Animal is contained in the concept Man, for by tradition it is considered impossible for something to be a man without being an animal, and, of course, the same tradition guarantees that the concept Man can be analyzed as Rational Animal.

When we consider the containment of concepts in complete individual concepts, however, the matter becomes a bit more complicated. Leibniz says, it will be remembered, that the concept (or property) King is included in the complete individual concept of Alexander the Great. But this inclusion relation cannot be exactly the same as that which holds between Animal and Man or between Plane Curve and Circle. For Man and Circle are complex concepts that contain, in the sense defined above, simpler ones like Animal and Plane Curve, while the complete individual concept of Alexander cannot contain King in that same way. It is not absolutely impossible for something to be Alexander without being a king; indeed, before 336 B.C. such was actually the case. The concept of Alexander seems to be a temporally ordered series of states, each of which is itself a "complete" property or concept—complete in the sense that it contains, for every property P, either P or the complement of P and not both. Thus, the property King is not, strictly speaking, contained in the concept of Alexander, but rather it is contained in some elements of the series of states that constitute that concept.

There is no evidence that Leibniz ever explicitly considered this asymmetry between individual and general concepts. Usually he seems to regard the complete concept of an individual simply as a complex property of the same type as any other complex property, with components that are less specific concepts and are ultimately analyzable into simples. Just as the concept Man is the concept Rational Animal, so the concept of Julius Caesar would be the concept Rational-Animal–Roman-General who subdued Gaul,

---

[12] If not obvious, this is evident from the text cited in n. 10.

defeated Pompey at Pharsalus, was assassinated in 44 B.C., and so on, including every property of Caesar.[13] Thus considered, an individual concept would be in effect a limiting case of a general concept, an *infima species* generated by the successive addition of components or "determinations" to a general concept, with results that become more and more specific, until finally it is "complete" and characterizes exactly one possible individual.[14] Leibniz's substitution of both proper names and general terms indifferently for the variables in expressions like "*A* is *B*" and his acceptance of both kinds of terms in subject or predicate positions and in compounds formed by juxtaposition (compare "the apostle who denied Christ is Peter" and "Peter the apostle who denied Christ is an existent thing") are further indications that he took individual concepts to be of the same type, as it were, as the others. But difficulties arise when we try to fit this interpretation together coherently with some of his other doctrines.

For monad names *M* and specifications of moments of time *t*, I shall use 'the *t*-stage of *M*' as short for 'the state of the monad *M* at the time *t*'. Thus, using this abbreviation, we may say of any 335 B.C.-stage of Alexander the Great that it contains—in the fundamental sense of "contain" as defined by Leibniz—the attribute King, while his 340 B.C.-stages do not. Then, in a *derivative* sense of "contain," we may say that the attribute King is contained in a complete individual concept, meaning thereby that it is contained, in the fundamental sense, in at least some of the *t*-states of the individual falling under that concept.

Now, it might seem preferable to treat the matter in a quite different and apparently simpler way in which, instead of taking the complete individual concept to be a temporally ordered series of states, we would consider it a complex property composed of component properties expressed by phrases like "was king in 336 B.C." This would harmonize better with much of what Leibniz says, as we have indicated above. Instead of trying to apply the Predicate-in-Subject principle to sentences like "Alexander is a king," we would apply it only to the corresponding sentences asserting that Alexander was a king at such and such times or during such and such intervals. After all, it appears that propositions, not sentences, are what Leibniz means to talk about, and it can be argued that on any occasion of its use the sentence "Alexander is king' will express some proposition that could be expressed by a sentence in which the relevant time or times are explicitly mentioned.

But this way of dealing with the matter would be hard to reconcile with various Leibnizian texts and doctrines. We may note that in our specific example he says several times that King—not King between 336 and 323 B.C.—is included in the complete individual concept of Alexander.[15] More important, though, are the systematic reasons against the interpretation in question. Leibniz defines the nonsimultaneity of two states of a substance as

---

[13] Cf. the description of Alexander's concept in n. 5.
[14] G II 54 (M 61).
[15] G IV 433 (L 307–8); cf. S 475–76, quoted in n. 1.

the inclusion in one of a property that is lacking in the other, and it is plain that in general he hopes to reduce temporal relations to nontemporal properties of the relata; if qualities had time specifications built in, as it were, this would make no sense.[16] Further, if such time specifications were built in, no unactualized individual concept would contain any property belonging to any individual in the actual world. Thus, for example, no member of any other possible world could have a property expressed by "was a king in 336 B.C."—that is, "was a king at a time 336 earth revolutions before the birth of Jesus Christ," since Jesus Christ would not exist in that world. (Specifying times with reference to any states of any other monad or monads would have the same effect.) But clearly Leibniz thinks of forming concepts of other possible individuals by taking different combinations of the same ingredients that form the concepts of actual individuals.[17] Though his doctrines imply that there is no cross-world identity of individuals, these same doctrines certainly require cross-world identity of properties. Thus although, because of "the interconnections of things," Adam would not have existed if any of the rest of us had not existed, God could have created a completely different first man with a completely different wife and progeny, and in that possible world there would be men in the same sense of "man" that there are in ours.[18]

For these reasons I believe that Leibnizian statements to the effect that an (incomplete) attribute or concept B is contained in a complete individual concept A are best interpreted as meaning that the concept B is a component of the relevant t-states of the concept A. If A and B are both general, the containment relation is as defined in chapter 4.

3. Truth Conditions

The singular affirmative essential proposition 'A is B' is equivalent to 'AB is absolutely possible'. Its truth value, therefore, will not fluctuate with time. For, according to Leibniz, until God created the actual world, there was no time, though he knew exactly what was possible and what was not. In other words, the range of possibilities does not depend on which of the possible worlds was chosen for existence, and hence it is independent of temporal variations in the actual world or in any of the other worlds that could have existed. (Note that this invariability of truth value holds even though the complete individual concepts that are the subjects of such propositions will be temporally ordered series of states.)

Similar considerations apply to the universal affirmative essential proposition 'Every A is B', which Leibniz makes equivalent to 'An A non-B is absolutely impossible'. Thus the absolute impossibility of a man who is not an animal does not depend on which possible world God created, and therefore

---

[16] GM VII 128 (L 666); F 482.
[17] I do not mean to imply that all properties are exemplified in the actual world.
[18] G II 42 (M 45).

it cannot vary with time, since each time series is relative to its own particular world.

For the corresponding existential propositions the case is different. Singular existential 'A if B' is equivalent to 'AB is an existing thing', and the truth value of such a proposition may be expected to vary with respect to different possible worlds and different times in those worlds. Again, the same holds for the universal existential 'Every A is B', which is equivalent to 'An A non-B does not exist'.

The truth criteria for essential propositions would therefore seem to be relatively simple, and those for existential propositions, as involving time, relatively more complex.

Still, even for essential propositions different interpretations, leading to different criteria, are compatible with the Leibnizian texts. For instance, in view of the special sense that Leibniz sometimes (but only sometimes) gives to the word "essential," according to which an essential property of an individual is a property that the individual has at all times, it would be natural to characterize the truth of singular affirmative essential propositions as follows:

(1) 'A is B' is true if and only if every t-stage of A contains B.

Here the variable "t" is to run over designations of times in the actual world, and also over designations of the "times" of the other possible worlds.[19] (There is, of course, no simultaneity relation between the stages of individuals in different possible worlds. It makes no sense to ask, "Did Bellerophon ride Pegasus before or after the birth of Christ?")

Applied to particular cases, the criterion just stated leads to such results as that essential "Alexander is a man" is true, essential "Alexander is a king" is false, essential "Don Quixote is a man" is true, and essential "Don Quixote is tilting at windmills" is false—this last because in the story of Don Quixote there was a "time" before he attacked the windmills. These results accord well with the aforementioned Leibnizian use of "essential."[20]

The corresponding criterion for universal affirmative essential propositions would be:

(2) 'Every A is B' is true if and only if, for every individual concept C and time t, if the t-stage of C contains A, then it contains B.

Thus, essential "Every man is an animal" will be true because, loosely speaking, every possible man, at every time in his world, is an animal; better, every

---

[19] G VII 564: "The imaginary possible participates just as much as the actual in the fundamentals of order, and a novel can be ordered with respect to space and time just as much as a true history." It will be noticed, however, that novels, including some to which Leibniz himself often refers, seem to order their events with respect to time in the actual world, which ought to be nonsensical on Leibnizian principles. In such stories, terms like "hour," "day," "year," could not have the same sense as they have in reports about the actual world; the same would be true of spatial terms like "meter."

[20] Cf. G II 258 (L 533).

t-stage that contains the concept Man contains the concept Animal.[21] By contrast, essential "Every man is liable to sin" is false for Leibniz, in view of his claim that although in the actual world every man is indeed liable to sin, there is a possible world in which this is not the case.[22] That is to say, there is a complete individual concept that has a *t*-stage containing the concept Man but not containing the concept Liable to sin.

It will be noticed that the above condition for the truth of essential 'Every *A* is *B*' is equivalent to '*A* contains *B*'. For '*A* contains *B*' means that it is absolutely impossible for something to fall under *A* without falling under *B* and this amounts to: no *t*-stage of any individual concept that contains *A* can fail to contain *B*.

Therefore, for the singular and universal affirmative essential propositions these criteria would agree exactly with the Leibnizian Predicate-in-Subject principle, though for the singular proposition "contain" must be taken in the derivative sense we have described above.

But I am inclined to believe that a somewhat different analysis more faithfully represents Leibniz's intuitions and intentions, and corresponds to the sense of "essential" in which he contrasts essential with existential propositions. In this sense one might want to say that although it is not simpliciter the case that King is essential to Alexander the Great, as is evident from the fact that he did exist for a time without being a king, it is essential to his individuality that this property belong to him in 336 B.C. That is, it was possible for Alexander to exist without being king, but it was not possible for him to exist in 336 B.C. without being a king. If a property belongs to a given individual at a given time, it is absolutely impossible that that individual should have existed without having that property at that time; in this respect Leibnizian doctrine seems to imply that every property of an individual is essential to it.

Following this track, we would need somehow to add a time parameter to our propositions. As has been noted earlier, there are at least three ways of doing so, as can be seen most clearly in the singular propositions. We can say that '*A* is *B*' is true at *t*, or that '*A* is (*B* at *t*)' is (timelessly) true, or that '(*A* is *B*) at *t*' is (again timelessly) true. For the reasons given at the end of the preceding section, it seems best to choose the latter mode. This amounts to adding the time parameter to the copula.

With reference to such propositions, as contrasted with the "timeless" ones we have been considering up to now, the truth condition for singular affirmative essential propositions would be the following:

---

[21] In a note to his edition of Nizolius (A.6.2.472 n. 86) Leibniz says that "Man is an animal" means "If something is a man, it is an animal," and that for the truth of the latter the existence of a man is not required, but that if one exists, he is an animal. In mathematical contexts, where the propositions are uniformly essential, Leibniz makes it clear that, e.g., to say "All rectangles are parallelograms" is equivalent to saying that the concept Parallelogram is included in the concept Rectangle (G VII 240).

[22] G VI 108.

(3) 'A is$_t$ B' is true if and only if the t-stage of A contains B.

Again, the variable "t" is understood to run over designations of times in the various possible worlds. Thus, although the timeless essential proposition "Hamlet is a boy" is not true, in the Hamlet story there are values of "t" such that the essential propositions 'Hamlet is$_t$ a boy' are true, for it is absolutely impossible that anyone should have been this very same person, Hamlet, and not have been a boy at those times. Correspondingly, in that possible world there are other values of "t" such that the essential propositions 'Hamlet is$_t$ a boy' are false. In this way we can deal with the fact that even nonexistent individuals can in a sense be said to have properties at one time that they lack at another.

It has been debated in the literature whether Leibniz was a "super-essentialist" or not, where a superessentialist is a person who holds that for every property P, if P belongs to a given individual, then that individual could not exist without having P.[23] In view of our analysis, the answer seems to be that if the word "essential" is used in Leibniz's own rather special sense, then he is no superessentialist, for he agrees that at one time Alexander had the property King and that at another time he lacked it. But if "essential" is used in what is probably its more usual sense in philosophical discourse generally, including Leibniz's own, then he is indeed a superessentialist, since he clearly holds that (in the same example) if Alexander had the property King at a certain time, then he could not have existed without having that property at that time.

For universal affirmative essential propositions, the corresponding criterion would be:

(4) 'Every A is$_t$ B' is true if and only if, for every individual concept C, if the t-stage of C contains A, then it contains B.

Thus if, as Leibniz seems to suggest, there are nonactual but possible men who, at least some of the time, are free of liability to sin, criterion (4) implies that some of the essential propositions 'Every man is$_t$ liable to sin' are false. Compare this with the discussion of criterion (6) below.

Coming now to the existential propositions, we recall once again that existential 'A is B' is equivalent to 'AB is an existent thing'. For example, "Socrates is old" is equivalent to "Old Socrates is an existent thing." For such propositions, when we add the time parameter to the copula, we obtain as a truth-condition (where t designates a time in the actual world):

(5) 'A is$_t$ B' is true if and only if the concept B is included in the t-stage of A and A belongs to the actual world.

Thus for most t in 1674 the existential propositions 'Leibniz is$_t$ in Paris' are true, while this is not the case for 1678. On the other hand, for all values of t the existential propositions 'Hamlet is$_t$ is a boy', as well as all other singular propositions about nonexistent individuals, are false.

[23] The term is due to Mondadori; cf. Mondadori (1973, 1975).

It must be acknowledged, parenthetically, that adding a temporal index to the copula in this way leads to complications in some of the propositional transformations that Leibniz proposes. Consider, for example, his treatment of "Peter is denying," an existential proposition that he tells us is equivalent to "Peter denying is an existent." Clearly, if "Peter is denying" means "Peter is now denying," then "Peter denying is an existent" must mean "Peter now denying is an existent," rather than "Peter denying is now existent." For, according to Leibniz, Peter, like every other monad, exists at all times if he exists at all. It seems clear, therefore, that when 'A is$_t$ B' is transformed into 'AB is an existent', the time index t must attach to the compound 'AB'; 'AB' must be the concept resulting from combining B with the t-stage of A. Thus, when an individual concept is one of the components, the composition of concepts has to be a different sort of operation from what it is otherwise. Further, if 'A is$_t$ B' is false, where A is the concept of an actual individual, the combination 'AB' will not even be a t-stage in the concept of any possible individual. Worse, if both A and B are complete individual concepts and are not identical, it is hard to see any plausible interpretation whatever for 'AB'. Leibniz does not, so far as I know, ever face these difficulties.

The universal affirmative existential propositions 'Every A is B' will also have to have a time parameter because it can (and often does) happen that sometimes all the individuals falling under A will fall under B and at other times this will not be the case. For the same reason as before, we add the index to the copula rather than to the predicate. Then, existential

(6) 'Every A is$_t$ B' is true if and only if, for every complete individual concept C belonging to the actual world, if the t-stage of C contains A, then it contains B.

Again, it seems safest to restrict t to designations of time in the actual world.[24]

Thus, all the existential propositions 'Every man is$_t$ liable to sin' are true because (according to Leibniz, as I read him) every actual person is at all times liable to sin. This case suggests that when dealing with existential propositions, we might reintroduce the notation 'Every A is B' for 'For all t, every A is$_t$ B', and, similarly, the notation 'A is B' for 'For all t, A is$_t$ B'.[25] And, since one of the advantages of propositions over sentences is supposed

[24] Thus, when the universal affirmative is taken existentially, Leibniz agrees with Hobbes. Cf. the quote from Hobbes cited at NE 450 n. 1: "When two names are joined together into a consequence, or affirmation, as thus, 'A man is a living creature', ... if the latter name 'living creature' signify all that the former name 'man' signifieth, then the affirmation, or consequence, is true; otherwise false."

Leibniz seems to hold that in the case of nonactual things "we cannot say whether they exist *now* or not" (see chap. 4, n. 20). Therefore, he perhaps would wish to say that such propositions as "Bellerophon is now riding Pegasus" and "All unicorns are now horses" are either nonsense or without truth value, and not false. In any case, they would not be true.

[25] More strictly, the sentence 'Every A is B' can be reintroduced as short for the meta-theoretical statement that all sentences 'Every A is$_t$ B' for all time designations t, are true; e.g., 'All men are liable to sin' could be short for "For every time designation t, 'All men are$_t$ liable to sin' is true." Needless to say, I am not claiming that Leibniz had any such scheme explicitly in mind.

to be that there are no clear criteria for determining how many there are, or of what sorts they are, we might postulate "standing" propositions corresponding to such sentences. Then, existential "All men are liable to sin" would be one such (true) standing proposition. "Adam is the first man" would be another.

Other examples of existential universal affirmatives would be "Every man is now old," which is false, and "Every man twenty feet tall is now short," which is true. (Here, instead of the indexical "now," I should more properly be using a designation of the time at which I am writing this, or the reader should substitute a designation of his or her present time; it seems safe to assume that nobody will be reading this at a time when everybody is old or there are people twenty feet tall.) "At the beginning of 1985 everybody is (was) in jeopardy from nuclear weapons" is true, while "At the beginning of 1934 everybody is (was) in jeopardy from nuclear weapons" is false.

As our examples show, it is not necessary for the truth of an existential proposition 'Every A is, B', or even for that of a standing proposition 'Every A is B', that the concept B be contained in the concept A. We are thus left to wonder whether in applying the Predicate-in-Subject principle to universal affirmative existential propositions, Leibniz was not confusing containment in the general concept itself with containment in the individual concept of every existent individual falling under the general concept, or whether he meant to apply the principle to essential propositions only.[26] I incline toward the former hypothesis. He sometimes writes as though he takes the subject of the universal proposition 'Every A is B' to be 'Every A'; he may then be led to apply his Predicate-in-Subject principle and conclude that 'Every A is B' is true if and only if B is included in every A, and, with his carelessness about distinguishing x from the concept of x, to take this last as equivalent to B's inclusion in every concept of an A.

4. Relativization to Possible Worlds

In relation to the possible-worlds scheme, it is evident that "exists" means "exists in the actual world" (or, more exactly, "falls under a complete individual concept belonging to the possible world that has been actualized"). This suggests generalizing the unqualified notion of truth to a notion of truth relative to a given possible world W.

Let us here follow the usage of Russell and say that a sentence or proposition is true or false "of" a possible world and not "in" it..[27] For we are not

---

[26] At G VII 212 (P 116) Leibniz says: "For 'Every man is an animal' is the same as 'Man A is an animal', 'Man B is an animal', 'Man C is an animal', and so on"; and, of course, a necessary condition for the truth of all these latter propositions is that the concept Animal should be included in the complete individual concept of every man. Leibniz notes, at A.6.1.183, that Aristotle expressed 'Every A is B' as 'B is in each A'.

[27] R 32. Medieval logicians had this same distinction in view when they replaced the simple locution 'P is true' by the more involved phrase 'things are as described by P'; as a critical

interested in what would have happened to the sentence itself if the given world had existed. We wish to say, for example, that "There are no sentences" is true of any possible world in which there are no people and hence no languages, even though *in* such a world the sentence "There are no sentences" would not even exist, let alone be true. Again, we shall want to say that the sentence "Either Socrates is mortal or it is not the case that Socrates is mortal" is true of all possible worlds, including, for instance, worlds in which the word "or" means what the word "and" means in ours. The point is less clear with respect to propositions, as contrasted with sentences, but even in this case the use of "in" might beg such questions as whether, if there were no people, and hence no thoughts, there would be no propositions. Besides, it is hard to know what could be meant by saying that so abstract an entity as a proposition is in a possible world, that is, could have existed.

Now, in relativizing the notion of truth to possible worlds, we must treat the nonactual possible worlds analogously to the actual, for, after all, they could have been actual, and the relationship we are attempting to explicate is one of meaning rather than of fact.

We have said that existential 'A is, B' is true of the actual world if and only if the complete individual concept A belongs to the actual world and its t-stage includes the concept B. So, generalizing, we may say that existential

(7) 'A is, B' is true of world W if and only if the concept B is included in the t-stage of A and A belongs to W.

Again, the variable "t" is to run over time designations for the world W.

For singular existential "standing" propositions we have, correspondingly,

(8) 'A is B' is true of world W if and only if all propositions 'A is, B' are true,

with the same restriction on "t."[28]

Thus, for all values of "t" for the actual world, the existential propositions 'Don Quixote tilts, at windmills' will be false, as Don Quixote does not exist; but there is a possible world with respect to which some of these propositions will be true and others false, since in that world Don Quixote tilts at windmills (only) some of the time. Of that world, too, various standing propositions, such as "Don Quixote is a man," are true.

For universal affirmative existential propositions, the truth criterion generalized to possible worlds would be:

---

example they gave the sentence 'No negative proposition exists'. This proposition cannot be true, they said, because if it were true, it would not exist; but things could perfectly well be as it describes, and indeed would have been so if there had been no people.

[28] Thus, if A is a complete individual concept belonging to the actual world, existential 'A is B' is true of of the actual world if and only if essential 'A is B' is true. Cf. Leibniz's assertion at C 272: *In veris individuis existentibus omnes propositiones etiam essentiales sunt simul existentiales.*

(9) 'Every A is, B' is true of world W if and only if, for every concept C belonging to W, if the t-stage of C contains A, it also contains B.

Here again, the inclusion of a concept B in a concept A is a sufficient but not a necessary condition for the truth of any of these existential propositions. This result is not some bizarre consequence of our particular analysis but, rather, is clearly implied by what Leibniz says. He considers the existential (standing) proposition "Every man is a descendant of Adam" to be true, that is, true of the actual world; but, although Being-a-descendent-of-Adam is part of every t-stage of the complete individual concept of every existent man, it is obviously not part of the concept Man. If it were, it would be absolutely impossible that there should be a man who was not a descendant of Adam, but Leibniz refers to other "series" of possible men, stemming from other possible first men.

The foregoing analysis treats universal affirmative existential propositions as having no existential import, which may seem paradoxical. In the "laugher" passage quoted earlier in chapter 3, section 3, Leibniz interprets them somewhat differently. There he presupposes, as he often does, that the subject of any true categorical proposition is a "true term," an *ens* or *possibile*. Representing 'Every A is B' as '$A = AB$', he obtains 'AB is an *ens*' from it together with the presupposition 'A is an *ens*', and he points out that if we take *ens* in the sense of *existens*, we give existential import to the original proposition. Thus, he seems to be telling us that existential 'Every A is B' implies 'AB is an existent thing' or 'An AB is an existent thing'. This is somewhat stronger than the *secundi adjecti* counterpart of existential 'Every A is B', namely, 'An A non-B is not an existent thing'.

If we use this passage as a guide, we may infer that Leibniz has another, and slightly different, method for dividing categorical propositions into essential and existential: where A is the subject term and B the predicate, assume A *est ens* in each case, and either interpret *ens* as referring to whatever is abstractly possible, or else take it as equivalent to *existens*. This would not lead to any change in the truth criteria for singular existential propositions, but for the existential universal affirmative we would now have:

(10) 'Every A is, B' is true of world W if and only if (1) the t-stage of at least one complete individual concept in W contains A, and (2) for every complete individual concept C in W, if the t-stage of C contains A, then it contains B.

Thus, this intepretation differs from the other in that existential import is built in. As a result, the inclusion of B in A is no longer either necessary or sufficient for the truth of existential propositions 'Every A is, B' and their standing counterparts—not necessary, because of cases like "Every man is now liable to sin" (which is true of the actual world), and not sufficient, because of cases like "Every man twenty feet tall is now a man" (false of the actual world). Neither "Every man is an animal' nor even "Every man is a man," as standing existential propositions, will be true of all possible worlds, though each is true of the actual world (in view of the fact that every monad exists throughout the history of the world).

It is interesting to note that the problems with universal affirmative existential propositions extend even to certain propositions appearing to have the form '*A* is *B*'. For example the indefinite proposition "Man is liable to sin," as an existential proposition, is presumably equivalent to the existential "All men are liable to sin," and hence would be a standing proposition true of the actual world, although Liability to sin is not contained in the concept Man. The existential proposition "[The] victor of Pharsalus was assassinated in 44 B.C. " is true of the actual world, though the concept Assassinated is not contained in the concept Victor of Pharsalus. Here again I conjecture that in applying his Predicate-in-Subject principle to propositions of the form '*A* is *B*', Leibniz would confuse the inclusion of *B* in *A* with the inclusion of *B* in the complete concepts of the individual or individuals falling under *A*.

It is worth mentioning that since Latin lacks the definite and indefinite articles, the relevant Latin phrases are not quite isomorphic with their translations into English and other languages that do have articles. This leads to difficulties about the structure and identity of the associated concepts. For example, is the subject concept of the last cited sentence "Victor of Pharsalus" or "*The* Victor of Pharsalus"?

5. Some Consequences

The Predicate-in-Subject principle is related in an interesting way to the grammatical transformations we have described in chapter 3. Recall once again that for every *tertii adjecti* proposition '*A* is *B*' there is an equivalent *secundi adjecti* proposition '*AB* is an entity'. Leibniz also considers '*AA* = *A*' to be a necessary truth,[29] and his famous Law authorizes the intersubstitutivity of identicals. Consequently, all the propositions, essential or existential, in the following series are equivalent when time is held constant:

A is B.
AB is an entity.
ABB is an entity.
AB is B.

Thus, to say '*A* is *B*' is, for Leibniz, always equivalent to saying '*AB* is *B*', and the predicate of the latter is explicitly contained in its subject.[30]

[29] G VII 245 (P 142); C 366 # 18 (P 56).

[30] Of course, there is the usual problem about what Leibniz means by "equivalent," "equipollent," and "is the same as" when he discusses the various "forms" of propositions. At C 378 # 83 (P 67) he argues that '*A* is *B*' is the same as '*A* = *AB*', "whence it is manifest that *B* is contained in *A*." If '*A* is *B*' is the same as '*A* = *AB*', it would seem to follow that it is also the same as '*AB* is *B*'. Note also that at G VII 218 (P 33) '*AB* is *B*' is called a *propositio per se vera*.

It should also be mentioned, however, that Leibniz is capable of the kind of fallacy involved

On the same basis we see that the following series of propositions are also equivalent to one another:

A is *A*.
AA is an entity.
A is an entity.

These transformations take on a particular interest when the propositions concerned are existential, that is, when *ens* means the same as *existens*. Leibniz says:

> If I say of an existing thing '*A* is *B*', it is the same as if I were to say '*AB* is an existent thing'; for example, "Peter is denying," that is, "Peter denying is an existent thing."[31]

In particular, existential '*A* is *A*' is equivalent to the proposition '*A* exists' and thus is false if *A* does not exist.[32]

Every singular existential proposition with an individual concept as subject is equivalent to an assertion that the corresponding individual exists; this fact plays a crucial role in Leibniz's theology. In deciding whether to create a world of which "Judas is going to sin" is true, God was simply deciding whether Judas-who-is-going-to-sin (*Judas peccaturus*) should exist. He could not first decide whether a certain individual was going to exist and then decide whether that individual was or was not going to sin. In determining to create *this* man, Judas, he settled the whole question at once. Anyone who was not going to sin would not have been this very same man. From Leibniz's point of view, therefore, God's choice was whether to create Judas or somebody else; the question was not whether Judas should sin, but whether Judas-the-sinner should exist.[33] No harm was done to Judas-the-sinner in creating him, for, according to Leibniz, existence is better than nonexistence.[34] Hence, God is not guilty of mistreating Judas, as he would have been if he had chosen to let Judas betray Christ and it had been possible for him to arrange that Judas should have existed without sinning in that way.

Incidentally, Leibniz's transformations can be imitated in the lower

---

in moving from 'Necessarily, if *P* then *Q*' to 'If *P* then necessarily *Q*'. At LH IV vii C 73r he argues that if '*A* is *B*' is true, then '*A* non-*B*' involves a contradiction; for if '*A* is *B*' is true, *A* coincides with *AB* and hence '*A* non-*B*' coincides with '*AB* non-*B*', which is manifestly contradictory.

[31] C 375 # 71 (P 65); cf. C 273.

[32] The passage (C 393, # 154, 155), cited by Fitch (1979), 35, as evidence that for Leibniz '*A* is *A*' is always true, does not say this. It only says that *he does not object* if someone wants to use signs in such a way as to make that turn out to be the case, and that *maybe* it would be better to do that and then not allow any deductions from '*A* is *A*' if *A* is not a *res*—this last, presumably, to block threatened fallacies. But see n. 31 to chap. 3.

[33] C 24, 520 (L 268); Grua 273, 314, 343, 371; G III 35; G IV 364; G VII 311–12; generalization at G III 33. See also FC 1 533–34. Furthermore, God did not will the sin, for to will sin is to delight in evil (*Confessio Philosophi*, 12r, ed. Saame, 74).

[34] G VII 304; cf. G I 221. On this ground, Russell (1945), 594, notes that children may be exhorted to be grateful to their parents.

predicate calculus with identity and descriptions, where, indeed, the proviso that the subject term have a denotation is superfluous (since, in effect, it is assumed that all individual constants denote). In view of the theorem

$$Fa \leftrightarrow F(\iota x)(x = a \ \& \ Fx)$$

we could say, if we agreed that sentences of the form

$$F(\iota x)(Gx \ \& \ Fx)$$

are analytic, that every atomic sentence is logically equivalent to an analytic sentence with the same predicate. Thus, "Caesar is a Roman" is logically equivalent to "the person who is Caesar and a Roman is a Roman," which amounts to Leibniz's "Caesar the Roman is a Roman."

Another point of Leibnizian doctrine that throws some light on his concept of truth is the principle (adopted from Descartes and the Scholastics) that "A nonentity has no attributes" (*Non entis nulla attributa sunt*). He cites this principle in various forms, typically in some such context as the following: "Suppose that N is not A, N is not B, N is not C, and so on. Then one can say that N is Nothing. This is what the common saying, that what is not has no attributes, refers to."[35] Such passages, of which there are many, reflect Leibniz's inclination to regard every proposition 'A is B' as false if the corresponding proposition 'A is an entity' is not true. In one place, referring to a proposal to represent 'No A is B' by '$AB \neq AB$', which latter he also reads as 'AB is not a thing', he says:

> This, however, presupposes denying every proposition in which there is a term that is not a thing [*res*]. So it remains that every proposition is either true or false, but that every proposition that lacks an existent subject, or a real term, is false. In the case of existential propositions this is somewhat remote from the ordinary way of talking. But there is no reason why I should care about that, since I am looking for a suitable notation [*propria signa*], not purporting to apply existing terminology [*recepta nomina*] correctly.[36]

Now, clearly the ambiguity of the word *ens* induces an ambiguity in the principle *Non entis nulla attributa sunt*. If *ens* is taken in the sense of *existens*,

---

[35] S. 472. Cf. S 474, C 252, 256, 266 # 20, 356, S 478. Couturat (CL 348 n. 2) mistakenly thinks *nihil* means "null set," and he accordingly says of Leibniz's definition: "Mais cette définition, inspirée, comme on voit, de la tradition scolastique, n'a aucune valeur. Tout au contraire, on définit à présent le zéro logique comme le terme qui est contenu dans tous les autres (en extension). . . ."

[36] C 393 # 153 (P 82). My translation of the words *cui deest constantia subjecti* as "that lacks an existent subject" has been challenged by one author (Fried 1978 and 1981, 62), who prefers Parkinson's "which lacks a consistent subject." Fortunately, at A.6.6.447 Leibniz tells us what *constantia subjecti* means: "The Scholastics have hotly disputed *de constantia subjecti*, as they called it, i.e., how the proposition made upon a subject can have real truth, if this subject does not exist (*si ce sujet n'existe point*)." Cf. Burkhardt (1980), 42. This error, together with failure to attend to Leibniz's distinction between existential and essential propositions (and to the systematic ambiguity of *ens* and *possibile*) leads Fried (p. 53) to accuse Mondadori (1975) and me (1972) of "a serious misinterpretation of the Leibnizian semantics." See also n. 31 to chap. 3.

the principle asserts, in effect, the falsehood of every existential proposition '*A* is *B*' having a subject term that does not denote an existent thing. If it is taken in the other sense, the same holds with "abstractly possible thing" substituted for "existent thing." Note that the passage just quoted refers to both cases.

Actually, the proposal to regard '*A* is *B*' as false if *A* does not denote anything is quite natural to philosophical authors writing in Latin.[37] (The same would be true for classical Greek.) Ancient and medieval philosophers seem always ready to infer '*A is*' from '*A* is *B*', and I believe it is also taken for granted by such authors that if '*A* is' is true, then at least some sentence '*A* is *B*' must also be true. The first half of this is contained in another principle cited by Leibniz, *Quod quid est, id est* (literally, "whatever is something, is"), which, of course, is the transpose of the principle that what is not has no attributes, isn't anything.[38]

As can be seen from the truth criteria stated earlier, the essential and existential interpretations of universal and singular affirmative sentences coincide, respectively, with the intensional and extensional interpretations of those sentences.[39] Thus, essential 'Every *A* is *B*' and '*A* is *B*' are true if and only if the concept *B* is included in the concept *A*, while the corresponding existential propositions are true of a world *W* if and only if the extension of *A* in *W* is included in the extension of *B* in *W*. (If existential propositions are treated in the second of our two ways, where existential import is presupposed, we must add the proviso that the extension of *A* is not empty; and in all cases appropriate adjustments must be made for the time parameter.)

All of this has concerned the truth of only two kinds of categorical proposition. As far as I know, Leibniz does not explicitly discuss the truth of the other kinds. But various remarks of his lead one to believe that he would reduce questions concerning the truth of these other kinds to questions concerning that of singular propositions, using a "substitution" interpretation of the quantifiers.[40]

Leibniz was not unaware of some of the problems with his analysis. One of these concerns the transformation of existential '*A* is *B*' into '*AB* is an existent'; thus, of "Peter is denying" into "Peter denying is an existent." In regard to the latter proposition he says:

> Here the question is how to proceed in analyzing it; whether the term "Peter denying" involves existence; or whether "Peter existent" involves denying—or whether "Peter" involves both existence and denying, as though you were to say "Peter is an actual denier," that is, "Peter is an existent denier", which is certainly true.[41]

---

[37] Thus, at A.2.1.227 Leibniz infers *sentiens ego sum* from *ego sum sentiens*. And the proposal is also quite natural to many authors *not* writing in Latin; cf. Quine (1961), 166.

[38] Grua 535; cf. S 478. G VI 603: "Monads, however, must have some qualities; otherwise they would not be things at all."

[39] For the extensional and intensional interpretations, see C 53 (P 20) and A.6.6.486; cf. C 292ff.

[40] Cf. n. 26.

[41] C 375.

The problem, of course, is that by the Predicate-in-Subject principle we seem forced to conclude that existence is part of the complete individual concept of Peter denying, that is, of Peter, and that in general if existential '*A* is *B*' is true, the concept of *A* involves existence.[42] But God is the only substance whose concept involves existence. Of created beings we must say that they might not have existed (or else God would have had no choice in creating them).[43] Leibniz does not offer a solution to this difficulty.[44]

In another fragment Leibniz observes that the transformation in question leads to a similar difficulty about necessity:

> Thus a disturbing necessity is involved. For example, "Every man sins," with the proposition taken as existential: "A nonsinning man is not existent," or "An existent nonsinning man is not an entity," that is, is impossible. Or, finally, "An existent sinning man is a necessary being."[45]

In this case he tries to extricate himself by suggesting that the necessity involved is not absolute necessity but "the necessity of the consequent," which he elsewhere calls "hypothetical necessity." We shall discuss this in chapter 6.

Leibniz is similarly puzzled when he finds that his transformations sanction the following propositions as equivalent:

> Every animal is an animal.
> An animal nonanimal is not an entity.
> An animal nonanimal is not possible.
> An animal animal is a necessary being.
> An animal is a necessary being.

He tries to get around this result by denying, oddly, that in this context, "animal animal" can be replaced by "animal."[46]

Two additional points need to be made apropos of these difficulties, lest the way out seem too easy. First, existence appears to be a predicate for Leibniz—at least, he treats it as such in the only place where he explicitly considers the matter.[47] And second, there is Leibniz's insistence, mentioned earlier, that the concept of an individual is not changed by God's actualization of that individual, and that the only individual whose essence involves existence is God himself. These doctrines seem clearly incompatible.

---

[42] However, at G VI 255 (H 270) (cf. Grua 303) we are told that the decree that an individual, e.g., Adam, should exist does not change the nature of the individual; on this basis, existence would not be a predicate. The same point is made elsewhere. On the other hand, at A.6.6.358 Leibniz says that existence *is* a predicate, and, in an unpublished text quoted by Schneiders (1978), 27, he says that existence is an *attributum affirmativum*.

[43] Grua 288.

[44] C 271.

[45] Ibid.

[46] C 272. Why doesn't he refer here to the ambiguity of *ens, possibile*, and *necessarium*?

[47] See n. 26. Also, at A.6.6.437, in connection with the ontological argument for the existence of God, he accepts Descartes's treatment of existence as a perfection. Cf. A.6.6.411 and G I 223, where existence is a quality of God. On the other hand, at G VII 311 the complete concept of any created individual contains what would happen to him *if he existed*—which confirms the usual doctrine that existence is not part of the concept of any being other than God.

6. Critique

The Predicate-in-Subject principle is initially implausible, and it will probably seem even more so when, in chapter 6, we consider its consequences in
relation to the distinction between necessary and contingent propositions. So
the question arises: how could Leibniz, or any other thoughtful theorist,
believe this principle to be obviously true?

Here is a line of argument that might lead one to such a conclusion.

In our use of language we apparently presuppose, or take for granted, that
the various expressions constituting our discourse are meaningful and that
their meanings are grasped with different degrees of exactness and adequacy
by different persons. Some speakers and writers use language relatively
sloppily, others relatively precisely, and the same person, at different times or
with respect to different expressions, may be more or less exact.

In theorizing about this, one can adopt the Humpty-Dumpty position
("When *I* use a word, it means just what I choose it to mean—neither more
nor less"), holding that each person, on each occasion, attaches his own
meaning to what he reads, writes, or says, and that all the multifarious meanings thus generated for a single sentence or other expression resemble one
another to a greater or lesser degree. On such a theory, when you and I seek
to communicate our thoughts to one another by means of language, the
degree of success depends on the degree of similarity of the (essentially
private) meanings we individually attach to the expressions used. The closer
we come to meaning the same thing by what we say, the better our
communication.

But there is another, more common and seemingly more satisfactory, way
of conceptualizing the situation. According to this, there is such a thing as *the*
meaning—or, in the case of real ambiguity, *the* meanings—of a linguistic
expression; different users of the language grasp this meaning more or less
adequately.

These two ways of viewing the matter need not be considered incompatible. We could try to define *the* meaning by reference to the private
meanings of some designated subclass of expert users, and then a person
could be said to grasp *the* meaning more or less adequately according as his
or her private meaning resembled the public meaning more or less closely.
Or, we could have a more abstract concept of *the* meaning of an expression,
which could allow for our intuition that any group of experts, no matter how
narrowly or broadly defined, could in principle be mistaken about the meaning of any given linguistic expression.

Leibniz's view of the matter is clearly the second. Like most authors, he
speaks of "the proposition that . . ." and "the concept . . ."—for example, of the
proposition that Man is a rational animal and of the concept Man. Only one
monad, namely, God, is deemed to comprehend these propositions and concepts perfectly; the understanding of the rest of us is always more or less con-

fused. In other words, the propositions and concepts Leibniz speaks of, which are designed to serve as the meanings of sentences and noun phrases, are not in your mind or mine, but reside in the mind of God.

Now the essential point here is not quite so theological as it may look. As we shall see, it has to do with deciding which properties must be attributed to the meanings of linguistic expressions if one is to make sense of the claim that different users of the language intuit those meanings with varying degrees of adequacy.

Leibniz is fond of distinguishing between two different kinds of ordering relations, namely, those with respect to which a maximum can be consistently postulated, and those with respect to which it cannot. For instance, the ordering relation "greater than" holds among the integers, but the notion of a greatest integer is inconsistent. Similarly, with respect to points on a rotating disk of infinite radius, some are moving faster than others, but there can be no fastest. The relation "knows more than," on the other hand, which is an ordering relation among minds, is considered by Leibniz to be essentially different from these. He says that there is nothing contradictory in the notion of a mind that knows everything that is the case. It is also possible in principle, he thinks, for there to be an individual who is omnipotent or who is maximally benevolent or who is both. (This, of course, is in effect part of his argument that the concept of God is consistent.)

Now, if we consider that the users of a given linguistic expression can understand it more or less adequately, we have in effect introduced another ordering relation. I believe that Leibniz would say that it is in principle possible to grasp the meaning perfectly, though such a degree of understanding is reserved to God. In other words, the notion of someone's understanding perfectly what is meant by the given linguistic expression is not inconsistent; it is not like the notions of greatest number and fastest circular motion.

At this point it probably should be mentioned parenthetically that, as the relevant phraseology is used by those philosophers and others who think along these lines, 'to grasp or be acquainted with the sense of N' does not imply 'to be acquainted with N', any more than 'to be acquainted with the brother of X' implies 'to be acquainted with X'. If we suppose, for example, that the thought expressed by *Es regnet* is the same as that expressed by "It is raining," it seems to follow that whoever has the thought expressed by "It is raining" has the thought expressed by *Es regnet,* even if he does not know that this thought is the sense of *Es regnet.* That a given sense or meaning is expressed by a given linguistic form is considered to be a contingent fact; the existence of propositions and concepts is supposed to be independent of that of linguistic expressions that may express them; one may grasp a meaning without being able "to put it in words"; one can "know" something without being able to "say" it. (I don't believe any of this, but I am trying to describe a line that many philosophers seem to follow.)

Thus, the perfect understanding that is attributed to God does not immediately imply his acquaintance with English or any other natural language, though the propositions he understands so well will surely include all truths, whether expressed in any language or not, that concern natural languages and what their constituent expressions express. At the same time, it is assumed that every well-formed expression in any natural language has a meaning, though there are many more meanings than expressions.

All of that said, let us consider one of Leibniz's favorite examples:

(1) Caesar crossed the Rubicon.

Grasping the sense of this sentence involves grasping the sense of its subject term, "Caesar," and that of its predicate, "crossed the Rubicon." Putting aside consideration of the latter for a moment, we can say that to understand (1) perfectly, one would need to know, at a minimum, exactly who is being talked about. To the extent that one has only a vague notion of who Caesar was, to that extent one does not understand what is asserted by sentences having "Caesar" as subject term. Thus, a perfect understanding would preclude confusing Caesar with any other individual, however similar; indeed, it would preclude confusing him with any other *possible* individual. In short, he who perfectly understood (1) would know exactly which possible state of affairs is thereby asserted to obtain, and he cannot know this unless his concept of Caesar is complete—that is, sufficient to distinguish this Roman general from any other actual or possible individual.

Therefore, *the* concept of Caesar, which is the meaning this term would have for someone who understood perfectly those sentences in which it serves as subject term, must be a complete individual concept, sufficient to distinguish the intended individual from any other, actual or possible.

From this, together with some rather common assumptions about concept composition it would seem to follow that if (1) is true, then the concept expressed by "crosser of the Rubicon" must be involved in the concept expressed by "Caesar"—that is, that its predicate is contained in its subject.

VI

Necessary and Contingent Truths

Like most of the other major philosophers of the seventeenth and eighteenth centuries, Leibniz endeavors to draw a clear distinction between necessary and contingent truths.[1] The underlying idea, agreed upon by all, is that a proposition is a necessary truth if it is true in fact and there are no conceivable circumstances of which it would be false, while a contingent truth is a proposition that is true but not necessary. Necessary truths are also called by Leibniz "truths of reason" and "eternal truths" (as well as "metaphysical truths" and "logical truths"), while contingent truths are also called "truths of fact" or "truths of existence." Sometimes he uses the term "absolute necessity" to characterize the kind of necessity under consideration here, because he elsewhere distinguishes hypothetical and moral necessity from this.[2]

1. Absolute Necessity

The distinction between the necessary and the contingent coincides with that between the a priori and the empirical. "Geometrical demonstrations," Leibniz says,

would be no less evident to a sleeping person than to one awake, if they happened to occur to the sleeper; and therefore they do not depend upon the credibility of the senses, but upon ideas or definitions, which (latter) are nothing else than the expressions of ideas.[3]

---

[1] G IV 357 (L 385), G VI 50 (H 74), A.6.6.361.
[2] C 17; G II 391 (M 41); and many other passages. At G VI 50 (H 74) the term "truth of reason" is extended to apply to physical laws. This is unusual.
[3] G I 205.

As examples of absolutely necessary truths Leibniz usually mentions, first of all, so-called identities, namely, propositions of the forms "*A* is *A*," "*AB* is *A*," "*ABC* is *AC*," and so forth. Then he mentions mathematical truths and also a few "disparities" like "heat is not color."[4] Presumably "Caesar is not Pompey" would qualify, too. He makes it clear that, for him, necessity belongs to propositions, not sentences; the proposition "Every multiple of 12 is a multiple of 4" is necessary and would be so even if "multiple of 12" (*Duodenarius*) and "multiple of 4" (*Quaternarius*) had been otherwise defined.[5] (Thus, in assessing the status of "Caesar is not Pompey" we would need to ask ourselves, "Could Caesar have been Pompey?" and not, "Could the names 'Caesar' and 'Pompey' have denoted the same individual?")[6] Examples of contingent truths, which he says are characteristically true "at a certain time" (*certo tempore*), are singular propositions like "I am alive," "the sun is shining," "this stone tends to fall," "the earth moves," and natural laws like "a body continues in uniform motion unless acted upon by some other body."[7]

Because the correct interpretation of what Leibniz says about necessity and contingency is a notorious *Streitfrage* among scholars, it seems best to begin our account by quoting some of his most typical pronouncements on this subject.

There are also two kinds of truths, truths of *reason* and the truths of *fact*. Truths of reason are necessary, and their opposite is impossible. Truths of fact are contingent, and their opposite is possible. When a truth is necessary, the reason for it can be found by analysis, resolving it into more simple ideas and truths until we reach the primary. . . . Primary principles cannot be proved, and indeed have no need of proof; and these are identical propositions, whose opposite involves an express contradiction.[8]

A truth is necessary when the opposite implies a contradiction; and when it is not necessary, it is called contingent. That God exists, that all right angles are equal to each other, are necessary truths; but it is a contingent truth that I exist, or that there are bodies which show an actual right angle.[9]

---

[4] The identities and mathematical truths are frequently cited. The disparities "Heat is not color," "Man is not Animal," and "Triangularity is not Trilaterality" are mentioned at A.6.6.362. At G III 550 we are told that it is a necessary truth that there are exactly three dimensions, neither more nor less.

[5] C 18.

[6] Nor is the question "Could a person who at one time is Caesar be Pompey at another time?" Cf. n. 68 to chap. 3, concerning "Appius" and "Valerius."

[7] C 18–20, 22; A.6.2.479.

[8] G VI 612 (L 646). The "opposite" of a categorical proposition is its contradictory: C 76, G VI 612 (L 646), G VII 211 (P 115), C 364–70 (P 54–60). An "express contradiction is a proposition '*A* is *B*' in which some component of the concept *A* is the complement of some component of the concept *B*, or vice versa, or it is a proposition '*A* is not *B*', where the corresponding proposition '*A* is *B*' is a so-called identity.

To say that a proposition is true solely by virtue of the meaning of its terms, and to say that it is reducible to an identity by a series of *definiens-definiendum* substitutions, are, for Leibniz, equivalent (G I 188).

[9] G III 400 (R 208); cf. G I 194 (L 187).

Hence we now learn that propositions which pertain to the essences and those which pertain to the existences of things are different. Essential surely are those which can be demonstrated from the resolution of terms, that is, which are necessary, or virtually identical, and the opposite of which, moreover, is impossible or virtually contradictory. These are the eternal truths. Not only will they hold as long as the world exists, but also they would have held if God had created the world according to a different plan. But existential or contingent truths differ from these entirely. Their truth is grasped a priori by the infinite mind alone, and they cannot be demonstrated by any resolution.[10]

As is evident from these quotations and many similar passages, two different (though at first sight perfectly compatible) characterizations of necessity and contingency are to be found in the Leibnizian writings. On the one hand, a necessary truth is defined as a proposition the opposite of which implies a contradiction, while correspondingly a contingent truth is defined as a true proposition that is not necessary. On the other hand, there is the presumption, almost never stated explicitly but always visible in the background, that a necessary truth is a proposition true of all possible worlds, so that a contingent truth will be a proposition true of the actual world but false of at least one of the other possible worlds.[11]

Each of these ways of looking at necessity and contingency is plausible enough. To say that a proposition is true of all possible worlds would seem to mean that it is true and that there are no conceivable circumstances of which it would be false, which amounts to saying that it is a necessary truth. And to say that its opposite implies a contradiction would seem to mean that if the opposite were true, that is, if things were not as described by the given proposition, a contradiction would have to be true, which cannot be the case—hence, again, there are no conceivable circumstances of which the given proposition would be false. Thus the two characterizations appear to be merely different ways of saying the same thing and are therefore perfectly compatible.[12]

[10] C 18 (S&G 348).

[11] Thus Kauppi (1960), 247, is strictly right in claiming that Leibniz never explicitly defines a necessary truth as a proposition true of all possible worlds, but the passage at C 18, quoted above, comes very close to this. It needs to be said, however, that except in the formal calculi, there is in general no way of telling whether Leibniz is defining a notion or just characterizing it. Obviously he is interested in the truth of the generalized biconditionals and doesn't care much about their status as "definitions" or "theorems."

Kalinowski (1983), 341, objecting to the use of the passage at C 18 as support for a "true of all possible worlds" definition of necessary truth, paraphrases the crux of that passage as follows: "Elles tiennent dans notre monde et tiendraient dans un autre si, par impossible, il existait (était créé par Dieu)." But the "*par impossible*," on which he places weight, does not correspond to anything in the original text and, indeed, goes counter to Leibniz's emphatic and repeated insistence that God could have done otherwise.

[12] Indeed, Leibniz's statement at Grua 390—that there are as many possible worlds as there are series of things that can be conceived without contradiction—amounts to saying that a proposition P is true of some possible world if and only if P does not imply a contradiction, from which it follows (by putting "not-P" for "P" and negating both sides of the biconditional) that a proposition P is true of all possible worlds if and only if not-P implies a contradiction.

Note that one of Leibniz's two characterizations of necessary truth applies to categorical propositions only, while the other applies to propositions of whatever structure.

But problems arise when these ideas are combined with Leibniz's state-ments about truth and with his division of propositions into essential and existential. The most serious difficulty is one he mentions himself: How is it possible for a proposition to be other than necessary if its predicate is con-tained in its subject? Since a contingent truth is a proposition that could have been false, the question is more trenchantly formulated as: How could or can 'A is B' be false if the concept B is included in the concept A, and hence if being B is part of what it is to be A?

In several passages Leibniz says that this problem bothered him for a long time, until at last he saw that the solution was to define a necessary truth as one that can be reduced to an identity (or the opposite of which can be reduced to a contradiction) in a finite number of steps, whereas a contingent truth is to be a proposition in which, though the predicate concept is con-tained in the subject concept, the reduction goes on to infinity.[13]

I have to confess that I can find no intuitive plausibility whatsoever in this "solution." It is hard to see what the length of the reduction of a proposition would have to do with whether the proposition is false of some possible world.[14] Nevertheless, let us look more closely at some of the texts in which Leibniz makes this point. The matter is so crucial that I shall quote rather extensively.

Having recognized the contingency of things, I raised the further question of a clear concept of truth, for I had a reasonable hope of throwing some light from this upon the problem of distinguishing necessary from contingent truths. I saw that in every true affirmative proposition, whether universal or singular, necessary or contin-gent, the predicate inheres in the subject or that the concept of the predicate is in some way involved in the concept of the subject. I saw too that this is the source of infalli-bility for him who knows everything a priori. But this fact seemed to increase the diffi-culty, for, if at any particular time the concept of the predicate inheres in the concept of the subject, how can the predicate ever be denied of the subject without contradiction and impossibility, or without destroying the subject concept? A new and unexpected light arose at last, however, where I least expected it, namely, from mathematical con-siderations of the nature of the infinite. . . .[15]

The criterion for distinguishing necessary from contingent truths emerges from the following feature, which only those who have in them a tincture of mathematics will easily understand: in the case of necessary truths an identical equation will be reached by carrying the analysis sufficiently far, which amounts to demonstrating the truth with geometrical rigor; whereas in the case of contingent truths the analysis proceeds to

---

[13] C 1, 2, 8, 17, 387, 407–8, G III 582 (R 221), G VII 309 (R 221–22). Direct and indirect proofs amount to the same thing; i.e., it makes no difference whether you reduce the proposition to an identity or reduce its opposite to a contradiction: G VII 295 (L 232).

LH IV, vii, C, 73–74 (Fasz. 2, # 103, 402): "Inference is of two sorts, *explicable*, when the series of substitutions is finite, in which case the premise is said to *imply* the conclusion, or *inexplicable*, when the series of substitutions is infinite, in which case the premise is said to *involve* the conclusion. The *impossible* is that which implies a contradiction; the *possible* is that which does not imply a contradiction."

[14] Here I have to disagree with Rescher (1967), 45–46.

[15] FC 179 (L 263–64); cf. G VII 309.

infinity, with reasons given for reasons, in such a way that there is never a complete demonstration although the underlying reason for the truth is always there, perfectly understood only by God, who, with one stroke of thought, goes through the whole infinite series.[16]

Leibniz then invokes a mathematical analogy:

It is possible to illustrate this with an appropriate example from geometry. Just as in necessary propositions by continued analysis of the predicate and subject one can reduce the thing to a point where it becomes apparent that the notion of the predicate is contained in the subject, so also in the case of numbers one can eventually reach the greatest common divisor by continued analysis (with alternative divisions); and as in the case of incommensurable quantities there is a proportion or comparison even though the resolution goes to infinity and is never terminated, as was proved by Euclid, so in contingent truths the connection of the terms, that is, the truth, is there even though it is not possible by substitution of identicals actually to accomplish a reduction to the principle of contradiction or of necessity.[17]

And again:

In order to fix our attention . . . an analogy comes to mind between truths and propositions which seems admirably to clarify the whole matter. . . . Just as the smaller number is contained in the larger in every proportion (or an equal in its equal), so in every truth the predicate is contained in the subject. And just as in every proportion between homogeneous quantities an analysis of equal or proportional terms can be carried out by subtracting the smaller from the larger, that is, taking away from the larger a part equal to the smaller, then subtracting the remainder from the smaller, and so on, either until there is no remainder or on to infinity; so also can be we establish an analysis of truths, always substituting for a term its equivalent, so that the predicate will be resolved into elements already contained in the subject. But just as in proportions the analysis is sometimes completed and we arrive at a common measure which is contained in both terms of the proportion an integral number of times, while sometimes the analysis can be continued to infinity, as when comparing a rational number with a surd (for example, the side of a square with the diagonal), so also truths are sometimes demonstrable or necessary, and sometimes free and contingent, so that they cannot be reduced by any analysis to identities as if to a common measure. This is the essential distinction between truths as well as proportions.[18]

The analogy with the Euclidean algorithm, as that algorithm is conceived by Leibniz, can be explained a little further. Suppose that a and b are two positive numbers (or magnitudes—for instance, line segments) with a the greater. Then either a and b are commensurable or they are not. If they are commensurable, that is, if there is a common measure (a rational number) c such that for some integers p and q, a equals pc and b equals qc, then the

---

[16] Grua 303; cf. FC 182, 184. FC 182 (L 265): "In contingent truths, however, though the predicate inheres in the subject, we can never demonstrate this, nor can the proposition ever be reduced to an equation or an identity, but the analysis proceeds to infinity, only God being able to see, not the end of the analysis, since indeed there is no end, but the nexus of terms or the inclusion of the predicate in the subject, since he sees everything which is in the series."

[17] Grua 303. Cf. C 2, 17–18.

[18] FC 183–34 (L 265–66).

Euclidean algorithm, in a finite number of steps, will give us such a common measure—in fact, the greatest such measure—and hence will give us explicitly the ratio p/q (in lowest terms) of a to b. This is supposed to be analogous to the case in which the proposition 'A is B' is necessary; in a finite sequence of steps we analyze the concepts A and B until the components of B are found to be components of A. If, on the other hand, a and b are incommensurable, the Euclidean algorithm goes on to infinity, producing an infinite series that converges on the true ratio. Leibniz insists that in this case, too, there is a ratio, even though the terms of the series only approach it more and more closely. Similarly, he suggests, in a contingent truth 'A is B' the concept B is indeed contained in the concept A, but the analysis would go on to infinity.

To apply the Euclidean algorithm to two numbers or magnitudes a and b, with a the greater, proceed as follows. First, subtract b from a as many times as possible—say, q_1 times—leaving r_1 as remainder, with $b > r_1 \geqslant 0$. If $r_1 > 0$, subtract r_1 from b as many times as possible—say, q_2 times—leaving the remainder r_2, with $r_1 > r_2 \geqslant 0$. If $r_2 > 0$, subtract r_2 from r_1 as many times as possible—say, q_3 times—leaving the remainder r_3, with $r_2 > r_3 \geqslant 0$. And so on. Thus, we are generating numbers satisfying the equations

$$(1) \qquad \begin{aligned} a &= q_1 b + r_1 \\ b &= q_2 r_1 + r_2 \\ r_1 &= q_3 r_2 + r_3 \\ &\quad * \\ &\quad * \\ r_n &= q_{n+2} r_{n+1} + r_{n+2} \\ &\quad * \\ &\quad * \end{aligned}$$

If one of the remainders is 0, suppose that r_n is the first such. Then r_{n-1} (or b, if $n = 1$) will be the greatest common measure (divisor, denominator) of a and b.

As an example,[19] Leibniz gives us $a = 17$, $b = 5$. Then we have

$$\begin{aligned} 17 &= 3 \times 5 + 2 \\ 5 &= 2 \times 2 + 1 \\ 2 &= 2 \times 1 + 0 \end{aligned}$$

So the greatest common measure in that case is 1, and the ratio is, of course, 17:5. If $a = 175$, $b = 21$, we have

$$\begin{aligned} 175 &= 8 \times 21 + 7 \\ 21 &= 3 \times 7 + 0; \end{aligned}$$

the greatest common measure is 7, and the ratio is 265:3.

[19] GM VII 23–24.

Leibniz notes that the series of quotients, $q_1, q_2, \ldots, q_n$ completely determines the ratio, for if the equations (1) hold, we have

$$(2) \qquad a/b = q_1 + \cfrac{1}{q_2 + \cfrac{1}{q_3 + \cfrac{1}{q_4 + \ldots}}}$$

Thus, in the case of $17/5$ the successive quotients are $3, 2, 2$, and in the case of $175/21$ they are $8, 3$. If, as in a geometrical example he offers,[20] the four quotients $2, 1, 1, 2$ are obtained before a zero remainder is reached, then the ratio a/b turns out to be $13/5$. Evaluation of the successive continued fractions (2) corresponding to the successive steps (1) of the algorithm would in this example generate the series

$$2, 3, 5/2, 13/5,$$

which alternates above and below the true ratio, approaching it more and more closely until it reaches it. If the successive quotients in a run of the algorithm were $1, 2, 2, 2, 2, 2, 2, 2, 2, 2$, the series generated would be

$$1, 3/2, 7/5, 17/12, 41/29, 99/70, 239/169, 577/408, 1{,}393/985,$$
$$3{,}363/2{,}378.$$

Here again the reader may verify that the successive terms approach the final value ever more closely, alternatively from above and below. If the above series of quotients continued repeating 2 to infinity, we would get an infinite series converging on the square root of 2.

So much for the analogy. It would be of great help in our attempt to understand Leibniz's doctrine on this subject if we had even one actual example of (the initial portion of) an analysis of a contingent truth. We do have examples, such as they are, for the necessary case. He proves that "every multiple of 12 is a multiple of 6" as follows:

If we understand by a ternary, a senary, and a duodenary, numbers divisible by 3, 6, and 12, respectively, then we can demonstrate this proposition: every duodenary is a senary. For every duodenary is a binary-binary-ternary, since this is the reduction of a duodenary into its prime factors ($12 = 2 \times 2 \times 3$), or the definition of a duodenary. But every binary-binary-ternary is a binary-ternary (this is an identical proposition), and every binary-ternary is a senary (by the definition of a senary, since $6 = 2 \times 3$). Therefore every duodenary is a senary (12 is the same as $2 \times 2 \times 3$, and $2 \times 2 \times 3$ is divisible by 2×3, and 2×3 is the same as 6; therefore 12 is divisible by 6).[21]

This proof has some obvious gaps, but we can see in a general way that Leibniz had in mind. For contingent truths, however, no such examples are available.

<hr>

[20] GM VII 267–68.
[21] FC 181–82 (L 265). Cf. C 11, 17, 240ff. Another example Leibniz frequently adduces is that of $2 + 2 = 4$. See G III 448ff., G IV 403, A.6.6.413–14, LH IV, vii, C, 71 (Fasz. 1, # 54, 169).

A Leibnizian "analysis" or "resolution" of a proposition '*A* is *B*' consists in making a succession of definitional replacements in the terms *A* and *B*.[22] If the proposition is a necessary truth, the succession of such replacements will eventually end in a so-called identity;[23] if the proposition is a contingent truth, the results are supposed to "converge upon," though never actually reach, a proposition in which the elements of the predicate term are somehow "explicitly" present in the subject term.[24] He says:

> A true contingent proposition cannot be reduced to identical propositions, but is proved by showing that if the analysis is continued further and further, it constantly approaches identical propositions, but never reaches them. Therefore it is God alone, who grasps the entire infinite in his mind, who knows all contingent truths with certainty.[25]

Thus, the idea seems to be that as we progressively analyze the concept of Caesar, or that part of it of which we are aware, we find it more and more understandable that a person with those attributes would cross the Rubicon.

> For if some man were able to carry out the complete demonstration by virtue of which he could prove this connection between the subject, who is Caesar, and the predicate, which is his successful undertaking, he would actually show that the future dictatorship of Caesar is based in his concept or nature and that there is a reason in that concept why he has resolved to cross the Rubicon rather than stop there . . . and why it was reasonable and consequently assured that this should happen.[26]

In some texts Leibniz concedes that the mathematical analogy is not perfect, for in the mathematical case we can sometimes calculate by other means the value of the ratio even when the series is infinite, whereas this never happens with a contingent proposition.[27] Obviously we need a better grasp of what he has in mind here, and especially of how the supposed feature of contingent truths is to be connected with the real basis of their contingency, which is that God could have chosen not to create this actual world.[28]

---

[22] C 258: *Resolutio est substitutio definitionis in locum definiti*. Cf. C 518, FC 181 (L 264).

[23] A.6.2.479: Propositions of reason follow solely from definitions. Cf. C 351, 518, A.2.1.95, 386.

[24] C 388 # 134 (P 77). Couturat (CL 213 n. 4), citing C 376–77 (P 66)—"But the concept of Peter is complete, and so involves infinite things; so one can never arrive at a perfect proof (of 'Peter denies'), but one always approaches it more and more, so that the difference is less than any given difference"—makes the obvious point that the terminology is borrowed from the calculus of infinitesimals. Cf. also C 374 # 66 and C 376–77 # 74.

[25] C 388 # 134 (P 77).

[26] G IV 437–38 (L 311). At A.6.2.480 Leibniz briefly considers the questions "How can definitions alone generate something new in the mind?" and "Aren't the new propositions only the old ones expressed differently?"

Another problem, pointed out in Maher (1980), 239, is this: Even if Caesar's concept is infinitely complex, "it would seem that any given predicate which is in the subject must emerge after a finite number of steps."

[27] C 272–73, 18. Cf. C 388 # 136 (P 77–78), Schneider (1974), 156, 287 n. 3).

[28] G IV 438 (L 311), A.6.6.446–7. Schneider (1974), 291 ff., makes a serious attempt to work out the analogy, but finally concludes (302), "Mir scheint daher, dass in der Leibniz-Forschung mit Recht wiederholt der Versuch von Leibniz kritisiert worden ist, das mathematische Konvergenz-modell auch auf Begriffe zu übertragen."

One wonders why, in seeking the "root of contingency," Leibniz did not make use of the fact that for any time t, the singular existential proposition 'A is$_t$ B' is false of the actual world if the actual world does not contain the individual concept A, or, what amounts to the same thing, if there is no existent individual falling under A. He is well aware that this applies even when the concept B is included in the concept A, as is evident when he equates singular existential 'A is A' with 'A exists'. So he has ready at hand, if he will only use it, an explanation of how, for example, the true proposition "Caesar crossed the Rubicon," although its predicate concept is contained in that of its subject, can nevertheless be false of some possible world (and indeed is false of every possible world not containing Caesar, or, more strictly, not containing Caesar's concept). Likewise, existential "Pegasus is a winged horse" is a falsehood, since no winged horse exists; but it would be true if Pegasus existed, and hence it is only contingently false. For all other types of proposition the crucial notion 'S is true of possible world W' could be defined recursively by reference ultimately to the singular atomic propositions 'A is$_t$ B', using perhaps a "substitution" interpretation of the quantifiers and treating disjunctions, conjunctions, conditionals, and negations in the obvious way. Thus Leibniz could save the possible-worlds analysis of contingency and necessity, maintaining at least for singular and universal affirmative propositions that the predicate's inclusion in the subject is a necessary or sufficient condition for their truth.[29]

But, for good or for ill, he did not do this. One line of thought that might have guided him is the following. The predicate of the contingent truth "Caesar crossed the Rubicon" must be contained in the subject, since anyone who really knew who Caesar was (in the sense of being able to distinguish him from all other possible individuals, however similar to Caesar they might be) would see that such a person would have to cross the Rubicon.[30] But, unlike what we find in a necessary truth like "A bachelor is a man," where a finite number of substitutions of *definiens* for *definiendum* convert the sentence into an explicit identity ("An unmarried man is a man"), there would seem to be no upper limit to the length of the analysis of Caesar's concept (that is, of what it is to be Caesar, that very man, as contrasted with anybody and everybody else) that might be required to reach the component "crossed the Rubicon" attribute. So, the difference between a necessary truth like "A bachelor is a man" and a contingent truth like "Caesar crossed the Rubicon" is marked by this difference in their analyses. We put aside, for the moment, questions about the *meaning* of the term contingent truth and instead look to

---

[29] Unless existential import is built in, as was described in chap. 5, sec. 4. Maher (1980) observes that the account of contingency proposed in this paragraph would imply that "Caesar is a man" is contingent. I see no implausibility in this, as the existential proposition "Caesar is a man" is equivalent to "Caesar the man is an existent," which would be false if Caesar did not exist. Leibniz would add, however, that (in his special sense of "essential") the attribute of being a man is essential to Caesar, as it is an attribute that he has *at all times.* Maher also objects that the proposed account would make (existential) "Caesar did not cross the Rubicon" necessary. Regarding this, see n. 35.

[30] See chap. 5, sec. 6.

its *extension*, trying to find a feature that is shared by all the propositions to which the term is in fact applied; that feature is apparently that they require an infinite analysis to reveal the presence of the predicate in the subject.[31]

This line of thought, which in its general outlines is frequently followed by philosophers in our own day, is, as I have argued elsewhere, seriously defective.[32] What a term means, and what the objects to which the term is in fact applied may have in common, are by no means necessarily the same. Leibniz would still owe us an explanation of how "Caesar crossed the Rubicon" could under any conditions have been false if crossing the Rubicon is a very part of what it is to be Caesar. His only way out, it seems to me, is to agree that the essential proposition "Caesar crossed the Rubicon" couldn't have been false, and that only the corresponding existential proposition implies Caesar's existence and hence is contingent.

Often Leibniz writes as though the distinction between necessary and contingent truths coincides with that between true essential and existential propositions, it being assumed here that we are dealing only with categorical propositions.[33] From what he says, it is clear that the intuition behind this is that insofar as the truth of a proposition depends on what exists and what does not exist, the proposition must be contingent (for God could have created a different series of individuals from the one he chose, and hence there is a possible world of which the proposition is false); while if, on the other hand, the truth of a proposition is independent of what exists or does not exist, that proposition must be necessary, or true of all possible worlds.

But this idea, like that concerning infinite analysis, collides with other Leibnizian doctrines clearly implying that some true existential propositions are true (at all times) of all possible worlds. If we obtain the existential interpretation of a sentence by transforming it into *secundi adjecti* form and then taking *ens* in the sense of *existens*, we find that every universal affirmative existential proposition of the form 'Every A is A' will be true at all times and of all possible worlds although it "concerns existence or nonexistence" (since its *secundi adjecti* counterpart is 'A non-A does not exist'). The same will hold of such propositions as "Every man is an animal" taken existentially, as well as of various other types of existential propositions.

This difficulty argues for the second way of defining truth conditions for existential propositions, as set forth in section 4 of chapter 5, which implies that no existential proposition of "Every A is B" form is necessary, that is, true of all possible worlds, unless the concept A is such that it is instantiated in every possible world. But such a concept would amount to *existens* or *ens*, for which we have to make exceptions anyway. The same point holds for the other types of existential categorical propositions: none will be true of a possible world unless the subject concept is instantiated in that world. Thus, with

<hr />

[31] Here cf. C 513, where Leibniz distinguishes between *what we take to be* true and *what absolutely is* true.

[32] Mates (1958).

[33] C 18; cf. C 376 # 74 (P 66).

a few dubious exceptions, on this interpretation the existential categorical propositions will all be contingent.[34]

Note that on either interpretation the existential proposition '*A* is *B*' will be false of all possible worlds if the concept '*AB*' is inconsistent. In particular, when a false existential proposition has a complete individual concept as subject (with the necessary specifications of time), it will be false of all possible worlds, and hence its negation will be a necessary truth. This has seemed counterintuitive to some commentators, but I am convinced that it represents the Leibnizian view. Thus, the existential proposition

(1) Socrates is tall

is false (at all times) of every possible world, for the concept Tall is not contained in the complete individual concept of Socrates, since he exists and is not tall. Hence its negation,

(2) Socrates is not tall

is true (at all times) of all possible worlds, and thus is a necessary truth. But that, I think, is exactly what Leibniz means to assert. Anybody, in any world, who was tall would not be our Socrates, that is to say that this individual would not be Socrates; in other words, it is absolutely impossible that Socrates should have been tall or should have had any attributes whatever other than the ones he does have. This point will be discussed more fully in chapter 7.

It is worth mentioning that some of the paradoxical aspect of the foregoing may be removed by distinguishing between denying the predication of Tall, on the one hand, and affirming that of non-Tall, on the other. Thus, existential

(3) Socrates is non-tall

would be true of the actual world but false of all others; hence, unlike (2), it would be contingent.[35]

---

[34] The exceptions I have in mind are negative identities like "Caesar is not Pompey." Cf. n. 4 above and Burk 134ff.

[35] Similarly, consider (with Fried 1981) the four sentences:

1. Ford is a Republican.
2. Ford is a non-Republican.
3. Ford is a Democrat.
4. Ford is a non-Democrat.

Taken as expressing existential propositions, (1) and (4) are contingent truths and their negations are contingent falsehoods; (2) and (3) express impossibilities and their negations are necessary truths. As regards (2), Fried assures us (p. 49), without evidence, that "Leibniz wants such a proposition to be contingently false." Does he? Leibniz would say, "Anybody who was not a Republican would be somebody other than Ford."

I cannot claim, however, that the Leibnizian texts are unambiguous on this point. At G IV 218 (H 235) he says that no contradiction follows from the falsehood "Spinoza died in Leyden," which seems analogous to (3), and "nothing would have been so possible." Yet he goes on to explain that the reason the proposition is false is that God chose a universe, a "sequence," not including that event. It seems that Leibniz has forgotten, for the moment, that his doctrines

Tangentially related to these matters is the claim, recently made by several scholars,[36] that Leibniz recognized certain truths as necessary although they do not satisfy his regular definition, that is, are not such that their opposites imply contradiction. The propositions they have in mind are negative identities such as:

Yellowness is not sweetness,
Square is not circle,
White is not red,
Warmth is not color,[37]

the terms of which are examples of what Leibniz calls *disparata.* He defines this word as follows: "*A* and *B* are *disparata* if *A* is not *B* and *B* is not *A*, as Man and Stone."[38]

But surely Leibniz would say that the opposites of these propositions do imply contradictions, however difficult it might be for us to see what the reductions would be. In the only passage in which he discusses the matter explicitly, he says that the propositions are "nearly" identities (in his sense of "identity," of course), which suggests that he thought the required reductions would not be very lengthy. Lest this seem too fantastic, we should recall that sometimes what he offers as "analyses" seem more causal than conceptual,[39] as, for example, when he analyzes Green as Yellow plus Blue.[40] In any case, actual reductions to identities are few and far between in the Leibnizian writings, and we don't even know how he would handle a mathematical example like "A square is not a circle."

The upshot of all this is, in my opinion, that the possible-worlds framework can be consistently applied at most to the semantics of *existential* propositions. If the inclusion of concept *B* in concept *A* is a necessary and sufficient condition for the truth of '*A* is *B*', as is the case when '*A* is *B*' is an essential proposition, then it seems impossible that this proposition should be true of some possible worlds and false of others. For the selection of a given possible world for existence cannot determine the relationships of the concepts that are in God's mind prior to Creation. The "infinite analysis"

---

imply that there is no possible world in which Spinoza does die in Leyden, for such a person would have been somebody else, not Spinoza.

S 478 seems to imply that nonpredicability of all purely positive terms is a sufficient condition for nonexistence. That is, '*A est non-ens*' is true if and only if, for all positive *B*, '*A est B*' is not true. But, on the other hand, note C 264: "*A non est B idem est quod A est non-B.*"

[36] Wilson (1969), 62–63; Poser (1969), 133; Schneider (1974), 251ff.; Burk 134–35.

[37] Cf. A.6.6.82 and 362.

[38] G VII 225; cf. C 47, 53, 62, 239, 363, G VII 237. LH IV vii C 38v: "*Disparata sunt quae specie differunt.*" (At A.6.6.362, however, Leibniz gives Man and Animal as examples of *disparata*.) Burk 110 argues that no two concepts are "completely" disparate. This is because he thinks that every pair of compound concepts have a common component. That view is surely mistaken, for any consistent combination of simple concepts and/or complements of simple concepts is a complex concept. In any case, Leibniz nowhere entertains the idea that disparateness comes in degrees.

[39] G IV 422–23 (L 291).

[40] A.6.6.403; G IV 426 (L 294).

account of contingent propositions may perhaps be accepted as a characterization of those propositions that we, in our ignorance, call "contingent,"[41] but it cannot intelligibly define the class of propositions that *are* contingent, being true of some possible worlds and false of others.

2. Hypothetical Necessity

Following a tradition extending back to Aristotle,[42] Leibniz attempted to distinguish absolute and hypothetical necessity. Unfortunately, the distinction seems to originate from a certain confusion that also goes back at least as far as Aristotle. It is the confusion of 'Necessarily, if P then Q' with 'If P then necessarily Q'.

In classical Greek, as in English and other modern languages, when a modalized conditional is to be expressed, one naturally puts the modal operator in the consequent: we say, "If Reagan was elected, then he must have received the most votes," instead of the more logically perspicuous but less idiomatic "Necessarily, if Reagan was elected, he received the most votes." Thus we make it appear that necessity is being conditionally predicated of the consequent, rather than unconditionally predicated of the whole.[43] If we add the true premise "Reagan was elected," we may go on (if we are philosophically confused enough) to detach by *modus ponens* the consequent, "Reagan must have received the most votes"; and then, since there was obviously no logical necessity that Reagan receive the most votes, we might suppose that some other kind of necessity is involved.

The tendency to fall into this kind of fallacy, which we may call the "fallacy of the slipped modal operator," is very strong, as one can verify for oneself by discussing it with friends who are not logicians. People want to say things like "Of course, it isn't really necessary that Smith have a wife, but *given that* (or *on the hypothesis that*) he is a husband, it *is* necessary."[44]

In the Sea Fight chapter of *De Interpretatione*,[45] Aristotle appears to argue as follows: If it is now true that something will be so, then it cannot not be so and will necessarily be so; and if it is now true that it won't be so, then

---

[41] Because we have to discover their truth a posteriori, i.e., by experience: C 17, FC 182, G III 259, G VII 44.

[42] Aristotle, *Physics* 200a12–14.

[43] A typical Leibnizian example in which the fallacy is clear is at G III 36: "Granted that, if God foresees something, it will necessarily happen, yet this necessity, since it is only hypothetical, does not negate contingency and freedom."

[44] So we find Leibniz saying, at C 271: "For even contingent propositions, on the hypothesis of the existence of things, are necessary. Just as it is impossible to take money away from Codrus, given that he doesn't have any."

Leibniz suspected that some sort of logical fallacy is involved when we say "What will happen, must happen," but he thought it resided in a "suppressed repetition" and that what is meant is more properly expressed by "What will happen, *if* it will happen, it must happen," or "Of what will happen, it is inconceivable that if it will happen it won't happen" (A.6.1.541). In this last rephrasal the modal operator clearly governs a conditional, as it should, but the triviality of the result seems not yet appreciated by Leibniz.

[45] *De Interpretatione*, chap. 9.

necessarily it won't be so; consequently, if it is now true that it will be so or it is now true that it won't be so, then either necessarily it will be so or necessarily it won't be so—everything that will happen, therefore, will happen necessarily, and nothing will come about by chance. The argument clearly rests on the fallacy we are discussing. Aristotle's tendency to let the modal operator "necessarily" slip over into the consequent of a conditional is also visible elsewhere in his logical writings. Thus, in the *Prior Analytics*[46] the slippage is visible in his statements of valid modes of the syllogism (for example, Barbara: "If *A* is predicated of all *B* and *B* of all *C*, then it is necessary for *A* to be predicated of all *C*"). And in the *Physics* passage in which the notion of hypothetical necessity is first introduced, we read: "If something is going to be a saw and do its work, it must necessarily be made of iron. But the necessity is hypothetical [*ex hypotheseos*]. . . ."[47]

Leibniz is interested in the distinction between the absolute and the hypothetical modalities primarily as a way of distinguishing logical from physical necessity.[48] He holds that many things that were antecedently possible, or possible per se, became impossible once God had created the actual world. Thus, given that God has created this world, it is impossible that a moving body should deviate from uniform motion unless acted upon by something else, though considered in itself this state of affairs is by no means impossible.[49] In other words, it is hypothetically impossible, though absolutely possible, for such a state of affairs to exist. In general, for Leibniz a proposition *P* is hypothetically necessary if and only if the conditional proposition 'If the actual world exists, then *P*' is absolutely necessary but *P* itself is not (or, what comes to the same thing, if and only if *P* is not absolutely necessary but the conjunction 'The actual world exists, and not-*P*' is absolutely impossible).[50]

Since the actual world is the set of complete individual concepts of actual individuals, to bring it into existence is to create an individual corresponding to each and every one of its constituent concepts. And because of the mutual mirroring of these concepts, if one such individual exists, they all will exist. Therefore, the proposition "The actual world exists" is equivalent to each and every proposition of the form '*A* exists', where *A* is any concept belonging to the actual world. So the absolutely necessary truth "If Caesar exists, then he

---

[46] *Prior Analytics* 25b37ff.

[47] *Physics* 200a12–14.

[48] At G VII 303 (L 487) he says: "The present world is necessary in a physical or hypothetical sense, not absolutely or metaphysically. That is, once it is established to be such as it is, it follows that things such as they are will come into being." Sometimes, however, Leibniz seems to define hypothetical necessity by reference to God's foresight; cf. G VII 389–90 (L 696). Further references on hypothetical necessity, from Poser (1969), 73n: G II 18, G III 400, G IV 437, G V 163ff., G VII 303, Grua 271, 273, 300, 305ff., 309, C 271, 525, GM III 576.

[49] Grua 288, C 22. Regarding such laws of nature, Leibniz says at C 20 (S&G 350): "Since the fact that the series [viz. this series of things, the actual world] itself exists is contingent, and depends on a free decree of God, its laws too, considered absolutely, will be contingent; hypothetically, however, if the series is supposed, they are necessary and so far essential."

[50] Cf. G VI 280–81: Thus, as concerns the devil, "it is written in the book of eternal truths, which contain all possibilities prior to any decree of God, that *if* he were once created he would freely turn to evil." So it is only hypothetically necessary that the devil sins. Grua 300: A contingent truth is necessary *ex posito decreto Dei*.

will cross the Rubicon" is equivalent to "If the actual world exists, then Caesar will cross the Rubicon," and hence the proposition "Caesar will cross the Rubicon," though not absolutely necessary, is hypothetically necessary. In fact, if P is any proposition true of the actual world, the proposition 'If P, then Caesar will cross the Rubicon' is again absolutely necessary and could be used to establish the hypothetical necessity of "Caesar will cross the Rubicon." Thus, we may say in general that a proposition P is hypothetically necessary if and only if, for some true proposition Q, 'If Q then P' is absolutely necessary though P is not.

It follows that the hypothetically necessary propositions coincide with the contingently true propositions.[51] This is what Leibniz has in mind when he tells us that those who, with ancient Diodorus Cronus, say that whatever is necessary has been, is now, or will be the case simply confuse hypothetical necessity with absolute.[52]

One important use Leibniz found for this doctrine was that it permitted him to concede to his critics that according to his philosophy, the proposition "Judas will sin" was indeed necessary. But he could then escape their strictures by the (perhaps somewhat sophistic) device of pointing out that the necessity was only hypothetical, not absolute.[53] To this, by redefining "free," he could add that it was not only hypothetically necessary that Judas should sin, but that he should sin freely.[54]

Leibniz says that he agrees with Aristotle in defining an act as free if it is spontaneous and deliberate or spontaneous involving choice.[55] His own phrase for the crucial feature is "rational spontaneity." An act is "spontaneous," he explains, if the principle (origin) of the act is in the agent.[56] Thus, he seeks to make the freedom of an act compatible with that act's being a hypothetically necessary effect of antecedent events, including motives or other causes, which, he says, "incline without necessitating, that is, without imposing an absolute necessity."[57] He rejects as "an impossible chimera" the

---

[51] C 271: For, on the hypothesis of the existence of things, contingent propositions too are necessary. Grua 273: "... *contingentia, seu ut ita dicam per accidens sive ex hypothesi necessaria*." LH IV vii B 3 40–49 (Fasz. 2, # 97, 369): contingent propositions are necessary *per accidens*.

Notice that the hypothetically possible, too, will coincide with the contingently true.

[52] G III 572 (L 661), G VII 409 (L 709), G VI 442, Grua 288, G VI 212ff. (H 230ff.), C 534. Cf. Mondadori (1983), p. 502. At Grua 289, Leibniz says that "no pentagon exists" is necessary if taken in the sense of "no pentagon has existed or ever will exist," but it is not necessary if we abstract from time. This means that "the actual series of things contains no pentagon" is a hypothetically necessary truth, but "no possible series of things contains a pentagon" is false.

[53] G VI 37, 123, 184, 284–85 (H 61, 144, 203, 298–99); G VII 302. The free actions of men are *certain*, according to Leibniz, because they are foreseen and, indeed, foreordained by God, but "infallible certitude is one thing and absolute necessity is another, as Augustine and Aquinas and other learned men recognized long ago" (from the "Metaphysical Discussion with Fardella," printed in Stein [1888], 322–26).

[54] Similarly, God created *Adam libere peccans* (G III 35).

[55] A.6.6.175–76, G VI 122 (H 143), G III 364.

[56] C 25, G VI 296 (H 309–10), Hansch (1728), 34.

[57] G VII 390 (L 697), C 504, G III 468. Note this explication of the famous phrase "inclines without necessitating." Cf. G II 46 (M 50), G VI 127 (H 148).

definition of freedom as "the power of acting or not acting, assuming that all requisites for the action are present."[58]

Thus, with his distinction of hypothetical from absolute necessity, and his special conception of freedom, Leibniz was able to deny that his version of determinism gave any excuse whatever to Judas or to any other malefactor. He emphatically rejects the "lazy sophism," which, as stated by him, is: "If what I ask is to happen, it will happen even though I should do nothing; and if it is not to happen it will never happen, no matter what trouble I take to achieve it." He comments:

> This sophism, which ends in a decision to trouble oneself over nothing, will haply be useful sometimes to induce certain people to face danger fearlessly. It has been applied in particular to Turkish soldiers: but it seems that hashish is a more important factor than this sophism, not to mention the fact that this resolute spirit in the Turks has greatly belied itself in our day.[59]

In fact, Leibniz was second to none in urging all of us to take purposeful action to bring about a better world. "I maintain," he said,

> that men could be incomparably happier than they are, and that they could, in a short time, make great progress in increasing their happiness, if they were willing to set about it as they should. We have in hand excellent means to do in ten years more than could be done in several centuries without them, if we apply ourselves to making the most of them, and do nothing else except what must be done.
>
> Indeed, there is nothing so easy as contributing to the solid well-being of men; and without waiting for universal peace or for the assistance of princes and states, even individuals already have the means to do it in part. One need only will . . .[60]

Leibniz also used the notion of hypothetical necessity in explaining his way out of the following puzzle. Since omniscience, omnipotence, and benevolence are defining characteristics of God, it seems absolutely necessary that God should will to create the best of all possible worlds and that he should be able to do whatever he wills; therefore, it seems absolutely necessary, and not contingent, that this, the best of all possible worlds, should exist. Leibniz agrees that it would indeed be absolutely impossible that God should create a world and not create the best; that is to say, it is absolutely necessary that if he created anything, he created the best.[61] But the nonexistence of this world would not imply a contradiction, and thus its existence is only hypothetically necessary.

Note that since a proposition is possible if its negation is not necessary, the corresponding "hypothetical" concept of possibility also turns out to coincide extensionally with that of contingent truth. Thus the fundamental ambiguity of the term *ens* spreads to its equivalent term *possibile*, with the

---

[58] Cf. G VI 131–32 (H 152), 288–89 (H 302–4), 296 (H 310).

[59] G VI 132 (H 153). For the term "lazy sophism" see Cicero, *De Fato* XII, 28–30.

[60] Klopp 10.8, translated in Riley (1972), 104.

[61] In par. 8 and 196 of the *Theodicy* we are told that if there had been no best possible world, God would not have created anything. Note that if the proposition "There is a best possible world" is absolutely necessary, Leibniz's solution collapses.

latter referring either to absolute possibility or to hypothetical possibility, that is, existence.[62] Given God's creation of this world, that, and only that, can happen in it which *does* happen in it. Whether Leibniz was clearly aware that his concepts of hypothetical necessity and possibility coincide with one another, and with that of contingent truth, I do not know.[63]

Finally, it should be mentioned that Leibniz also speaks occasionally of *moral necessity*. This may or may not coincide extensionally with hypothetical necessity. In one passage he says:

For we must distinguish between an absolute and a hypothetical necessity. We must also distinguish between a necessity which takes place because the opposite implies a contradiction (which necessity is called logical, metaphysical, or mathematical) and a necessity which is moral, whereby a wise being chooses the best, and every mind follows the strongest inclination.[64]

This, as well as other remarks in the same context, suggests that moral necessity is not the same as hypothetical necessity (though the same passage seems also to suggest—falsely, as we know—that absolute necessity is different from metaphysical necessity).

On the other hand, the morally necessary is sometimes defined more narrowly as that which proceeds from God's choice of what is best.[65] On that basis it would seem to be practically the same as the hypothetically necessary.[66] When Leibniz accuses Newton of confounding moral necessity with absolute necessity, he cites Diodorus, as he usually does in his strictures against confounding absolute with hypothetical necessity.[67] In some passages, however, he indicates that physical (hypothetical) necessity is a consequence of moral necessity, which again suggests a difference.[68] Perhaps the truth is that these various terms all differ in intension but coincide in extension. At least I know of no passage that is clearly inconsistent with that hypothesis.[69]

---

[62] For an example of *non ens* and *impossibile* referring explicitly to hypothetical impossibility, see C 271.

[63] A.6.1.86: ". . . as, so to speak, denying of it the hypothetical possibility of existence, i.e., that it was, is, or will be the case." Thus Leibniz had the components of this conclusion; whether he ever put them together is the question.

[64] G VII 389 (L 696). Grua 608: An action is morally necessary if it is what a good man must, as such, do. Cf. A.6.1.465, G VI 50, 255 (H 74, 270).

[65] G VII 409 (L 709).

[66] C 405: "The notion of existence is such that those states of the universe are existent which please God. And what freely pleased God is the more perfect."

[67] G VII 409 (L 709).

[68] G II 450 (L 604); G VI 50 (H 74).

[69] However, I grant that the following passages are not easy to reconcile with this interpretation. G II 419: "I, too, would not say that there was a moral necessity in Adam to sin, but only this: that an inclination to sin prevailed in him, and to that extent there was predetermination if not necessity." G II 420: "Therefore, it is preferable never to acknowledge moral necessity except as directed to the good, since one cannot suppose that the wise person can do anything bad. I may at some time have spoken otherwise; if so, it was an incautious remark. . . ." G II 423: "Since I am regarded as having attributed moral necessity to events, I wish to explain my intentions more distinctly. The choice of the whole series of contingent things as most appropriate had moral necessity, but this cannot be said equally suitably of the sins that are ingredient in it and were admitted as concomitant. Adam did not at first, when he was created, have a greater inclination to evil than to good, but only when the sin was at hand."

VII

Identity in the Actual World

If any single topic lies at the very heart of Leibniz's philosophy, it is that of identity. He thought and wrote about it from the beginning of his philosophical career (in his first publication, the *Disputatio metaphysica de principio individui*, 1663), and on the crucial point he never changed his mind: things are individuated by their "whole being": Every property of a thing is essential to its identity.[1] His metaphysics of monads is largely derived from this conception of what it is to be an individual, and his whole philosophy of language and logic is based on his metaphysics.

Thus, to be Julius Caesar, as contrasted with any other actual or possible individual, *is* to be a Roman general, to conduct the Gallic wars, to cross the Rubicon, to be victorious at Pharsalus, to be assassinated in 44 B.C., and so on, to a complete list of everything that ever happened or will happen to him. Contrary to much of the tradition, there is, in Leibniz's view, no reasonable way of sorting Caesar's attributes into two nonempty categories, such that he could have lacked those in the first category, at the times when he had them, and still have been Caesar, while the absence of any of those in the second

---

[1] G IV 18; see also chap. 8, n. 19. As I have explained elsewhere, the *Disputatio* thesis that things are individuated by their whole nature may also be interpreted in another way, to mean that no accident of any individual is an accident of any other individual, i.e., that no accident of any individual fails to distinguish that individual from every other actual and possible individual. If monad A is not identical with monad B, the wisdom of A is not the wisdom of B, even if both A and B fall under the concept Wise, and similarly for all other accidents of A and B, regardless of the concepts under which A and B may fall by virtue of those accidents. But, as we shall see below, the principle of the Identity of Indiscernibles ensures that although the individual accidents of A and B will be the ground of their falling under many concepts together, i.e., of their having many properties or attributes in common, there will always be some concept under which A falls and B does not, or vice versa. If we consider only the (logically independent) "simple" properties, we find that every such property of an individual A is essential to its identity in the sense that there is another possible individual that differs from A in that property alone. (Here, as usual, a more precise statement would have to take account of the time parameter.)

category would have destroyed his identity. The same is true of every other individual, actual or possible.

Consequently, in uttering a truth about an individual, we do no more than ascribe to him one of those attributes without which he would not be that same individual. The truth of "Caesar crossed the Rubicon" implies that the concept expressed by the predicate, "crossed the Rubicon," namely, the sense of those words, is involved in the concept expressed by, or the sense of, the proper name "Caesar." And the truth or falsehood of any proposition, however complex or general, comes down in the end to the truth or falsehood of propositions about individuals, for individuals are all there are in this or any other possible world. Such is the point of view from which Leibniz considers the topic of identity.

1 Two Criteria

Leibniz gives two criteria for identity or sameness; both occur in many texts, and there are passages in which he purports to derive each from the other.[2] The lesser-known but more frequently occurring statement is: *A* is the same as *B* if *A* is *B* and *B* is *A*.[3] The other is, of course, the much-quoted Leibniz's Law: *A* is the same as *B* if *A* can be substituted for *B* in any proposition whatsoever *salva veritate*.[4] In both cases it is clear from the context that "if" means "if and only if."[5]

Let us first examine the better-known of these two criteria. The following are typical of the passages in which this statement occurs:

Those things are *the same* of which one can be substituted for the other without loss of truth. Thus if there are *A* and *B*, and *A* is an ingredient of some true proposition, and on substituting *B* for *A* in some place a new proposition is formed which is also true, and this always holds good in the case of any such proposition, then *A* and *B* are said to be *the same*; and conversely, if *A* and *B* are the same, the substitutions I have mentioned will hold good. Things that are the same are also called *coincidents*; sometimes, however, *A* and *A* are called the same, whereas *A* and *B*, if they are the same, are called coincidents.[6]

Those things are *the same* or *coincidents* of which either can be substituted for the other everywhere without loss of truth—for example, Triangle and Trilateral. For in all

---

[2] G VII (P 35), G VII 225 (P 43), G VII 240–41 (P 136). Cf. C 362 (P 53), C 264.

[3] C 382 # 110 (P 72); S 475, 479; C 240. According to recent philosophical dogma, stemming mainly from Frege and Russell, the verb "to be" is ambiguous, having "identity" and "predicative" senses, and perhaps others. Leibniz here shows in effect how these "senses" can be defined in terms of a single, primitive sense. For more on this, see Mates (1979b), 216ff.

[4] C 35, 72, 259, 362 (P 53); S 475, 479; G VII 228 (P 122), 236 (P 131). At *Hyp. Pyrrh.* II, 227, Sextus Empiricus remarks that "because Alexander and Paris are identical, it is impossible that the proposition 'Paris is walking' be true but the proposition 'Alexander is walking' be false." As other antecedents, the following have been noted: Aristotle, *Topics* 152b27ff.; Plotinus, *Enneads* V, 7.2; Aquinas, *Summa Theologiae* Ia, qu. XL, a.1 ad. 3. Cf. Burk 229.

[5] For the second principle this is clear in the passage next quoted.

[6] G VII 228 (P 122). Note the confusion of the variables with their values.

the propositions about Triangle proved by Euclid, Trilateral can be substituted without loss of truth, and conversely.[7]

It is usual to point out that these formulations seem to involve a confusion of names with what they name.[8] Presumably it is the *names* that are to be interchanged, but the *things named* (or, in the case of general terms, the *extensions*) that are or are not identical. The name "Paris" is not identical with the name "Alexander," nor is "Triangle" identical with "Trilateral"; and, conversely, it would seem to make no sense to say that the man Paris can or cannot be interchanged with some component of a proposition, nor even that the set of triangles can be so interchanged.[9]

One must concede, however, that there are reasons for being hesitant about ascribing to Leibniz so egregious an example of confusion. For one thing, he explicitly discusses the importance of distinguishing the properties of names from those of the things named.[10] For another, in connection with Nizolius's nominalism he had given serious consideration to the nature of names and had even raised the relatively esoteric question whether names are not themselves universals and hence abstract entities.[11] But, more important than either of these points, we have seen that for Leibniz propositions and concepts are in the realm of ideas, intermediate between linguistic expressions and the real world to which they refer; hence, when he speaks of interchanging *terms*, which he often identifies with concepts, he may be thinking neither of names nor of the things named, but of concepts.

Accordingly, several commentators have attempted to rescue him from the appearance of confusion by interpreting his *salva veritate* principle as providing a criterion for the identity of concepts, and not for that of the things that fall under the concepts.[12] For example, Professor Ishiguro has taken the

---

[7] G VII 236 (P 131). Cf. G VII 196. Note that he asserts the applicability of the principle to such complex propositions as Euclid's theorems, but when he proves it, he considers only atomic propositions of the form '*A* is *B*'.

In another geometrical example, at LH IV vii B 2 8–9 (Fasz. 1, # 30, 90), he gives the three concepts: Square, Equilateral equiangular quadrangle, and Equilateral rectangular quadilateral.

[8] Cf. e.g., Quine (1960), 116–17. It is amusing that Leibniz alternates between the singular and plural forms, *idem* and *eadem*, in the statements of his principle. At G VII 206 he uses the term "equipollence" for the relation between *signs* that can be substituted for one another *salvis calculi legibus*.

[9] One might suppose that one could get some guidance for the proper interpretation of the principle by consulting the works of Leibniz's follower, Christian Wolff, whom he often praises to the skies. But there we find the following astonishing account:

Things are called the same if they can be substituted for one another *salvo* any predicate that pertains to one of them either absolutely or subject to a given condition. When the substitution is made, the result ought to be the same as if no substitution had been made. . . . For example, let us posit that weight *A* has been put in equilibrium with weight *C*. Now if you substitute weight *F* for weight *A*, the equilibrium with weight *C* will not be destroyed; so weight *F* will be the same as weight *A*. *Gesammelte Werke*, ed. Ecole, Hoffman et al. Hildesheim, (1962–), series 2, vol. 3, 148–49. Cf. C 389, 519; PLR 132.

[10] A.6.6.343ff.

[11] A.6.2.450 n. 14 (note by Leibniz in his edition of Nizolius): *Recte igitur dicitur nomina esse universalia, non res.*

[12] Ishiguro (1972), 32–33; Feldman (1970); cf. also the translations at S 302, 307. Unfortunately, I broached the idea myself in n. 15 to Mates (1968).

Kauppi (1968), 141, says that "the quoted definition has established a synonymy which holds

content of the principle to be the following: "To say of two concepts that they are identical is nothing more nor less than to say that one can be substituted for the other in all propositions (apart from special intensional contexts) without change of truth value of the proposition (which is a complex concept made up of concepts)."[13]

Now, Leibniz does sometimes state his principle as applying to what he calls "terms,"[14] and there is the often-cited passage in which he says flatly that a term is not a name but a concept signified by the name (although, oddly, two lines earlier in the same passage he declares that "for us, every simple term is a name").[15] And, as Professor Ishiguro correctly points out, he does consider propositions to be complex concepts that contain their subject and predicate terms as components.

But there are also at least two rather strong considerations arguing against the proposed interpretation: (1) It makes the principle nearly vacuous and (2) there are numerous texts with which it cannot be reconciled.

As to reason (1): Disregarding, for the moment, the obscurity in the notion that a proposition is "made up" of concepts for which other concepts can be "substituted,"[16] we see that if concept A is identical with concept B, then presumably the result of substituting B for A in a proposition P will not be some other proposition Q that has the same truth value as P, but will be just the proposition P itself. On the other hand, if concept A is different from concept B, and if the concept A is part of the proposition P, then the result of substituting B for A in P will be a different proposition P'. So the *salva veritate* clause in the principle would seem entirely superfluous, as would the reference to all propositions. Anyone who can recognize the same proposition twice (when he sees it with his mind's eye)—and anyone who cannot do this is in a poor position to be assessing the truth values of propositions— could on this basis be given the following simpler criterion: Let A and B be concepts, and let P be a proposition in which A occurs; then A is the same as B if and only if the result of replacing A by B in P is the same as P. In the application of the principle there would be no need to check truth values: if the result of the substitution is a different proposition, whatever its truth value, the concept substituted is a different concept; and if the result of the substitution is the same proposition, then presumably the truth value has not

---

between two designations if they have the same concept as their meaning." But, as she herself notices two pages later, the sentence "Johannes Kepler = the discoverer of the elliptical form of the planetary orbits" is true, even though the concepts expressed by the two designations can hardly be considered identical. See n. 20.

[13] Ishiguro (1972), 32–33.

[14] C 362 (P 53). LH IV vii C 71–72 (Fasz. 1, # 54, 169): "Two terms are the same if one can be substituted for the other *salva veritate.*"

[15] C 243 (P 39). At G III 224 it is indicated that notions = terms = concepts. In his "great principle" at G II 56 (M 63–64) he speaks of concepts *of* the terms of a proposition. At LH IV vii 7 C 107–9 (Fasz. 2, # 106, 411) he tells us that a *substance* is a *terminus completus*!

[16] See chap. 3, sec. 4.

been altered anyway.[17] But this makes the principle both trivial and circular, since, after all, propositions are concepts.

I have pointed out earlier, however, that concepts cannot very well be parts of propositions, for it would seem that the same concept can "occur" more than once in a proposition, while it makes no sense to say that the very same part occurs more than once in a whole. If this fact is taken into account—as, indeed, it usually is not—we can no longer assume that the result of replacing, in a proposition P, a concept A by a different concept B will always be a different proposition P'.[18] But sometimes it will. Hence there would still be no need for *salva veritate*; the criterion could be that concept A is the same as concept B if and only if, for every proposition P, the result of replacing A by B in P is P.[19] This makes the principle slightly less trivial but still circular.

The moral, I think, is that an absolutely minimum condition to be satisfied by any plausible interpretation of the Leibnizian criterion is that what are substituted for one another in applying the criterion shall not be the same as what are thereby determined to be identical or not identical. The interpretation to be offered at the end of this section satisfies that criterion.[20]

As to reason (2) for rejecting the interpretation that the *salva veritate* principle applies to concepts, consider the following passage:

> I have said that it is not possible for there to be two particulars that are similar in all respects—for example, two eggs—for it is necessary that some things can be said about one of them that cannot be said about the other, else they could be substituted for one another and there will be no reason why they were not better called one and the same.

---

[17] I suppose it might be argued that just as one could know that the height of a person A was the same as that of a person B without knowing whether or not A was identical with B, so also one could in certain cases ascertain that the truth value of a proposition P was the same as that of a proposition Q without being able to tell whether P was the same proposition as Q. I shall leave it to better metaphysico-epistemological heads than mine to determine whether this sort of thing can happen even when it is known that the proposition Q is the result of "substituting" one concept for another in the proposition P.

[18] See n. 16. Thus, the concept expressed by "Adam," together with that expressed by the open formula

x ate the apple that Eve gave x

or with the different one expressed by

x ate the apple that Eve gave Adam

will constitute the proposition "Adam ate the apple that Eve gave him."

[19] However, at G VII 228 Leibniz says that a *new* proposition P' may be formed by substituting B for A in a proposition P even though A and B are identical. If this is so, how can P be said to be "composed" of A et al.? And, if A and B are the same *concept*, how can a new proposition arise from the substitution?

[20] Herbert Knecht (1981), 233 n. 24, takes the principle to mean that concepts or propositions A and B are identical if the signs representing them are everywhere interchangeable *salva veritate*. However, if this were right, i.e., if Leibniz were talking about the identity or nonidentity of the intensions of the signs, he should not make an exception for the oblique (i.e., nonextensional) contexts. See sec. 2 below.

Moreover, if they have diverse predicates, the concepts, too, in which these predicates are contained, will differ.[21]

As I read this passage, Leibniz is saying that two eggs, however similar, will have diverse predicates ("else they [the eggs] could be substituted for one another"!) and that if they have diverse predicates, the concepts, too, will differ. He is clearly applying the *salva veritate* principle to the eggs, not to the concepts, and since he next states explicitly that the concepts will differ if the eggs differ, it can hardly be suggested that in this case when he says "eggs" he really means "concepts of eggs."[22]

For a second example, consider what happens when the proposed interpretation is applied in Leibniz's examples involving "Triangle" and "Trilateral." Leibniz is then understood to be telling us that the concept Triangle is the same as the concept Trilateral.[23] But compare the following statement:

Things that are in reality distinct are usually distinguished by the senses; things that are conceptually distinct, that is, things that are formally but not really distinct, are distinguished solely by the mind. Thus, in the plane, Triangle and Trilateral do not differ in fact [*re*] but only in concept, and therefore in reality they are the same, but not formally. Trilateral as such mentions sides; Triangle, angles. A trigon qua triangle has three angles equal to the two right angles; qua trilateral, it has two sides always greater than the third.[24]

This passage, which in other ways is hardly reassuring to anyone hoping to rescue Leibniz from use-mention confusion, says clearly enough that in the case of Triangle and Trilateral, which are among his standard examples for illustrating the *salva veritate* principle, the concepts are not the same.

Nor is the foregoing passage the only text in which Leibniz denies the identity of the concepts of Triangle and Trilateral. He does this at least twice in the *New Essays*, asserting that the two ideas, that is, triangularity and trilaterality are not the same.[25] In still another passage, "Equivalent terms are those by which the same objects are signified, as, for example, Triangle and Trilateral,"[26] he seems to be contrasting the equivalence of the terms with the identity of their extensions. And, as we shall see below, he offers the pair Triangle and Trilateral as an example of terms that cannot be interchanged in "reflexive" propositions even though they are "the same," because a reflexive proposition is a proposition that "does not so much speak about a thing as

---

[21] LH IV vii C 103–4 (Fasz. 1, # 58, 187); also S 476–77. On similar eggs, cf. Sextus Empiricus, *Adv. Math.* VII, 409; Cicero, *Acad.* II, 57 (quoted in Jungius [1957], 10).

[22] Cf. also LH IV vii B 3 24r: "*A* is *B* means that *B* can be substituted everywhere for *A*. It means also that *A* and some *B* coincide, or can be mutually substituted for one another." Thus, "Socrates is a man" means that Socrates coincides with some man. If this is about *concepts*, what concept is here said to coincide with *A*?—the concept "some man"?

[23] I should mention, however, that to explain why the substitutivity breaks down in certain oblique contexts, as noted by Leibniz, Professor Ishiguro (1972, 21–24) ascribes to him a distinction between the meaning of a term and the concept expressed by the term.

[24] LH IV viii 61r.

[25] A.6.6.363, 408.

[26] C 240 (P 36).

about our way of conceiving it." All of this appears to indicate that the concept of Triangle is not identical with that of Trilateral.[27]

But there is more. In the two *New Essays* passages just cited, Leibniz is making another point, and, in so doing, reveals that what we are encountering here is a fundamental, deep-rooted contradiction in his whole philosophy of language and logic. He says that the nonidentity of the ideas, or concepts, should not lead us to deny the identity of their objects; thus, from the fact that triangularity is not trilaterality, we must not conclude that the triangle is not a trilateral. (Other pairs offered to illustrate the same point are God and the omnipotent,[28] and the oblique sections of the cylinder and those of the cone.)[29] But, according to the Predicate-in-Subject principle, the truth of the two universal affirmative (essential) propositions, "Every triangle is a trilateral" and "Every trilateral is a triangle," guarantees that the concepts Triangle and Trilateral contain one another and hence are identical.[30] Thus his doctrines seem to imply that the two concepts both are and are not distinct. A similar problem arises for singular existential propositions: "Adam is the first man" and "The first man is Adam" are both true, and so the concept of The First Man is identical with the complete individual concept of Adam; yet we are given to understand that such a concept as The First Man does not suffice completely to determine an individual.[31]

Still another aspect of the same problem is this. In view of Leibniz's other criterion for identity, which postulates the equivalence of 'A is the same as B' with 'A is B and B is A', the Predicate-in-Subject principle implies that if 'A is the same as B' is true, then the concepts A and B are identical. Therefore, if 'A is the same as B' is true, it is the same proposition as 'A is the same as A', so that every true identity is trivial. The proposition that Caesar is the victor of Pharsalus is just the proposition that Caesar is Caesar. Thus Leibniz falls into the conundrum analyzed by Frege in the opening paragraphs of 'Über Sinn und Bedeutung.'[32] I know of no satisfactory Leibnizian solution for these difficulties.

It was mentioned at the outset of this section that there are passages in

---

[27] On the other hand, cf. C 52 (P 20): "Two terms which contain each other and are nevertheless equal I call 'coincident'. For example, the concept of a triangle coincides in effect with the concept of a trilateral—i.e., as much is contained in the one as in the other. Sometimes this may not appear at first sight, but if one analyzes each of the two, one will at last come to the same." Thus Leibniz may have realized that, as I point out in the next paragraph, other doctrines of his imply that the concept of Triangle is the same as that of Trilateral, after all.

[28] C 242 (P 38).

[29] A6.6.408.

[30] G VII 240 (P 136): "If A is in B and B is in A, then $A = B$." GM VII 261: "If A is in B and B is in A, then A and B coincide." Thus Leibniz means the same by the expression "coincide" and "are identical," though in gemetrical contexts he usually prefers the former.

[31] I am forced to conclude that even for singular terms N, like "the first man," Leibniz was confusing the concept N with the concept of the individual falling under N. Or, applying the Predicate-in-Subject principle, we reach such unfortunate results as that the essential proposition "The first man is Adam" will be false, while the essential proposition "Adam is the first man" will be true.

[32] Translated as "On Sense and Reference," in *Translations from the Philosophical Writings of Gottlob Frege* (1952, 56–78). But see n. 19 above.

which Leibniz tries to prove the equivalence of his two criteria for identity or sameness. One such "demonstration" runs as follows.[33] Suppose that '*A* is *B* and *B* is *A*' is true. Then, for any concept *C*, if '*B* is *C*' is true, '*A* is *C*' will also be true (by virtue of the axiom 'If *A* is *B* and *B* is *C*, then *A* is *C*'); while, for any concept *D*, if '*D* is *A*' is true, '*D* is *B*' will also be true. Thus *A* and *B* will be interchangeable in the subject or predicate position of any universal or singular affirmative categorical propositions in which they may occur. Leibniz illustrates:

> Every pious person is happy, and every happy person is pious. Also, every happy person is elect and every martyr is pious. Therefore, every pious person is elect, and every martyr is happy.[34]

(We may note that interchangeability in particular affirmative propositions could be shown in like manner, on the basis of the moods Disamis and Darii.) That we have '*A* is *B* and *B* is *A*' if *A* and *B* are everywhere interchangeable is presumably taken as obvious, on the basis of '*A* is *A*'.

Elsewhere Leibniz gives as a "most powerful axiom":

(1) If '*A* is *B*' is true, then *B* can be substituted for *A* in the predicate position of any other proposition *salva veritate*.[35]

Clearly, he holds this on the basis of a form of the syllogism in the mood Barbara:

(2) If '*A* is *B*' and '*C* is *A*' are true, then '*C* is *B*' is true.

Rewriting variables in (2) and commuting the antecedent, we have also

(3) If '*A* is *B*' and '*B* is *C*' are true, then '*A* is *C*' is true,

from which follows

(4) If '*A* is *B*' is true, then *A* can be substituted for *B* in the subject position of any other proposition *salva veritate*.

And from (1) and (4) there follows

(5) If both '*A* and *B*' and '*B* is *A*' are true, then *A* and *B* are substitutable for one another in (the subject or predicate positions of) any proposition *salva veritate*.

There are, of course, many ways in which Leibniz could have formulated his Law so as to avoid use-mention confusion. One such formulation would be as follows: For any names, definite descriptions, or general terms *T, T'*, and for any possible world *W*:

---

[33] G VII 225 (P 43). At G VII 223 (P 35) a somewhat more complex argument is given. Cf. LH IV vii B 2 8–9 (Fasz. 1, # 30, 90). See also n. 2.

[34] G VII 225 (P. 43).

[35] C 402–3 (PM 94–95).

The existential proposition '*T* is the same as *T'* ' is true of *W* if and only if '*T* exists' is true of *W* and *T* and *T'* are interchangeable in all (direct) contexts *salva veritate*[36]

and

The essential proposition '*T* is the same as *T'* ' is true if and only if *T* and *T'* are interchangeable in all (direct) contexts *salva veritate*.

Here we are interchanging terms in order to determine the identity of their extensions, and thus we are not caught in the aforementioned Catch-22 loop of trying, by the interchange, to determine the identity of the very entities we are interchanging.

It should be noted, however, that in the right-left direction these principles are trivial, since identity sentences themselves are among the contexts to which Leibniz applies the principle.[37] Thus, if *T* and *T'* are interchangeable in all direct contexts *salva veritate*, they are interchangeable in the direct context '*T* is the same as *T'* '.

2. Oblique Contexts

In a passage to which little attention was paid until recently, Leibniz says:

If *A* is *B* and *B* is *A*, then *A* and *B* are called the same. Or, *A* and *B* are the same if they can be substituted for one another everywhere (*excepting*, however, those cases in which not the thing itself but the manner of conceiving the thing, which may be different, is under consideration; thus Peter and the apostle who denied Christ are the same, and the one term may be substituted for the other, unless we are considering the matter in the way some people call "reflexive": for example, if I say "Peter, insofar as he was the apostle who denied Christ, sinned," I cannot substitute "Peter" and say "Peter, insofar as he was Peter, sinned").[38]

In another place he makes the same point about the terms "Triangle" and "Trilateral," explaining that it is not permissible to substitute the latter for the former in the proposition "*A* triangle, as such, has an angle-sum of 180 degrees," "since part of the content lies in that way of saying it."[39] Still another

[36] Of course, a more precise formulation would have to take account of the time parameter. Otherwise we shall generate examples of the notorious fallacy called *A dicto simpliciter ad dictum secundum quid*. E.g., from "What you eat today = what you bought yesterday" and "You bought raw meat yesterday," we would have to infer "You eat raw meat today."

[37] See pp. 135–36.

[38] LH IV vii 7 C 103–4 (Fasz. 1# 58, 185); also S 475. I have to assume that Leibniz is referring to the fact that "Peter sinned" is not a necessary truth, for he says elsewhere (Grua 358) that if Peter had not sinned, Peter would not have been Peter.

In this passage Leibniz uses "reflexive" to apply to cases he elsewhere calls "reduplicative." Other texts show that the reduplicative cases are considered by him to be a proper subclass of the reflexive cases; see A.6.1.89, C 402–3 (PM 94–95), and n. 42.

Burk 230 says that Angelelli (1967) was the first to notice the restriction to extensional contexts, but see pp. 518–19 of Mates (1968), which was a contribution to the 1967 International Congress of Logic and the Methodology of Science.

[39] C 261.

passage involving the same distinction occurs in some unpublished comments Leibniz wrote on a work by the Jesuit Aloysius Kümmeth:

> I would call *distinct* or *diverse* those things that accept opposite predicates, when we understand that they are not the same, but different. White Socrates [*Albus Socrates*] and musical Socrates [*Musicus Socrates*] are one and the same, for even though Socrates qua musical sings well, and qua white does not sing at all, nevertheless it is true that white Socrates does sing, and whatever can be said about musical Socrates can also be said about white Socrates, except for the predications we are here excluding.[40]

The reason for the breakdown of the *salva veritate* principle in these kinds of cases, according to Leibniz, is that the propositions concerned are "reflexive":

> For coincidentals can be substituted for one another (except in the case of propositions which you could call formal, where one of the coincidentals is taken in such a way that it is distinguished from the others; but these are reflexive, and do not so much speak about a thing, as about our way of conceiving it—where indeed there is a distinction).[41]

Elsewhere Leibniz contrasts reflexive propositions with those he calls "direct," giving as an example that if L is a direct proposition, 'L is true' will be reflexive.[42] Thus, it seems that a reflexive proposition R is one that concerns not only elements of the real world but also the concepts and propositions that are ingredients of R. (Of course, this is only a preliminary analysis, for, as I shall argue in a later chapter, talk of concepts and propositions is ultimately analyzable as talk about the states of a particular individual, namely, God.) As is apparent from the example about Peter, the presence of words like *quatenus* and *eatenus* (to which I would add *qua, eo ipso*, and some others) is a tip-off that the given proposition is reflexive and not direct. Obviously the distinction has medieval forebears and to some extent anticipates Frege's distinction between the direct and the oblique denotations of linguistic expressions.[43]

---

[40] LH IV vii 60r (see also LH 113).

[41] C 367 (P 56–57).

[42] C 363 (P 54). Cf. Kauppi (1960), 169 n. 2. At C 183–84 Leibniz says that in demonstrations he uses two "reflexive" principles ("that syllogistic forms are sound and that a contradiction is absurd"); he contrasts these with the "material" assertions that constitute the premises of the demonstration and that he takes (for purposes of refutation) from his adversary.

[43] In the important passage at C 402–3 mentioned earlier, Leibniz says that if a universal affirmative proposition 'All A is B' is true, then the predicate B can be substituted for the subject A *salva veritate* in any universal affirmative proposition 'All C is A' of which that subject (A) is the predicate. But what Leibniz adds is more interesting: "We must except, however, the reduplicative propositions, in which we are speaking of a term so strictly that we are unwilling to substitute any other, for they are reflexive and are to thoughts as material propositions are to words." Since material propositions are about words, this seems to imply that reflexive propositions are similarly about thoughts.

For an illuminating explication of this passage and the related category of "reduplicated" propositions, see Mugnai (1979), 82–92. For the origin of the medieval concern with reduplicative propositions, i.e., propositions expressed by sentences containing words like *qua, quatenus,*

Leibniz was also aware that his substitutivity principle breaks down when words are used to denote themselves:

Furthermore, it sometimes happens that our ideas and thoughts are the subject matter of our discourse and are the very things we wish to signify; and reflexive notions enter more than one might think into notions of things. Sometimes words themselves are spoken of materially, and in such a context one cannot precisely replace the word by its signification. ... This happens not only when one speaks as a grammarian but also when one speaks as a lexicographer, giving the explanation of a name.[44]

3. The Identity of Indiscernibles

Closely related to the criteria for identity is the Leibnizian principle commonly known as "the Identity of Indiscernibles."[45] The following are some typical statements of this principle:

It is not true that two substances may be exactly alike and differ only numerically, *solo numero*, and what St. Thomas says on this point regarding angels and intelligences (that among them every individual is an *infima species*) is true of all substances, provided that the specific difference is understood as geometers understand it in the case of figures.[46]

I infer from that principle [the principle of Sufficient Reason], among other consequences, that there are not in nature two real, absolute beings, indiscernible from each other; because if there were, God and nature would act without reason, in ordering the one otherwise than the other.[47]

There is no such thing as two individuals indiscernible from each other. An ingenious gentleman of my acquaintance, discoursing with me in the presence of her Electoral Highness the Princess Sophie, in the garden of Herrenhausen, thought he could find two leaves perfectly alike. The princess defied him to do it, and he ran all over the garden a long time to look for some; but it was to no purpose. Two drops of water, or milk, viewed with a microscope, will appear distinguishable from each other. This is an argument against atoms, which are confuted, as well as a vacuum, by the principles of true metaphysics.[48]

---

inquantum, prout, see Aristotle, *Prior Analytics* I, 38, and I. Angelelli's explication of that text, in the *Notre Dame Journal of Formal Logic* 19 (1978): 295–96.

    Possibly relevant here is Leibniz's distinction between *terminus* and *ens* (sense and denotation?) at G II 471; cf. Burk 231.

[44] A.6.6.287.

[45] For some recent discussions of this principle, see Schneider (1974), 330ff., and Khatchadourian (1969), Lorenz (1969), and Kauppi (1966).

[46] G IV 433 (L 308). Thus, a typical case of difference *solo numero* would be that of congruent geometric figures.

[47] G VII 393 (L 700).

[48] G VII 372 (L 687). Cf. A.6.6.231. The "ingenious gentleman" was one Carl August von Alvensleben; see G VII 563 and L 14.

    C. S. Peirce, in a review of Latta's translation of the *Monadology* (*The Nation* 68 [1899]: 210), says that the leaf story tends to support Leibniz's opponents more than it supports him. For, according to Peirce, Leibniz is not saying merely that in fact there aren't any two indiscern-

Another favorite example, besides the leaves and the drops of water or milk, involves the two eggs that are similar in all respects (see the "egg" passage quoted earlier.)[49]

The mathematical paper entitled *Specimen geometriae luciferae* casts some light (though certainly not enough) on the meaning of "differ ... *solo numero*." After asserting that things that cannot be discerned in any way, whether per se or per alia, are identical, Leibniz continues:

> But there are things that agree completely or are of the same stamp or model, and yet differ in number, for example, equal straight lines, two eggs completely similar [in shape], two impressions of the same stamp in uniform wax. It is clear that these cannot be discerned in any way if they are considered per se, even when they are compared with one another. They are discerned only by position in relation to external things. Thus, if two eggs are perfectly similar [in shape] and equal [in volume] and are placed next to one another, one can at least be distinguished from the other as more to the east or to the west, or more to the north or to the south, or above or below, or as closer to some other body located outside of them....[50]

At first sight this passage seems inconsistent with Leibniz's frequent assertions that there cannot be two eggs that are perfectly similar, but the context makes it reasonably clear that here he is referring exclusively to the geometrical features (that is, size and shape) of the eggs and their environment. So the principle of the Identity of Indiscernibles says that, unlike the situation in geometry (and with other kinds of abstracta and, perhaps, even with phenomena), in the real world of monads and monadic aggregates there cannot be two things that differ *solo numero*.[51]

Note, however, that "discernible" means discernible by God, not by us, which renders the principle immune to any empirically discovered purported counterexamples. "You see," Leibniz says,

---

ible things, but that it is inconceivable that there be such, and von Alvensleben's behavior shows that he, at least, was conceiving that there were or might be two indiscernible leaves in the garden. This argument is obviously defective, but the general woolliness of the notions of "concept of..." and "conceive that ..." (and their interrelations) stymies any attempt to explain just what is wrong with it. There seems to be no rule for deciding what concepts a person must have in order to conceive that something is the case. At any rate, Leibniz was not talking about von Alvensleben's concepts or conceivings, but of God's.

[49] The treatment of the egg example in the *Confessio Philosophi* (Saame, 124ff.) is puzzling, for there Leibniz says that two eggs could be so similar that even God himself couldn't give any other distinguishing feature than that at present one of them is in place *A* and the other in place *B*.

[50] GM VII 275. Earlier in the passage, "similar" has been explained as referring to species, where a species is, e.g., Circle, Ellipse, Triangle. Ibid., 265: "In congruent figures everything is the same except position, so that they differ *solo numero*." Cf. C 519 (L 268). LH IV vii B 2 57–58 (Fasz. 1, # 40, 139): "Things differ *solo numero* if they are distinguished only in time and space, or if they are indiscernible per se."

[51] Kuno Lorenz correctly points out (1969, 153ff.) that the principle does not apply to abstract objects like geometric figures; he cites C 519ff. In that text, however, Leibniz seems to be confusing (1) talking about abstract objects and (2) talking abstractly about, i.e., disregarding some of the individuating properties of, concrete individuals.

paradoxical as it may seem, it is impossible for us to know individuals or to find any way of precisely determining the individuality of any thing. . . . For any set of circumstances could recur, with tiny differences which we would not take in; and place and time, far from being determinants by themselves, must themselves be determined by the things they contain. The most important point in this is that individuality involves infinity, and only someone who is capable of grasping the infinite could know the principle of individuation of a given thing.[52]

Some scholars have considered the Identity of Indiscernibles to be just half, as it were, of the *salva veritate* criterion. They interpret the latter as a generalized biconditional: '*x* is the same as *y* if and only if whatever is true of *x* is true of *y*, and vice versa', or, perhaps equivalently, '*x* is the same as *y* if and only if every attribute of *x* is an attribute of *y*, and vice versa', and then they call the generalized conditional from left to right "the Indiscernibility of Identicals" and that from right to left "the Identity of Indiscernibles."[53]

Whether this is essentially correct I do not know. One apparent discrepancy is that Leibniz applies the Identity of Indiscernibles only to individual substances, whereas the *salva veritate* criterion is applied also to cases like *Felix et pius idem est* and *Triangulum et trilaterum idem est*, where the terms concerned are general, not singular.[54] Another question that arises is why, if the Identity of Indiscernibles is merely a special case of the *salva veritate* criterion, Leibniz seems to accept the relevance of empirical procedures like peering through the microscope at drops of water or hunting in the garden for pairs of exactly similar leaves. After all, that criterion is not put forward as a contingent truth.[55]

In any case, I should like to suggest that Leibniz's general metaphysical framework gives us a way of interpreting the principle that makes better sense of it: it becomes the statement that no two individual substances fall under exactly the same concepts, or, what comes to the same thing for Leibniz, that no two such substances have the same complete individual concept.[56] Bear in mind that, of course, no two substances have even one acci-

---

[52] A.6.6.289.

[53] Here cf. LH XXXV xii 73 (quoted in Kauppi [1966], 502 n. 18): "If there is a true proposition in which *A* occurs, and this proposition goes over into a false proposition by substituting *B* for *A*, then *A* and *B* are discernible. If *A* and *B* are discernible, then they are different; otherwise they would be the same or coincident."

[54] Of course, these Latin sentences are best understood as generalizations about individuals—e.g., "The happy men and the pious men are one and the same."

[55] See n. 58. Cf. the statement at G VII 394 (L 699) that "this supposition of two indiscernibles, such as two pieces of matter perfectly alike, seems indeed to be possible in abstract terms, but it is not consistent with the order of things, nor with the divine wisdom by which nothing is admitted without reason." Cf. R 56, G II 264 (L 534–35).

The Identity of Indiscernibles is derived from the principle of Sufficient Reason at various places in the Clarke correspondence, e.g., at G VII 372 (L 687), 393 (L 699), 394–95 (L 700).

[56] Parkinson (PLR 129) gives essentially the same interpretation of the principle. As indicated elsewhere, however, I must restrict "concept" to concepts that are "in the category of Quality."

At G IV 433–34 (L 308) Leibniz says that the Identity of Indiscernibles follows from the fact that every individual concept is complete. Just how does it follow? Maybe via the principle of Sufficient Reason, which itself is said to follow from the fact that every individual concept is com-

dent—let alone all accidents—in common; but plainly that is not what Leibniz is asserting here. He is saying, rather, that God's concepts, though certainly not ours, are fine-grained enough to distinguish each individual from all of the others.[57] It is obvious that by virtue of their accidents, any two individuals will fall together under a very large number of concepts, that is, will have a large number of attributes in common. But the principle assures us that however similar they may be, there will always be some concept under which one of them falls and the other does not. Thus God is able to tell them apart by their qualities; they are in principle *discernible.*[58]

On this interpretation, the principle of the Identity of Indiscernibles and the right-left half of the *salva veritate* criterion are related as follows. If A and A' are the complete concepts of two distinct individuals, then, by the principle, there will be a concept B that is in A but not in A', so that the essential proposition 'A is B' will be true, but 'A' is B' is false. Thus the principle implies the right-left half of the criterion. But the latter does not seem to imply the former. For, even waiving the fact that the criterion is said to apply to *all* propositions (explicitly including theorems in Euclid's *Elements*), and not just to propositions of "A is B" form,[59] the concepts involved in this interpretation of the principle must be limited to concepts from the category of Quality. Extrinsic denominations (Leibniz's term for what some philosophers now call "relational properties") are plainly intended to be excluded. If they are not, then, for example, since Caesar is distinct from Pompey, he of course will fall under the concept Distinct from Pompey while Pompey would not; and in general any two distinct things will trivially fall under different concepts.[60]

If this is correct, the Identity of Indiscernibles is not the complete obverse of the Indiscernibility of Identicals. For Leibniz employs the latter to make substitutions in just the sorts of relational sentences we have been considering.

---

plete or the predicate of a true proposition is contained in the subject. Perhaps the point is that if individuals A and B express the universe in different ways, they can't fall under all the same concepts.

[57] Thus, as Parkinson (PLR 133–34) points out, even if Princess Sophie and the gentleman had found two leaves that *they* could not distinguish, this would be nothing against Leibniz's principle.

[58] Note that Leibniz defines two things as similar in a given respect—i.e., with respect to a given concept—if they both fall under that concept; e.g., if x is red and y is red, then x and y are similar in that respect.

[59] In his derivations of the *salva veritate* criterion from the "A is B and B is A" definition (see p. 129), he applies that criterion only, or at least primarily, to universal or single affirmative categorical propositions.

[60] In the fourth letter to Clarke (G VII 374, L 688), Leibniz makes it clear that "discernible" means "discernible by an internal reason [property]"; with this he intends to rule out the sort of trivialization indicated. Also, at A.6.6.110 he says that any two things differ in *intrinsic denominations.* (See chap. 12, sec. 5, for a definition of this term.) This shows that Caesar must differ from Pompey in respects other than the extrinsic denomination "thing distinct from Pompey." The possibility of this sort of trivialization of the Identity of Indiscernibles has, of course, been noticed by many others besides Russell. One of the earliest was Black (1952), 153–54.

In the famous *Non inelegans specimen* he deduces "$A = C$" from "$A = B$" and "$B = C$" by substituting, on the basis of the *salva veritate* criterion, "C" for "B" in "$A = B$."[61] In the "Calculus of Real Addition" he proves "If $A = B$, then $B = A$" and "If $A = B$ and $B \neq C$, then $A \neq C$" by similar substitutions.[62] Thus, apparently the *salva veritate* criterion is indeed intended to apply to open sentences of the forms "$X = A$" and "$X \neq A$," and if the Identity of Indiscernibles were half of it, it would be trivial in the way suggested above.

Russell, in the Introduction to *Principia Mathematica*, makes a similar point when he cites Leibniz's Identity of Indiscernibles as an intuitive justification for *Principia*'s definition of identity. He says:

It should be observed that by "indiscernible" he cannot have meant two objects which agree as to *all* their properties. Some limitation of the properties necessary to make things indiscernible is therefore implied by the necessity of an axiom.

As is well known, in *Principia* the limitation was to so-called predicative functions of the types of objects in question.[63]

---

[61] G VII 231.

[62] G VII 236–37. At A.2.1.525, which does not deal with a formal calculus, the same move is made with respect to the natural language expressions "A and B are the same," "B and C are the same," "A and C are the same."

[63] *Principia Mathematica*, vol. 1, p. 57. Oddly enough, in Russell's introduction to Wittgenstein's *Tractatus*, p. xvii, he says that "the conception of identity is subjected by Wittgenstein to a destructive criticism from which there seems no escape." But on this subject we find in the *Tractatus* only such muddleheadedness as "Incidentally [*Beiläufig gesprochen*], to say of *two* things that they are identical is nonsense, and to say of *one* thing that it is identical with itself is to say nothing at all." For more on all of this, see Grelling (1926).

VIII

Cross-World Identity

The Leibnizian conception of necessary truth as that which holds of all possible worlds has enjoyed a renaissance in recent philosophizing about the semantics of modal logic. But in a number of respects the modern versions of the possible-worlds story do not jibe with the original. Some of the differences are perhaps inessential. Thus we now speak of *individuals* as existing in possible worlds, whereas for Leibniz these worlds—at least the nonactual ones—are made up of *individual concepts*; he does not believe in nonexistent individuals. And we say, perhaps carelessly, that sentences or propositions are true or false "in" possible worlds, whereas Russell is surely right in using the preposition "of"—at least, again, if we are talking about Leibniz's kind of possible world.

But a more consequential difference is this: for Leibniz each individual concept belongs to exactly one possible world, while in modern treatments the same individual can, and typically does, belong to many. Some recent writers feel quite strongly about this. To Saul Kripke, for example, it is completely obvious that Richard Nixon belongs to more than one possible world:

When you ask whether it is necessary or contingent that *Nixon* won the election, you are asking the intuitive question whether, in some counterfactual situation, *this man* would in fact have lost the election.

"Possible worlds" are *stipulated*, not *discovered* by powerful telescopes. There is no reason why we cannot *stipulate* that, in talking about what would have happened to Nixon in a certain counterfactual situation, we are talking about what would have happened to *him*.[1]

Leibniz, on the other hand, though he was well aware of the relation of the possible-worlds framework to the truth conditions for counterfactual

---

[1] Kripke (1972), 265, 267.

conditionals, would hold it absolutely impossible that Nixon should have had attributes other than the ones he did and does in fact have.[2] Here the modern view is surely the more intuitive—at least prima facie—and hence it is worth-while to look into Leibniz's grounds for holding the opposite. The preferred example, of course, is not Nixon, but Adam.

1. Adam's Concept

In a letter of 12 April 1686 to the Landgraf Ernst von Hessen-Rheinfels, through whose mediation he was exchanging philosophical ideas with the noted French Jansenist Antoine Arnauld, Leibniz wrote:

There is a possible Adam whose posterity is of a certain sort, and an infinity of other possible Adams whose posterity would be otherwise; now is it not true that these possible Adams (if we may speak of them thus) differ among themselves and that God has chosen only one, who is precisely ours?[3]

Arnauld did not grasp the significance of the parenthetical qualification "if we may speak of them thus," and in his reply he remarked:

Moreover, Monsieur, I do not see how, taking Adam as an example of an individual, several possible Adams are conceivable. It is as though I should conceive of several possible me's; a thing that is surely impossible. For I am not able to think of myself without considering myself as an individual, so distinct from every other actual or possible individual that I am as little able to conceive of several me's as of a circle that does not have all its diameters equal. The reason is that these various me's are differ-ent, one from the other, else they would not be *several*. There would have to be, there-fore, one of these me's that would not be me, an evident contradiction.[4]

Leibniz's response to this is very important to an understanding of his philosophy. It exists in two forms: one is a long memorandum headed *Remarks upon M. Arnauld's letter in regard to my statement that the indi-vidual concept of each person involves, once for all, all that will ever happen to him*; the other is his actual letter, dated 14 July 1686. In the relevant sections the two documents agree almost verbatim. I quote the memorandum:

I have said that the supposition from which all human events can be deduced is not simply that of the creation of an undetermined Adam [*un Adam vague*] but the creation of a particular Adam, determined in all circumstances, chosen out of an in-finity of possible Adams. This has given M. Arnauld opportunity to object, not without reason, that it is as little possible to conceive several Adams, taking Adam as an individual, as to conceive several me's. I agree; but in speaking of several Adams I do

---

[2] More precisely: for every attribute A and time t, if Nixon had A at t, it is absolutely impos-sible that he should have existed and not have had A at t. As explained earlier, I believe that this is Leibniz's view and that he did not incorporate the times into the attributes, as it were; see pp. 88–89. In his examples, the reference to time is usually tacit. See also n. 17.

[3] G II 20 (M 16).

[4] G II 30 (M 29).

not take Adam for a determined individual. I must, therefore, explain. This is what I meant. When we consider in Adam a part of his predicates, for example, that he was the first man, put into a garden of enjoyment, and that, from his side, God took a woman, and, if we consider similar things, conceived *sub ratione generalitatis* (that is to say, without mentioning Eve or Paradise or the other circumstances which constitute his individuality), and if we call the person to whom these predicates are attributed Adam, all this does not suffice to determine the individual, for there might be an infinity of Adams, that is to say, of possible persons to whom these would apply but who would, nevertheless, differ among themselves. Far from disagreeing with M. Arnauld in what he says against the plurality of the same individual, I would myself employ the idea to make it clearer that the nature of an individual should be complete and determined. . . . We must not, therefore, conceive of a vague Adam or of a person to whom certain attributes of Adam appertain when we try to determine if all human events follow from his presupposition, but we must attribute to him a concept so complete that all which can be attributed to him may be derived therefrom. . . . It follows, also, that if he had had other circumstances, this would not have been our Adam, but another, because nothing prevents us from saying that this would be another. It is, therefore, another. It indeed appears to us that this block of marble brought from Genoa would be wholly the same if it had been left there, because our senses cause us to judge only superficially, but in reality, because of the interconnection of things, the universe, with all its parts, would be wholly different and would have been wholly different from the very start if the least thing in it had happened otherwise than it has.[5]

This conclusion—that if Adam had had any attributes other than the ones he actually did have, he would not have been the same person—is frequently repeated by Leibniz, as applied both to Adam and to other individuals. Thus, in a note printed by Grua he says:

You will object that it is possible for you to ask why God did not give you more strength than he has. I answer: if he had done that, you would not exist, for he would have produced not you but another creature.[6]

Elsewhere he makes the same point about Jacob and Esau:

Hugo of St. Victor, asked why God favored Jacob but treated Esau with scorn, responded that no other reason can be given for this than that Jacob is not Esau,

"which," Leibniz adds, "is absolutely correct."[7] Still another example:

But, someone will object, whence comes it then that this man will assuredly do this sin? The reply is easy. It is that otherwise he would not be this man.[8]

And the point is made yet again in a comment on the interpretation of counterfactual conditionals:

---

[5] G II 42 (M 45); note particularly that in the general description there must be no mention of Eve or other individuals actually existing, for anybody from whose side *Eve* (and not just any woman) was taken would have been Adam himself. Cf. G II 54 (M 60–61), G VI 107–8, 363–64 (H 128–29, 370–71); S 476.

[6] Grua 327.

[7] Grua 314. Cf. G VII 311–12; G VII 74; C 26.

[8] G IV 455 (L 322).

Many future conditionals are inconsistent [*inepta*]; thus, when I ask what would have happened if Peter had not denied Christ, it is asked what would have happened if Peter had not been Peter, for denying is contained in the complete notion of Peter.[9]

In general, he tells us:

... if, in the life of any person, and even in the whole universe, anything went differently from what it has, nothing would prevent us from saying that it was another person or another possible universe that God had chosen. It would then indeed be another individual.[10]

Despite the doubts of some commentators, all of this makes it clear enough that Leibniz held that no individual could have had any attributes other than the ones it does have.

Insofar as these passages contain any argument for their thesis, it seems to be only that since there is no reason against the claim that the supposed individual is different from the actual individual, he *is* different. This is clearly an application of the principle of Sufficient Reason—namely, that whatever is the case, there is some sufficient reason why things are thus and not otherwise.[11] Adam and the supposed individual are the same or they are not. If they were the same, there would be some reason for it, but there is no such reason; ergo . . .

As is usual in Leibniz's applications of the principle of Sufficient Reason,

---

[9] Grua 358. This note continues in an interesting way:

But it *is* permissible [*excusabile*] that by the name Peter should be understood what is involved in those attributes [of Peter] from which the denial does not follow, while at the same time there must be subtracted from the universe everything from which it does follow; and then sometimes it can happen that the decision follows per se from the remaining things posited in the universe, but sometimes it will not follow unless there is added a new divine decree *ex ratione optimitatis*. If there is no *vinculum naturale* or consequence from the remaining things posited, it will not be possible to know what would have happened unless on the basis of a decree of God in accord with that which is best. Therefore, the issue depends either on the series of causes or on a decree of the Divine Will, and the "scientia media" [of Molina, on whom Leibniz is here commenting; cf. G VI 124–25 (H 145)] doesn't appear to help at all.

At the place where I have said "from which it does follow," the manuscript and Grua's text have (alas!) "from which it does not follow"; this, so far as I can see, must be an error.

[10] G II 53 (M 59–60). Still another relevant comment is at G VII 74: "The question why God has given more perfection of mind to this person than to that is one of those silly questions, like asking, when the shoe pinches, whether the shoe is too small or the foot too large."

It may seem that Leibniz is throughout confusing the trivially true

$$\Box[Fa \rightarrow (x)(-Fx \rightarrow x \neq a)]$$

with the dubious

$$Fa \rightarrow \Box (x)(-Fx \rightarrow x \neq a);$$

for example,

Necessarily, if Adam is bald, then no nonbald person is Adam

with

If Adam is bald, then any nonbald person would necessarily have been someone else, not Adam.

See my comments (chap. 6, sec. 2) on the "slipped modal operator."

[11] G VI 612 (L 646); G VII 199, 309; C 11, 25. See chap. 9, sec. 2.

it is unclear just what sorts of "reasons" he has in mind. In this instance one might suppose that he has reference to some form of Leibniz's Law and is saying that the only possible reason for holding Adam to be identical with some individual, actual or possible, would be that the two of them had every attribute in common, and that since, by hypothesis, that is not true in the present case, there *is* no reason. But why don't they have every attribute in common? An attribute, after all, is supposed to be what is expressed by a predicate; so why not consider predicates like "is bald," "is wise," as abbreviations for "is bald in the actual world," "is wise in the actual world," and for each world W add a battery of predicates like "is bald in W"? Then Adam, who (let us say) is five feet ten, could perfectly well have all attributes in common with an individual, Adam_1, who inhabited the nonactual world W and was like Adam in all respects except that he was five feet eleven (and had such other attributes as were implied by this difference in height). Both Adam and Adam_1 would have the attribute expressed by "is five feet ten in the actual world," and both would have that expressed by "is five feet eleven in world W." So the claim that individuals are identical if and only if they have all attributes in common does not prima facie rule out the possibility that the same individual could belong to two possible worlds, even if we grant Leibniz's further thesis that the individuals of a given world are so interconnected with one another that each "mirrors" all the others.

In the draft of the letter to Arnauld there is another passage that is somewhat relevant to this. In it Leibniz considers what it means to say that an individual existing at one time is identical with an individual existing at another.

Let a straight line, ABC, represent a certain time, and let there be a certain individual substance, for example, myself, which lasts or exists during this period. Let us take then, first, the I that exists during the time AB, and again the I that exists during the time BC. Now, since people suppose that it is the same individual substance that perdures, or that it is the same I that exists in the time AB while at Paris and that continues to exist in the time BC while in Germany, it must needs be that there should be some reason why we can say truly that I perdure or that the I which was at Paris is now in Germany. For if there were no reason, it would be just as right to say that it was another. To be sure, my inner experience convinces me a posteriori of this identity, but there must also be some reason a priori. It is not possible to find any other reason, excepting that my attributes of the preceding time and state, as well as the attributes of the succeeding time and state, are predicates of the same subject; *insunt eidem subjecto*. Now, what is it to say that the predicate is in the subject if not that the concept of the predicate is in some way involved in the concept of the subject? . . .[12]

I interpret Leibniz to be saying in this passage that although my memories are my basis for believing that "I, who now am in Germany, was previously in Paris," the statement obviously does not imply the existence of such

---

[12] G II 43 (M 46–47). Cf. G II 264 (L 535). On identity through time, see A.6.6.240ff.; Leibniz there asserts that x could be the *same monad* at times t and t' without being the *same person*.

memories and hence it means something else.[13] In general, when Leibniz looks for an "a priori reason" for a statement, what he produces is an explication of its meaning.

It might seem that in the quoted text the expressions "was in Paris during the time AB" and "was in Germany during the time BC" are intended to express attributes. As I argued in chapter 5, this must be incorrect; the attributes must be expressed by "is in Paris" and "is in Germany," and we should say that Leibniz had the first of these during the time AB and the second during the time BC.[14] Otherwise, if time is treated in the Leibnizian manner (that is to say, if we suppose that references to specific times are always eliminable in terms of references to the simple attributes of particular individuals), it would seem impossible for the concepts of individuals in different possible worlds to include any time-dependent attributes in common—a consequence that he clearly does not wish. Analogous considerations weigh against letting predicates containing a "possible-worlds" parameter express attributes; we would lose cross-world identity for any such attribute.

As an alternative to considering time references as built into properties, we are interpreting Leibnizian individual concepts not as complex attributes but as series of states (complex properties) ordered by time or some other relation as a parameter.[15]

Now, it might seem that if in effect Leibniz considered Adam's concept to contain a time parameter, he could just as well have built in a parameter relating to the different possible worlds. Thus the complete individual concept of Adam would not only indicate which attributes he had at which time, but which attributes at which (or other timelike relation) in which world. Just as, in the actual world, Adam has a given attribute at one time and lacks it at another, so also we could expect that in some other possible world Adam would have attributes he lacks in this. By framing the notion of complete individual concept along these lines, it would seem that Leibniz could allow the same individual concept to belong to more than one possible world and yet could retain the principle, so important to him, that every individual concept involves all that would ever happen to a corresponding individual and reflects all the other individual concepts that are compossible with it.[16]

---

[13] As concerns the relation of memory to personal identity, see Leibniz's discussion of "physical" and "moral" identity, A.6.6.236ff.

[14] There is, however, a problem about having the proper names "Paris" and "Germany" in the predicates. Paris and Germany are not substances, so presumably propositions that appear to be about them are analyzable as propositions about monads. But the problem would remain.

[15] In addition to the indirect support for such an interpretation, there are occasional relatively direct statements like the following at G II 136 (L 360): "Each of these substances contains in its nature *a law of the continuation of the series of its own operations*." Adam's concept therefore not only contains all of Adam's attributes; it indexes these attributes by time.

[16] Another relevant question is whether the complete concept of an individual contains attributes expressed by a modalized predicate, e.g., whether Peter's concept contains an attribute expressed by the predicate "is possibly saved." There are passages (G II 42, 46, 50–52) in which Leibniz seems to countenance this, but I cannot see any nontrivial way of interpreting such a view consistently within the general framework of his metaphysics.

However, although Leibniz could have considered the matter in this way, it is fairly obvious that he didn't. Let us look in other directions for clues as to what might have motivated his denial that an individual concept can belong to more than one possible world.

It is worth mentioning at this point that anyone who holds a view according to which the same individual concepts can belong to several possible worlds has to make the sorts of decisions involved in what Quine has called "essentialism."[17] In one way or another the question has to be faced of how similar (in what respects similar) an individual in one possible world must be to an individual in another possible world in order for them to count as one and the same individual. For example, it would have to be decided exactly which of Adam's attributes he could have lacked and still have been Adam. This amounts to the time-honored problem of distinguishing between the essential and the accidental (though not in the special Leibnizian sense of those terms).[18]

This problem is not much affected by the particular way in which the notion of individual concept is handled. If, with Leibniz, we consider Adam's concept to be just the sequence of his states and then try to go further and apply the name "Adam" also to some concept in another possible world, we shall have to give a criterion (presumably in terms of similarity) for deeming that other concept to be this sort of "counterpart" to the concept of Adam.[19] If, unlike Leibniz, we think of Adam's concept as indexed with respect to different possible worlds, we are still left with the problem of explaining how similar the sequences associated with the different possible worlds must be to one another in order to count as belonging to the concept of a single individual. No matter how the technical details are arranged, the problem of dividing each individual's attributes nontrivially into essential and accidental will remain in one form or another.

---

[17] Quine (1961), 22, 155–58; Quine (1960), 199–200.

[18] For the special Leibnizian sense, see A.6.6.305, G II 458, Grua 383. As we saw in chap. 5, in this sense an attribute is essential to an individual x if it belongs to x at all times (or, if any individual that lacked that attribute at any time would not be x), while an attribute that belongs to x at some times and not at others is an accidental attribute of x. In this sense, of course, Leibniz asserts that some of an individual's attributes are essential while others are accidental; e.g., the attribute "is a man" is essential to Alexander, and the attribute "is king" is accidental.

Curley (1982), 319, surprised at Leibniz's apparent adoption of an essentialist, rather than a "superessentialist," position at A.6.6.305, seems not to have noticed the ambiguity. Hunter (1981), trying to show that Leibniz did not consider every attribute of an individual essential to it, falls into the same trap. Apparently unaware of Leibniz's special sense described above, he finds it "irritating" that Leibniz uses the term "essence" occasionally as a synonym for "individual concept," as this does not fit in with the (erroneous) theory of his article. Additionally, he contributes his own measure of confusion to the discussion by assuming that whether Leibniz is an "essentialist" or a "superessentialist" depends on Leibniz's (as contrasted with our) use of "essence." He also, unfortunately, endorses the Fried mistranslation of C 393 #153 and the erroneous consequences that Fried draws from it (see chap. 5, n. 36).

[19] Thus Lewis (1968) defines the essence of an individual as the set of attributes he shares with all his counterparts, where, roughly, "your counterparts are men you *would have been*, had the world been otherwise."

So the crucial question amounts to the very question with which Leibniz had dealt in his first published work, namely, what is the essence of an individual?[20] It is said that the essence of man is rational animality, but this surely cannot mean that the essence of each individual man is just rational animality. It must apply only to the species. Otherwise, Adam would still be Adam no matter what attributes he had, provided only that he was a rational animal; he might, for example, have all the attributes of some other rational animal, say Moses, and still be Adam. Thus, presumably, rational animality is at most a part of the essence of the individual man; nothing could be Adam unless it was a rational animal, but many things can be and are rational animals without being Adam. So the question reduces to: what other attributes of the individual are to be added to his species essence in order to form his whole essence?

Leibniz's answer, of course, is in effect "all of them"; his opponents hope to make do with something less.[21] Their intuition is that, just as identity through time survives relatively slight changes in an individual but is destroyed when the changes are sufficiently great, so absolute identity should tolerate transworld differences if they are small enough. They would say that Adam could have had one less hair on his head and still have been the same individual, but that he couldn't have been a stone. For Leibniz, on the other hand, there is no coherent way in which the requisite distinction can be drawn.

2. The Double World

One's confidence that very slight changes in an individual would not destroy its identity may be shaken, however, if one reflects on the following interesting passage from the *New Essays*, where Leibniz attacks Locke's view (*Essay*, 2, xvii, 19) that personal identity consists not in the identity of substance but in the identity of consciousness.

In another region of the universe, or at some other time there may be a sphere in no way sensibly different from this sphere of earth on which we live, and inhabited by men each of whom differs sensibly in no way from his counterpart among us. Thus at one time there will be more than a hundred million pairs of similar persons, that is, pairs of persons with the same appearances and states of consciousness. God could transfer the minds, by themselves or with their bodies, from one sphere to the other without their being aware of it. . . .

---

[20] The constancy of Leibniz's view on this matter is documented by Saame in n. 207 (p. 191) of his edition of the *Confessio Philosophi*. He cites, with dates: A.6.1.3ff. (1663); Jag 44ff. (1676); C 518ff. (1680–84); G II 54 (1686); G IV 433 (1686); S 476ff. (1695?); G IV 512ff. (1698); A.6.6.229–32 and 306–10 (1704); G VI 608 (1714); G VI 598 (1714); G VII 372 and 393–95 (1716).

[21] Again, the point is that anyone who did not have those attributes *at those times* would not be Adam.

"But," Leibniz continues,

whether they are transferred or left where they are, what would your authorities say about their persons or "selves"? Given that the states of consciousness and the inner and outer appearances of the men on these two spheres cannot yield a distinction between them, are they two persons or are they one and the same? It is true that they could be told apart by God, and by minds which were capable of grasping the intervals [between the spheres] and their outer relations of space and time, and even the inner constitutions, of which the men on the two spheres would be insensible. But since according to your theories consciousness alone distinguishes persons, with no need for us to be concerned about the real identity or diversity of substance or even about what would appear to other people, what is to prevent us from saying that these two persons who are at the same time in these two similar but inexpressibly distant spheres, are one and the same person? Yet that would be a manifest absurdity.[22]

The emphasis throughout this passage is, of course, on appearance.[23] As I understand him, Leibniz is saying that there could exist, in some extremely distant portion of the actual world, another individual so like Adam that no created mind could tell them apart by any possible experience. Their bodies would appear identical in every respect; each man would be spatially and temporally surrounded by an immense environment sensibly indistinguishable from that of the other; and their conscious states, if we could somehow examine those, would also be indistinguishable. In a word, all the tests, and then some, by which in fact we distinguish things would fail, and yet there would be two individuals.

The point of this fanciful story is to cast light on our concept of identity.[24] It suggests that this concept—which, of course, is supposed to be the sense of the word "identity"—allows at least the abstract possibility that any one of us could have a practically indistinguishable (at the conscious level) double, indistinguishable from the "inside," as it were, as well as from the "outside."

---

[22] A.6.6.245. Note the assumption that the total population of the earth is about 100 million.

[23] G VI 363: There are many different possible persons who have all the properties *we* know of any given individual. Cf. A.6.6.289–90.

[24] A.6.6.314: ". . . these bizarre fictions have their uses in abstract studies, as aids to a better grasp of the nature of our ideas."

It should be mentioned that in the context in which this story appears, Leibniz is distinguishing so-called personal or moral identity, on the one hand, from real or natural identity (both relative to time) on the other, and that he is primarily interested in the former, whereas our present concern is the latter. (Cf. the definition of *persona* at Mollat [1893, 107] as "substance capable of rights and obligations and having or going to have reason and will.") The relation between the two kinds of identity seems to me to be this: X at time t is personally (i.e., morally) identical with Y at later time t' if and only if X at t is really identical with Y at t' and X at t is morally responsible for the actions of Y at t'.

At A.6.6.237 it *looks* as if Leibniz is countenancing the possibility that X at t might be morally identical with Y at t' even if they were not really identical, but I think that in that passage the clause ". . . if God were to change the real identity in some extraordinary manner" need only mean ". . . if the temporal development of the soul in question contained a discontinuity." At G VII 569 Leibniz says that not only the same real soul but also the same moral person exists through all time, "which renders it susceptible of rewards and punishments under the most perfect government, that of God."

On the whole different question of personal identity in Leibniz, see Scheffler (1976) and Jolley (1984, chap. 7).

Therefore, it seems, all of us must face the rather odd fact that we do not really know who we are, in the sense that we cannot, by means of any of our own attributes that we are aware of, distinguish ourselves from various other possible individuals who may exist in this actual world.[25]

Of course these considerations represent, at most, reasons that may have disinclined Leibniz to follow common sense in accepting a counterpart relation specified in terms of sensible similarity. Suppose, for example, he had agreed that Adam (who, let us say, had dark hair) could have had somewhat lighter hair—in other words, that there is a counterpart C of Adam, in a possible but nonactual world W, who is just like Adam in all respects open to empirical verification except that he has somewhat lighter hair. So we could say that if things were as represented by W, C would be Adam.[26] Now, suppose that from the point of view of world W, somebody is looking back at the actual world A. Adam's concept differs no more from C than C differs from it. Thus it should be as much a counterpart of C as C is of it.[27] But suppose that the actual world is double, as in principle it may be; then there is another individual, $Adam_1$, who has just as much claim to being C's counterpart in the actual world A as Adam does. Hence there would be somebody other than Adam of whom it could be said: he would be Adam if things were as represented by A, that is, if things were as they in fact are. But this is absurd. As Arnauld observed, there cannot be two individuals who are Adam. If, therefore, we restrict our consideration to sensible qualities, we perhaps have found an intuitive reason for denying that Adam could have had any attributes other than the ones he does have. Unfortunately, however, we cannot so restrict ourselves and remain within Leibniz's framework; according to him, every individual has infinitely many attributes that are not sensed.[28]

3. Continuity

There is, however, another argument that Leibniz might well have offered for his doctrine of the non-otherworldliness of actual individuals, and that would

[25] G II 46 (M 50): We have only confused experience of our own individual concepts. Another "proof" of the same point is at A.6.6.114, where it is argued that it is not absolutely impossible for a man to forget all he knows and later to learn things again—so that identity cannot depend on memory.

[26] See n. 19.

[27] For Lewis (1968), the counterpart relation is not symmetric. But I think that intuitively it ought to be. Ditto for transitivity.

[28] Perhaps the argument may be more easily generalized than I am allowing here. For we ourselves, as well as Leibniz, would probably grant that each of us not only has infinitely many attributes that are not sensed, but infinitely many attributes of which neither we nor anyone else is aware by any mode of cognition. If so, could not there be, in principle, two individuals so similar that we could not tell them apart by any means whatever? Then, both of these individuals will be counterparts of any possible individual that is a counterpart of either of them, and we are led again to the absurd statement that one of these individuals would be identical with the other if things were as they in fact are.

not involve a limitation to sensible qualities. This argument would rest upon his so-called principle of Continuity, which in one formulation goes as follows: "Jumps are impossible, not only in the case of motions, but also in the whole order of things and truths."[29] As Russell puts it:

If two substances differ by a finite difference, there must be, according to Leibniz, a continuous series of intermediate substances, each of which differs infinitesimally from the next. As he often expresses it, there is as little a hiatus, or vacuum of forms, as there is a vacuum in space.[30]

(Russell's use of the term "next" here is unfortunate, but the general idea of Leibniz's principle seems clear enough, at least for present purposes.) In illustrating his principle, Leibniz does not restrict himself to cases that concern substances, in his strict sense of that term, but considers such composites as men, animals, plants, fossils, and rocks. In one passage he says:

I think, therefore, that I have good reason for believing that all the different classes of being, whose union forms the universe, exist in the ideas of God (who has distinct knowledge of their essential gradations) only as so many ordinates of a single curve, where the totality of these ordinates does not allow the insertion of any others because that would indicate disorder and imperfection. Men are connected with the animals, these with the plants, and these again with the fossils, which will be connected in their turn with bodies that the senses and the imagination represent to us as perfectly dead and shapeless. Now, since the principle of Continuity requires that, as the essential determinations of one being approach those of another, so all the properties of the former must gradually approach those of the latter, it is necessary that all the orders of natural beings form a single chain in which the different classes, like links, connect so closely the one to the other that it is impossible for the senses and the imagination to fix the precise point where any one begins or ends; all the species which border on or which occupy, so to speak, the regions of inflection and retrogression (of the curve) have to be equivocal and endowed with characters which belong to the neighboring species equally.[31]

Now, since Leibniz postulates this sort of continuum among the concepts that are exemplified in the actual world, there is little reason to doubt that he held a similar view about individual concepts belonging to different possible worlds. Thus, in the letters to Arnauld he says that there are infinitely many possible Adams, who approach Adam in similarity the way ellipses approach a circle.[32] And in the *New Essays*, arguing against the "vacuum of forms," he says:

My view, in other words, is that there must be species which never did and never will exist, since they are not compatible with that succession of creatures which God has chosen. But I believe that the universe contains everything that its perfect harmony

---

[29] G III 635 (L 658); A.6.6.307; GM VII 25 (L 670–71); G III 52 (L 351); GM VI 130; G II 168 (L 516); B&C 556–59 (see W 184 ff.). I discuss the principle at greater length in chap. 9, sec. 3.

[30] R 64–65. Cf. Jag 28 (L 157).

[31] Guhrauer (1846), Anmerkungen zum zweiten Buche, p.32, trans. in NE 712–13, quoted and discussed by A. O. Lovejoy in Frankfurt (1972), 282–83.

[32] G II 20 (M 15).

could admit. It is agreeable to this harmony that between creatures which are far removed from one another there should be intermediate creatures, though not always on a single planet or in a single (planetary) system; and sometimes a thing is intermediate between two species in some respects and not in others. Birds, which are otherwise so different from man, approach him by virtue of their speech, but if monkeys could speak as parrots can, they would approach him even more closely.[33]

Thus the claim would be that for any two complete individual concepts, there is a series of intermediate concepts (belonging perhaps to different possible worlds) such that, for any concept C in the series, and any preassigned positive degree of similarity that one might wish to consider, there will be an interval around C in which all terms of the series are at least that similar to C. Actually, all that is needed for our present argument is the claim that any two complete individual concepts, whether from the same or from different worlds, can be joined by a discrete series of intermediate concepts in which each concept is enough like its predecessor to qualify as a counterpart of it. Then we would have the absurd consequence that every complete individual concept is a counterpart of every other complete individual concept.

These considerations may be illustrated in the case of Adam. Someone suggests, let us say, that although in fact Adam's hair was of rather fine texture, he could have had coarser hair, that is, would still have been Adam even if his hair had been somewhat coarser. And various others of his attributes will be regarded as similarly "nonessential." On the other hand, it is held that there are limits; Adam could not, for example, have had all the properties of an elephant or all those of Moses. The statements "Adam is an elephant" and "Adam is Moses" are considered not only factually false but also as expressing absolute impossibility.

Suppose, then, that Adam had had slightly coarser hair than he in fact did have; in the possible-worlds framework this amounts to the supposition that instead of the world of which we are a part there had been actualized a possible world W_1 of which "Adam has coarse hair" is true and which is maximally like our actual world in all respects except those involved with this hypothesis. Now, from the point of view of W_1 (pretending, as it were, that W_1 is the actual world), we ask, "Could Adam have been somewhat larger than he is?" "Could Adam have weighed 200 pounds instead of 150 pounds, as he does?" The answer is, presumably, yes. So we are led to consider another possible world W_2, of which "Adam weighs 200 pounds" is true and which is like W_1 in all other respects except ..., and so forth. Hence, "Adam has coarse hair and weighs 200 pounds" is true of W_2. (Note that simple attributes are always compatible and that Leibniz's doctrine applies in the first instance to simple attributes only.) In this way, step by step, we reach a possible world W_n of which "Adam has *very* coarse hair over his entire body, weighs about two tons, has a long trunk, and so forth, and so on" is true. But that, of course, is admitted to be impossible.

[33] A.6.6.307.

The foregoing, I suppose, is just an elaboration of the simple and obvious point that the concept of any individual, by a series of the same sort of relatively "slight" changes that are not regarded as crucial for identity, could be gradually transformed into the concept of anything whatever. Once we allow that an individual could have had *some* attributes other than the ones that individual does have, there is no "natural" place to draw the line.[34] In short, there is no plausible way of dividing the attributes of an individual nontrivially into the essential and the accidental.

As this may seem to some readers to be merely an example of the ancient *sorites* or "heap" fallacy, the following observation by Leibniz is relevant:

> All those concepts to which the heap argument of the Stoics is applicable—as, for example, wealth, poverty, baldness, heat, cold, lukewarmness, light, dark, large, small—taken absolutely are vague, imaginary, indeed false or without definite form. Only those concepts to which this objection cannot be made are purely and certainly understood by us. For the former ones involve reference to our opinion, which varies; for example, what seems cold to one person seems hot to another and indeed [cold and hot] to the same person at different times. The same with poverty. In one respect we affirm a person to be poor, but in another respect we deny it. If poverty taken absolutely were a valid notion, it would have to be defined by a certain number of obols, and then it is indeed necessary that at some point, if at all, a poor person will become nonpoor by the addition of 1 obol. Hence the laws remedy this sort of defect by defining a pauper as a person who doesn't have a certain number of solidi or by defining an adult as a person over twenty-five years of age.[35]

The individual concepts that make up the series cited in our continuity argument are not "vague," "imaginary," or "without definite form" (for they are God's concepts, not ours, and hence are completely idealized). Also, the concept Being a concept of Adam is not one of those "vague" concepts like Being poor, Being bald, Being small; it is not the kind of concept with respect to which there can be a sequence of objects such that the first terms of the sequence fall under it, the last do not, and yet there is no intervening place in the sequence where there is a clear change. The concept Being a concept of Adam is already definite in the way that the concept Being poor becomes definite when defined by a certain number of obols. Hence the heap fallacy is not relevant.

4. Rigid Designators

At the outset of this chapter I mentioned that there is a fundamental difference of outlook between Leibniz and most of the contemporary philosophers who have recently considered the subject of cross-world identity. For Leibniz, the connection between words and concepts is primary and direct,

---

[34] Regarding an analogous matter, Leibniz says, at G IV 556 (L575): "For this involves merely a matter of more or less, which does not alter matters in the realm of possibilities."

[35] LH 117–18; Fasz. 2, 426.

while that between words and their denotations is indirect, mediated by the relevant concepts. Words are symbols for thoughts and only indirectly refer to whatever objects, if any, these thoughts may be about. This holds for proper names as well as for all other types of expression. It is not the case, Leibniz would say, that we succeed in directly associating a proper name with a definite individual and then, as we discover properties of that individual, gradually build up a concept or intension to go with the name. Rather, to the extent that we understand what we are saying when we use the name, we already have some sort of concept attached to the name, and then we gradually narrow down the range of possible individuals who could fall under the concept. We form the concept X by learning the use of the expression X as a part of the language, and not by abstracting qualities from what we may take to be the designatum of X. From this point of view, it is not as though we know from the start exactly *which* individual we are talking about, and as though over time we find out more and more attributes of that individual and can intelligibly speculate as to what would have happened if that very same individual had had properties other than the ones he does have.

Now, it might be supposed that, at least in very favorable though artificial circumstances, we can (and do) indeed manage to attach a proper name to a definite individual and then, as we discover the properties of that individual, use the name in making true assertions, including counterfactual conjectures, about it. So I might point to somebody or something and say, "By 'Nixon' I mean *this man*; now, what if Nixon had not resigned the presidency?"

Of course, with almost all the proper names we use (including, needless to say, the cherished example "Nixon") we have never carried out any such deictic or dubbing performance. But even when we have, it is by no means clear that by using a name introduced in this way we can formulate an intelligible question about what would have happened if some individual had had attributes other than the ones he does have. For Leibniz will ask, "Exactly which individual are you talking about?" It will be of no avail to resume the pointing while reiterating, with whatever emphasis, THIS MAN, for Leibniz's question amounts to "Who is *this man*?" We can hardly claim that by pointing we have singled out and identified a particular individual, if at the same time we have to admit that there may be many individuals such that, for all we know, any one of them might have been the one in front of us at the time when we did the pointing. In introducing a name or making an identification, the demonstrative pronoun "this" is effective only to the extent that the speaker and the audience can distinguish the intended object from the rest of the objects in the world. As mentioned earlier, Leibniz is willing to go the whole way in this direction and argue that even in the case of our own individual concepts, to say nothing of those of others, we have only confused experience, so that in a real sense we do not even know precisely who we ourselves are.[36]

---

[36] Cf. G II 46 (M 50).

At any rate, whatever the right view about these matters may be, we should take note that Leibniz agrees with his opponents on one important point, namely, that proper names, unlike such descriptions as "The first man," are what are today called "rigid designators";[37] they designate the same thing in every possible world in which they designate anything. But for Leibniz this is because no proper name designates anything in more than one possible world.

[37] Kripke (1972), 269–70.

🔲🔲🔲🔲🔲🔲🔲🔲🔲🔲🔲🔲🔲🔲🔲🔲🔲🔲🔲🔲🔲🔲🔲🔲🔲🔲🔲🔲🔲🔲🔲🔲🔲🔲

IX

"Two Great Principles" and Two Lesser Ones

In sections 31 and 32 of the *Monadology*, Leibniz says:

> Our reasonings are based upon two great principles: the first, the *Principle of Contradiction*, by virtue of which we judge that false which involves a contradiction, and that true which is opposed or contradictory to the false; and the second, the *Principle of Sufficient Reason*, by virtue of which we observe that there can be found no fact that is true or existent, or any true proposition, without there being a sufficient reason for its being so and not otherwise, although we cannot know these reasons in most cases.[1]

Similarly, in the *Theodicy*:

> I have remarked . . . that there are two great principles, namely, that of *Identity* or of *Contradiction*, which says that of two opposed propositions one is true and the other is false, and that of *Sufficient Reason*, according to which there is no true proposition for which anyone with the requisite knowledge to fully understand it could not see the reason.[2]

and

> There are two great principles of our reasoning; one is the *Principle of Contradiction*, which asserts that of two contradictory propositions one is true and one is false; the other is the *Principle of Determining Reason*, that nothing ever happens without there being a cause or at least a determining reason for it. . . .[3]

In interpreting these two principles, Couturat and others[4] have suggested that the first amounts to the claim that every analytic proposition is true,

---

[1] G VI 612 (L 646); G VII 309.
[2] G VI 413–14 (H 418–9).
[3] G VI 127. There are literally dozens of other references in the Leibnizian corpus to these "two great principles."
[4] CL 213–17; R *v.* Rescher (1979) 23ff., in a variation on this, has the principle of Sufficient Reason as "Every true proposition is analytic," the principle of Identity as "Every finitely analytic

while the second asserts that every true proposition is analytic, so that both together are equivalent to the statement that in every true proposition the concept of the predicate is contained in the concept of the subject. With this suggestion in mind, let us now take a closer look.

1 The Principle of Identity or of Contradiction

The first thing that meets the eye when we survey the passages in which Leibniz states this principle is that he pays no attention whatever to a number of distinctions that today would be thought important or even essential. Clearly, he regards all the following statements as alternative formulations of a single law:

1 A proposition cannot be true and false at the same time.[5]
2 A proposition is either true or false.[6]
3 *A* is *A* and cannot be non-*A*.[7]
4 Of a pair of contradictories, one is true and one is false.[8]
5 The same thing cannot be and not be.[9]

Indeed, in one text he seems to include under the same heading almost the entire theory of truth and falsity:

First of all, I assume that every judgment (that is, affirmation or negation) is either true or false and that if the affirmation is true the negation is false, and if the negation is true the affirmation is false; that what is denied to be true—truly, of course—is false, and what is denied to be false is true; that what is denied to be affirmed, or affirmed to be denied, is to be denied; and what is affirmed to be affirmed and denied to be denied is to be affirmed. Similarly, that it is false that what is false should be true or that what is true should be false; that it is true that what is true is true, and what is false false. All these are usually included in one designation, the *principle of contradiction*.[10]

Perhaps it is not too surprising that in view of the obviousness and seeming triviality of Tarski equivalences like "'Snow is white' is true if and only if snow is white," most of these multifarious formulations would appear to Leibniz (and to many others) to amount to the same thing. But it is more puzzling that such formulations as "*A* is *A*" or "Every identical proposition is true and its contradictory is false"[11] should be considered equivalent to the rest of them. There is no doubt, however, that this was Leibniz's view. In many places he uses phrases like "the principle of Contradiction or, *what amounts to the same thing*, that of Identity," and he indicates in other ways that for him the two principles coalesce.[12]

---

proposition is necessarily true," and the principle of the Best as "Every infinitely analytic proposition is contingently true."

[5] G VII 355 (L 677).
[6] A.6.6.361–62.   [9] Grua 20.
[7] G VII 355 (L 677).   [10] G VII 299 (L 225).
[8] G VI 127.   [11] G VII 309.
[12] G IV 359 (L 385); G V 14; G VII 309, 355 (L 677); G VI 413; C 1.

Actually, it is not difficult to see why Leibniz might look at things in this way. We have only to keep in mind that, for him the proposition '*A* is *B*' (essential) is equivalent to the generalized conditional 'If something is *A*, then it is *B*'. Thus, taking "Nothing both is *A* and is not *A*" as the principle of Contradiction, and "*A* is *A*" as the principle of Identity, we see that while the former is equivalent to "If something is *A*, then it is not not-*A*," the latter is equivalent to "If something is *A*, then it is *A*," and that these last are plainly equivalent to one another. I do not vouch for the soundness of this line of argument, but I do believe that it accurately reflects Leibniz's way of thinking about the matter.[13]

We have seen (in chapter 7) that the principle of Identity plays a central role in one of Leibniz's ways of defining necessary and contingent truth. He says that '*A* is *B*' is a necessary truth if, and only if, by means of a finite series of definitional replacements in *A* and *B* it can be reduced to the form '$A_1 A_2 \ldots A_n$ is $B_1 B_2 \ldots B_m$', where each B_i is one of the A_i's. (Or, equivalently, it is necessary if and only if its contradictory, '*A* is not *B*', can by such replacements be brought to a form in which some component of the predicate is the complement of some component of the subject.) It is therefore clear that Leibniz wishes his principle of Identity to cover not only propositions of the form "*A* is *A*," but also those of such forms as "*AB* is *A*," "*ABC* is *AC*," and, generally, "$A_1 A_2 \ldots A_n$ is $B_1 B_2 \ldots B_m$," where every B_i is one of the A_i's.

Hence, if we are to judge by the use to which Leibniz puts this principle, its content is, as Couturat has asserted, that every explicitly analytic subject-predicate proposition is true. The word "explicitly" must be added here because we are not told, either by Leibniz or by any of his modern expositors, whether the propositions obtained at the successive steps of this sort of reduction are or are not to be considered identical with the original proposition—for example, whether the proposition "Bachelors are unmarried" is or is not the same proposition as "Unmarried men are unmarried."

2. The Principle of Sufficient Reason

The second "great principle" so often cited by Leibniz is that of Sufficient Reason: Nothing comes to pass without a reason (*nihil fit sine ratione*). As with the principle of Contradiction, so this principle, too, is put forward in many different versions that are by no means obviously equivalent. In addition to the five formulations already quoted, here are a few more:

There must be a sufficient reason for anything to exist, for any event to occur, for any truth to obtain.[14]

---

[13] Cf. PLR 61.
[14] G VII 419 (L 717).

Nothing occurs for which it would be impossible for someone who had enough knowledge of things to give a reason adequate to determine why the thing is as it is and not otherwise.[15]

There is no proposition (other than identicals) in which the connection between subject and predicate cannot be distinctly explained.[16]

The principle that a reason must be given is this: that every true proposition not known per se has an a priori proof, or that a reason can be given for every truth, or, as is commonly said, everything has a cause.[17]

Nothing exists without a reason. For nothing exists without the aggregate of all its requisites. (A requisite is that without which the thing cannot exist; the aggregate of all requisites is the full cause of the thing.)[18]

Nothing exists without a reason, or there is no effect without a cause.[19]

Whether this principle plays as great a role in "all our reasoning" as Leibniz seems to think it does[20] is open to question. But there is no question that he uses it frequently in his own philosophizing.[21] Some of the arguments in which it appears are, in very condensed form, as follows:

1. *On absolute space*. If space were absolute, there would be no reason why the physical universe should be oriented as it is rather than in some other way, for example, with east and west reversed. Therefore, space is not absolute.[22]

2. *On absolute time*. Similarly, if time were absolute, God would have had no reason to begin the world at one time rather than another. Therefore, time is not absolute and the world is eternal.[23]

3. *On atoms*. If God had created two things that differed *solo numero*, he would have had no reason to put one of them in one place and the other in another, rather than vice versa. Therefore, there do not exist two things that differ *solo numero*, and such atomic theories as postulate the contrary are false.[24]

4. *On the existence of God*. God exists, for otherwise there would be no sufficient reason why this possible world rather than some other exists.[25]

---

[15] G VI 602 (L 639).

[16] C 513.

[17] G VII 309: . . . *et principium reddendae rationis, quod scilicet omnis propositio vera, quae per se nota non est, probationem recipit a priori, sive quod omnis veritatis reddi ratio potest, vel ut vulgo ajunt, quod nihil fit sine causa*. Cf. VII 301.

[18] Grua 267.

[19] C 519. Other statements are at C 11, 25. For a really early statement of the principle, see Plato, *Timaeus*, 28a4–6.

[20] See G VII 301.

[21] The principle appears in Leibniz's works from the very beginning; cf. A.6.1.490 (from 1668), A.2.1.23 (from 1669). See O. Saame's edition of *Confessio Philosophi*, 145 n. 28.

[22] G VII 364 (L 682); cf. G II 515, III 595.

[23] Grua 270; G II 515.

[24] C 519 (L 268).

[25] G VI 603 (L 639); cf. G VII 356 (L 677–78). G II 424: If no series were best, God would have created nothing, for he cannot act without a sufficient reason.

5. *On Archimedes' De Aequilibrio*. Archimedes, in his book *De Aequilibrio*, was obliged to make use of a particular case of the great principle of Sufficient Reason. He takes it for granted that if there be a balance in which everything is alike on both sides, and if equal weights are hung on the two ends of that balance, the whole will be at rest. This is because no reason can be given why one side should go down rather than the other.[26]

In chapter 8 we have seen that Leibniz also employs the principle in a series of arguments of the form: there is no reason for P; therefore, not-P. Presumably such arguments are enthymemes for arguments of the form: either P or not-P; if P, then there is a sufficient reason for P; but there is no sufficient reason for P; therefore, not-P. We have earlier noticed two examples of this sort of reasoning:

> ...It follows, also, that if he had had other circumstances this would not have been our Adam, but another, because nothing prevents us from saying that this would be another. He is, therefore, another.[27]

> ...If, in the life of any person, and even in the whole universe, anything went differently from what it has, nothing would prevent us from saying that it was another person or another possible universe which God had chosen. It would then indeed be another individual.[28]

In all of his uses of the principle it is evident that Leibniz tacitly places limits on the kinds of reasons that are to be considered. In the argument concerning the balance, for example, it is assumed that the only relevant reasons would refer to physical features of the balance, the weights, and the surrounding environment. Indeed, it is clear that not even all such features are regarded as relevant. After all, everything can't be "alike on both sides" of the balance, or else, on Leibnizian principles, there wouldn't be two sides. So, some features must be excluded. Thus, the tacit conditions of the Archimedean argument would presumably be violated if, the equal weights being made of iron, a magnet that is close to one side of the balance causes that side to go down. We are also left to wonder, in this case and in similar cases, why Leibniz's principle does not call for a sufficient reason for balance as well as for imbalance. He seems to assume gratuitously that if the equal weights (and by what criterion are they equal?) do not balance, that calls for an explanation, whereas if they do balance, nothing more need be said about it.

Similarly, in the arguments about space and time, only "internal" proper-

---

[26] G VII 356 (L 677), 301 (L 227); C 519 (L 268), 402. At C 514 Leibniz argues that Euclid's axiom that the results of adding equals to equals are equal also follows from the principle because no reason could be given for their being diverse!

[27] G II 42 (M 46). Cf. C 374 (P 64 n. 1).

[28] G II 53 (M 59–60). At G II 43 (M 46), in a similar argument, he draws a weaker conclusion: "...there must of necessity be a reason for the true statement...that I who was in Paris am now in Germany. For if there is no reason, one would be as justified in saying that it is another person."

ties of the universe—properties that would be the same no matter when or where it was located—were to be considered by God. No doubt speculation in these matters is best left to the theologians, but one might suppose that God, like any ordinary workman, would act to produce an artifact when and only when he felt that he was quite ready. And when a workman feels that he is quite ready is surely not determined exclusively by the design and materials of the contemplated product.

In any case, when the possible reasons are restricted in this way, the principle that there must be a sufficient reason for whatever happens seems to lose whatever vague plausibility it has when it is stated simpliciter.

We should take note, however, that in most of the aforementioned applications the relevant individuals are not simple substances. Perhaps the principle applies to aggregates only by weak analogy with the way it applies to monads. And in the latter connection, at least, it seems intended merely as a corollary of the definition of truth, or of the Predicate-in-Subject axiom, as has been argued by Couturat, Rescher, and Parkinson. In support of this interpretation, Parkinson[29] quotes Leibniz's remark that the principle of Sufficient Reason "is contained in the definition of truth and falsity," and he points to such passages as the following:

> It is evident, therefore, that all truths—even the most contingent—have an a priori proof, or some reason why they are truths rather than not. And this is just what is meant when it commonly said that nothing happens without a cause, or, that there is nothing without a reason.[30]

Thus, the sufficient reason for the truth of "Caesar crossed the Rubicon," for example, would be found in the complete individual concept of Caesar, involving perhaps that he was angry with Pompey, that he considered a good offense to be the best defense, and so on.[31] In other words, anyone who really knew who Caesar was, that is, who knew in full what kind of individual he was, would know why he chose to cross the Rubicon; and, in general, to discover the reason for the truth of the essential proposition 'A is B' is to analyze the concept A far enough to reveal the concept B as contained in it.[32] In contingent truths, where the analysis would go on to infinity, we mortals can only achieve a probable opinion, presumably by analyzing the subject term to a point where we can discern some sort of tendency. The root of all this is, once again, Leibniz's idea that every question can be resolved into a question of which individuals exist or of what would be the case if this one or that one did exist.

We might ask ourselves: what's wrong with this idea, anyway? Well, for one thing, it seems to make it impossible for anyone to be mistaken about the

---

[29] PLR 66.

[30] G VII 301, as translated by Parkinson. Cf. G IV 436–37 (L 310–11), C 405, 519.

[31] C 26: If Peter acts differently from Paul, the reason for this can only be found in Peter-ness and Paul-ness.

[32] G II 46 (M 50): To say that the predicate is in the subject is to say that there is always something to be conceived in the subject which serves to explain why this predicate pertains to it.

accidents of any individual. Whoever appears to believe something false of individual x has not fully grasped the complete individual concept of x, and hence the belief is not really about x. This result obviously does violence to our intuitions. We may note, however, that while, on Leibniz's doctrine, I cannot believe of Caesar that he died in bed, I can mistakenly believe that the proposition "Caesar died in bed" is true. For I can fail to understand or grasp that proposition (that is, the sense of the sentence "Caesar died in bed") to the extent requisite for investigating its truth. Hence the clash with intuition may not be quite so serious as it appears at first. Nevertheless, it cannot be denied that Leibniz comes uncomfortably close to holding the curious doctrine that "every assertion is true in the sense intended."

Leibniz's use of the principle of Sufficient Reason in proving the existence of God calls attention to another deficiency of that principle. He argues as follows. We can ask not only why a particular state of the world should exist, but also why there should be a world at all and why it should be structured according to one set of laws rather than another. In the first of these cases, we can give a reason for the particular state by referring to preceding ones and citing natural laws that link them to the one in question, but in the other two cases there must be some other sort of reason. Then he continues:

> The reasons for the world therefore lie in something extramundane, different from the chain of states or series of things whose aggregate constitutes the world ... and since there is no reason for an existing thing except in another existing thing, there must necessarily exist some one being of metaphysical necessity, or a being to whose essence belongs existence.[33]

Thus Leibniz moves us from the relatively innocuous admission that it makes sense to ask certain Why questions, to the much stronger conclusion that there is a necessary being, and the principle of Sufficient Reason has been shifted from the claim that nothing happens without a reason to the very different claim that everything has a cause. Indeed, from several of Leibniz's formulations quoted earlier in this section it can be seen that he notices no difference here. With very few exceptions he appears to use the terms "reason" and "cause" interchangeably.[34]

This tendency on Leibniz's part to confuse reasons and causes can be explained, if not justified. It is not peculiar to him, and in fact it goes back through the history of philosophy to Plato and Aristotle and their use of the Greek word *aitia*, which was later translated into Latin as *causa* and eventually into English as "cause." Every beginner in philosophy has been puzzled

---

[33] G VII 303 (487). G II 264: the reason for the existence and harmony of the monads is in that *res* we call "God." Cf. A.6.6.98. G II 271 (L 538): to ask why there is perception and appetition in monads is to inquire about something ultramundane and to demand reasons of God.

[34] At C 533 he asserts straight out that "*Causa* is nothing else than *realis ratio* [real reason]." G II 233: the causes of eternal monads will have to be *rationes extraneas*. A.6.2.483: *Ratio sufficiens est qua posita res est*. A.6.6.118: "Hunger has *particular reasons* that do not always exist." Cf. the proof of the principle of Sufficient Reason at A.6.6.483, in which the sufficient reason for a thing's existence or occurring is identified with all the "requisites" for its occurring or existing; a *ratio sufficiens* is defined as *qua posita res est*, and a *requisitum* is *quo non posito res non est*. At

by Aristotle's doctrine of the "four causes," since only his so-called efficient causes seem to deserve the name at all. Aristotle was of course philosophizing in Greek, and the crucial word was *aitia*. As both he and Plato usually employ this word, *x* is an *aitia* of *y*'s being in such and such a condition if *x* is prominently mentioned in an appropriate answer to a question as to why *y* is in that condition.

This becomes clearer if we consider the following four Aristotelian questions and answers.[35]

1. Why did the Persians invade Attica? Because the Athenians had raided Sardis.
2. Why is this statue so heavy? Because it is made of bronze.
3. Why is he taking after-dinner walks? Because of his health.
4. Why is the angle *A* inscribed in a semicircle a right angle? Because it is equal to an angle *B* that is half of a straight angle.

In each case the *aitia* is what is mentioned most prominently in the answer.

Thus, in the first example the Athenian raid on Sardis is the *aitia*; this *aitia* is a so-called efficient cause. In the second example the *aitia*, according to Aristotle, is the bronze, the material cause. The third example is supposed to illustrate the final cause, which in this case is health. And in the last example the *aitia* is, oddly enough, the angle *B*, which is the formal cause.[36] We see, therefore, that Aristotle is in effect noticing four different kinds of answers that can be given to Why questions; only one of these types of answer mentions what we today would call a "cause."

Plato's use of *aitia* is similar, and in the same way it gives rise to texts that in translation seem rather odd. In Leibniz's favorite passage from the *Phaedo* (97C-99B),[37] where Socrates complains that Anaxagoras did not stick to his

---

Grua 267 Leibniz states that the aggregate of all requisites is the "full cause" (*causa plena*) of the thing.

A passage that seems clearly to make causes a subclass of reasons is the following, from LHI, 4, 3, 1–4 (Fasz. 2, #69, 236):

Axioma Magna

Nothing is without its reason.

Or, what is the same, nothing exists without its being possible (at least for an omniscient being) to give a reason why it exists rather than not, and why it is in this condition rather than in some other. Whence it follows that nothing is, per se and absolutely speaking, undetermined [*indifferens*], and the indifference of things is only a figment of our ignorance, like what the pagans call Fortune. But, somebody will say, if nothing is without its cause, then there will be no first cause and no ultimate termination. The response is that though indeed nothing is without its reason, it does not follow that nothing is without its cause. For a cause is a reason for the thing that is outside the thing, or a reason for the production of the thing; though it is indeed possible for the reason for a thing to be internal to the thing itself. This would be the case with all things that are necessary, like mathematical truths that contain their own reasons, and God, who, alone among existing things, is the reason for his own existence.

[35] Here I follow the excellent account in Vlastos (1978). The relevant references to Aristotle are given in his n. 7.

[36] One might have thought that it would at least be the proposition that angle *A* is equal to angle *B* and angle *B* is half of a straight angle; and in other instances propositions do serve as *aitiai*; e.g., the premises of a valid syllogism are said to be *aitiai* of the conclusion.

[37] Cf. G III 54–55 (L 353). This passage (and Leibniz's translation of it) are discussed at some length in Mates (1973). Leibniz also has praise for the *Parmenides* and *Timaeus* (cf.

announced doctrine that *nous*, or intelligence, is ultimately responsible for everything, our English translations have Socrates ridiculing the suggestion that the *cause* of his sitting there in a bent position is that his sinews, by relaxing and contracting, have brought his skeletal frame into that configuration. "The true cause," he says, "is that the Athenians decided to condemn me and that I, for my part, have thought it best to sit here." But what Socrates is really concerned with is the *aitia*, and not the cause; and the *aitia* must be something prominently mentioned in an appropriate answer to the question "Why are you sitting here?"—so that obviously it would be his own decision and that of the Athenians.

Thus, in philosophical discourse the Latin word *causa* (and consequently some of its derivatives in modern languages) acquired from *aitia* a sense that does not jibe with that of "cause" in ordinary English. It covers not only what we call "causes" but also many other things as well, including in certain cases the propositions that we would call "reasons."

Now reasons, it seems to me, belong to the category of *propositions* (thoughts, the senses of declarative sentences); they are good or bad, true or false, and they stand in logical relations to one another and to that for which they are the reasons. Causes, on the other hand, would seem to be things or events or circumstances—with all of which, unlike reasons, it makes sense to associate spatiotemporal coordinates.[38] The propositions that $2 + 3 = 5$ can serve as a reason, for example, in relation to the proposition that $2 + 3$ is a prime number, but, considered as an abstract entity, it can hardly be a cause. *My belief* in the truth of the proposition, which, unlike the proposition itself, is something that occurs within a certain time span, can indeed be a cause, perhaps, of my saying that at least one prime number is the sum of two others. But the proposition itself is supposed to be timeless.

We do indeed speak of reasons for actions, and actions occur in a space-time frame. But it seems to me that when we speak of the reasons for someone's action, we are referring to certain propositions concerning the agent's wants, beliefs, or other attitudes that motivate his action. "What was his

---

A.6.2.475 n. 93), and he translated most of the *Theaetetus* into Latin. Portions of the following paragraphs are from the cited paper.

[38] At A.6.6.475 Leibniz says: "A reason is a known truth whose connection with some less well known truth leads us to give our assent to the latter. But it is called a 'reason', especially and par excellence, if it is the cause not only of our judgment but also of the truth itself—which makes it what is known as an 'a priori reason'. A *cause* in the realm of things corresponds to a *reason* in the realm of truths, which is why causes themselves—and especially final ones—are often called 'reasons'."

LH IV vii B 57–58 (Fasz. 1, #40, 137): "The cause is the thing the existence or mode of existence of which is the reason for the existence of another thing, called the effect." This might be interpreted to mean something like: x is the cause of y if and only if 'A exists' is a reason for 'B exists', where x falls under the individual concept A and y falls under the individual concept B.

G IV 422 (L 291): "A concept is obscure which does not suffice for recognizing the thing represented, as when . . . I consider some term which the Scholastics had defined poorly, such as Aristotle's entelechy, or cause [*causa*] as a common term for material, formal, efficient, and final cause, or other such terms of which we have no sure definition." Cf. Grua 269, PLR 65n. and 66.

reason for driving so fast?" "Because he wanted to avoid the five o'clock traffic." The reasons themselves, which are propositions, do not cause the actions; rather, it is the agent's attitude that has the causal efficacy. Likewise, as regards the motivating attitudes, their causes are one thing, and the reasons that would be given to justify them are another.

Of course, in giving reasons we may mention causes. Indeed, it can happen that the very sentence expressing (having as its sense) the reason can also refer to (have as denotation) a state of affairs that is the cause. If I support my claim that there will be an eclipse tomorrow, I shall probably give reasons in which reference is made to certain circumstances that will cause this occurrence. But the causes of the eclipse are still not to be confused with the reasons that may be adduced for the claim that an eclipse will take place.

The connection of all this with Why questions is evident.[39] When we ask a question of the form "Why is such and such the case?" we are asking in the first instance for a reason, not a cause. Strictly speaking, the answer would express a proposition and should not be a name or a description. (When we do accept a phrase like "because of his health" as an answer to "Why is he taking after-dinner walks?" such a phrase may be viewed as elliptical for a clause containing a sentence, "Because he wishes to be healthy.") The reason given may or may not refer to a cause, but it will not itself be a cause. If a question of the form "Why is such and such the case?" makes sense, then there must be a reason why such and such is the case, but it does not at all follow that there must be a cause. Yet that is just what Leibniz seems to be assuming.

Having been presumptuous enough to accuse Leibniz of confusing reasons and causes, I shall go the rest of the way and conjecture a train of thought that could have led him to this confusion.

Note first that, whether intentionally or by inadvertence, Leibniz does not respect the distinction, which many of us nowadays find so fundamental, between propositions and the objects they are "about." This is evident from various features of his analysis. For one thing, he applies the terms "true" and "false" indifferently to propositions (as expressed by sentences) and to individuals or classes (as denoted by names and descriptions). For another, he intends the substituends for the variables in formulas like "A is B" to include not only names of individuals and classes but also infinitive phrases ("for man to be an animal") that express propositions; thus, as we have seen, he analyzes 'If A is B, then C is D' as 'For A to be B is for C to be D', managing in this way to bring it under the general "A is B" form.[40] It is further clear that when he appends the phrase "is true" to individual and class names, he uses it to mean practically the same as "exists"; this suggests that he also considers the

---

[39] Leibniz himself points out the centrality of Why questions in connection with the principle of Sufficient Reason, which is in effect the statement that every Why question about the actual world has an answer. See the *Confessio Philosophi* 7r (Saame, 40). In his letter of March 1706 to Princess Sophie (*Correspondance de Leibniz*, ed. O. Klopp, Hanover, 1874, vols. 3, 172), Leibniz says: "Un des grandes principes dont je me sens, est celui qui porte que rien n'est sans raison, ou bien qu'il y a toujours *un pourquoi*" [Leibniz's emphasis].

[40] C 389 (P 78); cf. C 363 (P 54).

truth of propositions to consist in the existence of something, presumably a corresponding state of affairs.

The next step, I think, is to confuse a state of affairs with a complex object having the components of that state of affairs as parts. Thus one might suppose that to assert that the book is on the table is to assert the existence of the fact that the book is on the table, or that there *is* such a state of affairs; and one might then go on to identify this fact or state of affairs with a complex object consisting of the book and the table arranged in the requisite positions relative to each other and to the earth.

From this point of view, therefore, the sentence would be the name of an object having as parts the objects named by the parts of the sentence. Such a complex object could, of course, be a cause. Thus, a sentence that expresses (that is, has as its sense) a reason that there will be an eclipse of the sun tomorrow—for instance the sentence "Tomorrow the moon will come between the earth and the sun"—could be considered as denoting an object or a fact that will cause the eclipse.

If these are the lines along which Leibniz was thinking, then the error here, as in so many other philosophical tangles, is simply the failure to distinguish the sense of linguistic expressions—particularly, of sentences—from their denotation or reference. Even if we were to agree that a sentence expressing the reason why there will be an eclipse refers to or denotes a state of affairs that can plausibly be considered to cause the eclipse, we should not conclude that in this or any similar case a reason is the same as a cause. For although the cause may be the denotation of the sentence in question, the reason is its sense, the proposition that it expresses.

In sum, then, we can say that the principle of Sufficient Reason, interpreted as a claim about reasons, is, as Couturat has maintained, just a rather trivial corollary of the Predicate-in-Subject principle. But when it is interpreted as concerning causes, it amounts to the so-called law of universal causation. By confusing reasons and causes, Leibniz gets the odd result that if it makes sense to ask 'Why is A B'? there must be some cause for A's being B—for example, there must be a cause to explain why the laws of physics hold or why the sum of the angles of a triangle is 180 degrees or why something, rather than nothing, exists.

3. The Principle of Continuity

We have briefly considered this principle in chapter 8 in connection with the conditions for cross-world identity. There we were only interested in Leibniz's application of it to yield the conclusion that "there is no vacuum of forms." But he applies it in many other ways and in many other areas.

One of the best statements of the principle and of its significance for Leibniz is found in a letter he wrote to Bayle's *Nouvelles* as part of a controversy with Nicolas de Malebranche and the Abbé Catelan. Leibniz observes that certain of Malebranche's proposed physical laws violate a "Principle of General Order":

This principle has its origin in the *infinite* and is absolutely necessary in geometry, but it is effective in physics as well, because the sovereign wisdom, the source of all things, acts as a perfect geometrician, observing a harmony to which nothing can be added. This is why the principle serves me as a test or criterion by which to reveal the error of an ill-conceived opinion at once and from the outside, even before a penetrating internal examination has begun. It can be formulated as follows. "When the difference between two instances in a given series or that which is presupposed can be diminished until it becomes smaller than any given quantity whatever, the corresponding difference in what is sought or in their results must of necessity also be diminished or become less than any given quantity whatever." Or, to put it more commonly, "When two instances or data approach each other continuously, so that one at last passes over into the other, it is necessary for their consequences or results (or the unknown) to do so also." This depends on a more general principle, that "As the data are ordered, so the unknowns are ordered also" (*Datis ordinatis etiam quaesita sunt ordinata*).[41]

Elsewhere he compresses the principle into the maxim that "Nature never makes jumps,"[42] or "No transition happens by a leap."[43] "This holds," he says, "not only of transitions from place to place, but also of those from form to form or from state to state."[44] He adds that experience confutes all sudden changes; what pass for such are always found, on closer examination, to be merely changes that are greater or more rapid than the ordinary.[45] Besides, it is agreed on all hands that motion, transition from place to place, is continuous; the same a priori reasons, whatever they are, will apply to transitions from state to state.[46]

Leibniz's favorite examples to illustrate the application of his principle are from geometry and mechanics. The most frequently occurring geometrical example concerns the fact that the various conic sections can be continuously transformed into one another by gradually tilting the intersecting plane. Thus, if a right circular cone is cut by a plane parallel to its base, the intersection is, of course, a circle. If the plane is then gradually tilted, using a diameter of the circle as the axis, the intersection becomes an ellipse. As the tilting is increased and the plane approaches a position parallel to one of the elements of the cone, the ellipse (with its foci becoming farther and farther apart) approaches a parabola. When the plane becomes parallel, the intersection *is* a parabola. If the plane is tilted still farther in the same direction,

---

[41] G III 52 (L 351); cf. G VI 321 (H 333–34). Leibniz's manuscripts also contain a Latin version of this letter, which differs considerably from the French. In the Latin version the principle is stated as follows: When the particular cases or data continuously approach each other until at length one goes over into the other, then the same must happen in the corresponding consequences or results (or unknowns) (GM VI 129). He refers to this again at GM VI 250 (L 447) and at GM IV 93 (L 544).

[42] A.6.6.56; G VII 567; G I 403.

[43] G II 168 (L 515).

[44] G II 168 (L 516, R 222–23).

[45] G III 634 (L 658).   [46] G II 168 (L 516).

164   *The Philosophy of Leibniz*

the parabola becomes a hyperbola. Thus, the parabola can be regarded as a limiting case of the ellipse or of the hyperbola.

In view of this, Leibniz says, theorems about ellipses and hyperbolas can be carried over to parabolas. For example, an important theorem about the ellipse is that all the rays from either of its foci intersect, when reflected, at the other; thus, as the foci become more and more distant from one another, the reflected rays from either of them become closer and closer to parallel; at the limit, the reflected rays from the focus of the parabola *are* parallel. We therefore see, Leibniz says, that this fact about parabolas is only a corollary of the cited theorem about ellipses.[47]

The examples from mechanics are designed not only to illustrate the application of the principle but also, as he says in the passage quoted above, to show how it can be used "to reveal the error of an ill-conceived opinion at once and from the outside, even before a penetrating internal examination is begun." Descartes, in the second part of his *Principles of Philosophy*, had set forth several "rules" describing collisions of a pair of perfectly elastic (*perfecte dura*) bodies, B and C.[48] According to the first rule, if B and C are of equal mass and collide while moving in opposite directions at the same velocity, both will be repelled, with the velocities remaining the same but directions reversed. Leibniz has no quarrel with this. But the second rule says that if the conditions are the same except that the mass of B is greater than that of C, then after the collision B will continue in the same direction with the same velocity as before, while C alone will be deflected, moving now with its former velocity but in the opposite direction, so that B and C together will move in the original direction of B.

Leibniz argues that if these two rules were both true, there would be a discontinuity in nature. For as the mass of B is continuously decreased toward equality with that of C, the result of the collision should continuously approach that described in the first rule. But Descartes's second rule has B retaining the same velocity and direction after its collision with C, no matter how little B's mass exceeds that of C, until suddenly, when B and C are equal in mass, B's motion is completely reversed and it bounces off with undiminished velocity in the opposite direction. An adequate account, Leibniz insists, must provide that

if B is gradually diminished, its advance also will diminish continuously until, when a certain ratio is reached between B and C, B will at length come to rest and then, by a continuous diminution, be turned into contrary motion; this will gradually increase until finally, when all inequality between B and C is removed, the motions end in the rule for equality, in which the regressive motion of each body after collision is equal to its progressive motion before collision, as the first rule states.[49]

[47] GM VI 129–30; cf. G III 51–52 (L 352), G IV 375–76 (L 397–98).

[48] Descartes, *Principia Philosophiae*, Part 2, sections 46–52 (*Oeuvres*, ed. Adam and Tannery, Paris, 1964, vol. viii-2, 68–69).

[49] G IV 376–77 (L 398–99); cf. A.2.1.470. For a useful discussion of the principle, particularly in relation to this case, see Seager (1981), 485ff.

Another application of the principle in the domain of physical theory is Leibniz's use of it to rule out the existence of a vacuum.[50] Apparently he thought that an empty space would be the kind of "gap" or "leap" the principle excludes. We may mention parenthetically that he also argues for this conclusion on the basis of the Identity of Indiscernibles (as one empty space would be completely indiscernible from another)[51] and on that of the principle of the Best (as more is better, in the case of existence),[52] as well as on that of the principle of Sufficient Reason ("because there is no reason for limiting or ending, or for stopping at any particular place").[53] But underlying all of this bad reasoning, probably, was his feeling that the notion of action at a distance was a mere scholastic superstition, so that the undeniable fact of gravitational attraction must involve the presence of bodies between and surrounding the bodies attracted.[54]

The principle of Continuity is also cited against the existence of rigid atoms. Leibniz says:

> Matter, according to my hypothesis, would be divisible everywhere and more or less easily with a variation which would be insensible in passing from one place to another neighboring place; whereas, according to the atoms, we make a leap from one extreme to the other, and from a perfect incohesion, which is in the place of contact, we pass to an infinite hardness in all other places. And these leaps are without example in nature.[55]

In the field of psychology Leibniz uses the principle as support for his thesis that there are unconscious perceptions. "It asserts," he says, "that we pass always from the small to the large, and vice versa, through the intermediate magnitudes in degree and quantity; and that motion never arises immediately from rest nor is reduced to it except through a smaller motion. And all this leads us to conclude rightly that noticeable perceptions also come by degrees from those which are too minute to be noticed."[56]

As is only too obvious, none of these various formulations and purported applications of the principle of Continuity is quite clear. Instead of our having a good understanding of the principle and its alleged consequences, and of seeing just how the consequences follow from it, we have to use, as an aid to interpretation, the fact that Leibniz *thought* that such logical relationships obtained.

So, in view of all this, what are we to conclude about the meaning of the

---

[50] Jag 28 (L 157).

[51] G VII 372 (L 687).

[52] G VII 303–4 (L 487).

[53] G II 475 (L 608).

[54] At G VI 599 (L 637) Leibniz argues that plenitude, i.e., the nonexistence of a vacuum, implies that everything is connected and each body acts on every other, etc., and he says that from this it follows that "each monad is a living mirror, or a mirror endowed with an internal action, and that it represents the universe according to its point of view and is regulated as completely as is the universe itself."

[55] GM II 156 (R 235).

[56] A.6.6.56. At G III 635 (L 658) Leibniz uses the principle to argue against metempsychosis.

principle? Clearly, the terminology employed by Leibniz supports Couturat's opinion that the principle must have been suggested to him by his work on the infinitesimal calculus, where every function considered was assumed to be continuous and everywhere differentiable.[57] And the principle obviously reflects Leibniz's belief that whenever one physical quantity or state is a function of another, that function is continuous. (That is—roughly—for every argument x_0 in the range of significance of the function, the limit of the function values as their arguments approach x_0 is the function value for the argument x_0.) In the cases to which this aspect of the principle applies, Leibniz's reasoning is relatively clear.

Consider, for example, the quoted critique of Descartes's rules about collisions. The principle implies that if the body B's velocity depends on its mass, then by a suitably small change in B's mass its velocity can be made to increase or diminish by however small amount may be desired. Thus, if B will have a given velocity in the cases in which the masses are equal, that velocity can be increased or diminished however slightly one wishes by making a suitably small change in B's mass. In the geometrical example, the shape of the curve can be changed as slightly as one may wish (that is, by a finite amount within any preselected range) by making a suitably small change in the tilt angle of the intersecting plane. Since that angle can be altered gradually, there can be no "jumps" in the series of resulting curves.

But how the principle, as thus interpreted, yields the conclusions about the nonexistence of vacuums and indiscernible atoms, or the existence of petite perceptions or the continuity of forms, is less clear. As is all too often the case with Leibniz, we can see—perhaps "feel" is the more appropriate word—that he has an important idea, but neither he nor we can formulate it with anything like satisfactory precision.[58]

4. The Principle of the Best

Leibniz accepts the Socratic principle that nobody desires what he really considers to be bad for himself, or, more generally, that everyone desires only

---

[57] CL 235 n. 1.

[58] This is not to say that it is without content. Attempts to express the same idea continue to this day. Hermann Weyl (1956), 1833, writes: "In studying a function one should let the independent variable run over its full range. A conjecture about the mutual interdependence of quantities in nature, even before it is checked by experience, may be probed in thought by examining whether it carries through over the whole range of the independent variables. Sometimes certain simple *limiting cases* at once reveal that the conjecture is untenable. Leibniz taught us by his principle of Continuity to consider rest not as contradictorily opposed to motion, but as a limiting case of motion. Arguing by continuity he was able a priori to refute the laws of impact proposed by Descartes. Ernst Mach gives this prescription: 'After having reached an opinion for a special case, one gradually modifies the circumstances of this case as far as possible, and in so doing tries to stick to the original opinion as closely as one can. There is no procedure which leads more safely and with greater mental economy to the simplest interpretation of all natural events.'"

what he deems to be best.[59] Applying this to God, of whom it can be said that (1) if he deems something to be the best, then it *is* the best, and (2) if he desires that something happen, then it *does* happen, we infer that the actual world, which God created, is the best of all possible worlds.[60] This general principle, and sometimes the special case of its application to God's creation of the actual world, is called by Leibniz the principle of the Best.[61] Its importance, for him, has to do with the nature of explanation.

As we have seen in our discussion of the principle of Sufficient Reason, Leibniz observed that in many cases questions about the actual world require answers referring to what is best, or is thought to be best, rather than to mechanical causes. His doctrine on this point might be summarized as follows. There are at least four different categories of Why questions. (1) There are questions like "Why is the mine full of water?"—where the answer might be "Because there has been no wind to operate the pumps." In these the indicative form of the given interrogative is a contingent proposition describing a particular state or group of states of the actual world. In such cases one may properly answer by mentioning other states of the actual world—"other links in the chain," as Leibniz puts it—together with laws that characterize the ways in which the various states of the world are related to one another. (2) But one can also raise more general questions about why the world is so constructed that these laws obtain, for example, "Why do bodies attract one another with a force inversely proportional to the square of the distance between them?" or "Why is energy conserved?" Questions like these amount to questions of why this world, instead of one of the infinitely many other possible worlds, exists; and such questions, according to Leibniz, are only answerable by reference to God's having chosen this world above all of the others on the basis of his knowledge of what is best. Nor do all questions in this second category concern general physical laws. Also included would be questions as to why a particular monad exists, for in effect these too ask why the actual world rather than some other possible world was chosen for existence.[62] Thus, the most general and the most particular contingent facts are explicable only by reference to what is best. (3) Why questions can also be raised with respect to necessary truths. If we ask "Why?" with respect to an assertion like "The square root of 2 is irrational," an appropriate answer

---

[59] G VII 389 (L 696); G VI 128 (H 148). LH IV iii C 12–14 (Fasz. 2, #85, 305): If the necessity of choosing the best destroyed freedom, it would follow that neither God, the angels, the saints, nor we ourselves act freely, for in acting we are determined by the greater good, real or apparent.

[60] Grua 493: "This is the best [possible world]" is a contingent truth. Cf. Grua 336, 351. At Grua 311 Leibniz says that God is necessarily he who wills the best, but God is not he who necessarily wills the best.

[61] G I 328 (L 209–10): "God acts in the most perfect manner possible." L 218: "God made everything in the greatest perfection of which the universe is capable." G IV 428–29 (L 304–5): God could not have made things better. G IV 438 (L 311): "God assuredly always chooses the best." G II 581 (L 664): "God has chosen the best possible plan." A.6.1.86, 30; Grua 253, 297, 299, 414; A.6.6.179.

[62] G VII 390 (L 697): "A contingent which exists owes its existence to the principle of what is best, which is a sufficient reason for the existence of things."

would be a proof of that assertion. (4) But if we ask a Why question with respect to a mere identity like "Why are all black cats black?"—there is no answer. Here, he says, we hit rock bottom with the giving of explanations.[63]

Thus, Leibniz believes that many meaningful and important questions about the actual world require answers that refer to what is best. Indeed, he occasionally implies that even some of the questions in category (1) require such answers. Thus, as we have mentioned before, he agrees that any reasonable answer to the question "Why is Socrates sitting here in prison and not running away?"[64] must make reference to what has seemed best to Socrates and to the Athenians who condemned him. Therefore, when Leibniz says that "the particular events of nature can and ought to be explained mechanically, though without forgetting their ends and uses,"[65] the qualification must not be overlooked. Indeed, if he does agree fully with Socrates, he must concede that there are cases in which mechanical explanations of "particular events of nature" are entirely inappropriate.[66]

When "the principle of the Best" refers to God's actualization of the best, or most perfect, of the possible worlds, the term "best" is frequently explained as meaning "simplest in hypotheses and richest in phenomena."[67] Leibniz insists, against some unspecified opponents whom he characterizes as "the new Scholastics," that the standard of goodness must be objective and absolute, independent of God's will. For if whatever God did would have been *eo ipso* good, as the opponents held, God would not be praiseworthy for having chosen the best.[68] Thus, in creating the actual world, God's task was to maximize its variety while minimizing the complexity of its laws. In view of this, when explaining natural phenomena, the scientist should give preference to the simplest hypotheses, for they are the ones most likely to be true.

---

[63] Cf. Leibniz's 1671 letter to Wedderkopf (A.2.1.117–18), also published—and with better punctuation—in Trendelenburg (1855), 2, 189 ff.: "...Behold! Pilate is damned. Why? Because he lacks faith. Why does he lack faith? Because he previously lacked the will to attend. Why that? Because he did not understand the urgency of the matter, or the advantage of attending. He did not understand because the causes of understanding were not there. For it is necessary that everything be ascribed to some reason, nor can we stop until we have reached the *prima*.... What, therefore, is the ultimate reason for the divine will? The divine intellect. For God wills what is best; he understands which things are maximally harmonious and selects them, as it were, from the infinitely many possibles. What, then, is the reason for the divine intellect? The harmony of things. What is that for the harmony of things? There is none. For example, no reason can be given why 2 is to 4 as 4 is to 8, not even the divine will. For this depends upon the essence itself, or the idea, of the things...."

[64] *Phaedo* 97c ff.

[65] G III 55 (L 353).

[66] Cf. G VII 419 (L 716): "All the natural forces of bodies are subject to mechanical laws, and all the natural powers of spirits are subject to moral laws. The former follow the order of efficient causes, and the latter follow the order of final causes. The former operate without liberty, like a watch; the latter operate with liberty, though they exactly agree with that machine which another cause, free and superior, has adapted to them beforehand." So perhaps Leibniz would say that insofar as the question concerns Socrates' *soul*, it is to be answered in the manner that Socrates suggests, while if it concerns his *body*, a mechanical explanation is called for.

[67] G IV 431 (L 306); cf. G VI 241, 603 (L 639).

[68] G IV 428–29 (L 304–5).

Concerning the perfection of monads, as contrasted with that of bodies and other phenomena, Leibniz tells us that it is proportional to the distinctness of the given monad's perceptions, and that a monad does not have knowledge of what it perceives unless the perception is distinct.[69] One would therefore suppose that the most perfect world would be one in which every individual clearly perceived (and thus had perfect knowledge of) every other individual.[70] Leibniz never explains why such a world is impossible, nor does he explain why a world consisting of relatively perfect monads would be a world that was "simplest in hypotheses and richest in phenomena."

When it comes to applications of the principle, we find very few. Usually it is only mentioned (instead of being used), and this occurs in metatheoretic comments to the effect that it is the only possible reason for the truth of such and such contingent proposition. Socrates had expected that Anaxagoras would explain among other things, why it is better that the planets follow the orbits they do, and he was greatly disappointed when Anaxagoras merely invoked the same kinds of mechanical causes he had heard about elsewhere. He would have been equally disappointed in Leibniz, who argued that the planets follow their courses because they are carried along in a vortex of surrounding (though invisible) matter.[71]

I have been able to find only one text in which Leibniz attempts to justify particular physical laws on the basis of the principle of the Best. That is the paper entitled *Tentamen anagogicum* (An anagogical essay in the investigation of causes).[72] There he tries to prove various laws of catoptrics and dioptrics, for example, that the angles of incidence and reflection for a reflected ray of light are equal, by using as a general principle that a ray of light moves from one point to another by the easiest (with respect to time) and the simplest (having no "twin") path. The proofs are very obscure, far inferior to the clear reasoning of his mentor Huygens on the same subject.

---

[69] G VI 604 (L 640); cf. G II 451 (L 605): ". . . in the monads themselves, domination and subordination consist only in degrees of perfection."

[70] Our model in chap. 4 shows that a perfect mirroring of all monads by all monads would not necessarily destroy their individuality.

[71] GM II 141–42 (L 414–15); L 217.

[72] G VII 270–79 (L 477–84). For an explanation of the term "anagogical" see L 484 n. 2.

□□□□□□□□□□□□□□□□□□□□□□□□□□□□□□□□□□□□□□

X

Leibniz's Nominalism and the *Lingua Philosophica*

A very important aspect of Leibniz's metaphysics—and one that has too often been neglected by expositors and interpreters—is his tendency toward nominalism. There can be little doubt that he was a nominalist—certainly in the earlier portion of his philosophical career, and, in my opinion, in the later as well.[1] This does not mean, of course, that he was a nominalist in every sense in which that term has been used by historians of philosophy. Nor does it mean that he was a nominalist in the sense in which *he* used the term (though he tells us that, with reservations, this was indeed the case). Rather, the sense of "nominalist" I have in mind here is the sense it bears in current Anglo-American philosophical discussion about so-called ontological commitment.[2] According to this, a nominalist, as contrasted with a Platonist, is one who denies that there are abstract entities, asserts that only concrete individuals exist, and in consequence considers that all meaningful statements appearing to be about abstract entities must somehow be rephraseable as statements more clearly concerning concrete individuals only.[3] Properly speaking, "concrete" and "abstract" refer to terms or concepts, not to elements of reality. Concrete terms are those under which individuals fall,

---

[1] Thus, I agree on this with Gottfried Martin (cf. Martin 1967, 141). It is sometimes held that Leibniz started out as a nominalist and later found himself forced toward realism. C. S. Peirce (*The Nation* 68 [1889]: 210) was an early proponent of this view. But I can find no evidence that clearly supports it.

[2] Cf. Quine (1961), 9ff., 117–18, 128–29; Quine (1960), 233ff.

[3] Burkhardt, who strenuously objects to calling Leibniz a nominalist, describes the position as "ontological individuation," the doctrine that there are only individuals. This seems indistinguishable from what I am calling "nominalism," unless it accepts the existence of what Leibniz calls *abstracta singularia*. Cf. Burk 333 and Burkhardt (1974), 59ff. Cf. also LH IV i 9 1–17, as edited by Jolley, SL 7 (1975), 161ff., especially p. 183.

such as "man" or "Caesar," while abstract terms are those like "humanity" or "heat."[4]

Note that a nominalist is perfectly well entitled to use abstract terminology, provided that he has a way of eliminating it in favor of the concrete; consequently, from the fact that a philosopher uses abstract terms it does not follow that he is not a nominalist. Lack of attention to this has given rise to a considerable amount of futile argument among historians of philosophy, including commentators on Leibniz.

It is true that Leibniz seldom emphasized this feature of his philosophy, especially in his later years. Perhaps this can be explained by the fact that nominalism was not a popular doctrine, and, although Leibniz was not the intellectual coward that Russell makes him out to be, he also did not go out of his way to dispute received opinions.[5] Be that as it may, much of his philosophical activity and many of his doctrines become more understandable when one keeps in mind that he did not believe in the existence of abstract entities of any sort.

1. That Only Individual Substances Exist

One of the few explicit statements of Leibniz's nominalism is found in a draft entitled *De accidentibus*, for which Grua conjectures the date of 1688. After wrestling with issues related to the question whether the accidents of substances should themselves be considered parts of reality, Leibniz concludes (in a rather deliberative vein):

> Up to now I see no other way of avoiding these difficulties than by considering abstracta not as real things [*res*] but as abbreviated ways of talking [*compendia loquendi*]—so that when I use the name *heat* it is not required that I should be making mention of some vague subject but rather that I should be saying that something is hot—and to that extent I am a nominalist, at least provisionally. . . . There is no need to raise the issue whether there are various realities in a substance that are the fundaments of its various predicates (though, indeed, if it *is* raised, adjudication is difficult). It suffices to posit only substances as real things [*res*] and to assert truths about these. Geometricians, too, do not use definitions of abstracta but reduce them to concreta; thus Euclid does not use his own definition of *ratio* but rather that in which he states when two quantities are said to have the same, greater or lesser ratio.[6]

---

[4] LH IV vii C 101 (Fasz. 1, #57, 181–83).

[5] Thus, he once wrote: "Metaphysics should be written with accurate definitions and demonstrations, *but nothing should be demonstrated in it that conflicts too much with received opinions*. Thus this metaphysics will be able to be received *if it is once approved*; then afterward, if any examine it more profoundly, they will hold the consequences to be necessary" (Lestienne [1962], 14 n. 1 [emphasis Leibniz's]; cf. Adams [1982], 283 n. 64).

[6] Grua 547. Cf. A.6.6.217 and Mugnai (1976), 133ff. At G IV 433 (L 307) an accident is defined as "a being whose concept does not include everything that can be attributed to the subject to which the concept is attributed." At A.6.6.333 accidents are spoken of as "beings added to a substance." But compare G II 458: Every accident is a kind of abstraction; only substances are concrete. (For the ambiguity of "accident," see chap. 11, sec. 2.)

Regarding Leibniz's use of the expression *compendium loquendi*, cf. G II 305: It is therefore

In addition to this relatively definite statement we have Leibniz's well-known and very favorable remarks about medieval nominalism. In the preface to his edition of Nizolius he declares that the nominalists were the most profound of all the Scholastic sects, and that their approach to philosophy is the one most agreeable with what he calls "the present-day reformed way of philosophizing." He has high praise for William of Ockham, whom he explicitly classifies as a nominalist, and for Thomas Hobbes, whom he dubs a "supernominalist."[7] Although he does dispute Hobbes's contention that what is true and what is not true depends only on the human will (because the assignment of names to things is arbitrary), he makes it plain that he does not regard this erroneous view as part of nominalism but rather as something that Hobbes has added.[8]

Speaking for himself in the same preface, Leibniz says, "'It appears certain that the passion for devising abstract words has almost entirely obfuscated philosophy for us; we can well enough dispense completely with this procedure in our philosophizing. For concreta are really things [*vere res sunt*]; abstractions are not things but modes of things."[9] To this he adds: "Therefore, if anyone wishes to give a perfect exposition of the elements of philosophy, he must abstain from abstract terms almost entirely."[10]

A little farther on in the same preface Leibniz takes regretful note of the fact that even Hobbes felt obliged to admit some usefulness for abstract

---

a *loquendi compendium* when we speak of one [whole], where there are more things than can be assigned to any one whole, and we treat as a magnitude what does not have the properties of such.... *Philosophice loquendo*, I do not speak of infinitely small magnitudes any more than of infinitely large, nor more of infinitesimals than of infinituples. For I treat them all *per modum loquendi compendiosum* for fictions of the mind, useful for calculation, like imaginary roots in algebra.

[7] G IV 148 (L 127ff.). Burk (410–11) classifies Ockham as a *psychologistischer Konzeptualist*. Cf. Boehner in Ockham (1957), xi: "It seems justifiable to consider Ockham as the central figure of a new movement, known as the school of the nominalists, the *schola* or *via nominalium*."

[8] G IV 148 (L 127ff.); cf. A.2.1.227–28. At A.6.2.429 n. 3 he notes that, as in arithmetic, true propositions remain true when the notation is changed.

Couturat (CL 468ff.) says that Leibniz rejected not only the nominalism of Hobbes but also nominalism "pure and simple, such as that put forward by Nizolius." He then proceeds to interpret Leibniz's critique of Nizolius's crude reductions—e.g., the suggestion that "sheep" means the totality of all sheep, considered as a huge, widely distributed herd—as evidence that Leibniz rejected nominalism. Couturat's further discussion shows that he uses "nominalist" in such a sense that a nominalist cannot agree that there are necessary truths. He does not seem to realize that a nominalist can accept *any* forms of words as *compendia loquendi* for expressions not implying the existence of abstract entities.

[9] G IV 147 (L 126); cf. A.6.6.217. LH IV vii B 3 40–49 (Fasz. 2, #97, 357): ... *nam si humanitas est res aliqua, utique intelligi potest essentiam eius ab ipsa re esse distinctam, et habebimus si ita fingere placet quandam* humanitalitatem; *et hoc ibit in infinitum. Unde scholasticorum tricae circa abstracta.*

[10] G IV 147; cf. S 472. C 243: *In lingua rationali videndum an non abstractis absinteri possit, aut saltem quousque possit.* LH IV vii C 101 (Fasz. 1, #57, 182): "If the heat is a different entity from the hot object, humanity will also be a different entity from the man, but humanity is neither a substance nor an accident. To avoid this sort of nonsense it is better to abstain regularly from abstracta, or at least to reduce [or return] the subject afterwards to concreta."

terms. Hobbes based this on the observation that, for example, it is one thing to double what is hot but another to double the heat. Leibniz replies that the doubling of heat can perfectly well be expressed by means of concrete terms exclusively—for example, by saying that the thing has been made twice as hot as it was.[11]

Elsewhere, again using his favorite example of "heat" and "hot," he makes the point that if abstractions are admitted, we shall also have to admit, on the same basis, abstractions of abstractions, and so on, ad infinitum: "It is well here to get rid of abstract concepts, since they are not necessary, and especially since there would result abstractions of abstractions. Thus in place of 'heat' we shall consider 'hot'; for otherwise one could next invent a 'heatness,' and so on, ad infinitum."[12]

In the *New Essays* and elsewhere Leibniz makes the additional points that "indeed, knowledge of concrete things is always prior to that of abstract ones—hot things are better known than heat,"[13] and "scientific knowledge is not about universals, but about particulars, even possibles."[14]

From all of this, together with many other obiter dicta to the same effect, it is clear enough that Leibniz would agree wholeheartedly with that notorious pronouncement of present-day nominalism: "We do not believe in abstract entities."[15] He does not believe in numbers, geometric figures, or other mathematical entities,[16] nor does he accept abstractions like heat, light, justice, goodness, beauty, space or time, nor again does he allow any reality to metaphysical paraphernalia such as concepts, propositions, properties, possible objects, and so on. The only entities in his ontology are individuals-cum-accidents, and sometimes he even has his doubts about the accidents.[17]

[11] G IV 147; cf. C 390. A.6.6.179: attributing power to heat or to other qualities is to attribute it to bodies insofar as they have the qualities.

[12] C 512–13. Cf. n. 9 above and G IV 147 (L 126). At SL VII (1975, 187) he puns that if we go this route with the term *ens*, we shall be multipyling entities beyond necessity, proceding from *ens* to *entitas* to *entitatitas*, and so on, in infinitum.

[13] A.6.6.145.

[14] A.6.2.461 n. 49. At A.6.2.448 n. 8 Leibniz says that when *omnis* is applied to a singular noun, e.g., to the noun *homo*, the proposition is "figurative"; the "figurative" *omnis homo est animal* is synonymous with the "proper" *omnes homines sunt animalia*. "Thus," he says, "the supposition that universals, in addition to singulars, are real arises from language."

[15] N. Goodman and W. V. Quine, "Steps toward a Constructive Nominalism," *Journal of Symbolic Logic* 12 (1947), 105–22. At C 437 Leibniz says ". . . *abstracta sunt entia* . . .", and he does the same at LH IV iii C 85r and elsewhere; this means only, I think, that abstract terms are not nonsense, and it does not imply that abstracts exist (or subsist).

[16] C 8; G II 101. G IV 491: A number, e.g., 1/2, is only a relation. G IV 569 (L 583–84): "However, mathematicians do not need all these metaphysical discussions, nor need they embarrass themselves about the real existence of points, indivisibles, infinitesimals, and infinites in any rigorous sense. In my reply I pointed this out, and in the same year I suggested that the mathematicians' demand for rigor in their demonstrations will be satisfied if we assume, instead of infinitely small sizes, sizes as small as are needed to show that the error is less than that which any opponent can assign, and consequently that no error can be assigned at all."

[17] A.6.6.217. G V 132: There are only substances and their modes or modifications (qualities); to these the understanding adds relation. SL VII (1975), 189: *Sic substantia universalis, seu Homo in genere non Res est sed Terminus. Homo qui universalis sit non datur, itaque abstinere philosophi possent multis quaestionibus inanibus, et parcere chartae, vel potius tempori lectoris et suo.* G II 101 (M 126–27): "Our mind notices . . . relationships." LH IV vii C

2. Nominalistic Rephrasings

Unfortunately, Leibniz does not give us any general instructions for eliminating from our discourse the abstract terms that, according to him, contri-
bute so much to obfuscation in philosophy.[18] If meaningful sentences
containing such words are only *compendia loquendi* for sentences plainly
referring only to individuals, there should be some way of retrieving the
unabbreviated versions, so that just what we are talking about will be clearer.
Leibniz does deal with a few particular cases, and he provides hints as to how
certain other classes of cases could be handled. Thus, as we have mentioned,
in his comment on Hobbes he indicates that such a statement as

The heat of x has been doubled

is a *compendium loquendi* for

x is twice as hot as it was.

For

The duration of x is eternal,

he offers

x lasts eternally.[19]

In another place he suggests in effect that occurrences of the abstract term
"animality" (*animalitas*) can be eliminated in favor of the predicate "x is an
animal" (tò *aliquid esse animal*).[20]

But more interesting, perhaps, are his attempts to eliminate not only
abstract terms like "animality" and "heat," but also various general nouns,
adjectives, and verbs that Platonists have regarded as standing for universals.
Thus, he proposes to get rid of "man" in "Man is an animal" or "Every man is
an animal" by using instead "All men are animals," which gives the metaphysical semanticist less excuse for postulating a universal Man, or by using
"If somebody is a man, then he is an animal," which, with the general terms

---

73–74 (Fasz. 2, #103, 406): *Ens omne singulare seu individuum est, sed Termini sunt vel
singulares vel universales. . . .*

   [18] As we have mentioned earlier, he does, however, criticize some crude reductions by
'Nizolius. Nizolius first proposes to analyze *omnis homo est animal* into *omnes homines sunt
animalia*. With this, Leibniz has no quarrel. But then Nizolius takes *omnis homo* and *omnes
homines* to stand for the aggregate of all men. Leibniz notes that this sort of analysis would lead
to the absurdities that the aggregate of men is an animal and that every man is the whole aggregate of animals. Instead, he says, *omnes homines sunt animalia* just means that if you take Titius
or Caius or any other man, you will find that he is an animal. Note well that Leibniz corrects
Nizolius in this nominalistic way, rather than by asserting that *omnis homo est animal* is about
the concept Man. A.6.2.430–31.
   [19] G VII 403 (L 705).
   [20] C 389 #139 (P 78).

occurring only as parts of the predicates, is plainly about individuals and not about manhood.[21]

There are also some interesting analyses in which number words (remember that he denies the existence of numbers) are eliminated. The statement

Peter and Paul are two apostles,

which might appear to be about the number two as well as about Peter and Paul, is in effect analyzed as

Peter is an apostle and Paul is an apostle and it is not the case that Peter is Paul and Paul is Peter.[22]

Further examples of the elimination of these sorts of expressions will be given in the next section and in chapter 12.

Assertions like

The concept of Adam contains everything that can be attributed to him,

which contain Leibniz's own fundamental metaphysical terminology of concepts, propositions, properties, ideas, and the like, might seem more recalcitrant. But a method of treating these will appear if we bear in mind three points. First, it must be noted that ideas, for Leibniz, are only dispositions of minds to think in certain ways; an idea of a thing is a disposition or a capacity to think of that thing.[23] I interpret this to mean, or at least to imply, that statements which seem to be about certain ephemeral entities called "ideas" can in principle be rephrased to make it clear that they are only about states of individual monads. Leibniz makes the point—by no means original with him—that having an idea at a given time does not require having an actual thought at that time but only a disposition to think in a certain way if requisite conditions obtain. Thus, to use an ancient example, the man who is asleep nevertheless has an idea of justice, because when awake and the topic is raised, he can consider whether some action is just or unjust. Hence, for Leibniz, to say that this or that idea is in somebody's mind is not to say that his mind is a kind of receptacle containing entities having an ontological status different from that of individuals like you and me, but only to say that among the attributes of the person in question is the disposition to think in a certain way.

The second point is that the concepts to which Leibniz refers are highly idealized. When he says that the concept of Adam contains everything that can be attributed to him, he is obviously not referring to your concept of Adam or to my concept of Adam, which are bound to be incomplete and in some respects vague and confused. Rather, he is referring to the concept of Adam that would be held by a mind not limited by the various weaknesses

---

21 A.6.2.448 n. 6, 451 n. 18, 472 n. 86.
22 C 239–40 (P 36).
23 See chap. 3, n. 9.

that affect us mortals; in short, he is referring to God's concept of Adam.[24] This sort of idealization, I believe, applies not only to complete individual concepts but also to their less-complete components, for presumably God's perfect concept of Adam is made up of perfect component concepts of Rational, Animal, and First, etc. Propositions, as compound concepts, are also idealized. The truth that Adam was the first man is not your thought or my thought to that effect, for these again are contaminated by the vagueness and confusion in our concepts of Adam and the other elements involved.[25] It is rather to be identified with God's thought.

Third, it appears that all the denizens of Leibniz's "region of ideas" are themselves only concepts or compounds or series of concepts. No example is ever given of an idea that is clearly not a concept. Properties, attributes, notions, and terms (subjects and predicates, general and singular) are, all of them, concepts. Possible worlds are congeries of complete individual concepts, and even propositions, as we have been noting, are considered by Leibniz as combinations of concepts and as concepts themselves. Therefore, if there is a way of translating talk about concepts into talk about concrete individuals, it will apply to all of these other items, too.

With these points in mind one can make a plausible conjecture, at least in a general way, as to how statements about the Ideal world could be treated nominalistically. God is the individual substance par excellence. Like any other monad, he is characterized by various individual accidents that are the foundation of the truth of what is said about him. By virtue of some of these accidents we can say truly that he has certain capacities, that he could have created a world with such and such features. Thus, he could have created a world in which there was no sin, though he didn't.[26] Now this fact might be rephrased as "there is a no-sin possible world that God could have made actual," but the ontological commitment in the rephrasal would be only apparent. A cabinetmaker who is about to make a table can make it in any one of an infinite number of shapes and sizes; but if we describe this situation by saying "there are infinitely many possible tables, any one of which our cabinetmaker can bring into existence," we must not take too literally what

---

[24] Among the many passages in which this is made clear, the following are typical. G II 131: "Can it be denied that everything (whether genus, species, or individual) has a complete notion, according to which it is conceived by God, who conceives everything perfect? . . ." G VII 310: God's mind is the region of ideas and truths. LH IV vii C 108v: *Idea est conceptus in mentis agentis*. Jág 6: Only God has a complete idea of *circle*; we do not.

[25] Cf. G IV 422 (L 290).

[26] G VI 108. See also chap. 4, n. 3. Of course, there is the difficulty, with which Leibniz contended through most of his philosophical life, that he wants also to say that God's nature is to will only the best. Cf. Adams (1982), 247ff. Even if this world is the best, however, it would not follow that God couldn't have created any world other than this, for "could" and "will" generate oblique contexts. In saying (G VI 216, H 233), apropos this problem, that the objects of will must not be confused with the objects of power, was Leibniz in effect rejecting *willing* as one of the things we can or cannot do? He says somewhere that we don't desire to will what we shall will, but to will the best.

Cf. the discussion in Adams (1982), 255ff., regarding "this = the best" as contingent; Grua 351, 305ff., 336, 493. Adams thinks that what is involved is the scope of the descriptive phrase.

we have said. It is only a rather fancy way of saying that the cabinetmaker has a certain capacity. Its truth value is completely determined by the properties of the cabinetmaker. Similarly, Leibniz's often-repeated statement that the actual world is only one of infinitely many possible worlds, which appears to commit him to an elaborate ontology of abstract entities, need only be understood as a statement about the capacity of a single individual substance, namely, God, to act in various ways.[27]

The same approach would seem to work for concepts generally. For example, the claim that Adam's concept contains everything that can be predicated of him could be reduced to the assertion that God, in considering whether to create Adam, was aware of all that would happen to him; it is, again, a statement about God.[28] That Adam is an object falling under the concept Man means, perhaps, that in deciding to create Adam, God *eo ipso* decided to create a man.[29] For another example, to say that the proposition that Adam is the first man involves the concept of Adam is to say that in order for God to consider whether to make the first man Adam, he had to consider Adam. And so on.

I am not really concerned with these conjectural reductions in detail, much less ascribing them to Leibniz. They are only suggestions as to how he could have proceeded. But I do hold that when he tells us that possible worlds, concepts, and propositions exist only in "the region of ideas" or in "the mind of God,"[30] what he intends is not that there are two kinds of existence, namely, in the mind of God and out of the mind of God, but rather that statements purporting to be about these kinds of entities are only *compendia loquendi* for statements about God's capacities, intentions, and decrees.

It must be granted that in some of the passages in which Leibniz explicitly discusses or implicitly indicates the sort of ontology to which he subscribes, he writes as though there were two basically different realms or domains of being, namely, the Real and the Ideal. This has tempted expositors to suppose

---

[27] Or, perhaps, God's capacity to think in certain ways. At G VII 263 (L 207) we learn that an idea of a thing is a disposition or a capacity to think of that thing; at G VI 253 the possible worlds are described as "plans"; at G II 51 (M 57) Leibniz speaks of the infinite number of possible "ways of creating the world according to the different plans that God could form." At G IV 556 (L 575) possible worlds are "in God's mind." At G VII 190 Leibniz almost gives a nominalistic analysis of assertions to the effect that a proposition or thought *P* is true. Noting that possible, not necessarily actual, thoughts are concerned, he offers essentially the following: if anyone should think in this way, he would think truly.

[28] LH IV vii C 111–14 (Fasz. 2, #107, 417): "When God conceived the substance of Peter, he *eo ipso* conceived everything that has happened or will happen to him." Grua 311: For God to have a complete concept of possible Peter is for him to know completely what would be true of Peter if he existed.

[29] Or, that the proposition "Adam is a man" is a truth, i.e., that it exists in God's intelligence, or, in other words, simply that God knows that Adam is a man.

[30] G VII 305 (L 488), 311; G VI 614–16, sections 43 and 53 (L 647–48); cf. G VI 362–63 and A.6.6.447. A.6.6.87: Truths are dispositions to think. G VI 440: "The very possibility of things that do not actually exist has its reality founded on the divine existence, for if God did not exist, nothing would be possible." Cf. G VI 226–27, Grua 393. The statements that possible worlds "have their reality in the mind of God" I interpret to mean that the objective counterparts of propositions about possible worlds are states of the individual substance that is God.

that he is one of those philosophers who think that existence comes in several varieties, often described with the help of the treacherous little word "as" (Latin *qua*). Thus, one hears that although Hamlet does not exist as a real, flesh-and-blood person, he does exist as a character in Shakespeare's play or he does exist as a figment of someone's imagination. Or, reaching gratefully for the word "subsist," proponents of this point of view sometimes will tell you that although Pegasus, Hamlet, & Co. do not exist, they subsist (which is supposed to be less ephemeral than not being around at all).

I think it clear that Leibniz does not subscribe to any of this. He does not think that there really is anything other than reality. There are indeed intelligible statements that give the appearance of being about things other than the Real, but they must be understood as rephraseable into statements in which it is clear and explicit that what is being spoken about is some part of reality.[31] Leibniz agrees with Berkeley's dictum that one should "think with the learned but speak with the vulgar"; and so, although on occasion he finds it convenient to express himself as though there were a "region of ideas" in addition to the actual world of individual substances, his serious view is that there is only one domain, namely, the Real.

3. Nominalism and the Reform of Language

This nominalistic metaphysics provides the basis and motivation for much of what Leibniz says about language. If the real world consists exclusively of individual substances-with-accidents, it is natural to suppose that it could in principle be completely described by a set of propositions of '*A* is$_t$ *B*' form, where *A* is the complete individual concept of a given substance, and *B* is a concept under which the substance falls at time *t* by virtue of one or more of its accidents. Further truths could be generated from these by making "reflexive" propositions about them. Thus, passing from propositions to sentences, one might suppose that whatever can be said at all, at least in the indicative or descriptive mode, could be said by means of a language in which all declarative sentences were obtained by the above-mentioned means from a core of atomic sentences of the form '*A* is$_t$ *B*', where *A* expresses a complete individual concept and *B* expresses a concept under which individuals can fall. In such a language, Leibniz appears to have thought, all inferences would be purely formal; the unwieldiness could be remedied by introducing abbreviations, *compendia loquendi*.

Leibniz regarded the natural languages as very far from satisfying this sort of ideal.[32] Not only was he bothered by such obvious features as their vagueness and ambiguity of vocabulary and irregularity of syntax, but he con-

---

[31] Thus, sometimes Leibniz makes statements in the material mode that, if they were properly put into the formal mode, would be seen to be statements about reduction. E.g., when he says (G IV 559, L 577–78) that aggregates of substances are only "results," he is best understood as saying that any statement about such an aggregate is reducible to statements about its components.

[32] Leibniz's studies of natural languages were very extensive and no doubt affected his con-

sidered them encumbered by all sorts of unnecessary complications. For example, he believed it possible to get along in Latin without any of the oblique cases, and he found all differences of gender, number, tense, person, and mood equally superfluous.[33] As empirical evidence for this hypothesis he occasionally mentions a certain Dominican priest from Persia, whom he had met in Paris and who spoke with great fluency a broken Latin in which such differences were entirely neglected. Nevertheless, Leibniz says, there was no difficulty in understanding him.[34] Obviously his point is that many of the grammatical features of natural languages are inessential to their functioning and could be dropped without loss if we set out to simplify and rationalize such languages. Leibniz reinforces this point by taking note of several artificially simplified languages that had actually been constructed in his day on the basis of Italian, French, German, and Latin, and that were being successfully used.[35]

In line with such ideas we find in the *Nachlass* a large number of notes and jottings in which Leibniz seems to be trying to reduce particular Latin sentences to combinations of '*A* is *B*' sentences in which nouns and adjectives appear in the nominative case only.[36] A sampling of such entries follows.

Titius is wiser than Caius, that is, Titius is wise, and qua wise is superior insofar as Caius qua wise is inferior.[37]

Caius is slain by Titius, that is, in the respect in which Titius is a slayer, in that respect Caius is slain.[38]

The Ethiopian is white of teeth, that is, the Ethiopian is white in that the teeth, which are parts insofar as the Ethiopian is a whole, are white.[39]

Paris is Helen's lover, that is, Paris loves and *eo ipso* Helen is loved.[40]

Peter writes beautifully, that is, Peter writes something beautiful (or Peter writes, and what Peter writes is beautiful).[41]

---

ception of what an ideal language would be like. Heinekamp (1972) provides a detailed account of this subject.

[33] C 286 (P 13); cf. C 244 (P 13), 287 (P 14–15), 290 (P 16), 353, 357. C 281–82: All verbs may be eliminated in favor of the single verb *est*. C 433: The distinction between substantive and adjective is dispensable. A.6.2.486: Every oblique case of a noun can be resolved into the nominative [but Leibniz uses oblique cases of relative pronouns in order to do it]. LH IV vii B 40–49 (Fasz. 2, #97, 376): Declension of adjectives is unnecessary in view of the fact that the substantives are declined; similarly, there is no need for number in the verb, for the noun shows this sufficiently. Likewise, it is unnecessary for verbs to indicate person, when we have the pronouns "I," "you," "he," etc.

[34] C 286 (P 13); A.6.6.279; CL 59 n. 2.

[35] A.6.6.278.

[36] Cf. C 357. C 35: all propositions are analyzable into combinations of the particles *est*, *et*, *non*, etc., and nouns in the nominative case.

[37] C 280.

[38] LH IV vii B iii 60r.

[39] Cf. Jungius, *Logica Hamburgensis*, 92.17. The white-toothed Ethiopian first appears at Aristotle *De Soph. El.* 167a10–13.

[40] C 287.

[41] C 244.

Peter stands handsomely, that is, Peter is handsome insofar as he is standing.[42]

Men are writing, that is, Titius is writing, Caius is writing, Titius is a man, Caius is a man.[43]

Peter is similar to Paul . . . is reduced to the propositions Peter is A now and Paul is A now.[44]

Evander's sword, that is, the sword that is property insofar as Evander is owner.[45]

Now property is what is acted upon insofar as somebody acts and insofar as he is just. Thus, when everything is reduced to the nominative, we have: The sword is Evander's, that is, if the sword is acted upon when Evander acts, Evander is to that extent just, or if the sword is acted upon insofar as Evander acts, then in that respect Evander is just.[46]

Evander's sword is excellent, that is, the sword is excellent which, if it is acted upon because Evander acts, Evander is not therefore unjust.[47]

This villa is at a distance of one mile (literally, a thousand paces) from the city, that is, this villa is a terminus insofar as the city is a terminus and insofar as the path between is terminated and is a whole insofar as its thousandth part is a pace.[48]

I send you John's money for exchange, that is, I am the sender of John's to-be-exchanged money, of which you will be the receiver. (I call the money "to-be-exchanged" [*cambiata*] in order to avoid the abstract "exchange" [*cambium*]. A sender of what is to-be-exchanged [*missor cambiati*] can be called in one word an "exchender" [*campsor*].)[49]

I act through [*per*] an attorney, that is, I act insofar as [*quatenus*] the attorney acts. But this does not appear to express satisfactorily that my act and the attorney's act are one and the same. So, rather, I act as [*ut*] the attorney acts. Thus, I bring suit through an attorney, that is, I am quasi he who brings the suit. . . .[50]

These curious entries, which Leibniz calls "analyses," "reductions," or "resolutions,"[51] apparently represent his attempts to show, in a variety of particular cases, that by means of just two kinds of propositions we could in principle say everything about the world that we now say by means of a much wider variety of structures. The two kinds in question are (1) propositions of 'A is, B' form, where in most cases A is a complete individual concept and B

---

[42] Ibid.

[43] Ibid.

[44] Ibid. Cf. LH IV vii C 98 (Fasz. 1, #56, 17): "Her skin is like milk"—the similitude is resolved into two propositions, e.g., "Her skin is A" and "Milk is A." Thence arises the relation of similarity.

[45] LH IV vii B iii 26r (Fasz. 2, #95, 350).

[46] Ibid. He goes on to say: "Thus it is only a question of those conjunctions which connect propositions. Indeed, the word *quatenus* [insofar as] should be further explained this way: if the sword is acted upon because Evander acts, it is not the case that Evander is therefore unjust."

[47] Ibid.

[48] LH IV vii B iii 60r.

[49] Ibid. Cf. C 239.

[50] LH IV vii B iii 60r.

[51] A.2.1.457: "*Analysis* is nothing else than substituting simples in the place of composites, or principles in the place of derivative propositions, i.e., to resolve theorems into definitions and axioms, and, if need be, to resolve the axioms themselves into definitions." A.2.1.398: "*Demonstration* is nothing else than the resolution of truths into other truths already known."

is any concept whatever, and (2) "reflexive" propositions about propositions of type (1).

Notice that in the gallery of analyses just set out, some of the cases provide a logically equivalent proposition, and some do not. As an analysis of

Titius is wiser than Caius,

Leibniz proposes the reflexive proposition

Titius is wise, and qua wise is superior insofar as [*quatenus*] Caius qua wise is inferior

This is a proposition about Titius, Caius, and the four type (1) propositions "Titius is wise," "Titius is superior," "Caius is wise," "Caius is inferior"; its reflexivity is indicated by the presence of the operators *qua* and *quatenus*. Clearly, the reflexive proposition is intended to be equivalent to the original; indeed, in the manuscript Leibniz has crossed out previous attempts, each time adding a note to the effect that it does not include this or that fact (for example, that Titius is wise), which is implied by the original. On the other hand, for

Men are writing

Leibniz gives

Titius is writing, Caius is writing, Titius is a man, Caius is a man.

We may interpret this as a collection of type (1) propositions or as a conjunction of these. Either way, however, it is obviously not put forward as equivalent to the original proposition. Instead the point seems to be merely that on any occasion when "Men are writing" could be truly asserted, there would be a group of propositions like those mentioned, though of course not necessarily the very same ones, that together imply "Men are writing" and would be made true by whatever substances-with-accidents were making "Men are writing" true. Another example of this kind of case is the "resolution" of

A is similar to B

into

A is red and B is red.[52]

Leibniz is surely not telling us that two things are similar if and only if they are both red. The point again must be that whenever 'A is similar to B' is true, there will be a couple of true propositions of the form 'A is C' and 'B is C' that imply it and are made true by the same substances-with-accidents that are the ground of its truth.

Thus, for the second kind of case, too, Leibniz could just as well have proposed reflexive analyses that would be equivalent. For example,

'A is similar to B'

---

[52] LH IV vii C 17r. Cf. the definition of "similar" at GM VII 19 (L 667).

he could have given

For some concept C, the propositions 'A is C' and 'B is C' are true,

and in a similar way he could have analyzed

Men are writing

as

For at least two individual concepts A, the propositions 'A is writing' and 'A is a man' are true.[53]

This subject will come up again when we consider what Leibniz has to say about relations and about relational propositions. Before leaving it now, however, we should observe that the term "reduction" (*reductio*) and its cognates are used by Leibniz in a rather broad sense to cover several kinds of processes and results. In line with the classical sense, he speaks of the reduction of moods of the syllogism to one another, or, more generally, of the reduction of one problem to another. Sometimes, however, he "reduces" one *proposition* to another, as when "Some man is learned" is reduced to "A learned man is an entity."[54] In such cases it is usually clear that the result of the reduction is intended to be logically equivalent to the proposition reduced.[55] But, as has been pointed out above, there are instances in which this is not so. In these cases it seems that all that is required for a proposition A to be reducible to propositions of simple categorical form is that on any occasion on which A could be truly asserted, there will be other propositions (perhaps different ones on different occasions) that have the requisite simple form and are such that A follows from them and they are made true by whatever states of affairs are making A true.

If we ask why Leibniz was interested in reducing all of the Latin language to a regimented portion of it in which nouns, pronouns, and adjectives occur in the nominative case only, the answer seems to be that he conceived this as preliminary to constructing the formalized language of which he dreamed.[56] If we ask why he thought it possible to make such a reduction, the answer, as we have suggested before, seems to lie in his metaphysics: if the world consists exclusively of substances-with-accidents, our descriptive thoughts about it must ultimately be to the effect that the substance or substances falling under one concept also fall, or fail to fall, under another; for the accidents of a substance determine under which concept it falls, and thinking descriptively

---

[53] C 363 (P 54): If L is a direct proposition, 'L is true' is reflexive.

[54] C 233.

[55] In fact, at C 244 it is indicated that at least in some cases the results of reductions are to be substitutable for the reduced expressions *salvo sensu*. In analysis, propositions are "resolved" into definitions and axioms, i.e., into other propositions (G I 205). At A.2.1.497 Leibniz says that [the concepts of] heat, cold, and colors, which are *protonoemata secundum nos*, "can nevertheless be resolved, for they have their causes." Elsewhere, he "resolves" green into yellow and blue. What the "resolution" of one concept into another amounts to is very unclear, to say the least.

[56] G VII 28ff.

about a substance consists in taking it to fall under this or that concept.[57] Contrary to what some commentators appear to have believed, there is no opposition between these two aspects of his attempted reductions.

4. The *Lingua Philosophica*

No reader of Leibniz can fail to be impressed by the multifarious and remarkable schemes his fertile mind was continually putting forward for the betterment of mankind. There were his great plans for reconciling the Catholics and the Protestants (thus reducing the chances for another Thirty Years' War) and for solving the problem of making adequate medical care available to everyone. There were medium-scale projects like those for founding learned societies, pumping water out of the Harz silver mines, persuading Louis XIV not to attack northern Europe, and keeping Venice from sinking further into the sea. And there were innumerable small designs such as those for a better wheelchair, a better clock, and a mechanism to help a coach wheel go over obstacles more easily.

But in some ways the grandest scheme of all, which Leibniz apparently pursued from the beginning of his career to the end,[58] was that of setting up a *Lingua Philosophica*, an artificial language in which the structure of human thought would be perfectly represented—or at least more perfectly represented than it is by any existing natural language.[59] References to this project, often accompanied by extravagant claims of the great benefits that were to flow from it, fill his writings; and, as we have seen in the preceding section, many of his most tantalizing philosophical texts appear to be notes or parts of preliminary studies directed toward the creation of such a language.

In Leibniz's day great advances had recently been made in mathematics—not least, of course, by Leibniz himself. This welcome development was largely due, in his opinion, to the improved notations that had come into use. It could not be ascribed to the genius of the mathematicians themselves, as he explains in an amusing passage, for when they venture out of their own field, the results show that in intelligence they do not in the least excel the rest of mankind.[60] Instead, the progress in mathematics results from the admirable quality of its language (and, no doubt, the language in turn is improved by the progress of the subject). If only we could find characters or signs fitted to express all our thoughts as felicitously as the signs of arithmetic express our thoughts about numbers, we could reason about everything as rigorously and smoothly as we do in algebra or geometry.[61]

---

[57] C 395 (P 84): "Every proposition which is commonly used in speech comes to this, that it is said what term contains what." LH IV vii B 3 25–26 (Fasz. 2, #95, 350): "In a rational grammar it is possible to dispense with abstract nouns."

[58] G VII 185ff. (L 222ff.).

[59] Other names for the *Lingua Philosophica* were *lingua rationalis* and *lingua universalis*. See Arndt (1967), 71.

[60] C 335.

[61] C 155.

Leibniz hoped to derive two principal advantages from the *Lingua Philosophica*, although there were to be several less-important "fringe benefits," too. First, the language was to make possible a so-called Art of Reasoning (*Ars ratiocinandi* or *Ars iudicandi*). By arranging the syntax in such a way that all valid inferences would be formally valid (that is, such that every inference of the same form would be equally valid), he expected to extend the rigor of mathematics to reasoning in general.[62] His goal, he tells us, was "to employ signs that are so constructed that all inferences that may be drawn proceed immediately from the words or characters themselves." For an example of what he has in mind, we are to consider the inference: David is the father of Solomon; therefore, Solomon is the child of David. "This *consequentia*," he says, "cannot be demonstrated from the Latin words unless they are resolved into other equipollent ones."[63] The suggestion is that when the given inference, which in its present form is sound but not formally sound, is transformed by replacing "father of" and "child of" by suitable defining expressions, the transform of the conclusion will be a formal consequence of the transform of the premise. Likewise, in reducing "Peter is similar to Paul" to "Peter is now A and Paul is now A," he seeks to convert the sound, though not formally sound, inference, "Peter is similar to Paul; therefore, Paul is similar to Peter," into a formally sound inference based on the commutativity of "and."[64]

Leibniz further assumed (mistakenly, as we now realize) that if all valid inferences in a language were formally valid, there would necessarily be an algorithmic decision procedure for determining whether or not given inferences were correct. In this way much useless argument could be avoided; the disputants would simply sit down together and say, *calculemus*.[65] In a

---

[62] C 153, 156, 176, 244, 284–85. Thus, in his view a prime advantage of the binary notation is that it permits a greater number of arithmetic identities to become algorithmically demonstrable. As an example of what he means, he offers (C 285):

for $3 \times 3 = 9$.

$$
\begin{array}{r}
11 \\
11 \\
\hline
11 \\
11 \\
\hline
1001
\end{array}
$$

[63] C 284. Cf. A.6.6.479, C 427. On this example and its history, see Burk 66 and his notes.

[64] C 244. In another place he analyzes "A is simultaneous with B" into "A exists today and B exists today," presumably with similar purpose.

In many passages Leibniz seems to suppose that all formally valid inferences can be made by substitutions. Cf. C 261, 327, 351, 407, 496. Also, in his formal calculi he allows rewriting of free variables, which he obviously interprets as depending on the fact that if an inference is sound for any individuals (assigned to the free variables), it is sound for all. See, e.g., G VII 224 (P 42–43).

[65] G VII 125, 200; C 156, 176; A.1.4.315; Bodemann 82. In LH IV vii C 160–61 (Fasz. 1, #60) Leibniz argues as follows:

"Children, who have only a little experience, are nevertheless able to understand a great deal that a skilled instructor explains to them, even if he doesn't show them anything but only describes. Therefore, it is necessary that concepts of all those many things are latent in them and arise from the few with which they are already acquainted.

Thus an intelligent and attentive child, however inexperienced, can understand an instructor discoursing

deductive science with a complete set of true axioms, the same procedure would, of course, decide truth as well as validity.

Leibniz acknowledged, however, that there would be one exception to all of this:

> Note that this language is indeed an adjudicator of controversies, but only in non-supernatural matters and not in those of revelation; for the terms occurring in the mysteries of revealed theology are not susceptible of such analysis, else they would be perfectly understood and there would be no mystery in them. And when common words must be transferred to talk of revelation, they acquire a different, loftier sense.[66]

The second major advantage to be provided by the *Lingua Philosohpica* was that it would promote the Art of Discovery (*Ars inveniendi*). Leibniz says that an ingeniously designed notation could serve as a *filum Ariadnaeum*, stimulating and guiding the mind to new discoveries.[67] As noted above, he attributed the great progress in mathematics to just this cause. Besides the languages of algebra and geometry he mentions as an example the notation he had recently introduced for the differential and integral calculus.[68] Perhaps he had in mind his representation of the derivative as the quotient dy/dx of two infinitesimal "differentials." Though this device is misleading, suggesting, as it does, that dy and dx are two functions, the quotient of which is the function that is the derivative of y with respect to x, it does have heuristic value, making such theorems as

$$\frac{dy}{dv} \cdot \frac{dv}{dx} = \frac{dy}{dx}$$

and

$$\frac{dy}{dx} = \frac{1}{\dfrac{dx}{dy}}$$

seem obvious.[69]

---

about mathematics, morals, jurisprudence, and matters metaphysical—he will understand, I say, at least at the time when they are presented to him, even though, because of lack of experience, he is unable to retain them or put them to practical use.

It follows irrefutably that if somebody entered in a catalog all the primitive concepts which that child has, with a letter or character assigned to each, together with all the concepts composed of these (i.e., all the concepts which could be explained to that child without putting anything new before his eyes), he would be able to designate [all of these] with combinations of those letters or characters. . . .

This designation of concepts will have the virtue that the same relation will obtain among the characters as among the concepts, which is not the case in ordinary speech. . . .

Thus I assert that all truths that can be demonstrated about things expressible in this language with the addition of new concepts not yet expressed in it—all such truths, I say, can be demonstrated *solo calculo*, or solely by manipulation of characters according to a certain form, without any labor of the imagination or effort of the mind, just as occurs in arithmetic and algebra.

[66] C 285.

[67] A.2.1.241; cf. A.2.1.428.

[68] G VII 21; cf. GBr xiv and Gerhardt (1848), 134.

[69] For a brief and lucid account of how the notion of the infinitely small "differentials" has been rescued in Abraham Robinson's "nonstandard analysis," see Oberschelp (1969).

Thus, the primary benefits to be derived from the new language were to be an *ars iudicandi* and an *ars inveniendi*. But there would be some important by-products. For example, users of the rational language would find it impossible to talk nonsense. In a famous passage, wonderful for its optimism, Leibniz says:

> Now the characters that express all our thoughts will constitute a new language that can be written and spoken; this language will be very difficult to construct, but very easy to learn. It will be quickly accepted by everybody on account of its great utility and its surprising facility, and it will serve wonderfully in communication among various peoples, which will help get it accepted. Those who will write in this language will not make mistakes provided they avoid errors of calculation, barbarisms, solecisms, and other errors of grammar and construction. In addition, this language will possess the wonderful property of silencing ignoramuses. For people will be unable to speak or write about anything except what they understand, or if they try to do so, one of two things will happen: either the emptiness of what they put forward will be apparent to everybody, or they will learn by writing and speaking; as indeed those who calculate learn by writing and those who speak sometimes meet with a success they did not imagine, the tongue running ahead of the mind. This will happen especially with our language, on account of its exactness. So much so, that there will be no equivocations or amphibolies, and everything which will be said intelligibly in that language will be said with propriety. This language will be the greatest instrument of reason.[70]

And still another benefit to flow from the rational language would be the propagation of the faith:

> Where this language can once be introduced by missionaries, the true religion, which is in complete agreement with reason, will be established, and apostasy will no more be feared in the future than would be an apostasy of men from the arithmetic or geometry which they have once learned. So I repeat what I have often said: that no man who is not a prophet or a prince can ever undertake anything of greater good to mankind or more fitting for the divine glory.[71]

Leibniz also claims that whoever learns the *Lingua Philosophica* will in effect learn an encyclopedia.[72] The reason for this is that the predicate concept of every true proposition is contained in the subject, and the *Lingua Philosophica* will perfectly represent all propositions.

How was this wonderful instrument of reason to be constructed? The leading idea was the so-called Law of Expressions: "The law of expressions is this: the expression of a given thing [*res*] is to be composed of the expressions of those things the ideas of which compose the idea of the given thing."[73]

---

[70] C 156–57 (W 16). Cf. G III 605 (L 654); GM I 186 (L 166); G VII 4n., 23, 205; A.2.1.428; Burk 190.

[71] G VII 188–89 (L 225).

[72] A.2.1.240. Cf. Schulz (1970), 133.

[73] Bodemann 80–81. Cf. C 50 (P 17); GM VII 8; G VII 22–23; A.2.1.240. In "The Philosophy of Logical Atomism" (reprinted in *Essays in Logic and Knowledge*," ed. R. C. Marsh, London, 1956, vol. 5, 197–98), Russell adopts a similar idea himself: "In a logically perfect language there will be one word and no more for every simple object, and everything that is not sim-

When deciphered, this rather involuted statement means, I think, that just as a complex concept is composed of simpler ones, so the linguistic expression representing that concept is to be composed of expressions representing its components. To prevent unwieldiness of the notation, Leibniz also contemplates introducing further terms by explicit definition;[74] but when all defined terms are eliminated, we should be able to tell, just from the representing linguistic expressions themselves, whether one given concept is included in another. Or, at least, we shall be able to tell this if we are sufficiently wise and the case does not involve infinite analysis. All simple propositions, of course, assert such inclusion. Consequently, just as the mathematician can calculate with the signs alone, without having to expend time and intellectual effort in referring back to their meanings until the conclusion is reached, so also the user of this new language will be able to proceed in the same way, because the signs are isomorphic with the concepts they represent.[75]

Clearly, the whole scheme depends on two fundamental features of Leibniz's philosophical outlook. First, there is his nominalistic metaphysics: if all there is, ultimately, is substances-with-accidents, then all that can be said about it, descriptively at least, should be sayable by means of simple 'A is, B' propositions, where A refers to a substance and B to one or more of its accidents (or to the substance by virtue of one or more of its accidents). Add to this his conceptualistic philosophy of language: between language and the world, and linking them, is the region of ideas or concepts; concepts are simple or complex, with the complex formed from the simple by an operation corresponding to the concatenation of adjectives or nouns, possibly supplemented by some sort of complementation; propositions are a special kind of concept, having other concepts as terms; and so all thought about the world,

---

ple will be expressed by a combination derived, of course, from the words for the simple things that enter in, one word for each component."

Note that Leibniz does not say that the expression of a thing is to be composed of the expressions of its parts. Thus, I do not agree with Patzig (1969), 36, that to construct his artificial language Leibniz would need a complete knowledge of reality. The project would presuppose, as Leibniz admits (G III 216), "the true philosophy," i.e., the complete analysis of thoughts. Cf. C 28 and G VII 84 # 10. The *Nachlass* contains many lists of definitions, which Leibniz may also have considered preliminaries to the philosophical language. Cf. C 437–510.

[74] C 326.

[75] Leibniz calls this "blind reasoning," G VI 423 (L 292); C 256–57. A.6.6.185–86: "... on topics and in circumstances where our senses are not much engaged, our thoughts are for the most part what we might call 'blind'—in Latin I call them *cogitationes caecae*. I mean that they are empty of perception and sensibility, and consist in the wholly unaided use of symbols, as happens with those who calculate algebraically with only intermittent attention to the geometric figures which are being dealt with. Words ordinarily do the same thing, in this respect, as do the symbols of arithmetic and algebra. We often reason, in words, with the object itself virtually absent from our mind." Cf. A.6.6.188f., 191, 202, 254, 259, 275, 286. Sometimes, however, he seems to mean by "blind thoughts" thoughts that contain a "gap." The topic is discussed in detail in M. Dascal, *Leibniz's Semiotic* (forthcoming), chap. 4, sec. 8.3.

It is interesting to note that one of Leibniz's objections to natural languages is that they contain expressions the sense of which is not a function of the senses of their parts. This, he observes, is sometimes true even of whole sentences, e.g., of *multa cadunt inter calicem supremaque labra* (something like "There is many a slip 'twixt the cup and the lip"). C 352.

and even "reflexive" thought about thought, consists of entertaining, comparing, analyzing, or synthesizing concepts. If, therefore, we can set up an isomorphism between our concepts and the linguistic expressions that represent them, we should be able to reason using the signs instead of the concepts themselves. Since signs are relatively permanent and easily identifiable by sense perception, whereas getting a concept clearly before the mind may take a great deal of time and effort, a properly constructed notation will enable us to carry out long and complex reasoning that we could not manage otherwise. That, with all its obvious weaknesses and shortcomings, is the gist of Leibniz's scheme.

The idea of constructing an improved language was by no means original with Leibniz. Indeed, such proposals were commonplace in his day. He himself describes several artificial languages that had already been created and were more or less successfully in use. These included, besides the well-known *Lingua Franca*, which was based on Italian and was used in the commerce of the Mediterranean, certain languages (*Rothwelsch, Lingua Zerga*, and *Narquois*) that were derived from German, Italian, and French and were coined by thieves so that they could be understood only by the members of their own gangs.[76] Leibniz also mentions two artificial languages that were not based on natural languages, namely, those invented by Dalgarno and Wilkins.[77] He admired these but regarded them as inferior in essential respects to what he himself was proposing to create. Some notes he wrote at the front of his copy of Dalgarno's *Ars signorum* are instructive:

> This invention was pursued and carried through to completion by John Wilkins, bishop of Chester, a distinguished philosopher, mathematician, and theologian, who is one of the founders of the Royal Society. His work on Philosophical Characters, published in London, seems excellent. However, as I pointed out to Robert Boyle and Henry Oldenburg, these distinguished men [Dalgarno and Wilkins] do not seem to have grasped the magnitude or the true use of the project. For their language or notation only accomplishes the facilitation of communication between people who speak different languages; but the true Characteristica Realis, as I conceive it, ought to be accounted one of the most effective instruments of the human mind, having immense potential for [aiding the] discovery, retention, and evaluation [of knowledge]. For it does in all subject matters what is done in mathematics by arithmetic and algebraic notation, the great power and admirable uses of which are well known to the experts.[78]

To this one must add, however, that while Wilkins and Dalgarno brought their projects to completion, Leibniz's much more ambitious plan remained only a dream.

---

[76] A.6.6.279.

[77] John Wilkins, *Essay toward a Real Character and a Philosophical Language*, London, 1668; George Dalgarno, *Ars signorum: Vulgo character universalis et lingua philosophica*, London, 1661.

[78] Trendelenburg (1867), vol. 3, 31–32.

XI

Leibnizian Substances

Any thoughtful person who studies the history of Western philosophy, and who is not content merely to acquire a measure of skill in manipulating the accumulated jargon thereof, will sooner or later have to ask himself what all those great philosophers could possibly have meant by the term "substance," which plays so central a role in most of their theorizing. I wish I could offer a satisfactory answer to this question, especially in relation to the philosophy of Leibniz, but I cannot. The literature on the subject is remarkably unhelpful. Only a few relatively determinate features of the matter can be discerned through the murky metaphysical mist.

1. Substance, Simple and Complex

The root idea behind the concept of Substance seems to be that, contrary to appearances, the things that constitute the changing world around us are in reality composed of, or in some way result from, a few kinds of relatively permanent entities or stuff, and that their attributes can be explained and predicted as somehow depending on the attributes of those basic materials. In particular, the observed changes in everyday objects, including their origination and destruction or dissolution, are to be explained as resulting from changes in, or recombination of, the underlying ingredients, which, whether they themselves change or not, are assumed to retain their identity through such episodes.

The underlying stuff may be something that occurs overtly and is postulated also to occur covertly, as when the pre-Socratic philosophers theorized that everything is made of water or of air, or it may be held to consist of very small particles or other entities with which we are not directly acquainted and which are only detectable through the observable effects they are supposed to produce. Thus, the distinction between appearance and reality, which is originally drawn *within* the domain of our experiences, is shifted over into a distinction *between* the world as experienced and the world as it really is. The real world is deemed to be composed of substances, which "stand under" or "lie behind" our everyday experience; these substances are assigned certain attributes, or properties, often identical with (or at least similar in kind to) those with which we are acquainted in experience; and the observed features of the world of experiences are accounted for by reference to the attributes of the postulated underlying entities.

Scientists and philosophers have shared these assumptions, but from that common starting point they have gone their different ways. By and large, the scientific mind is content to seek *relatively* fundamental substances that stand behind our experience, and to theorize laws governing the behavior of such entities and their connections with what can be observed. For the scientist there is no presumption that these relatively fundamental substances will not later be found themselves to depend on, or be composed of, things that are still more fundamental; indeed, historically that is precisely what has happened over and over again. There is no reason to suppose that this quest for the fundamental will ever terminate.

Philosophers, on the other hand, have interested themselves more in the question of just what properties any ultimately fundamental substances would have to have, and, depending on their answers to this question, they have proposed various kinds of entities as filling the bill. There has been little if any philosophical activity directed toward formulating laws governing the actual operations of the primary substances thus postulated, or describing in detail how appearances depend on the states of these substances. Thus Leibniz, for example, tells us that the phenomena we experience are confused expressions of a universe of basic substances, the monads, but he gives us no details as to exactly how this works. Typically, the philosopher's hypotheses, in contrast to those of the scientist, are neither verifiable nor even confirmable.

Aristotle, whose doctrine has had maximal influence on what philosophers have said about this topic, states in the *Categories* that in the most fundamental or "primary" sense of the term a substance is *that which is neither predicable of nor present in anything else*.[1] Thus, if a term B names a primary substance, then in every true sentence of the form 'A is B' the term A will name that same substance; and (in view of Aristotle's technical use of the phrase "present in") if x is a substance, then there is no other y such that the existence of x depends on that of y, that is, such that x could not have existed unless y existed.[2] Consequently, for Aristotle the primary substances

---

[1] *Categories* 2a11, repeated practically verbatim by Leibniz in LH IV viii 29 102 (see LH 124).

[2] Leibniz uses *inesse* in this same sense of "present in," as is evident from his explanation of the part-whole relation (GM VII 274): "It is obvious that the part is in [*inesse*] the whole, or if the whole is posited, the part is immediately posited *eo ipso*, or if the part and the various other parts

turn out to be concrete individuals, including human beings like Socrates or Callias, as contrasted with universals and with all other candidates for this fundamental status.

From the second part of Aristotle's definition it would seem to follow that no substance has any parts (other than itself), for the part-whole relation is such that if x is a part of y, then that very same thing y could not exist unless x existed.[3] So his two conditions together imply that a substance, in what he calls "the primary and truest and most definite sense of the term," is a concrete individual that has no parts, an *individuum*. We may note, incidentally, that if this interpretation is correct, then in speaking of Socrates and Callias, Aristotle must be referring to their souls or minds as contrasted with their bodies.

Plato's substances were the Ideas, which were themselves supposed to be absolutely unchanging, but in terms of which the changes in "the world of sights and sounds" were in some sense explained. For the apple to change from green to red is for it to participate first in the Idea of Green and then in the Idea of Red. Strictly speaking, we should not say that the color of the apple changes: the greenness does not change into redness; it is the apple that changes color. This is a paradigm of a philosophical theory. The ancient atomists, on the other hand, advanced theories that belong at least in the gray area between science and philosophy.

In Leibniz's day the Cartesians were saying that the three primary substances were mind, matter, and God. Much of Leibniz's controversial writing is directed against this doctrine. Spinoza, on the other hand, had come to the conclusion that there was after all only one substance, namely, God. He thought that this conclusion followed from the definitions (as proposed by him) of the terms "God" and "substance."

Leibniz's own view is in some respects Aristotelian,[4] though in others it diverged very significantly from that tradition. For him, the only true substances are the individuals he calls "monads." These monads are like human souls or minds; in fact, the set of monads just *is* the set of human souls together with all other similar beings whose perceptions differ in distinctness from those of human souls.[5] Thus, on one side of man there are God and the angels; on the other, animals, plants, and various entities that can be said to

---

are posited, the whole is posited *eo ipso*; so that the parts taken together, plus position, differ only in name from the whole, and the name of the whole is used for them in reasoning only *compendia causa*. Cf. GM VII 19.

[3] A.6.6.238. Thus, in the "Metaphysical Discussion with Fardella" (Stein 1888, 323), Leibniz argues that a body cannot be a substance, for each body has parts, which again are bodies. G II 120 (M 153): A part is an immediate requisite of the whole and homogeneous with it.

[4] LH IV vii C 101 (Fasz. 1, #57, 182): "In short, a substance is that which 'stands under' [*substat*] other things, and under which nothing else stands; or, it is a subject in which other things inhere and which itself does not inhere in any other subject."

[5] Cf. G II 481: "Monads are nothing else than representations of phenomena with transition to new phenomena; it is manifest that representation in them is perception and that transition is appetition."

have perceptions only if we use that term in Leibniz's very abstract sense. Hence, Leibniz would agree with Aristotle that Socrates and Callias are substances and whiteness is not. He also accepts the Aristotelian condition that a term denoting a primary substance should not be predicable of anything other than itself. But a central tenet of his philosophy prevents him from accepting the second Aristotelian condition, that each substance exists independently of all the rest.

In a text dating from the very beginning of his philosophical career, Leibniz defines "substance" as "*ens* that subsists per se."[6] Even at this early date, however, he imposes on the Aristotelian formula the novel interpretation that an *ens* subsisting per se is one that has a principle of action in itself, that is, is capable of initiating action. Later, as he developed his doctrine of the "universal" interconnection of things," he realized more clearly that he could not consistently define a substance as that which does not depend for its existence on the existence of anything else. For, as we have seen, he held that any two monads in the actual world—for example, Adam and Eve—are such that neither could have existed without the other. He also pointed out that since substance and accidents depend on one another— Socrates could not exist without his wisdom, and his wisdom could not exist without Socrates—they cannot be distinguished in the traditional way by characterizing accidents as dependent and substances as independent. And further, even if "dependent" were understood as referring to causal dependence instead of to logical dependence, then all the created monads, though they would be independent of one another, would be dependent on their creator, God, and hence would no longer qualify as substances; the result would be Spinozism.[7]

So Leibniz gave up the traditional conception of substance and instead offered a different one.[8] In a well-known passage in the *Discourse on Metaphysics* he attempts to define an individual substance by reference to features of its concept: "It is of course true that when a number of predicates are attributed to a single subject while this subject is not attributed to any other, it is called an individual substance."[9] He adds, "But this is not enough, and such a

    [6] A.6.1.508 (L 115), probably from 1668.

    [7] G IV 364 (L 389); Loemker's translation should read: "I do *not* know . . .." At G II 451 (L 605) Leibniz says that "accident" can't be defined as "that which requires to exist in a substance," for substances require other substances. He prefers to define an accident as "a modification of something entirely other" or (at G II 457, L 605) as "that which depends upon a substance as ultimate subject." G II 458 (L 606): To inhere in a subject is to be a mode or state of the subject. G VI 582 (L 620): "In the end only God can be thought of as independent of every other being. Shall we then say, as does a certain innovator who is only too well known, that God is the only substance and that created beings are only his modifications?"

    [8] Parkinson (PLR 124) points out that Leibniz still used Aristotle's definition occasionally; he cites C 403, G II 457, S 477.

    [9] G IV 432–33 (L 307). LH IV vii C 104r (cf. S 463, 477): "Further, a singular substance is that which cannot be said of anything else. Or, if a singular substance is said of anything, they will be the same. Thus if from the fact that *A* is *B* it can be concluded also that *B* is *A*, or *A* and *B* are the same, *A* or *B* is called a singular substance or a thing subsisting per se; e.g., if it is said that Peter is the apostle who denied Christ, then, since it is known that there is only one such apostle,

definition is merely nominal."[10] In other words, he considers the possibility of defining an individual substance as anything the concept of which appears as subject in a number of true propositions but as predicate in only those true propositions of which it is also the subject. But such a definition, he says, would be "nominal," giving us merely a criterion (Aristotelian "property") of individual substantiality, and not the essence. So he continues:

> The subject term [of a true proposition] must always include the predicate term in such a way that anyone who understands perfectly the concept of the subject will also know that the predicate pertains to it. This being premised, we can say it is the nature of an individual substance or complete being to have a concept so complete that it is sufficient to make us understand and deduce from it all the predicates of the subject to which the concept is attributed.[11]

Thus, in effect, he defines an individual substance as whatever falls under a complete concept.

A concept is *complete* (and thus is a concept of an individual substance) if and only if it contains every property of whatever falls under it. A concept that is not complete, one that does not contain every property of whatever falls under it, is a concept of an accident.[12] Thus, the concept of Alexander is complete, for it contains every property of every X of which you can say truly 'X is Alexander'. The concept of King, on the other hand, is not complete and hence is the concept of an accident, for it does not contain every property of Alexander though you can say truly "Alexander is king."

It is not very easy to see much difference between Leibniz's preferred definition and the one he puts down as "merely nominal." The merely nominal definition says, in effect: you can recognize a concept A as being the concept of an individual substance if (1) there are true essential propositions

---

or since it can be inferred vice-versa that the apostle who denied Christ is Peter, it follows that the apostle who denied Christ will be a person or a singular substance. . . .'

[10] At G VI 294 (L 231) Leibniz explains that real definitions differ from nominal definitions in that they require a demonstration of possibility, and at G VI 500 (L 548) he explains further that "the purpose of nominal definitions is to give marks sufficient to aid in recognizing things. For example, assayers have marks by which they distinguish gold from all other metals, and even if a man has never seen gold, these marks could be taught him so that he could recognize it." Cf. A.6.6.293, G VII 293, G IV 423, and G II 63 (M 72).

From Leibniz's point of view, one trouble with a definition that is only nominal is that in employing it to make the kinds of substitutions involved in analytic proofs, we have no assurance that we shall not be led to contradictory results (since an impossible concept contains complementary components) (GM IV 481–82). Cf. G II 63, G VII 294 (L 230–31). Thus, although Hobbes was right in thinking that nominal definitions are arbitrary, he was wrong in concluding therefrom that necessary truths are arbitrary, for their proofs require real definitions, and whether concepts are consistent does not depend on us (A.2.1.504, 529).

Also, at A.6.6.300 and 311, Leibniz, again considering "gold" as a typical sortal word, distinguishes the "inner nature" from the "outer signs" of such substances, and he says that when we do not know the inner nature, our nominal definitions will be based on the outer signs and will be merely provisional, i.e., may have to be changed in the light of new discoveries.

[11] G IV 433 (L 307). At G VI 581–82 (L 620) there seems to be confusion of (1) a concept C's being a concept of an independently existing thing and (2) C's being conceived independently of any other concept.

[12] Ibid. But cf. the discussion of "containment" in chap. 5, sec. 2.

of the form '*A* is B ', and (2) no essential proposition '*C* is *A* ' is true unless *A* is the same as *C*. Now, if *A* is a complete concept and thus contains every attribute of everything that falls under it, then clearly conditions (1) and (2) hold. For, in general, essential '*A* is *B*' is true if and only if whatever falls under *A* must fall under *B*. But the implication in the other direction is less clear, as is Leibniz's reason for preferring the second definition over the one he calls "merely nominal."

There are many other texts, however, in which Leibniz gives, or hints at, a quite different definition, one reflecting his view that the only individual substances are minds and other mindlike beings. In an illuminating, quasi-autobiographical passage he explains that when reflecting on the notion of substance, he begins with himself, as a paradigm case: ". . . And since I conceive that there are other beings who also have the right to say 'I,' or for whom this can be said, it is by this that I conceive what is called *substance* in general."[13] He adds that it is the consideration of himself that also provides him with other concepts in metaphysics, such as those of cause, effect, action, similarity, and even with those of logic and ethics. In terms of Wallace Matson's aptly characterized distinction of the "inside-out" and "outside-in" approaches to metaphysics, Leibniz is clearly an inside-outer.[14]

When he is thinking along these lines, Leibniz defines the notion of substance in terms of the most salient characteristics that all those paradigm cases—that is, all those minds—seem to him to have in common: they *act*. So we find him declaring that an individual substance is "whatever has within it active force"—"short of annihilation, a monad cannot cease to act."[15]

This, I fear, is another example of the application of an analytic method that has a long history of the introducing confusion into philosophy. Namely, in seeking to grasp the sense of some general term (or to find the "essence" of the corresponding notion), one surveys the domain of individuals to which the term is in fact applied by those who use it, and one looks for the most striking feature that all or most of the individuals have in common; when such a feature is found, it is deemed essential. In other words, what may be at best merely an Aristotelian "property" is taken instead as definitive and is often at odds with the "dictionary definition" of the term in question. This method leads Leibniz to definitions of "substance" that seem to have little connection with one another; we are left to wonder what reason he could possible have had for holding that those and only those entities that "have within them active force" also have "concepts that contain every attribute of whatever falls under them."

At any rate, it clear enough that for Leibniz the only substances are the

---

[13] G VI 501 (L 549).

[14] Matson (1968), 287–88. Leibniz seems largely to have ignored the problem that the existence of other minds poses for inside-outers. At G III 339 he suggests the feeble argument that since nature is uniform in its fundamentals, there must be souls associated with other bodies, whether human or not, as there are in the case or cases with which we are immediately acquainted.

[15] G IV 470 (L 433), 479 (L 454).

monads, even though it is quite unclear how he reached this conclusion. When he comes to listing general properties of these entities, however, he seems to rely in some cases on the Aristotelian criteria. Thus, he tells us that the monads have no parts and hence can begin and end only by a miracle; he concludes that every monad begins at the Creation and perdures through all time.[16] He also preserves a kind of independence of his substances from one another even though they are not independent with respect to existence. "No created substance exerts a metaphysical action or influence upon another," he says,

> for, to say nothing of the fact that it cannot be explained how anything can pass over from one thing into the substance of another, it has already been shown that all the future states of each thing follow from its own concept. What we call causes are in metaphysical rigor only concomitant requisites.[17]

In other words, changes in one created individual never really cause changes in another; what we call "causes" are simply concomitant changes. As the passage quoted above shows, Leibniz seems to think that this follows from his thesis that the future states of any individuals are completely determined by its past states. But surely that inference is a non sequitur. Even if we keep in mind that for him a cause is an *aitia*, that is, something prominently mentioned in an appropriate answer to a Why question, it would seem that there are many cases in which the actions of one monad would be caused by those of another.[18]

In some passages Leibniz extends the term "substance" to cover animals and other organic beings, which are certain collections of monads arranged in a hierarchy dominated by a single monad of the type he calls a "soul." When he is attending to the distinction between individuals and aggregates of individuals, he uses the term "composite substance" to apply to such collections, reserving "simple substance" for the monads themselves.[19]

2. Accident

The correlative term to "substance" is, of course, "accident." In much of the tradition, and for Leibniz, this term has two senses: either it refers to a so-

---

[16] G VI·607 (L 643), 598 (L 636), 479 (L 454). Thus the immortality of the soul is established by an argument, plainly fallacious, borrowed from Plato's *Phaedo*.

[17] C 521 (L 269). At G IV 495 Leibniz does state, however, that just as a Copernican can truthfully speak about the sun rising, and a Platonist about the reality of matter, and a Cartesian about that of sensible qualities, *provided that this sort of talk is properly understood*, so also he himself can say, if properly understood, that one substance is the cause of a change in another.

[18] I have discussed this matter at length in Mates (1973).

[19] At A.6.6.213 he calls these composite substances *choses substantielles*; at G III 657 they are called "true substances"; cf. G VII 553. At C 13, 438, and 536 he uses the term *substantiata*.

In his March 1706 letter to Princess Sophie (*Correspondence de Leibniz*, ed. O. Klopp, Hanover, 1874, vol. 3, 173), Leibniz says that a complex substance is like a herd of sheep, "which has no reality beyond that which is in the sheep." This, I suggest, is in effect Leibniz's way of saying that any proposition appearing to be about a herd or kind should be reducible to propositions about the individuals that make it up.

called Predicable—along with Genus, Species, Property, and Differentia—or it is a collective term for the last nine Predicaments, or Categories.[20]

In the first of these senses it is contrasted with "essence," and Leibniz does occasionally use the word in this sense, though with a certain twist of his own. We have seen that his views about identity imply that no individual could at any time have had any properties other than the ones that it did in fact have at that time. Consequently, if "essence" is used in its traditional sense, we have to say that every property of every individual is essential to that individual. To avoid having to say this, and to preserve a distinction between the essential and the accidental properties of individuals, Leibniz makes a typically Leibnizian move; as we have seen, he redefines "essential" and "accidental" in such a way as to yield the desired results. Some of an individual's attributes pertain to it at all times, while others pertain to it at some times and not at others; thus the attribute King characterizes Alexander during part of his history only, whereas the attribute Man applies to him at all times. Attributes like the former are called "accidental" by Leibniz; like the latter, "essential."[21]

But in most cases Leibniz uses "accident" in its predicamental or categorical sense, where it is the correlative of "substance."[22] The accidents of a substance at any given time are what is happening to it at that time, and this consists simply of its thoughts and perceptions.[23]

> Nothing can in fact happen to us except thoughts and perceptions, and all our future thoughts and perceptions are only the consequences, however contingent they may be, of our preceding ones, so that if I were capable of considering distinctly everything that is happening to me or appearing to me at this hour, I could see in it everything that will ever happen or appear to me.[24]

Although the relevant texts are by no means unambiguous, and although Leibniz's use of the crucial terminology fluctuates from one passage to another, Kenneth Clatterbaugh has made a good case for his thesis that Leibnizian accidents are individual to their substances.[25] That is, no accident or

---

[20] See chap. 12, sec. 2, of this book, and Jungius, *Logica Hamburgensis*, p. 9 #43 and p. 18 #3. At A.6.2.457–58 n. 5, Leibniz says that he prefers "mode" to "accident," "because many modes are such that they cannot be absent without the destruction of the subject, e.g., the heat from the fire." Here, presumably, he is referring to the first of the two senses of "accident."

[21] G II 458 (L 606), Grua 383, A.6.6.305. Cf. chap 5, p. 90 ff., and chap. 8, n. 18; what I tell you at least three times is true.

[22] Cf. e.g., G II 504 (incorrectly translated at L 614). Sometimes, as at SL VII (1975), 187–18, Leibniz seems confusedly to be ascribing both senses to the term simultaneously, saying, e.g., that wisdom is not an accident of God (presumably because it is essential) and then speaking of quantity, quality, action, passion, etc., as accidents.

[23] Hansch (1728), 32: An accident is a mode of a finite substance.

[24] G IV 440 (L 312). "Thoughts" (*pensées*) is used in a wide sense; e.g., pains are thoughts. G II 70 (M 86).

[25] Clatterbaugh (1973). To the same point see Mugnai (1978), 5, and Burk 333, who cites (p. 375 n. 296) G II 458, A.6.6.145, LH IV vii C 107r. At A.6.6.328 the birth of Jesus Christ and the passing over of the angel that caused the death of the Egyptians' firstborn without harming those of the Hebrews are given as examples of individual accidents (of Jesus Christ and the angel, respectively).

mode can belong to two substances.[26] Hence, as we have noted earlier, the accidents of a substance are not to be confused with the concepts (properties, attributes) under which it falls, for Leibniz tells us that any two substances will have some properties in common. The accidents of a monad are in the domain of reality, not in the region of ideas; they are "ways of being" of substances.[27]

We have noted in the preceding section that Leibniz occasionally extends the application of the term "substance" to certain kinds of composite entities. He makes a corresponding extension for the correlative term, "accident." Again, his use is neither completely consistent nor unambiguous, but one scheme worth noting is found in a chart adjoined to his 19 August 1715 letter to Bartholomew des Bosses, with whom he had an extensive philosophical correspondence during the years 1709–15.[28] According to that chart, every created entity is either a "unity per se" (*unum per se*, or *ens plenum*) or a "unity by aggregation" (*unum per aggregationem, semi-ens, phaenomenon*). A unity per se, or substance-cum-modifications, is either simple (a monad) or composite (an animal or other organic being); the latter kind of entity is a collection of monads that endures through time (though not necessarily with the same constituents)[29] and adheres to a dominant monad. A unity by aggregation is a semisubstance-cum-semiaccidents, for example, an army of men, a herd of animals, a heap of sand, a house, a rock, a cadaver. The semiaccidents are the appearances of the semisubstances and include the perceived qualities, both primary and secondary, of bodies.

In other places Leibniz seems to have different classifications in mind. But despite the varying terminology, the underlying doctrine is fairly clear. The real world consists of monads-with-accidents; these monads perceive one another with varying degrees of clarity (lack of confusion); if monad A's perceptions of monad B are clearer than B's perceptions of A, then A may be called "active" or "dominant" relative to B.[30] An aggregate of monads (no spatial proximity is implied) may be so organized that its various constituents form a hierarchy, headed by a single monad that immediately dominates a group of other constituents, which in turn immediately dominate other groups, and so on. In this case the structured aggregate is an animal or a plant

---

[26] A.6.6.224: There is nothing "as inconceivable as an accident's passing from one subject to another." G II 221: There is no mode that is simultaneously in two subjects. G II 458 (L 606): "The same modification cannot be in many subjects at the same time." G II 517: "Nor, I think, would you accept an accident that was simultaneously in two subjects, with one foot, as it were, in one and the other in the other." Similarly, G II 481 and many other passages.

[27] G II 183 (L 519), G II 233. Thus Clatterbaugh (1971) is mistaken in asserting (p. 241, passim) that for Leibniz, two substances cannot have a common property; the passages he cites in support of this concern accidents, not properties. Leibniz's fluctuating use of the relevant terms make such a mistake understandable, however. "Ways of being": A.6.6.379.

[28] G II 506 (L 617).

[29] I owe to Robert Sleigh the undoubtedly correct observation that in this text *semper perstat* is better translated as "always endures" than as "always remains unchanged" (as at L 617). For Leibniz stresses that the monads dominated by a given soul are constantly coming and going, particularly in great changes like birth and death.

[30] Cf. G II 451 (L 604–5).

or a still-lower entity, depending on how clearly the dominant monad perceives the rest.

Every monad dominates some aggregate, its body.[31] If the dominant monad is a "soul," defined as a monad in which perception is relatively distinct and is accompanied by memory, then the aggregate is an animal. If the dominant monad does not have memory, the aggregate is a plant or something still farther down the line. An aggregate of monads dominated by a "spirit," defined as a soul that in addition has apperception or consciousness and thereby is capable of reason, is a human being or one of the "higher intelligences."

Thus, as Rescher puts it, in man and the animals the dominant monad is a sort of central receptor for the perceptions of the remaining monads, which in turn serve, so to speak, as organs of sense and activity.[32] Thus, the monads constituting the eye express (perceive) certain states of the monads constituting the environment; the monads of the optic nerve express the states of those of the eye; and so on, until the dominant monad has the experience we call "seeing." This type of hierarchy of the monads in an aggregate is called by Leibniz the "substantial bond" (*vinculum substantiale*) of the aggregate, and only aggregates characterized by such linkage are to be considered composite substances.

3. Perception

As just mentioned, the individual created monad's perceptions of an aggregate of monads will be more or less confused. Such perceptions are *phenomena*. Leibniz divides phenomena into those that are well founded (*bene fundata*) and those that are not. A well-founded phenomenon is one that corresponds to a composite substance—to an aggregate of monads organized by a *vinculum substantiale*—or that, as Leibniz says, "does not defeat the expectation of one who proceeds by reason."[33] Our perceptions of physical objects and even of such things as rainbows fall into this class.[34] To the rational mind they give information about the nature of the external world. On the other hand, the phenomena presented to us in dreams, hallucinations, mirages, and other such experiences are not well founded; although they are indeed confused perceptions of actual states of affairs, they are so confused as not to give even a distorted representation of the way things are; they show

[31] G VII 365 (L 683). This, however, is contingent; as Parkinson notes (PLR 137), Leibniz holds that God could deprive a created substance of *materia secunda*, i.e., of body. See G II 325, G VII 529.

[32] Rescher (1979), 115. A.6.6.117: The soul "always expresses its body, and this body is always affected in infinitely many ways by surrounding things, though often they provide only a confused impression."

[33] G II 276.

[34] Rainbows and parhelia are his favorite (special) examples of *phenomena bene fundata*. Cf. G II 262, 268, 276, 306, 390, 435.

an apparent unity where there is no corresponding unity in the actual world of monads.

Leibniz holds a very abstract view of perception, a view that, however, is in certain respects quite similar to what some recent philosophers have advocated. For him, A perceives B (where A is a monad and B is a monad or an aggregate of monads) if and only if the state of A expresses that of B. And the relation of expression, as we have seen earlier, is very abstract and general.[35] Thus, in perception it is no more necessary for the state of the perceiver to resemble the state of the perceived than for the string of symbols constituting an algebraic equation to resemble the circle defined (expressed) by that equation.[36] All that is required is that from the nature of the perception it should be possible to infer, via some law or laws, corresponding features of what is perceived.

Locke had concluded, in the case of his so-called secondary qualities, that they "in truth are nothing in the objects themselves but powers to produce various sensations in us by their primary qualities,"[37] but he considered our ideas of primary qualities—namely, of solidity, extension, motion or rest, number, and figure—to be representations of qualities actually in the bodies perceived. According to this, when I perceive a grain of wheat that has been divided into two parts, the color I see is simply a result in me of interaction between my sense organs and the colorless particles constituting the object, but the division of my perception into two portions represents a similar division really existing in the object. The perceived brownness is "in" me, with no similar counterpart outside me, while the perceived twoness corresponds to an actual twoness in the object itself. Berkeley, as everyone knows, challenged this primary-secondary distinction, concluding that all the qualities are on a par and none of them are copies or representations of features of an "external" object.

Leibniz agrees that the distinction is untenable and that none of our perceptions are qualitatively similar to the features perceived,[38] but he does not join Berkeley in abolishing the "external" world. In his copy of Berkeley's *Principles* he wrote:

> There is much here that is right and that is in accord with my own opinion, but it is expressed more paradoxically. For we don't have to say that matter is Nothing; it suffices to say that it is a phenomenon, like a rainbow, and that it is not a substance but a result of substances. ... For the true substances are monads, or perceivers. The author should have advanced further, all the way to the infinite monads constituting everything, and to their preestablished harmony.[39]

---

[35] See chap. 2, pp. 37ff. Cognition, too, is defined as "the expression or representation of external things in the individual" (LH IV vii C 111–14; Fasz. 2, #107, 418).

[36] Except in a very abstract sense of "resemble." Cf. A.6.6.131ff.

[37] Locke, *Essay*, II, viii, 9–10.

[38] A.6.6.130ff. G IV 367 (L 391): Colors, etc., do not exist in real things.

[39] See Kabitz (1932), 636, and Robinet (1983). Leibniz does agree, however, that it is impossible to prove that there exist bodies, i.e., substances that are external to us and that appear to cause our perceptions. LH IV vii C 65 (Fasz. 1, #49, 161).

In short, for Leibniz the rational man's perceptions do give him information about a world external to himself, but this is not because the world is qualitatively similar to his perceptions; rather, the information is only gleaned via scientific laws that allow us to conclude, from the features of the phenomena, the structure of the world they express. Our problem, in short, is to discover the laws that relate appearance to reality. This view is related to, but still quite different from, Russell's thesis (as found in *Human Knowledge* and elsewhere) that our perceptive experiences give us knowledge only of the structure, and not the qualities, of the physical world.[40]

Although each monad in the universe perceives every other monad at all times, the perceptual states of the different monads differ in their "point of view" as well as in the degree of clarity with which they represent a given portion of the whole.

Just as the same city viewed from different sides appears to be different and to be, as it were, multiplied in perspectives, so the infinite multitude of simple substances, which seem to be so many different universes, are nevertheless only the perspective of a single universe according to the different points of view of each monad.[41]

It is not obvious how monads can have a "point of view," since it is expressly stated that they do not exist in space. Our model in chapter 4, however, shows that there is nothing particularly puzzling about how different monads can express or "mirror" the same monad without themselves being exactly alike.[42] Indeed, it seems that this mirror feature automatically results in any model that satisfies the other conditions specified by Leibniz.

By contrast, the postulation of different degrees of clarity in the perceptions of monads appears to be completely ad hoc. Despite its obvious utility for his system, Leibniz's only explicit argument for it is that "otherwise each monad would be a divinity."

The nature of the monad being to represent, nothing can limit it to representing only a part of things, though it is true that its representation is merely confused as to the details of the whole universe and can be distinct for a small part of things only, that is, for those which are the nearest or the greatest in relation to each individual monad. Otherwise each monad would be a divinity.[43]

The utility, however, is clear enough. Leibniz needs to account somehow for the obvious fact that our perceptions of bodies, that is, of certain monadic aggregates, appear unitary although his doctrines imply that each monad in the aggregate is perceived individually. He also needs to explain how it can

---

[40]   Russell (1948), 256.

[41]   G VI 616 #57 (L 648).

[42]   Vittorio Mathieu states that if it were not for the relative confusion and obscurity in the perceptions of the various monads, these monads could not differ from one another (Mathieu 1969, 11). But our model shows that this is not the case.

[43]   G VI 616–17 #60 (L 648–49). From the "Metaphysical Discussion with Fardella" (Stein 1888, 323): ". . . when I perceive one thing or one state of a thing, I always confusedly perceive the whole universe, and the more perfectly I perceive one thing, the more properties of other things thereby become known to me."

be, on his theory, that we are more clearly aware of our own bodies than of the rest of the world and that in general we are more clearly aware of bodies that are relatively close to us than of things relatively distant.[44] And, finally, he needs to explain how his theory of monadic perception is compatible with the observed fact that people and other living creatures differ greatly among themselves in their knowledge of the world—not to mention the postulated fact that only one monad, namely, God, knows everything. These needs constitute the *hoc* of the aforementioned ad hoc.

Thus, by positing monadic confusion, Leibniz endeavors to account for our perception of physical objects via the claim that we confuse into single phenomena all our "petite" or unconscious perceptions of the individual monads in the underlying aggregates. We fail to distinguish the individual perceptions, he says, "in much the same way as when I hear the noise of the sea, I hear all of the particular waves which make up the noise as a whole, though without discerning one wave from the other."[45] (If he were alive today, he could illustrate the same point with a plethora of more graphic examples, ranging all the way from van Gogh paintings to motion pictures and television images.) That we perceive some things more clearly than others, as well as that some souls are better informed and wiser than the rest, is "explained" similarly.

No doubt the most striking way in which Leibniz has anticipated modern theories of perception is in his insistence, as against Locke, Berkeley, Descartes, and many others, that there are unconscious perceptions.[46] He argues for these on abstract grounds, but he also endeavors to give empirical evidence for the hypothesis. Abstractly, he reasons that a monad cannot exist without having some affects, and the affects of monads are their perceptions; therefore, every monad is perceiving at all times.[47] To this hardly convincing pronouncement he adds the following empirical considerations, using the term "perception" in its more familiar sense.[48]

1. Whether or not we are conscious of our perceptions depends on our attention. After we have lived near a mill or a waterfall for some time, we no longer take notice of the sound even though our sense organs continue to be affected as before; the independent evidence for general psychophysical parallelism supports the conclusion that in such a situation we are still, though unconsciously, perceiving the sounds.[49]

[44] C 13, G VI 617 #62 (L 649).
[45] G V 16 (NE 15). Cf. A.6.6.54, G VI 534 (L 557), G II 91, 113 (M 114, 145).
[46] Thus sensation (*sensio*) is only one kind of perception (*perceptio*): "sensation is perception that involves something distinct and is conjoined with attention and memory" (G VII 330). He goes on to say that to be in a stupor is to be experiencing a confused aggregate of many petite perceptions, with none that stands out to excite the attention.
[47] G VI 610 #21 (L 645). At A.6.6.118 he offers the further a priori argument that there must be some thought that is not thought of, else there would be an infinite regress.
[48] A.6.6.112: The petite perceptions manifest themselves through their consequences.
[49] A.6.6.53–54, 116.

2. Sometimes we let a perception pass by unnoticed, but if someone calls our attention to it immediately afterwards—for example, makes us notice some noise that was just heard—we remember it and are conscious of having perceived it earlier.[50]

3. "The loudest noise in the world would never waken us if we did not have some perception of its start, which is small, just as the strongest force in the world would never break a rope unless the least force strained it and stretched it slightly, even though the little lengthening which is produced is imperceptible." In other words, if we hear absolutely nothing when we are asleep, we cannot be wakened by a loud sound.[51]

4. Similarly, since on being wakened from a stupor we feel ourselves becoming aware of our perceptions, we must have had them immediately beforehand although we were unconscious of them.[52]

Leibniz concludes:

In short, insensible perceptions are as important to pneumatology [psychology] as insensible corpuscles are to natural science, and it is just as reasonable to reject the one as the other on the pretext that they are beyond the reach of our senses. Nothing takes place suddenly, and it is one of my best-confirmed maxims that *nature never makes leaps*. . . . It implies that any change from small to large, or vice versa, passes through something which is, in respect of degrees as well as of parts, in between; and that no motion ever springs immediately from a state of rest, or passes into one except through a lesser motion. . . . All of which supports the judgment that noticeable perceptions arise by degrees from ones which are too minute to be noticed.[53]

Leibniz regarded the doctrine of petite perceptions as an important element in his overall philosophy. He specifically mentions at least four ways in which it contributes: (1) By virtue of it he is able to hold "that the present is big with the future and burdened with the past, [and] that all things harmonize." (2) "These insensible perceptions also indicate and constitute the same individual, which is characterized by the vestiges or expressions which the perceptions preserve from the individual's former states, thereby connecting these with his present state." (3) "It is also through insensible perceptions that I account for that marvelous preestablished harmony between the soul and the body, and indeed amongst all the monads or simple substances, which takes the place of an untenable influence of one on another. . . ." (4) ". . . it is these minute perceptions which determine our behavior in many situations without our thinking of them, and which deceive the unsophisticated with an appearance of *indifference of equilibrium*—as if it made no difference to us, for instance, whether we turned left or right."[54]

---

[50] A.6.6.54.

[51] Ibid. Obviously, he is relying here on his principle of Continuity; the change from sleep to waking, as well as that from silence to a loud sound, cannot be instantaneous.

[52] G VI 610 (L 645).

[53] A.6.6.56.

[54] A.6.6.55–56.

Although, as we have mentioned above, Leibniz was familiar with Berkeley's *Principles*, it is all too evident that he nowhere attempts seriously to meet Berkeley's point that we cannot even imagine what a sound that is not heard, a color that is not seen, an odor that is not smelled, would be like—so that the hypothesis that there are such things is scarcely intelligible. Superficially it may seem that Leibniz need not quarrel with such an argument, for he does not say that there are sounds that are not heard, but only that there are sounds that are not consciously heard. But clearly, what Leibniz means by "consciously heard" is what Berkeley means by "heard"; hence Berkeley's point is not met. Leibniz's opponents will, of course, not grant his assumption that whenever there are sensory processes resembling those that normally accompany perception, there must be some sort of perception whether the perceiver is aware of it or not.

Finally, in an essay entitled "On the Method of Distinguishing Real from Imaginary Phenomena" (date unknown),[55] Leibniz tackles, without success, the sempiternal philosophical problem of how to distinguish veridical perceptions from nonveridical. His proposed criteria are the same as those relied on by Berkeley and Hume: force, vivacity, and coherence with antecedent and consequent phenomena. But, alas, Leibniz is unable to offer any good reason why the phenomena satisfying these criteria should be just those phenomena that are *bene fundata*. Indeed, in a letter to Simon Foucher he shows in a graphic example how the use of these criteria could lead one to take a real situation for a vision, and he asks rhetorically, "Since reality has thus passed for a vision, what is to prevent a vision from passing for reality?"[56]

Thus, while resisting the simple Cartesian explanation that otherwise God would be a deceiver, Leibniz seems unable to produce anything essentially better.[57] This puts him in a much worse position than that of Berkeley and Hume, for he is endeavoring to distinguish among phenomena in terms of their correspondence, or lack of it, with an external world, while they can *define* a veridical perception as one characterized by the aforementioned perceptible features. Thus, in the *Theodicy* he is driven back to a Santayana-style "animal faith": "We do not comprehend the nature of [for example] odors and savors, and yet we are persuaded, by a kind of faith which we owe to the evidence of the senses, that these perceptible qualities are founded upon the nature of things and are not illusions."[58]

[55] G VII 319ff. (L 363ff.). Cf. LH IV iii 5e 2 (Fasz. 2, # 83, 296), where dreaming experience is distinguished from waking experience by its "incoherence."

[56] G I 373 (L 154).

[57] G II 496 (L 611); cf. G IV 493. G II 496 (L 611): "Not from necessity, therefore, but by the wisdom of God does it happen that judgments formed upon the best appearances, and after full discussion, are true. . . ." G IV 367 (L 391–92): "Through previous sins, moreover, souls have deserved . . . such a life of deception, in which they snatch at shadows instead of things."

[58] G VI 74 (H 97).

4. Bodies

The physical world consists of bodies existing in space and time. Occasionally Leibniz speaks as though bodies were aggregates of monads,[59] in the way that a herd is an aggregate of individual animals (where the relation of ingredient to aggregate is the part-whole relation and not that of member to class). This account of the relation between monads and bodies fits in with a little story told by Michael Gottlieb Hansch:

> I remember that once, when Leibniz and I met in Leipzig and were drinking caffè latte, a beverage which he greatly savored, he said that in the cup from which he was drinking there might be, for all we know, monads that in future time would become human souls.[60]

But Leibniz's considered view is that "strictly speaking, matter is not composed of monads but results from them, since matter or extended mass is nothing but a phenomenon, like the rainbow or parhelia."[61] Monads are not truly ingredients of corporeal substances, he says, but are only "requisites."[62] They are not parts of bodies;[63] a part must be homogeneous with the whole,

---

[59] C 13–14 (PM 174–75). G II 301: There is no part of matter, or part of a part, that does not contain monads.

[60] Hansch (1728), 135. Voltaire, in a critique *Éléments de philosophie*, pt. 1, chap. 8) that has been justifiably neglected, goes further with this thought, in a direction characteristic of him, by ascribing to Leibniz the claim that even a drop of urine or a bit of excrement contains an infinite number of monads, each of which is perceiving, from that point of view, the entire universe. See also n. 12 to chap. 13.

[61] G II 268 (L 536). G IV 559 (L 577–78): Compound things are "merely the results" of monads; cf. G III 363. G II 118 (L 343): Bodies are only well-founded phenomena. G III 567n.: Material things and their motions are only phenomena. G II 436: A body is an actualization of phenomena proceeding beyond mere congruence (which dreams would have). GM II 537: "Matter per se, or *moles*, which one can also call *materia prima*, is not a substance; indeed, it is not even an aggregate of substances, but something incomplete. *Materia secunda*, or *massa*, is not a substance but *substances*; thus, not the herd, but the animal, not the fishpond, but the individual fish is one substance. Cf. A.6.6.434: ". . . secondary matter, i.e., the heap or mass of bodies."
G II 626: Bodies are no more true substance than are rainbows and parhelia. On the rainbow, see n. 34. Parkinson (1982, 5) cites G IV 495 as showing that Leibniz came to regard physical things as entities that are independent of the existence of minds, but I find nothing in that text to imply that the world contains anything other than monads.
As regards this whole issue, it is possibly significant that in the chart at G II 506 (L 617) it is indicated that some aggregates of substances *are* phenomena, so that perhaps we should not be attempting to distinguish (1) the individual substance, (2) an aggregate of individual substances, and (3) the phenomenon arising when the individuals in the aggregate are confusedly perceived.
Finally, there is the following peculiar statement at G II 435 (L 600): "If this substantial chain of monads were absent, all bodies along with all their qualities would be nothing but well-founded phenomena, like a rainbow or an image in a mirror—in a word, continued dreams in perfect agreement with each other . . . ." I am inclined to agree with Broad (1975), 124, when he suggests that Leibniz did not himself hold the *vinculum substantiale* theory but only put it forward for Bartholomew des Bosses' consideration.

[62] G II 435 (L 600). The "Metaphysical Discussion with Fardella" (Stein 1888, 323): A monad is not a part of a body, but an internal, essential requisite, just as a point is not a part of a line but is required that the line exist.

[63] G II 451 (L 604): Monads are not in bodies. GM III 537: "Even though the body of an animal, or of me considered as an organism, is composed of innumerable substances, neverthe-

and anyway the monads do not exist in space and consequently cannot be adjacent to one another.[64] But bodies are infinitely divisible and actually divided; there is no body that does not have parts that are smaller bodies.[65] There is no such thing as a perfect vacuum; every portion of space is filled with bodies.

Leibniz also holds, however, that although bodies exist in space, they have no determinate shape. In a very Platonic passage, he says that a body

... is only a phenomenon or a well-founded appearance, as are space and time also. It does not even have the exact and fixed qualities which could make it pass for a determined being ... because in nature even the figure, which is the essence of an extended and bounded mass, is never exact or rigorously fixed, on account of the actual division of the parts of matter to the infinite. There is never a globe without irregularities, or a straight line without intermingled curves, or a curve of finite nature without being mixed with some other, and this in its small parts as in its large.[66]

In the physical world, all action is mechanical.[67] The notion of action at a distance through empty space is a scholastic superstition.[68] Also, since there is no vacuum, the motion of any one body requires the motion of every other body in the universe.

... the very smallest body receives some impression from the slightest change in all the others, however distant and small they may be, and must thus be an exact mirror of the universe. The result is that a sufficiently penetrating spirit could, in the measure of his penetration, see and foresee in each corpuscle everything which has happened and will happen in that corpuscle, indeed, everything that has happened and will happen both within and outside of that corpuscle.[69]

Thus the mutual "mirroring" of monads has its counterpart in the physical world. The reason for this is that the states of any body express and are

---

less these are not parts of the animal nor of me." Cf. G II 305 (R 252), 436 (R 256). But in response to a question from Lady Masham, Leibniz says: "The question whether it (the soul) is or is not a part (of the body) is nominal; for its nature does not consist in extension, but it corresponds to the extension that it represents; thus one should place the soul in the body, where the point of view from which it represents the universe is located. To want to go further and give souls dimensions is to want to imagine souls as bodies" (Letter of 30 June 1704, G III 357). Lady Masham (G III 350–51) quite properly found it puzzling that Leibniz refers to the monads in-differently as "simple beings," "forms," "souls," "primitive forces," or "atoms of substance," when these various terms seem not even to refer to entities of a single category.

[64] G VII 365–66 (L 683).

[65] G VII 394 (L 699). GM III 592: "You ask how I divide a portion of matter into the substances of which it is composed. I answer that there are as many substances in it as there are animals or living beings or the like; therefore, I make the division in the same way as in the case of a herd or of a fishpond, except that the liquid [air or water] that is between the animals of the herd or the fish in the fishpond, as well as the liquid and other material that is in each fish or animal, must in my opinion be regarded as a new fishpond to be further divided, and so on, ad infinitum."

[66] G II 118–19 (L 343).

[67] G III 607 (L 655).

[68] G III 535, 580 (L 663). G VI 541 (L 587): A body never receives a change in motion except by another (contiguous) body that pushes it.

[69] G IV 557 (L 576), C 15.

expressed by the states of the monads in the aggregate with respect to which it is "well founded," and since the states of monads (and aggregates of monads) express one another, the states of the corresponding bodies will be similarly related.

To explain the occurrence of a given event in the physical world, we must cite laws that connect it to the occurrence of other events; similarly, mental events are to be explained by reference to other mental events.[70] The pre-established harmony among the states of monads induces in particular a derivative harmony of the states of a given mind and those of its body, namely, the body "resulting" from the monadic aggregate over which the given mind is dominant. As we noticed in the previous section, this harmony, or complete psychophysical parallelism, gives Leibniz one of his arguments for the existence of petite perceptions. But doubtless its principal theoretical advantage, from his point of view, was that it enabled him to answer (or, perhaps, to avoid) the difficult question of how the body and the mind could affect one another. His answer, of course, was that they can't (and don't need to).

There is no proper causal interaction between states of different monads, but if a state of monad A expresses a state of monad B "more distinctly" than the state of B expresses the state of A, "one calls it a cause" (and the other an effect). The same usage is carried over to bodies. Thus, although when a ship is in motion on the sea, the motion is entirely relative and we could say either that the ship is pushing the water back or that the water is pushing the ship forward, we attribute causality to the ship rather than to the sea because by reference to it we can explain "distinctly" what happens. Similarly, we attribute pains to bodily movements rather than vice versa. But these causal connections are only apparent; actually, the state of any monad is caused only by other states of that monad and ultimately by God.[71]

5. Leibniz on the Mind-Body Problem

Since bodies are only phenomena, whereas minds are real, one would suppose that the mind-body problem, the problem of how the mind can act causally on the body, would simply disappear. But Leibniz does not seem to be content to leave it at that.

We have seen that he has a great deal to say about bodies. Since phenomena do not really exist, all such statements should somehow be analyzable into statements about the perceptions of monads. But Leibniz gives no clues as to how such reductions could be accomplished; we can only conjecture that he would have followed a phenomenalistic line, as suggested by his

---

[70] G IV 560 (L 578): "Everything occurs in the body as if there were no soul, just as everything occurs in the soul as if there were no body."

[71] G II 69 (M 84).

comment on Berkeley's *Principles*. At any rate, when he considers the mind-body problem explicitly, he goes off in another direction.

Consider, for example, the note entitled "How the Soul Acts on the Body."[72] He begins this short statement by declaring that the soul acts on the body in the same way in which God acts on the world, that is, not by miracles but through the laws of mechanics.[73] He continues:

> Therefore, if *per impossibile* all minds were destroyed but the laws of nature continued to hold, everything would remain the same as if there were minds, and books would be written and read by human machines which would not understand anything. Of course we know it is impossible that the laws of mechanics should continue to hold in the absence of minds. For the laws of mechanics are the decrees of the divine will, and the special laws governing each body (which follow from the general laws) are decrees of its soul or form, directed toward its good or to perfection. Therefore, God is the mind that leads everything to general perfection. And the soul is that sentient force which in each individual tends toward its special perfection. For souls came into being when God impressed on each thing a tendency [*conatus*] toward its special perfection, in order that from the resulting conflict the maximum possible perfection should arise. Everything that occurs in nature can be demonstrated both by final causes and by efficient causes. Nature does nothing in vain; nature acts by the shortest routes, provided that they are regular.... Souls do not act in bodies *extra ordinem*. Nor does God so act in nature, even though some things do appear to occur *extra ordinem*, since from the beginning reality was so constituted that the general order will involve something extraordinary in the particular case.[74]

This account is obviously puzzling and unsatisfactory in several respects. First, we are invited to consider what would happen if the realm of bodies remained as it is but there were no minds. Given that bodies are only phenomena, so that statements purporting to be about bodies will be only *compendia loquendi* for statements about how things appear to minds, the hypothesis seems so self-contradictory that there is no nontrivial criterion for deciding whether this or that follows from it. Leibniz does, of course, characterize it as *impossible*, but not because bodies are only phenomena. Instead, he ignores this aspect of the matter and offers as his reason a claim that the *laws* governing bodies are decrees of a mind, a mind which found it best so to arrange things that the physical world proceeds in a completely regular way (though occasionally, to one who sees only a part of the whole, there may appear to be irregularities).

A second puzzle in the passage is the suggestion that the special laws governing the body of an individual person or other entity are the "decrees" of the soul of that person or entity, though at the same time they are supposed to follow from the general laws of mechanics, which are decrees of God. According to this, it would seem that we, all of us, are issuing a great many "decrees" of which we are totally unaware.

---

[72] LH IV vi 12f 15 (Fasz. 1, #26, p. 74); the same point is made at Grua 266.
[73] Though God is definitely not the soul of the world. Cf. LH I xx 408 (Fasz. 1, #13, p. 50).
[74] See n. 72.

But these puzzles aside, the upshot of the passage, as I read it, is that the mind does not act on the body. The body goes its way in accord with the "physicomechanical" laws, and the mind develops according to laws described as "ethicological."[75] Any appearance of causal interaction must arise from the preestablished harmony between the states of a monad and those of "its" body. In other words, Leibniz subscribes to the view now called "psychophysical parallelism." In a letter to Lady Masham he explains that he reached this view by reflecting that there is no way to explain how the mind can give an acceleration to the body, or how the body, acting in accord with the laws of mechanics, can produce a perception. He adds, incidentally, that this harmony of the mental and the physical is what led him to his general doctrine of the preestablished harmony.[76]

The content of this chapter is admirably summed up in a rather remarkable encomium that Leibniz wrote about his own system:

This system appears to unite Plato with Democritus, Aristotle with Descartes, the Scholastics with the moderns, theology and morality with reason. Apparently it takes the best from all systems and then advances further than anyone has yet done. I find in it something I had hitherto despaired of—an intelligible explanation of the union of body and soul. I find the true principles of things in the substantial unities which this system introduces, and in their harmony which was preestablished by the primary substance. I find in it an astounding simplicity and uniformity, such that everything can be said to be the same at all times and places except in degrees of perfection. I now see what Plato had in mind when he took matter to be an imperfect and transitory being; what Aristotle meant by his "entelechy"; in what sense even Democritus could promise another life, as Pliny says he did; how far the skeptics were right in decrying the senses; why Descartes thinks that animals are automata, and why they nevertheless have souls and sense, just as mankind thinks they do. How to make sense of those who put life and perception into everything ... How the laws of nature—many of which were not known until this system was developed—derive from principles higher than matter, although in the material realm everything does happen mechanically ... I see everything to be regular and rich beyond what anyone has previously conceived; with matter everywhere organic—nothing empty, sterile, idle—nothing too uniform, everything varied but orderly; and, what surpasses the imagination, with the entire universe being epitomized, though always from a different point of view, in each of its parts and even in each of its substantial unities ... Well, sir, you will be surprised at all I have to tell you, especially when you grasp how much it elevates our knowledge of the greatness and perfection of God.[77]

---

[75] G III 657.
[76] G III 340–41; cf. G VI 541 (L 587).
[77] A.6.6.71–73.

XII

Relations and Denominations

The proper understanding of Leibniz's views about relations has been and still is the subject of much dispute among commentators. As we have seen, his nominalistic metaphysics provides no place in the real world for anything other than individual substances-with-accidents. These accidents themselves are said to be individual, in the sense that the same accident cannot be in more than one substance, whether simultaneously or at different times, for such an accident would be a kind of universal. Consequently relations, considered as accidents of multiple substances, are not real.[1] Reality consists exclusively of individual substances in whatever conditions they are at any moment of time; it does not consist of substances, accidents, and relations. Relations, Leibniz says, are only *entia rationis*; they belong in the "region of ideas."[2] Further, as we shall see, even in the region of ideas they occupy a secondary status; they are only what are called "results," that is, by-products of concepts of a more fundamental type.[3] Obviously this ontology differs basically from what is tacitly or explicitly assumed in most metalogical theorizing these days, when a model or model structure involves one or more nonempty sets together with properties and relations among the elements of those sets.

In my opinion, the exegetical controversies arise from at least four distinguishable but interrelated sources. (1) The term "relation" is used in several senses by Leibniz, as well as by the tradition within which he writes and by the

---

[1] Grua 266: Relations are not real; they are *ideae imaginariae*. Cf. Grua 547, G VII 401 (L 704).

[2] Relations are *entia rationis*: G V 132, 210, 246; G II 486, 517. For *ens rationis* see PLR 41 n. 2. G II 96: An *ens rationis*, e.g., *a pair* of diamonds, "is useful only for abbreviating our thoughts and representing phenomena."

[3] Relations are "results": Grua 547; C 9; LH IV viii 60r; LH IV vii C 74r; G II 226 (L 525), SL VII (1975), 188. Cf. the definition of "result" at GM VII 21–22 (L 669). G II 471 (1712): "Let us see whether it wouldn't be better to remove relations from the class of *entia*."

people with whom he corresponds. (2) Leibniz's ever-present carelessness about use and mention often makes it unclear whether he is talking about sign, sense, or denotation—that is, about linguistic expressions, concepts, or the real world of concrete individuals. (3) Lack of clarity as to what constitutes a Leibnizian "reduction" infects the debate about whether Leibniz thought that all relational propositions are reducible to nonrelational ones. (4) Some of the disputants have employed their own metaphysical term, "relational property," without giving any practicable method for determining whether or not a given predicate expression represents one of these properties.

1. The Principal Texts

Among the many relevant texts, the most frequently cited are the following (a number of others are given in section 7 below):

> You will not, I believe, admit an accident which is in two subjects at once. Thus I hold, as regards relations, that paternity in David is one thing, and filiation in Solomon is another, but the relation common to both is a merely mental thing, of which the modifications of singulars are the foundation [*fundamentum*].[4]

> And here it may not be amiss to consider the difference between place and the relation of situation which is in the body that fills up the place. For the place of A and B may be the same, whereas the relation of A to fixed bodies is not precisely and individually the same as the relation which B (which comes into its place) will have to the same fixed bodies; but these relations agree only. For two different subjects, as A and B, cannot have precisely the same individual affection, it being impossible that the same individual accident should be in two subjects or pass from one subject to another. But the mind, not contented with agreement, looks for an identity . . . and conceives it as being extrinsic to the subject; and this is what we here call *place* and *space*.[5]

> I shall give yet another example to show how the mind uses, upon occasion of accidents which are in subjects, to fancy to itself something answerable to those accidents out of the subjects. The ratio or proportion between two lines L and M may be conceived in three ways: as a ratio of the greater L to the lesser M, as a ratio of the lesser M to the greater L, and, lastly, as something abstracted from both, that is, the ratio between L and M without considering which is the antecedent or which the consequent, which the subject and which the object. . . . In the first way of considering them, L the greater, in the second, M the lesser, is the subject of that accident which philosophers call "relation." But which of them will be the subject in the third way of considering them? It cannot be said that both of them, L and M together, are the subject of such an accident; for, if so, we should have an accident in two subjects, with one leg in one and the other in the other, which is contrary to the notion of accidents. Therefore we must say that this relation, in this third way of considering it, is indeed out of

---

[4] G II 486 (L 609). As I read this passage, David's paternity and Solomon's filiation (as distinct from paternity and filiation in general) *are* the "modifications of singulars" (i.e., of David and Solomon) on which the "merely mental" relation is founded.

[5] G VII 400–401 (L 703–4).

the subjects; but being neither a substance nor an accident, it must be a mere ideal thing, the consideration of which is nevertheless useful.[6]

It is apparent from these and other texts that Leibniz uses the word "relation" in at least two, and possibly three, senses. In one sense, a relation would be an accident that was in two substances at once; and since in reality there is no such thing as that kind of accident, relations in this sense are declared by Leibniz to be "merely mental" or "merely ideal." They are not even "true ideas" but are characterized as "*ideae imaginariae*, to which nothing corresponds in reality."[7] In a second sense, a relation is a legitimate kind of accident, namely, "that accident which philosophers call 'relation'," indicated by such terms as "David's paternity" and "Solomon's filiation" or "paternity-in-David" and "filiation-in-Solomon." When the word is used in this way, Leibniz has no quarrel with relations. Third, Leibniz sometimes says that "relations are truths," evidently using the term "relation" to signify a certain kind of true proposition. Thus his claim that relations are reducible may mean that certain propositions are reducible to other propositions, or it may mean that certain kinds of terms are reducible to other kinds of terms; Leibniz probably would not have regarded the difference as very important.

2. Terminology

Some of the definitions in Joachim Jungius's *Logica Hamburgensis*, which was Leibniz's favorite logic text,[8] throw a certain amount of light on the latter's use of the principal terms involved here.

The term "accident," Jungius says, either refers to one of the five Predicables—the other four are Genus, Species, Differentia, and Property[9]— or is a collective term for the last nine of the ten Predicaments (Aristotle's Categories), which are Substance, Quantity, Quality, Relation, Place, Time, Posture, State, Action, and Passion.[10] As we have noted earlier, Leibniz most often uses it in its "predicamental" sense, taking it and "substance" to cover the whole of reality.[11]

Jungius's section on the term "relation" and its cognates and associates includes the following points.[12] (The terminology and examples are largely the same as what one finds in Leibniz.)

The category *Relation* is called by the Greeks *kategoria tōn pros ti*, that is, the category of those things that [are] "to" something.

---

[6] G VII 401 (L 704).
[7] Grua 266 (see sec. 7).
[8] Leibniz considered Joachim Jungius (1587–1657) one of the greatest mathematicians and philosophers of his time, comparable with Descartes and even with Aristotle. For references, see CL 73–74, n. 4. Cf. C 345 and Kangro (1969).
[9] Jungius (1957), 9, #43. This is the sense in which "accidental" is opposed to "essential."
[10] Op cit., 18, #3. Cf. G IV 35, where Leibniz reduces all the categories to the first four.
[11] G II 504 (L 614, but not translated correctly).
[12] Jungius (1957), 41 ff.

This category has the peculiarity that the greater part of the things contained in it are better expressed by concrete terms than by abstract.

Relata (*ta pros ti*) are terms which are said to be what they are "of" something else, or which in some manner or respect refer to something else.

A *relation*, also called *habitudo, schesis*, and *respectus*, is an accident with respect to which the subject is described as a relatum to something, as, for example, Masterhood (*dominium*) is a relation, since Simo, who is the subject of Masterhood, or in whom (as in a subject) Masterhood inheres, is called Master of Davus with respect to that accident; and Slavery (*servitus*) is a relation, since with respect to it Davus, in whom (as a subject) slavery inheres, is called Slave of Simo.[13] Also, Equality is a relation, since with respect to it a line, which is its subject, is said to be Equal to another line.

The *terminus* of a relation is that thing to which the relation relates, or that in which the relation itself is terminated, as, for example, the terminus of the Masterhood which is in Simo is Davus, and conversely the terminus of the Slavery which is in Davus is Simo. Again, the terminus of the equality by which the area of a certain triangle is said to be equal to that of a certain square is the area of the square; and the terminus of the equality by which the area of the square is called equal to that of the triangle is the area of the triangle.

A pair of relata are *correlates* if they commute as subject and terminus, that is, if the subject of one is the terminus of the other and vice versa; thus Father and Child are correlates since, for example, David, the subject of one relation, which the philosophers call Paternity,[14] is the terminus of the other relation, which they call Filiation and which is in Solomon as a subject; and in turn Solomon is the terminus of Paternity, which is in David. So also Teacher and Student are correlates, since the subject of the former relation, for example, Aristotle, is the terminus of the latter; and correspondingly Alexander, who is the subject of the latter relation, is the terminus of the former.

Sometimes we speak as though there were one relation between two terms, although in fact two relations should always be understood. Thus we say that there is friendship between Orestes and Pylades, when in fact the friendship that Orestes feels toward Pylades is one thing, and that which Pylades feels toward Orestes is another. So also partnership between two merchants, equality between two figures, distance between two bodies.

We cannot assume, of course, that Leibniz follows Jungius's use of this terminology exactly, and the nominalistic emphasis in Leibniz's writings is not so obvious in the *Logica Hamburgensis*.[15] Still, I know of no text in which Leibniz clearly deviates from the senses defined in these passages.

Particularly interesting is the example concerning Orestes and Pylades. Its point could be stated in Leibnizian style as follows: the friendship that Orestes feels toward Pylades is one thing, and the friendship that Pylades

---

[13] Simo and Davus are characters in Terence's play *The Woman of Andros*.

[14] Note the reference to "the philosophers"; cf. the Leibniz text quoted on p. 210 above. "Rich" and "noble" would be other examples of "what the philosophers call 'relation'," "for 'rich' refers to money, and 'noble' refers to parents"; A.6.2.459 n. 45.

[15] Though at op. cit., p. 55, #14, Jungius says, "In fact nothing exists in reality besides *singulars*; universals depend upon our way of understanding." And he seems to regard relations, or at least some relations, as *entia rationis*; cf. op. cit., p. 54, #9.

feels toward Orestes is another, but there is no such thing as *the* relation of friendship between Orestes and Pylades. It is this point of view, embellished with the metaphysical remark about the fundamentum, that is expressed by Leibniz in the famous David-Solomon passage quoted above. What "the philosophers"—that is, the illuminati—refer to under the heading "relation" are really individual accidents of the related individuals, for example, the friendship of Orestes toward Pylades, or David's paternity of Solomon; but what other people have in mind under that heading has no counterpart in the real world, for there cannot be an accident that is in more than one subject.[16]

3. Sentences and Propositions, Predicates and Properties

At this point we need to consider once again the distinctions, so frequently ignored by Leibniz and by many of his commentators, between a sentence and the proposition it is supposed to express and between a predicate and the corresponding property. Philosophers who use these terms seem inclined at first to assume uncritically that for every grammatical sentence there is a proposition that is its sense or meaning (although, because of the limitations of language, there may be propositions for which there are no corresponding sentences), and, similarly, that for every grammatical predicate there is a property (though, again, the converse does not necessarily hold). But they are soon led, by reasoning that is often highly questionable, to make exceptions to this. For example, we are sometimes told that there are no propositions corresponding to the Liar sentence and its relatives.[17] Further, the conditions under which two sentences express the same proposition, or two predicates the same property, are never satisfactorily stated, and various formal features of the linguistic entities are often uncritically projected onto the propositions and properties they are supposed to express.

In the controversy about Leibniz's doctrine of relations these difficulties and their attendant confusions are especially bothersome. Some propositions are said to be of "subject-predicate form," while others are considered "relational" (and Leibniz is deemed to have made the mistake of supposing that no propositions are relational); but it is granted that this difference in structure cannot be read off in any simple way from that of the corresponding sentences. An analogous distinction is propounded between so-called relational and nonrelational properties. In both cases we are told that in order to determine what kind of meaning-entity we are confronting, we must begin by subjecting the sentence or predicate to "logical analysis."[18] This may lead to such "insights" as that, despite appearances, the proposition expressed by "Smith is bald" is relational, involving a relation between Smith and his head, while that expressed by "Smith is weary" is nonrelational. Or, one may be told

---

[16] G VII 401 (L 704, R 252).
[17] Kneale (1971), 321.
[18] Cf. Ishiguro (1972), 92 n. 1.

that all propositions are relational, or that none are; no workable criterion is given. At any rate, in the present connection one thing is relatively clear: if every predicate (or, as we might say, every open sentence with one free variable) expresses a property, then some of Leibniz's most well known principles and analyses become utterly trivial.

We have seen earlier that this is the case with the Identity of Indiscernibles, the principle that no two individuals have every property in common. For if the individuals A and B are different, and if 'different from B' expresses a property, then that will be a property that A has and B lacks.[19] Or, recall Leibniz's analysis of

(1) Peter is similar to Paul

as

Peter is now A and Paul is now A,

for some property (concept) A.[20] If "similar to Paul" expresses a property, the analysis is completely nugatory, for (1), of course, is equivalent to

Peter is now similar to Paul and Paul is now similar to Paul,

and thus, trivially, there is a concept A such that

Peter is now A and Paul is now A

is true. Again, regarding the man in India whom Leibniz so often mentions as having undergone a change when his wife died far away in Europe,[21] the point could have been established simply by observing that after her demise the man has the property expressed by "is a man whose wife has died," which he lacked beforehand, and that therefore he has changed. And any leaf A in the garden at Herrenhausen will differ from any other leaf B by having such properties as 'is other than B' or 'is at a distance from B', which, of course, B will lack.

I do not believe that such trivialities are what Leibniz had in mind. Surely it is not by chance that he resolves

A is similar to B

into

A is red and B is red

rather than into

A is similar to B and B is similar to B,

or that he declares that the relation common to David and Solomon is "founded on the modifications of *singulars*" instead of simply on a property

---

[19] Cf. chap. 7, p. 135.
[20] Chap. 10, p. 180.
[21] G VII 321 (L 365); LH IV vii C 108r (see sec. 7, p. 225); A.6.6.227 (see sec. 7, p. 226).

of David expressed by the predicate "is the father of Solomon." And, in his repeated statements that relations are only "results," he can hardly mean merely that if Simo has the property expressed by "is the master of Davus," then the relational proposition "Simo is the master of Davus" is true. Rather, in these cases he usually refers to his metaphysical doctrine that the states of every individual substance "reflect" those of every other individual substance;[22] by this he shows that what is involved here, once again, is the nominalistic claim that the truth or falsity of all propositions, relational or not, is completely determined by the individual accidents of individuals.

Thus, to the extent that one knows the accidents of individuals, one also knows, as a by-product, the relational truths about those individuals.[23] If you know how tall Smith is and you know how tall Jones is, you don't need any more information about the real world (which, of course, does not contain such abstracta as numbers) in order to assess the truth value of "Smith is taller than Jones."

Finally, in this connection it is interesting to note that in Leibniz's condensation of Plato's *Theaetetus*, at the point (155c) where Socrates expresses amazement that he has become smaller than Theaetetus without having changed, Leibniz adds a marginal comment: "This is a noteworthy difficulty, and one of great importance in other connections. I do not understand how Plato's own reply, that everything flows, responds adequately to the difficulty."[24] If Leibniz thought that every predicate expresses a property, some of them "relational" and some of them "nonrelational," he ought to have noted, instead, "*Of course* Socrates has changed: he now has the relational property 'smaller than Theaetetus', which he previously lacked." Leibniz's claim, instead, is that Socrates has changed, but in some less trivial way; he says that every relation requires a "fundament taken from the predicament of Quality or an intrinsic accidental denomination."[25]

4. Reducibility and Dispensability

Now, none of the recent commentators deny that in at least one sense of the term "relation" Leibniz considers relations to be, as he says, "unreal," "merely mental," "merely ideal." It is hard to see how they could. What they do deny is that for him, relational propositions are somehow reducible to nonrelational propositions; and they assert that while seeming to reject relations, he not only countenances but actually cannot get along without so-called relational properties, which, to a nominalist, ought to be every bit as suspect as relations themselves.

[22] LH IV vii C 17r (see sec. 7, p. 224).
[23] LH IV viii 60v (see sec. 7, p. 224).
[24] FC 108. At LH IV vii C 107–8 (Fasz. 2, #106, 112) Leibniz says in a marginal note that when matters are rightly considered, it is seen to be impossible for a (true) proposition about something to become false without some change occurring in that thing.
[25] C 9.

The doubts about reducibility are based in large part on the mistaken assumption (which I formerly shared) that if a proposition P is reducible to a proposition Q, then P and Q must be logically equivalent. We have seen in chapter 10 that in some cases the result of the reduction is indeed equivalent to the proposition being reduced; usually, in such cases, that result is a reflexive proposition. But in other cases there is no equivalence, and it is fairly clear that Leibniz claims only that on any occasion on which the original proposition could be truly asserted there are some direct propositions that (1) are of simple categorical form, (2) together imply the original proposition, and (3) are made true by whatever individuals-cum-accidents are the ground of the truth of the original proposition on that occasion.

Thus, on one occasion of its use,

Socrates is similar to Plato

would be reducible to the pair of propositions

Socrates is wise, Plato is wise,

while on another occasion it would be reducible to

Socrates is a man, Plato is a man,

(supposing, falsely, that "wise" and "man" represent simple attributes). Similarly,

Paris loves Helen

would be reducible to some propositions that have the forms "Paris is X" and "Helen is X," with simple attributes (or "intrinsic accidental denominations") X, and that depict those modifications of singulars that are the ground of its truth. The reflexive sentence

Paris is a lover, and *eo ipso* Helen is a loved one,

which Leibniz offers as a paraphrase of "Paris is Helen's lover," seems to me to point the way to such a reduction. It tells us that those "facts" or individuals-cum-accidents that make "Paris is a lover" true also make "Helen is a loved one" true; presumably, if those facts were more narrowly described, the resulting propositions (unlike the pair "Paris is a lover," "Helen is a loved one") would actually imply that Paris loves Helen. The subjects of those resulting propositions would still be "Paris" and "Helen," but the predicates would be concepts from the category of Quality and, above all, not "extrinsic denominations" like "lover of Helen" or "beloved of Paris."[26]

Russell, Broad, Rescher, and some other commentators seem to have assumed not only that the results of reductions would be logically equivalent

---

[26] I think that Hintikka (1972), 167, is right in doubting that the predicates would have to be simple concepts.

At LH IV vii B 3 26r, Leibniz gives another analysis of "Paris loves Helen": "Paris loves Helen, i.e., Paris thinks that Helen is a source of future delight to him."

to the propositions reduced, but also that these resulting propositions would involve only truth-functional connectives and operators. Broad even takes Leibniz to be saying in effect that for every relation R there are predicates F, G, such that the definition

$$(x)\,(y)\,(xRy \leftrightarrow (Fx\ \&\ Gy))$$

holds.[27] But, as every beginning logic student knows, the pair of formulas

$$(x)\,(Ey)\,xRy \qquad (Ey)\,(x)\,xRy$$

are not equivalent, whereas the pair

$$(x)\,(Ey)\,(Fx\ \&\ Gy) \qquad (Ey)\,(x)\,(Fx\ \&\ Gy)$$

are equivalent, which shows that for some relations R no such definition will be possible.

Russell and Rescher do not go so far as this, but they do join Broad in arguing that Leibniz's doctrine of the reducibility of relations to properties of the things related will get him into logical difficulties, particularly in the case of certain asymmetric relations.[28] Consider, as an example (not theirs), the relational proposition

(1) Theaetetus is taller than Socrates,

and suppose that the ground of the truth of this proposition consists of accidents that would support assertion of the two propositions

(2) Theaetetus is 6 feet tall,
(3) Socrates is 5 feet tall.

It is argued that these two propositions do not by themselves imply (1), but only when supplemented by the further proposition

(4) $6 > 5$,

which is considered relational. If we try to generalize the purported reduction, so as to obtain an equivalence, we come out with something like

(5) $(x)\,(y)\,(x$ is taller than y iff $(Em, n)\,(x$ is m feet tall $\&\ y$ is n feet tall $\&\ m > n))$,

in which the right side still makes reference to an asymmetric relation. So, allegedly, the relation "taller than" between Theaetetus and Socrates has not yet been reduced to properties of the things related, nor has it been shown to be grounded in the accidents of those individuals.

I find this argument unconvincing. Leibniz would indeed say, I think, that (1) above is reducible to the propositions (2) and (3);[29] his examples of

[27] Broad (1975), 39.
[28] Russell (1926), 58–59; Russell (1959), 55; Rescher (1967), 71 ff.
[29] Cf. the text quoted in n. 44 to chap. 10. There the relational proposition is to be "resolved"

reduction show that in reducing a given proposition to sets of propositions of "*A* is *B*" form, it is not necessary that the result of the reduction be logically equivalent to the original. It is only required that it implies it; and (2) and (3) certainly imply (1) (that is, it is absolutely impossible that (2) and (3) be true and (1) be false).[30]

5. Denominations

In the so-called region of ideas, the counterparts of declarative sentences are propositions or thoughts; correspondingly, the counterparts of definite or indefinite descriptions (or abbreviations of such) are *denominations*. Thus, the ontological status of denominations is that of concepts; in short, a denomination is a kind of concept.[31]

Now, suppose that a given individual *I* falls under a given denomination *D*. If one of the descriptions with which *D* is correlated makes a reference, via a name or a quantified variable, to some individual or individuals other than *I*, then *D* is called an "extrinsic denomination" of *I*. Otherwise, *D* is called an "intrinsic denomination" of *I*. Thus, the indefinite description "a man" represents an intrinsic denomination of Adam, while the definite description "the husband of Eve" represents an extrinsic denomination of him. Similarly, "the husband of somebody" represents an extrinsic denomination of Adam, and "a person who is identical with somebody" represents an intrinsic denomination of him (maybe). "This man" and "that man," as short for "the man closer to me," "the man farther from me," both represent extrinsic denominations of any individuals to which they are applicable; and in the same way the inclusion of the words "now," "here," "there," "I," "you," "they," and the like, usually result in the denomination's being extrinsic.[32]

I certainly do not myself believe that these notions are satisfactorily

---

into two propositions about the relata, and the relation is said to "arise" (*oritur*) from these two propositions.

[30] Some who think that (1) does not follow from (2) and (3) may be confusing the *consequence* relation with that of *formal consequence* (with respect to some vaguely intuited notion of logical form).

[31] G II 56 (M 63): The concept of an individual substance contains all its denominations. C 520: The concept of the subject denominated must involve the concept of the predicate, and so whenever the denomination of a thing is changed [i.e., I presume, whenever some denomination no longer applies to the thing], there must be some change in the thing itself.

[32] C 19, 244 (P 13–14); G VII 321 (L 365). *Studia Leibnitiana* VII (1975), 186: "Fake jewel" is an extrinsic denomination of *x* because it applies to *x* in relation to *our opinion* of *x*.

The distinction in question (as also that between "intrinsic" and "extrinsic" relations) is Scholastic. Suarez, in his *Disputationes Metaphysicae*, pp. 1011–1020, discusses the view that all *entia rationis* are extrinsic denominations; the proponents of this view argue that such expressions as "known thing" and, indeed, all universal and generic terms, do not apply to a thing except by virtue of its relations to other things. Suarez also mentions (op. cit., p. 868) that Scotus defined an intrinsic relation as one that arises necessarily when the relata are posited; thus the notion seems similar to or identical with that of "internal relation" and carries all the same cargo of (largely use-mention) confusion.

sharp,[33] but perhaps they are determinate enough to permit us to consider the well-known Leibnizian thesis that "there are no purely extrinsic denominations."[34]

What does Leibniz mean by a "*purely* extrinsic denomination"? I conjecture that he would define it along the following lines: A denomination of an individual I is *purely extrinsic* if and only if it is not reducible to intrinsic denominations of I, where a denomination D, as denoting an individual I, is *reducible* to the denominations D_i, as denoting individuals I_i, respectively, if and only if 'I is a D' follows from the set of propositions 'I_i is a D_i,' and the same accidents are the ground of the applicability of the denominations D_i to the I_i and the denomination D to I.[35]

Thus, in effect I am interpreting denominations in general as properties, and extrinsic denominations, perhaps, as what some recent commentators are calling "relational properties." Leibniz's dictum that "there are no purely extrinsic denominations" becomes, therefore, the assertion that every relational property of an individual is reducible, in his sense of "reducible," to nonrelational properties of that and other individuals; and thus is "grounded" in the accidents of those individuals.[36]

It is occasionally argued[37] that Leibniz could not have held such a view, because it is too plainly inconsistent with some of his pronouncements. In support of the claim that he must retain, if not relations, then at least the so-called relational properties, the following passages are cited:

In my opinion there is nothing in the world of created substances which does not need, for its perfect concept, the concept of every other thing, since each thing involves the others in such a way that, supposing it did not exist or were otherwise, all things in the universe would be different from what they now are.[38]

[33] Particularly as regards the notion of reference via a quantified variable.

[34] A.6.6.227; C 9, 520, 521; G VII 311. LH IV viii 61r (see sec. 7, p. 225). Cf. Grua 387. With this account cf. Mugnai (1978), 13 ff. Kulstad (1980) argues (p. 427) that for Leibniz every predicate is an intrinsic denomination. This amounts to the claim that there are no extrinsic denominations at all, or, at least, none that succeed in denominating anything. But Leibniz's addition of the modifier "purely" is not superfluous here. The concept First man is included in Adam's concept; it is an extrinsic denomination, but not purely extrinsic (as it is reducible to intrinsic denominations under which Adam falls).

Not everyone agreed with Leibniz's usage. Chauvin's *Lexicon* (s.v. *Denomination*, p. 171) reports that "the more careful philosophers point out that, properly speaking, there are *no* intrinsic denominations, since 'to be denominated' is nothing else than to get a name or an appellation from the name of another thing; but every name is extrinsic to the thing named."

[35] Leibniz also speaks of intrinsic and extrinsic denominations of classes, e.g., races of people, and of substances, e.g., gold; A.6.6.400–401.

[36] J. W. Nason, in a recently republished essay (1981), ascribes to McTaggart the insight that "every relation generates relational qualities in the things related"—e.g., A loves B if and only if A is a lover of B. Nason concludes that reducing relations to this sort of qualities "is verbal and not real." He should have concluded that the whole issue of whether all propositions are of subject-predicate form or some are relational is a paradigm case of a pseudo problem based on use-mention confusion.

It is a testimonial to the infinite possibilities of scholarship that one commentator (McCullough 1978, 263), despite all of Leibniz's pronouncements about the ideality of relations and extrinsic denominations, concludes that *all* properties of monads are relational.

[37] E.g., by Hintikka (1972), 165.

[38] G II 226 (L 524–25).

There is no term so absolute or so detached as not to involve relations and the perfect analysis of which does not lead to other things and even to all others.[39]

But Leibniz distinguishes sharply between the concept of one individual *needing* that of another, and the one concept *including* the other.[40] The concept of *A needs* or leads to the concept of *B* if and only if some part of the first expresses the second. The concept of *A* would *include* the concept of *B* if it were impossible for something to fall under the first without falling under the second, or, perhaps, if every component concept of the second were a component of the first. To conceive of Paris's love, the concepts of both Paris and Helen may be necessary, and to conceive of David's paternity or Solomon's filiation will involve the concepts of both David and Solomon. Paris's love and David's paternity are nevertheless individual accidents of Paris and David, respectively, but the narrowest concepts (*infimae species*) under which they fall, like the complete concepts of individuals, will be very complex. They will need, but not include, the concepts of Paris and David. Similarly, the concept of Adam needs, but does not include, that of Eve. Hence I interpret the passages in question to mean only that, ultimately, every individual concept needs every other, and not to be in any way inconsistent with Leibniz's denial of the reality of relations or to imply that any "relational properties" are included in such concepts.

It is, of course, important to remember, in considering these matters, that the states of one monad can express those of another even if none of the properties of either monad are in any sense "relational." We have seen this clearly enough in our numerical model of the possible worlds. Every complete concept expressed every other, and hence the states of the individual monads were the ground of innumerable relational truths although none of the simple properties were presumed to be relational. For example, two of the monad states mentioned there are the ground of the relational truth

With respect to property P_3, monad 5 in the year 10 was like monad 2 (Adam) in the year 20,

and of the extrinsic denomination of Adam as

Monad that in the year 20 had a property that monad 5 had in the year 10.[41]

A paradigm case in which a relation is obviously grounded in the accidents of the relata is the relation of Difference. If *A* is wise and *B* is not wise, *A* is different from *B*. We do not need to postulate that *A* has, in addition to wisdom, a relational property expressed by the predicate "different from *B*" or that *B* must have in addition a relational property expressed by "different from *A*"; *A*'s being wise and *B*'s being not wise *result*, to use the

[39] A.6.6.229.
[40] G II 226 (L 524).
[41] Chap. 4, p. 82.

Leibnizian term, in the difference, which thus is a *mere resultant*. Such relational properties would be extrinsic denominations of A and B, and any such denominations are reducible to intrinsic denominations, which are properties in the category of Quality.

6. Summary

The traditional conception of substance, deriving ultimately from Aristotle's *Categories*, is such that the existence of any individual substance is independent of that of any other individual substance. As we have seen in the preceding chapter, Leibniz, with his doctrine of the "universal interconnection of things," cannot accept this traditional conception[42] completely, but he seems nevertheless to use certain principles that are consequences of it. For instance, he insists that no accident can be in two substances at once. Bearing in mind that for him the accidents of an individual are "in" that individual—that is, have reality only insofar as that individual exists—one sees that if the same accident were in two substances, A and B, it would be impossible for A to exist without B, and for B to exist without A, contrary to the traditionally postulated independence. Another consequence is that there are no purely extrinsic denominations. For if there were a denomination—for example, "husband of Eve"—under which an individual A could fall only if some other individual B existed, then it would be impossible for A to exist unless B existed, contrary again to the traditional independence of individual substances.

But Leibniz denies the claimed independence, and in fact he asserts that the existence of each individual in the "series of things" is impossible without that of every other individual in the series. So, instead of arguing along the lines of the preceding paragraph, he appears to take the "no accident in two subjects" principle as self-evident and to obtain the "no purely extrinsic denomination" principle as a consequence of it plus the assumption that the ground of the applicability of any such denomination would have to be such an accident. The same "no accident in two subjects" principle seems also to be the basis of his more general claim that there are no irreducible relational propositions. Indeed, in view of the fact that any singular proposition 'ARB' is equivalent to 'A is an R of B', the question whether 'ARB' (for example, "Paris loves Helen") is reducible would amount to the question whether the denomination "an R of B' ("a lover of Helen") is a purely extrinsic denomination of the individual falling under A.

In sum, I conjecture that the metaphysics underlying what Leibniz has to say about denominations and relational propositions is as follows. Concepts,

---

[42] Thus, at G II 451 (L 605) he says: "If an *accident* is defined as that which requires [*exigat*] to exist in a substance, I fear that in order to explain its formal reason, we must find a reason why it thus requires. For certainly a substance also often requires [*exigit*] another substance; it would have to be explained what this 'existing in' [*inesse*] is in which the nature of an accident is usually located. My own answer to this would be that it is the modification of something entirely other."

though not a part of reality, come in various types. The main classifications are (1) simple and complex and (2) complete and incomplete. All incomplete concepts are concepts "of" the individual accidents of individual substances; complete concepts are "of" the substances. Extrinsic denominations, with which I am inclined to identify what recent authors are calling "relational properties," are reducible to intrinsic denominations, that is, to those concepts that are themselves simple or are compositions of such simples. Thus, the much-discussed relational properties are twice-removed from the real world of monads. Relational propositions are similarly reducible to nonrelational propositions, the predicate concepts of which are intrinsic denominations of the individual substances that fall under their subject concepts. To say that the relational propositions and extrinsic denominations are mere "resultants" amounts to saying that they are thus reducible: on any given occasion of the use of a relational proposition or extrinsic denomination there will be non-relational propositions or intrinsic denominations, respectively, that imply it and that are made applicable by the same individual accidents of individuals. This sort of reduction deserves the name "reduction" because if a true proposition P, as asserted on a given occasion, is reducible in this sense to a group of propositions Q_i, the latter propositions could equally truly have been asserted that occasion in place of P and would have had all of P's consequences.

How Leibniz would have handled cases in which the relational proposition is not itself asserted but is part of a more complex assertion, or cases in which, in effect, quantified variables are involved, is not clear. Perhaps such a proposition as

Whoever steals Helen becomes an enemy of Menelaus

would first be interpreted metatheoretically, as a reflexive proposition about all propositions of the form "X steals Helen" and "X becomes an enemy of Menelaus," but Leibniz gives us no clues as to how to proceed.

7. Some Additional Texts

Because the texts relevant to this controversial subject are strewn all through the Leibnizian corpus, many of them unpublished, the following gallery may assist the reader in coming to his or her own conclusions about what Leibniz had in mind.

Grua 266: It is no wonder that the number of all numbers, or that of all possibilities, all reflexions or all relations, are not distinctly understood, for they are *ideae imaginariae*, nor does anything correspond to them in reality; so if there is a relation between A and B and this relation is called C, and a new relation between A and C is considered, called D, and so on, ad infinitum, it is clear that we would not say that all these relations are true and real ideas. For those things only are intelligible which can be produced, that is, which have been produced or are being produced.

Grua 547: For if we deny all reality to accidents, as if they were only relations, we get stuck again. For a relation, since it results from a state of things, never comes into being or disappears unless some change is made in its fundament.

C 9: And in the universe, place and position, quantity (number, proportion) are only relations, resulting from other things which per se constitute or terminate change.... Considering the matter more accurately, I saw that they are only mere results, which themselves do not constitute any intrinsic denomination, and thus are only relations which need a fundament from the predicament of quality or an intrinsic accidental denomination.

G VII 284: Axiom. Whatever is extrinsically distinguishable from something else, is distinguishable *per se ipsum*. Thus a sphere can be distinguished from a cube either by consideration [that is, intrinsically] or by operation [that is, extrinsically]: by consideration, since it does not have vertices while the cube has eight; by operation, since if both are put on an inclined plane, the sphere descends by rolling, the cube by sliding.

A.6.6.227: Relations and orders are some kind of *entia rationis*, although they have their fundament in things; for one can say that their reality, like that of eternal truths and of possibilities, comes from the supreme reason.

A.6.6.265: Relations have a reality dependent upon the mind, like truths; but not the mind of men, since there is a supreme intelligence which determines them all for all time.

A.6.6.358: I have already pointed out that all relation involves either comparison or concurrence. Relations of comparison yield identity and diversity, in all respects or in some only, which make things the same or different, like or unlike. Concurrence includes what you call coexistence, that is, connectedness of existence. But when it is said that something exists or possesses real existence, this existence itself is the predicate; that is, the notion of existence is linked with the idea in question, and there is a connection between these two notions. Or the existence of the object of an idea may be conceived as the concurrence of that object with myself. So I believe we can say that there is only comparison and concurrence; but that the comparison which indicates identity or diversity, and the concurrence of the thing with myself, are the relations which deserve to be singled out from all the others.

A.6.6.145: I believe that qualities are just modifications of substances, and that the understanding adds relations. More follows from this than people think.

A.6.6.142: I take relation to be more general than comparison. Relations divide into those of comparison and those of concurrence. The former concern agreement and disagreement (using these terms in a narrower sense), and include resemblance, equality, inequality, and so forth. The latter involve some connection, such as that of cause and effect, whole and parts, position and order, and so forth.

A.6.6.146: ... only a congruity or relation, of which the fundament is in that which is found in each of the singular substances separately.

Grua 539: From these definitions it can be shown that the same subject can have several attributes, even contradictory ones, that is, that it can change. It must be shown, however, that there cannot be several subjects of the same attribute. Therefore it appears that something must be added to the definition, namely, that while it can happen that some attribute, for example, a relation, involves in its essence the existence of several things, it involves the one differently from the way it involves the other; thus paternity involves the two individuals David and Solomon, but differently in the two cases, and it involves David more closely, since from it he is denominated Father.

A.6.6.227: Ph. I believe that there is 'relation only betwixt two things'.

Th. But there are instances of relations between several things at once, as occurs in an ordering or in a genealogical tree, which display the position and the connections of each of their terms or members. Even a figure such as a polygon involves the relation among all its sides.

C 434: The relation of thing to thing is either of comparison or of connection. A relation of comparison is either of similarity or of dissimilarity. To this belongs analogy or the comparison of similar things.

A relation of connection is either of subject and adjunct, or adjunct and adjunct, or subject and subject. However, note that it is possible for an adjunct to be again a subject, as heat is the subject of magnitude.

The connection of subject and adjunct is expressed by *in*, as in "Learning in a man is praiseworthy." There does not exist in Latin an expression for the reciprocal relation of the man to learning, unless you want to say that "A man with learning is praiseworthy." But the word *with* signifies any connection, not specifically the one here concerned.

LH IV viii 60r: Besides substances, or ultimate subjects, there are the modifications of substances, which can be produced and destroyed per se; and further there are relations, which are not produced per se but result when other things are produced, and have reality in our intellect—indeed, they are there when nobody is thinking. For they get that reality from the divine intellect, without which nothing would be true.

Bare relations are not created things, and they are solely in the divine intellect, without the addition of any free choice; and such are whatever result from posited things, as the totality of an aggregate. Hence they are not entities, for every entity which is not God is created; rather, they are truths.

LH IV viii 60v: The foundation of a predicamental relation seems to be an absolute accident or modification . . . as the point does not augment the line, so the relation does not augment the subject.

LH IV vii C 17r (Fasz. 2, #99, 380): Relations are either of comparison or of connection. A relation of comparison arises between A and B from the fact that A occurs in one proposition and B in another proposition; a relation of connection arises from the fact that A and B are in one and the same proposition which cannot be resolved into a relation of comparison. For otherwise a relation of comparison may be a relation of connection, for it is possible for one proposition containing A and B to be formed, namely, A is similar to B. But that is resolved at length into two, of which one concerns B separately, and the other concerns A separately. For example, A is red and B is red, and therefore A is similar (in this respect) to B. By A and B are understood things [*res*] or individuals, not terms. But what shall we say about these: A exists today, and B exists today, or A and B exist simultaneously? Will this be a relation of comparison or of connection? The case is the same with coexistence in the same place.

LH IV vii C 74r (Kauppi 1960, 49 n. 1): A relation is an accident which is in several subjects and is only a result or supervenes with no change made on their part if several things are thought of at once; it is *concogitabilitas*.

LH IV vii C 35: A relation is the *concogitabilitas* of two things.

LH IV vii C 47: A relation is that according to which [*secundum quod*] two things are thought of at once.

LH IV vii C 107v-108r (Fasz. 2, #106, 413): A relation seems difficult to distinguish from other predicates, for any action requires something that is acted upon, magnitude consists in comparison, quality in a disposition to action. Therefore, extrinsic denominations, which arise and disappear without any change in the subject itself but only because a change comes about in something else, appear to pertain properly to Relation; thus a father becomes a father when the child is born, even if he happens to be in India and thus is not affected. Thus my similitude to someone else arises without any change in me, solely by change in the other person. It must be admitted, however, that speaking rigorously there is no extrinsic denomination in reality, since nothing happens anywhere in the universe which does not affect every existent thing in the universe.

G II 226 (L 525): For just as relations result from a plurality of absolute terms, so qualities and actions also result from a plurality of substances. And just as a relation is not compounded from as many relations as there are correlates, so neither are the other modes which depend upon many things resolvable into many modes. It does not follow, then, that a mode which requires many things is not a unity but a composite of many modes.

G II 517 (Broad 1975, 36–37): The relations which connect two monads are not in either the one or the other, but equally in both at once; and therefore, properly speaking, in neither but only in the mind. ... I do not think that you would wish to posit an accident which would inhere simultaneously in two subjects—one which, so as to speak, has one leg in one and another leg in the other.

LH IV viii 61r: In my opinion all extrinsic denominations are founded in intrinsic denominations; and a thing seen really differs from when it is not seen, for the light rays reflected from the thing even produce some change in it.

G VII 321 (L 365): That all existing things are thus interrelated can be proved, moreover, both from the fact that otherwise no one could say whether anything is taking place in existence *now* or not, so that there would be no truth or falsehood for such a proposition, which is absurd; but also because there are no extrinsic denominations, and no one becomes a widower in India by the death of his wife in Europe unless a real change occurs in him. For every predicate is in fact contained in the nature of the subject.

C 520 (S&G 342): It follows also that there are no purely extrinsic denominations, which have absolutely no foundation in the thing itself denominated. For the concept of the subject denominated must involve the concept of the predicate. Hence as often as the denomination of the thing is changed, some variation must occur in the thing itself.

C 8: This consideration is of maximum importance both in philosophy and in theology, namely, that because of the interconnection of things there are no purely extrinsic denominations. And it is not possible for two things to differ solely in place and time, but always some other internal difference must intercede.

A.6.6.401: Suppose for instance that the imaginary 'Australians' swarmed into our latitudes: it is likely that some way would be found of distinguishing them from us; but if not, and if God had forbidden the mingling of these races, and if Jesus Christ had redeemed only our own, then we should have to try to introduce artificial marks to distinguish the races from one another. No doubt there would be an inner difference, but since we should be unable to detect it we should have to rely solely on the extrinsic denomination of birth, and try to associate with it an indelible artificial mark which would provide an intrinsic denomination and a permanent means of telling our race apart from theirs.

C 244 (P 12–13): A pronoun is a noun put in place of another noun, that is, designating another noun, though not explaining any attribute of it, but only an extrinsic denomination relative to the discourse itself. An example is "this," that is, what is shown, what is spoken about, what is present. "That" and "this" differ as the nearer and the farther. "I": that is, the one now speaking. "You": that is, the one now listening to hear what is said.

C 19 (S&G 349): For God perceives in any individual substance from its very concept the truth of all its accidents, calling in nothing extrinsic, since any one at all involves in its way all the others and the whole universe.

C 521 (S&G 342): Every individual substance involves in its perfect concept the whole universe, and all existences in it past, present, and future. For there is nothing on which some true denomination cannot be imposed from some other thing, at least by way of comparison or relation. Moreover there is no purely extrinsic denomination. The same thing is shown by me in many other ways agreeing with one another.

A.6.6.227: Ph. However, a change of relation can occur without there having been any change in the subject: Titius, 'whom I consider today as a father, ceases to be so tomorrow, only by the death of his son, without any alteration in himself.'
     Th. That can very well be said if we are guided by the things of which we are aware; but in metaphysical strictness there is no wholly extrinsic denomination, because of the real connection amongst all things.

G VII 398 (L 702): If space is the property or affection of the substance which is in space, the same space will be sometimes the affection of one body, sometimes of another body, sometimes of an immaterial substance, and sometimes perhaps God himself, when it is void of all other substance, material or immaterial. But this is a strange property or affection, which passes from one subject to another. Thus subjects will leave off their accidents like clothes, that other subjects may put them on. At this rate how shall we distinguish accidents and substances?

LH XXXV xii 74: If there are two true propositions that differ only in that in one *A, B, C* occur where *L, M, N* occur directly in the other, there is said to be the same relation among *A, B, C* as among *L, M, N*, and so forth. Hence, if there is the same relation among *H, A, B, C*, as among *H, L, M, N*, there will be the same relation among *A, B, C*, and *L, M, N*.

A.6.6.110: Every substantial thing, be it soul or body, has its own characteristic relation to every other, and the one must differ from the other by intrinsic denominations.

XIII

Space and Time

Leibniz regards spatial and temporal relations as prime examples illustrating his doctrine of the unreality of relations. And he considers as essentially relational all propositions ascribing spatiotemporal position or movement to bodies. It makes no sense, according to him, to say absolutely 'Body *B* has moved' or 'Body *B* is in such and such a place'; the position, movement, or rest of a body is always relative to that of other bodies that serve as a frame of reference.

1. The Controversy with Newton

Leibniz's views on space and time are set forth most fully in five letters written in the last year of his life to Dr. Samuel Clarke.[1] Clarke, whom Voltaire in his *Lettres sur les Anglais* described as "a veritable reasoning machine," was a noted theological controversialist, author of *A Demonstration of the Being and Attributes of God*.[2] His responses in this correspondence with Leibniz are now known to have been framed by Newton, since they have been found in outline form among Newton's manuscripts.[3] Newton himself, however, did not deign to argue directly with the annoying German who he believed (or pretended to believe) had plagiarized his discovery of the differential and integral calculus. In the exchange, Clarke had the last word, publishing his fifth reply after Leibniz's death; but it is generally conceded

---

[1] G VII 352–440 (L 673–721 which uses Clarke's translation of Leibniz's letters).

[2] Samuel Clarke, *A Demonstration of the Being and Attributes of God, the Obligations of Natural Religion, and the Truth and Certainty of the Christian Revelation, More Particularly in Answer to Mr. Hobbs, Spinoza, and their Followers*, London, 1705–1706; Voltaire, *Lettres sur les Anglais*, VII, in *Oeuvres*, Paris, 1821, Lequien, vol. 26, 33 ff.

[3] Cassirer (1943), 366 n. 1; cf. Parkinson (1969), 79.

that on every important point (as well as on some trivial ones, such as the meaning of the Latin word *sensorium*), Leibniz won the argument.[4]

Leibniz's letters to Clarke contain at least a half dozen formulations along the following lines:

> As for my own opinion, I have said more than once that I hold space to be something merely relative, as time is, that I hold it to be an order of coexistences, as time is an order of successions. For space denotes, in terms of possibility, an order of things which exist at the same time, considered as existing together, without inquiring into their particular manner of existing. And when many things are seen together, one perceives that order of things among themselves.[5]

Essentially the same definitions appear in many other places in the Leibnizian writings. For example, "Space [*spatium*] is an order of coexisting things or an order of existence for things that are simultaneous; time is an order of existence of things that are not simultaneous."[6]

To understand these statements, we need to know, first of all, what "things" Leibniz has in mind here. They cannot very well be the monads, for each monad is said to exist through all time, and hence the question whether it is or is not "simultaneous" with some other monad does not make sense. For the case of time, monad states, as contrasted with the monads themselves, are obvious candidates; and sometimes Leibniz appears to be referring to them. But on such an interpretation space will be an order of monad states, whereas Leibniz frequently says that monads do not exist in space. Other candidates (for which there is also considerable textual support) are bodies or, better, states of bodies or of aggregates of bodies. These, of course, are in the realm of phenomena.

I think that on the whole the best interpretation is that in effect there are two kinds of Leibnizian space-time, one for the real world of monads and another for the phenomenal world of bodies. In the crucial respects the two domains are analogous, and in particular they both exhibit the preestablished harmony, with each element reflecting every other. Hence we may conjecture that often he is not motivated to make clear whether he is talking about states of monads or of bodies. In some passages, however, he assumes that physical events occur simultaneously with mental events, or before or after them, thus implying that they are in a common time frame. And when he says "there are souls everywhere, as there are bodies everywhere,"[7] he seems to have forgotten his warning that to speak of monads as being in space is only "to use certain fictions of our minds when we desire to visualize conveniently what can only be understood."[8]

---

[4] A relatively lucid discussion of the controversy, with further references, can be found in the Cassirer article cited above. Leibniz's comments on *sensorium* are at G VII 365, 374–75, 410.

[5] G VII 363 (L 682).

[6] GM VII 18. It is unclear whether we should translate the definitions as "space is *an* order" or as "space is *the* order," and similarly for time. Cf. G VII 376–77, 395, 400, 415 (L 690, 700, 703, 713–14); GM III 756; G IV 491, 568 (L 583).

[7] G VI 545 (L 590).

[8] G II 450–51 (L 604).

At any rate, when Leibniz says that monads do not exist in space, we can interpret him as meaning at least that they do not exist in the same space with bodies or other phenomena. They do have their "points of view," nevertheless, and the totality of these can constitute a kind of monad space, just as he says the totality of "places" constitutes the space of the physical world.

Another question raised by passages like those quoted above is, what does he mean by "order"? At one place he says, "Order is a relation of a number of things, through which each of them can be distinguished from all of the others."[9] But this isn't much help. In the fifth letter to Clarke, where he is clearly speaking, at least primarily, of the spatial relations of bodies, he explains that by the "order of coexistence" of a group of bodies he means their "situation" or distance from one another. He continues:

When it happens that one of those coexistent things changes its *relation* to a multitude of others, which do not change their relation among themselves, and that another thing, newly come, acquires the same relation to the others, as the former had, we then say it is come into the *place* of the former; and this change we call a *motion* in that body wherein is the immediate cause of the change.[10]

He explains further, however, that it is not strictly possible that the aforementioned "multitude of others" should not change their relations among themselves, for everything is constantly changing and *eo ipso* is changing its relations to everything else.

But if we suppose or feign that among these coexistents there is a sufficient number of them which have undergone no change, then we may say that those which have such a *relation* to those fixed existents, as others had to them before, have now the same *place* which those others had. And that which comprehends all those places is called *space*.[11]

Here the notion of place must not be confused with that of situation. The situation of a body at a given time seems to be considered an individual accident of that body; no two bodies ever have exactly the same situation. But two bodies can successively occupy the same place. Place is a "merely ideal thing," which we conceive because "the mind, not contented with an agreement [between the situation of body A at time t_1 and that of body B at time t_2], looks for an identity, for something that should be truly the same, and conceives it as being extrinsic to the subject: and this is what we here call *place* and *space*."[12]

Leibniz gives us few further particulars about the "orders" of space and

---

[9] LH IV viii 29 102 (see LH 124).

[10] G VII 400 (L 703).

[11] Ibid. It is easy to see why, from the point of view of expressed in this quotation, Leibniz would have trouble with the notion of empty space. The basic concept, for him, was not *place* but *sameness of place*: A, at time t, occupies the same place as B at time t'. One could define, à la Frege, *the place of A at time t* as the set of all B such that for some t', A at time t occupies the same place as B at time t'. But this would not provide a sense for the predicate *is a place*, nor a fortiori, for *is a place that nothing occupies*.

[12] G VII 401 (L 704).

time. As concerns time, the central notion is obviously that of simultaneity. We should like an analysis of that relation as holding between a pair of monad states or of states of bodies. But, so far as I know, the only explication that Leibniz offers is the following:

> If a number of states of things are posited to exist which involve no opposition, they are said to exist *simultaneously*. Thus we deny that what occurred last year and what occurred this year are simultaneous, for they involve incompatible states of the same thing.[13]

Now, as was obvious in our model of the possible worlds, any two monad states of the same monad are incompatible; that is, in every case there will be at least one simple property P such that one state contains P and the other contains the complement of P. So the stated criterion yields the trivial result that no two monad states of the same monad will be simultaneous. Presumably the same holds for the states of bodies.

But what is needed is a criterion for the simultaneity of the states of different things. With this, Leibniz gives us no help. Rescher[14] has suggested that, given two monads A and B, a state s_1 of A is simultaneous with the uniquely determined state s_2 of B that is most similar to s_1; but I have not been able to find any text supporting this. Another suggestion would be to define a pair of states as simultaneous if they "reflect" one another in some special (perhaps, particularly simple) way. This is how we arranged things in the model.

Leibniz does give us a criterion, such as it is, for determining which of two states is prior and which is posterior:

> If one of two states which are not simultaneous involves a reason for the other, the former is held to be *prior*, the latter *posterior*. My earlier state involves a reason for the existence of my later state. And since my prior state, by reason of the connection between all things, involves the prior state of other things as well, it also involves a reason for the later state of these other things and is thus prior to them. *Therefore, whatever exists is either simultaneous with other existences or prior or posterior.*[15]

Since any given state of a monad reflects, expresses, determines, all other states of that monad, future and past,[16] the phrase "involves a reason for," as used in this account of prior and posterior, must mean something other than "express" and its synonyms. I suspect that Leibniz is once again confusing reasons and causes, as was discussed earlier.

---

[13] GM VII 18 (L 666); F 482.

[14] Rescher (1979), 85: Rescher's chapter "Space and Time: Motion and Infinity" is far and away the best available account of this entire subject.

[15] GM VII 18 (L 666). LH IV vii C 71–72 (Fasz. 1, #54, 170–71): "That is *prior by nature* which is more simple to understand . . . of two contradictory singular states. That which is *prior by nature* is called *prior in time*." Cf. LH IV vii B 2, 37 (Fasz. 1, #37, 128–29). G VI 215 (H 238): "The objection is raised that it is necessary *ex hypothesi* for the future to happen, as it is necessary *ex hypothesi* for the past to have happened. But there is this difference, that it is not possible to act on a past state—that would be a contradiction—but it is possible to produce some effect on the future."

[16] G IV 433 (L 308): "There are at all times in the soul of Alexander traces of all that has happened to him and marks of all that will happen to him and even traces of all that happens in the universe . . .."

If, however, in a concession to ordinary usage, Leibniz is allowing the causal relation to hold not only between successive states of one monad or body but also, especially in the case of bodies, between states s_1 and s_2 of different things, then the above-quoted criterion for prior and posterior would apparently justify our defining one state as simultaneous with another, if and only if it is neither prior nor posterior to it. For, as he indicates, his doctrine of the universal interconnections of things implies (1) that if a state s_1 of A involves a reason for (or cause of) a state s_2 of B, then every state simultaneous with s_1 also involves a reason for (or cause of) every succeeding state of that monad. Rescher[17] notes that in *Process and Reality* Whitehead utilized this way of defining "simultaneity." Perhaps Leibniz could follow suit; of course, the quoted criterion for prior and posterior already contains the term "simultaneous," but in a seemingly inessential way.

For space, too, he gives us no specific characterization or analysis of the order to which he refers. We shall see in the next section that he thought he could define a wide variety of geometric figures in terms of a single quaternary distance relation that holds among x, y, z, and u when x is as far from y as z is from u. It would be interesting to have at least some hints of just what sorts of individual accidents he thought x, y, z, and u must have in order to stand in that relation.

When all is said and done, what is most clear about Leibniz's views on space and time is that he considers the spatial and temporal relations of things in the actual world to be completely determined in each case by the individual accidents of the relata. In deciding to create those particular things, God *eo ipso* decided how they would be spatially and temporally related to one another.[18] Other possible worlds have other "spaces" and "times," but there is no distance between the things in the nonactual worlds and those in ours, nor, presumably, is their any simultaneity relation between the different time series.

That other possible worlds have their own times and spaces is stated explicitly in an opuscule written in 1686.[19] Leibniz first notes, in a manner reminiscent of Berkeley and Hume, that we can make judgments about the existence of physical objects only on the basis of what he calls "the congruence" of perceptions.[20] It is by our awareness of the lack of such congruence that we distinguish between our waking and our dreaming experiences. Further, he explains that "to perceive congruently is to perceive in such a way that a reason can be given for everything and everything can be predicted."[21]

---

[17] Rescher (1979), 105 n. 2.

[18] G VII 405 (L 707): "Thus it appears how we are to understand that God created things at what time he pleased, for this depends upon the things which he resolved to create. But things being once resolved upon, together with their relations, there remains no longer any choice about the time and the place, which of themselves having nothing in them real, nothing that can distinguish them, nothing that is at all discernible."

[19] Jag 105–18.

[20] Jag 106.

[21] Jag 108.

Then, repeating that "we call *body* whatever is perceived congruently," he continues:

and [we call] *space* that which makes many perceptions cohere with one another at the same time—for example, I go by one route to a certain place, by another to another, and by a third to a third, and so on; then, assuming the unity of space I calculate how much time it will take me to go from one of the remaining places to another. The idea of space, therefore, is that by which . . . we separate the place and, as it were, the world of dreams from ours. . . . It follows that a perception is different from the cause of its congruence. And it follows further, on the assumption that there are minds having perceptions not congruent with ours, that there can be an infinity of other spaces and other worlds which are such that there is no distance between them and ours. And as the world and space of dreams differ from ours, so too they could have other laws of motion. . . . Whoever asks whether there could be another world and another space is just asking whether there are [better, could be] minds having nothing in common with our own.[22]

In the *New Essays*, too, Leibniz says that space and time concern the possible as well as the actual.[23]

We have seen that although each monad has in some metaphorical sense, "*ut sic dicam*," a "point of view," Leibniz prefers to say that the proper inhabitants of space are bodies, not monads.[24] Further, he holds that space and time are continuous, from which he infers that their parts, which (by the definition of "part") must be homogeneous with them, are also continuous. As continuity implies infinite divisibility, their parts must also be infinitely divisible. Leibniz seems to suppose further that whatever is in space occupies a part of space and must itself be infinitely divisible; of course, only bodies, not monads, satisfy this condition.[25] He does agree, however, that in a derivative sense a monad can have a position in phenomenal space through that of the body it dominates.[26] Perhaps this is the key to reconciling some of the apparent inconsistencies in his account.

As for the dispute with Newton, one of the clearest and most succinct

---

[22] Jag 114.

[23] A.6.6.153–54. G IV 491: Space is an order of possibles as well as of actuals.

[24] Russell (R 122) appears to be correct in asserting that when Leibniz was young, he regarded minds as occupying points in space, while later he denied this. In support, Russell cites G II 372 (where Leibniz himself says as much) and G I 52–54, 61. Typical statements of the later view are G II 444 (L 602): "In themselves monads have no situation [*situs*] with respect to each other, that is, no real order which reaches beyond the order of phenomena," and G II 370: "I do not consider it fitting, however, to think of souls as if they were in points." Cf., on the other hand, G II 339 (L 255): "A simple substance, though it has no extension in itself, yet has position, which is the foundation of extension, since extension is the simultaneous continuous repetition of position." Cf. G II 253 (L 531). Other relevant texts are G II 451 (L 604), G III 357, 623, G VII 366 (L 683), C 15. For contrary evidence, see G VI 107 (H 128), where Leibniz implies that different possible worlds are obtained by filling time and space in different ways, and G VI 545 (L 590).

In sec. 8 of the *Monadology* (G VI 608), which was written in 1714, Leibniz seems again to imply that monads exist in space, or, at least, if monads were indistinguishable, then "when motion occurred, each place would always only receive the equivalent of what it had before, and one state of things would be indistinguishable from another."

[25] Cf. PLR 164 ff.

[26] G II 253 (L 531).

statements of the Leibnizian objection to the notion of absolute space and time is found in the third letter:

> I say, then, that if space was an absolute being, there would something happen for which it would be impossible there should be a sufficient reason. Which is against my axiom. And I can prove it thus. Space is something absolutely uniform and, without the things placed in it, one point of space does not absolutely differ in any respect whatsoever from another point of space. Now from hence it follows (supposing space to be something in itself, besides the order of bodies among themselves) that 'tis impossible there should be a reason why God, preserving the same situations of bodies among themselves, should have placed them in space after one certain particular manner and not otherwise; why everything was not placed the quite contrary way, for instance, by changing east into west. But if space is nothing else but that order or relation, and is nothing at all without bodies but the possibility of placing them, then those two states, the one such as it now is, the other supposed to be the quite contrary way, would not at all differ from one another. Their difference therefore is only to be found in our chimerical supposition of the reality of space in itself. But in truth the one would be exactly the same thing as the other, they being absolutely indiscernible, and consequently there is no room to inquire after a reason of the preference of the one to the other.[27]

Actually, this statement seems to contain two interwoven arguments, one showing that the supposition of absolute space would violate a form of the so-called principle of Sufficient Reason, and the other showing that it would violate the principle of the Identity of Indiscernibles. Since Leibniz thought that the principle of the Identity of Indiscernibles followed from the principle of Sufficient Reason,[28] it is not surprising that he mentions both of them here.

The first argument is as follows. To suppose, with Newton, that space exists independently of the bodies that are located in it is to suppose that at the creation of the physical world God did something without having a sufficient reason; namely, he placed the universe in space in its present orientation rather than in some other that would have conserved all the relative distances and directions of the constituent bodies. The second argument, more interesting to us because it is less theological, is that if Newton's view is correct, at least two distinct states of affairs were possible: one, that the physical universe be situated in space in its present orientation; the other, that it should instead be in the situation that would result from rotating it 180 degrees around a north-south axis while keeping all internal spatial relations the same. But the consequent is false, for the supposedly distinct states of affairs would be indiscernible and hence identical.

Similarly, Leibniz says, if God changed the size of everything in the same proportion, the bodies we use as measures would be equally affected with all the rest, and hence we could not know how much things had been changed. The implication again is that the supposed change is chimerical, and that the two hypothetical states are identical.[29]

Leibniz carries over the same arguments in the case of time. To suppose

---

[27] G VII 364 (L 682). [28] G VII 372 (L 687). [29] GM VII 276.

that God might have created the same world some millions of years sooner, he says, is to suppose that God might do something without a reason, and it is also to suppose that at the Creation God had before him various distinct but indiscernible possibilities.[30] Likewise, the supposition that time could be stretched, with all durations increased proportionally, is a vacuous hypothesis, and it is absolutely impossible for there to be times in which nothing is happening.[31]

In other formulations of the arguments that depend on the Identity of Indiscernibles, Leibniz comes close to employing what is now called the Verifiability criterion of meaning:

I have demonstrated that space is nothing else but an order of the existence of things, observed as existing together; and therefore the fiction of a material finite universe moving forward in an infinite empty space cannot be admitted. It is altogether unreasonable and impracticable. For, besides that there is no real space out of the material universe, such an action would be without any design in it; it would be working without doing anything, *agendo nihil agere. There would happen no change which could be observed by any person whatsoever.*[32]

Again, "Motion does not indeed depend upon being observed; but it does depend upon it being *possible to be observed*. There is no motion when there is no change that can be observed. And when there is no change that can be observed, there is no change at all."[33] And, "There is no mark or difference whereby it would be possible to know that this world was created sooner."[34]

In all these passages Leibniz seems clearly to be implying that any circumstance not observable in principle is a circumstance that cannot exist.[35] This is not quite the Verifiability criterion of meaning, but note that Leibniz, like many other philosophers before and since, often supposes that there are no such things as *impossible concepts* and hence that the linguistic forms purporting to express such concepts are in fact meaningless.

In still other texts, Leibniz asserts flatly that there was no time before the world began, "so that the question why it did not begin sooner is otiose."[36] I suppose that he would not have cared much whether the propositions (better, sentences) in question are classified as nonsense or as necessarily and trivially false.

There is, of course, more to Leibniz's doctrine about space, time, and motion than the mere assertion that they are relative. Like all other relations, these kinds of relation are purely ideal, founded on the accidents of the particulars related.[37] For example, if we can say truly that '*A* is two feet from *B*',

[30] G VII 373 (L 688); cf. G VII 364 (L 682–83), G II 515.
[31] G VII 415 (L 714).
[32] G VII 395–96 (L 700).
[33] G VII 403 (L 705).
[34] G VII 404–5 (L 705–6).
[35] Jag 14 (December 1675): "To be [*esse*] is nothing else than to be capable of being perceived [*percipi posse*]."
[36] Grua 270.
[37] G VII 396 (L 701). For Leibniz, of course, when objects are in relative motion, it makes

then there must be some (nonrelational) qualities of *A* and *B* (and possibly other bodies) that make this proposition true. But unfortunately we are given no details or even clues as to how, in general, propositions about space, time, and motion are to be reduced to propositions ascribing qualities to the bodies concerned. (Paradoxically, Newton, though seemingly defeated in his argument with Leibniz about these matters, with his famous bucket experiment provided an empirical criterion, the shape of the surface of the water in the bucket, for determining whether the water was in motion or at rest—seemingly just the sort of property for which Leibniz was asking.)

Finally, with respect to relativity we must note with Rescher[38] that Leibniz can hardly be regarded as a precursor of Einstein and modern relativity theory, for such notions as that the duration of a time interval between two events depends on the frame of reference in which the events are observed, or that the inertial mass of a body is different for observers whose velocities relative to that body are different, are completely foreign to Leibniz's way of thinking.

2. *Analysis Situs*

Writing in the summer of 1716 to des Bosses, Leibniz adds an interesting comment to his usual point about the relativity of space:

> If someone tries to conceive the whole universe moved in space while the distances of things from one another are preserved, he will not succeed, for absolute space is something imaginary *and there is nothing real in it except the distance of bodies*.[39]

Perhaps this view—that given the distances of things from one another, all other spatial facts about them are *eo ipso* determined—is part of what motivated Leibniz to create his *analysis situs*, a scheme for reducing all geometrical propositions to propositions about the distance of points from one another.

In an early letter to Huygens[40] he indicates his dissatisfaction with the usual algebraization of geometry, and he says that what is needed is a notation that directly expresses *situs* (the situation of points relative to one another) in the way that algebra expresses magnitude. With an appropriately

---

no literal sense to ask which of them are really in motion and which really at rest. But he has a criterion to explain ordinary usage, in which we do ask such questions. G II 473: "That object is said to be moved which has in it the cause of change of position, or from which a reason can be given for its exchange of one position for another—and if it yields a sufficient reason, then it alone is in motion and the others are at rest, while if it yields less than a sufficient reason, all are in motion at once." He clearly has in mind examples such as a ship moving relative to the sea. Cf. G VII 400–401 (L 703–4).

[38] Rescher (1979), 84.

[39] G II 515. This was one of the last letters Leibniz wrote. At the close he apologizes to des Bosses for his shaky handwriting.

[40] GM II 17 ff. (L 248 ff.).

designed calculus utilizing such a notation, it would be possible to prove geometrical theorems simply, directly, and rigorously, instead of via the complications of analytic geometry and the sloppy inferences from figures and the informal explanatory remarks that accompany ordinary geometrical proofs. Leibniz says that he has found such a notation. He tells Huygens that he is apprehensive lest his idea of an analysis situs be lost if he does not have the time to carry it out, and for that reason he is sending along "an essay which seems to me to be important and which will at least suffice to make my plan more plausible and easier to understand." He adds, "If, therefore, some circumstance prevents its perfection at present, this essay will serve as a witness to posterity and give occasion for someone else to carry it through."

In the accompanying essay[41] Leibniz explains the mutual "situation" (*situs*) of a finite set of points in three-dimensional Euclidean space essentially as follows. The points $x_1, x_2, \ldots, x_n$ have the same situation among themselves as the corresponding points $y_1, y_2, \ldots, y_n$ have among themselves—in symbols $x_1, x_2, \ldots, x_n \star y_1, y_2, \ldots, y_n$—if and only if the figure obtained by joining with straight lines all pairs of points x_i, x_j is congruent with the figure obtained by joining all corresponding pairs of points y_i, y_j. For example, the vertices of the triangle ABC in that order have the same situation as the corresponding verticles of the triangle DEF, that is, ABC $\star$ DEF.

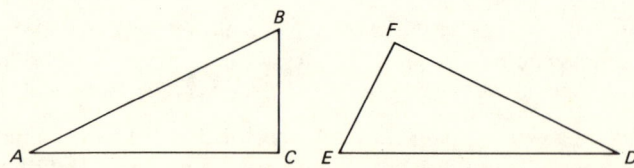

Thus, the mutual situation of a sequence of points is completely determined by their distances from one another. (Leibniz vacillates between saying that under these conditions the situations are the same or saying only that they are congruent.)

Leibniz is aware that he could have defined all these relations in terms of the single quaternary relation $x_1 x_2 \star y_1 y_2$. For example, $x_1 x_2 x_3 \star y_1 y_2 y_3$ holds if and only if $x_1 x_2 \star y_1 y_2$, $x_1 x_3 \star y_1 y_3$, and $x_2 x_3 \star y_2 y_3$ all hold. In other words, sameness of situation generally is definable in terms of sameness of distance.[42]

In terms of this concept of situs he shows how various figures may be simply defined. The locus of all points x satisfying

$$ab \star ax,$$

[41] GM II 20 ff. (L 249 ff.).
[42] GM V 157 (44) and (45), GM VII 264.

where a and b are given distinct points, is the surface of a *sphere* whose center is the point a and whose radius is the line ab. The locus of all points x such that

$$ax \star bx,$$

where again a and b are distinct points, is a *plane* bisecting the line ab and perpendicular to it. For any three non-colinear points $a, b, c,$ the locus of all points x such that

$$ax \star bx \star cx$$

is a *straight line*.[43] And a *circle* is the locus of all points x satisfying

$$abc \star abx,$$

where again a, b, c are three distinct points. The center of this circle will lie on the line ab, and the circle will be in a plane perpendicular to that line.

Using these definitions, Leibniz demonstrates some theorems about intersections.[44] Typical is the following proof of the theorem that the intersection of a plane and a sphere is a circle.[45]

Let the point a be the center of the sphere; let the line ab be perpendicular to, and bisected by, the intersecting plane; and let c be any point on the intersection of the sphere and the plane. Thus this intersection is the locus of all points x such that $ax \star bx$ and $ac \star ax$. Since c lies on the intersection, we have

$$ac \star bc.$$

Now, suppose

(1) $\qquad\qquad\qquad ax \star bx$ and $ac \star ax.$

Then

$$bc \star ax \text{ (since } ac \star bc),$$

and hence

$$bc \star bx.$$

Adding to this the trivial $ab \star ab$, we have the three congruences $ab \star ab$, $bc \star bx$, $ac \star ax$, from which follows, by "composition,"[46]

(2) $\qquad\qquad\qquad abc \star abx.$

Therefore, (1) implies (2), and the locus of all points satisfying (1) is included in the locus of all points satisfying (2), which latter is a circle. Leibniz omits

---

[43] At GM VII 262 he defines 'x lies on the straight line ab' as '$(y)((xa \star ya$ & $xb \star yb) \to x = y)$' or as '$(y)((abx \star aby) \to x = y)$'.

[44] Cf. C 550.

[45] GM II 24–25 (L 253). Leibniz ignores the limiting cases.

[46] See n. 42 above.

the argument to show that, conversely, (2) implies (1), perhaps regarding it as too trivial.

Huygens was not impressed by this. At first he did not even bother to reply, but after another letter from Leibniz he responded with the observation that the theorems Leibniz had managed to prove were not exactly news to geometricians; and in a fatherly tone he advised him to quite wasting his valuable time on such things. Leibniz wrote back that his calculus had two great advantages:

First, with this calculus I can express perfectly the whole nature and definition of the figure (which algebra can never do, for, saying that $x^2 + y^2 = a^2$ is the equation of a circle, it has to explain by a diagram what x and y are, that is, that they are straight lines perpendicular to one another and that one comes from the center of the circle, the other from the circumference). I can do this for all figures, for all of them can be defined in terms of spheres, planes, circles, and straight lines, for which I have already done it. The points of the other curves can always be found by means of straight lines and circles. Also, every machine is only a certain figure, which I can describe with this notation, and I can explain the change of situation it makes, that is, its movement. *Second*, when one can express perfectly the definition of a thing, one can also find all its properties. This notation will serve well for finding beautiful constructions, because the construction and the calculus correspond—though I do not claim that by means of it one can always find the very most beautiful construction. I confess, however, that argumentation is ineffective here, and that it would be more appropriate to *do* these things than to prove them feasible.[47]

Huygens was still not persuaded, and after one more try Leibniz gave up on him. But the *Nachlass* contains numerous other letters in which, over the remainder of his life, Leibniz tried to convince some of his other correspondents (for example, Tschirnhaus, Arnauld, Jakob Bernoulli, Placcius, Remond, and L'Hospital)[48] of the value of his calculus.

He also wrote several short essays about it. In one of these he achieves some additional generality by introducing, along with the relation of congruence or sameness of situation, that of *similarity*.[49] This is defined in terms of the more general notions of *quantity* (or *magnitude*) and *quality*. Leibniz explains that a *quantitative* sameness or difference of two things is one that can only be ascertained by observing them together or by comparing each with some third thing, whereas a *qualitative* sameness or difference can be ascertained by observing them singly.[50] If two things differ at all, they differ in quantity or in quality or in both. Therefore, if two different things do not differ in quality, they differ only in quantity and hence can be distinguished from one another only by observing them together or by comparing them with a third thing.

Leibniz defines things as *similar* if they do not differ in quality, and as

---

[47] GM II 30–31.
[48] References to these letters are given on pp. 614–15 of Freudenthal (1954).
[49] GM V 178–83 (L 254–58).
[50] GM VII 18–19 (L 667).

equal if they do not differ in quantity.[51] Since form (shape) is the only quality of geometric figures, a pair of such figures will have the same shape if and only if they cannot be distinguished without observing them together or comparing them with another figure.[52] Figures are *congruent* if they are similar and equal.[53]

It follows, Leibniz says, that if two geometric figures are similar, every ratio of parts in the one will be the same as the ratio of the corresponding parts in the other; otherwise a distinction would appear even when each was viewed by itself.[54] For instance, a pair of nonsimilar triangles might be singly distinguishable because in one of them, but not in the other, the ratio of the longest to the shortest side is 2:1.

On the basis of these explanations, Leibniz endeavors to establish such very general propositions as that the perimeters, areas, and volumes of similar figures are proportional to the lengths, squares, and cubes of the corresponding sides. He has us consider, for example,[55] a pair of circles, with diameters *AB* and *LM*, respectively, circumscribed by squares *CD* and *NO*.

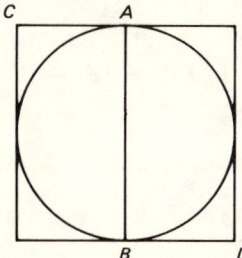 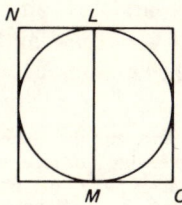

The figures *ABCD* and *LMNO* are similar, he says, because the circles are similar, the squares are similar, and the relation of circle to square is the same in both. Therefore, the area of the circle *AB* is to the area of the square *CD* as the area of the circle *LM* is to that of the square *NO*, or *alternando*, the areas of the circles are to each other as the squares of their diameters. In the same way, he adds, it can be seen that the volume of a sphere is proportional to the cube of its diameter, and that in general the aforementioned proposition holds.

As this rather loose argumentation clearly shows, even in geometry Leibniz considers himself to be talking about the physical world. In his characterization of such fundamental notions as those of similarity and congruence, he speaks of "observing" geometric figures, of "bringing them

[51] Ibid. and GM V 179 (L 254).
[52] GM VII 30; cf. LH IV vii C 71–72 (Fasz. 1, #54, 170), and LH IV vii B 2 57–58 (Fasz. 1, #40, 138).
[53] GM V 179 (mistranslated at L 255).
[54] GM V 181 (L 255).
[55] GM V 182 (L 257).

together," or of "considering them one at a time"—locutions that more properly apply to the realm of phenomena than to abstract mathematical entities or the real world of monads. So his efforts in geometry are relevant enough to his physical and metaphysical views about space, time, and motion; but, though relevant, they are obviously far from successful. Leibniz comes nowhere near establishing that the propositions and concepts of geometry can in general be reduced to the concept of distance, nor does he ever explain how the basic relations of congruence and similarity can be analyzed in terms of qualities of whatever occupies the positions concerned.[56]

Before leaving this topic, we must mention a curious historical fact about the use of the terms *analysis situs, geometria situs*, and *calculus situs*, which Leibniz employed as synonyms. Although for him the situs of a sequence of points is completely determined by the distances between them and is altered if those distances are altered, his admirer Euler, in the famous 1736 paper solving the Königsberg Bridge problem and its generalizations, used the term *geometria situs* in such a sense that the situs remains unchanged under topological deformations. He mistakenly credits Leibniz with originating this concept. Eventually, "analysis situs" became the standard name for what we now call "topology," and it is sometimes not realized that Leibniz used the term in an entirely different sense and hence can hardly be considered the founder of that part of mathematics.[57]

---

[56] C9: . . . distance and the degrees of distance involve the degree of expressing in itself the remote thing, of affecting it or receiving an affection from it.

[57] Freudenthal (1954), 616. On the question of the relation between Leibniz's analysis situs and the *Geometrische Analyse* of H. Grassman, see Echeverria (1979).

XIV

Concluding Thoughts

In this book I have attempted to set forth what appear to me to be the metaphysical foundations of Leibniz's philosophy. As philosophers ourselves, however, we are interested not only in finding out what our illustrious predecessors have thought and said, but also in considering whether, or to what extent, their doctrines are acceptable—that is, not to mince words, whether what they said is *true*. Of course, some historians regard such an attitude as the height of naïveté, even though, from the time of Socrates on, it has clearly been the attitude of nearly all the major philosophers themselves. Historians of this type, who naturally consider themselves more sophisticated than the rest of us, hold that there are no objective criteria in philosophy; each philosopher's outlook is supposed to be determined in large part by the intellectual and social environment; each must be "understood in his own terms"; only our contemporaries can properly be subjected to a scrutiny that makes use of modern distinctions and insights.

It is noteworthy that when these relativists set about considering a philosopher "in his own terms," they usually focus their attention on everything *but* his own terms. Instead, they treat us to speculations on "where he got" this or that idea, and whom he influenced by passing it on. (For ideas are themselves assumed to have a history, to exist through long periods of time; even if you are an Aristotle or a Leibniz or a Newton, you can't just think up an idea on your own; you have to "get" it from somewhere or somebody, or at least you have to put it together from pieces that you get from these outside sources.) This point of view places much emphasis on classifying the philosopher: was he a rationalist or an empiricist? a nominalist or a realist? a monist or a pluralist? In short, where does he stand in the stream of Western thought? Indeed, some people seem to think that is all there is to the history of philosophy.

But no philosopher worth his salt, and least of all, one of the major historical figures, would wish to be treated in this rather insulting, socio-anthropological way, that is, to have his doctrines merely recorded and made ready for museum exhibition as curiosities to amuse the casual visitor. No philosopher wishes his readers, contemporary or future, to be deflected from the philosophical issues by questions as to what circumstances—psychological, social, political, economic—could have led him to say the things he says. In short, no one wishes serious philosophical thoughts to be treated as of "purely historical" interest. We owe it to a Plato, an Aristotle, a Leibniz, or a Hume to subject his ideas to the most careful and penetrating scrutiny of which we are capable, using every distinction and insight, no matter what its source, that has any merit. In my opinion, if he is not worth reading that way, he is not worth reading at all.

It needs to be added, I suppose, that in taking this attitude toward the historical figures in philosophy, we do not propose to deprive ourselves of any information that would aid us in understanding what they meant by what they said. Sometimes attention to the views and usages of their contemporaries or predecessors can be of some help in this regard. But the yield from this sort of information is always miniscule in comparison with what one gains from a really careful, thoughtful, critical reading of the author himself.

Now, as the Germans say, *zur Sache*! The first thing that has to be acknowledged in a critique of Leibniz's metaphysics is that it shares the vulnerability of all metaphysics to the logical positivists' charge of *Nonsense*. If paradigm cases of absolutely unverifiable propositions are wanted—propositions that are not even in principle confirmable—this is the place to look. The Leibnizian hypotheses, one and all, are so constructed as to be completely immune to any possible refutation or disconfirmation. "This is the best of all possible worlds," he says, and if it seems to some of us (or indeed to any number of mortal observers in a finite time) that in at least a few respects things could have been better, that is irrelevant. For only God sees the whole picture, the beauty of which is actually increased by the features that appear evil to a more limited view.

Further, this best of all possible worlds, the real world that lies behind what appears to sensory perception, is composed of (of all things!) *souls*; it is chock-full of souls. How does Leibniz know that? Not by looking around, not by deriving testable consequences from the hypothesis. He knows the existence of his own mind by introspection; as for the others, he concludes their existence from the goodness of God, which requires the existence of everything that is compossible with what exists. Nothing that can be observed would ever be accepted by Leibniz as casting the slightest doubt on this ontology. The same holds for the Identity of Indiscernibles, the principles of Sufficient Reason and of Continuity, and all the rest of the story.

There is a certain irony in this because, as we have seen in chapter 13, Leibniz's own arguments against absolute space and time come very close to invoking a verifiability criterion of meaning. He says that "the fiction of a material finite universe moving forward in an infinite empty space cannot be admitted," "is altogether unreasonable and impracticable," for it would be "acting without acting"; that is, "there would happen no change that could be observed by any observer."[1] In another formulation he concludes that "when there is no change that can be observed, there is no change at all."[2] And in an opuscule of 1675 he goes so far as to assert in general that "to be [*esse*] is nothing else than to be capable of being perceived [*percipi posse*]."[3] But either he never thought of applying this to the fundamentals of his philosophy, or, what I hope is more probable, he is using "perceive" and "observe" in that very abstract sense in which we are perceiving everything that happens in the universe, whether we know it or not.

In any case, it is clear enough that the Leibnizian metaphysics is a network of completely unverifiable principles, and hence that it would qualify, on the basis of the Verifiability criterion, as "devoid of cognitive content."

Now, by "verifiable" most of the positivists mean "verifiable in the given," and it is not exactly news that Leibniz did not regard conscious sensory experience as the only source of knowledge and meaning. So the foregoing comments may seem little more than an elaboration of the obvious fact that he was no empiricist. But what if the sense of "verifiable" and "confirmable" is extended to include other methods of verification and confirmation? After all, there are relatively well-determined methods by which mathematicians establish the truth of their theorems, although such theorems make no predictions about what will be seen, heard, touched, tasted. When a mathematical hypothesis is put forward, everyone considers it open to refutation until it has been proved true. There is an undeniable vagueness about the notion of proof, but, roughly speaking, we can say that to prove a mathematical statement is to deduce it from other statements that are taken as self-evidently true (where which statements are taken as self-evident varies, within reasonable limits, from person to person and from time to time). The "experience" of the positivist, therefore, could be enlarged to include the experience of proof, so that on this basis one could be said to know the meaning of a grammatically well-formed sentence to the extent that one knew what would count for or against its truth.

Even on this relaxed standard, however, it is doubtful that Leibniz's metaphysics will qualify as meaningful. He does purport to deduce his main principles from certain theological propositions that he plainly regards as self-evident. But here, unlike the situation in mathematics, there is little agreement on what is self-evident, and the rigor of Leibniz's metaphysical "proofs" is far below the minimum normally required in mathematical discourse. Still, he did find correspondents with whom he shared enough theological assumptions to permit rational argumentation, and in some instances he was even able to prove a metaphysical point to an opponent's satisfaction.

[1] G VII 395–96 (L 700).   [2] G VII 403 (L 705).   [3] Jag 14.

Consequently, if we relaxed the meaning criterion still further by adding, as parameters, the set of shared assumptions and the group of persons who share them, we could concede at least a certain sort of content to the Leibnizian principles. If S is a well-formed sentence, we might say that any member of a group G of persons who accept a set A of propositions as self-evident knows (for purposes of discourse on that subject within G) the meaning of S to the extent that he knows what experience or proofs (on the basis of A) would count for or against the truth of S.

Something like this is the best I can do for Leibniz, but unfortunately those of us who cannot accept the fundamentals of his theology are left with the conclusion that we have at most a very provisional understanding of what he is up to.

In this book I have not attempted to give a systematic account of Leibniz's theology and its implications, but, as suggested above, an essential feature of his reasoning on matters metaphysical is its dependence on a background of assumed truths about the existence and nature of God. So far as I can see, he has no doubt whatever about the existence of God, whom he considers to be in essence a being that is omniscient, omnipotent, benevolent, and completely rational.

Sometimes the dependence is a fairly straightforward relation of implication between the theological principles (usually supplemented by some other assumptions, tacit or expressed) and the metaphysical thesis in question. This is the best of all possible worlds, because God created it, was completely benevolent, and had the power to do anything possible. There are "other minds"—indeed, the actual world contains every soul that is compossible with yours or mine—because existence is better than nonexistence and God wouldn't have left out any good that could have been included. Time and space are not absolute, because if that were true of either of them, God would have done something, (namely, created the world when or where he did rather than otherwise) without a sufficient reason; but God is not irrational. There must have been a unique best world, for otherwise God would not have created anything, since, again, he does nothing without a reason. The Identity of Indiscernibles must hold, for if there were an individual that was not in principle distinguishable from some other individual, there would be things that God could not know.

In other cases, Leibniz seems content to argue that his doctrines are more consistent with the assumed theology than are those of his opponents. He boasts that his theory of the preestablished harmony ascribes greater wisdom and power to the Creator than does occasionalism or the other rival theories; the artisan who can make a pair of machines that will stay synchronized indefinitely is more skilled than one who has to adjust them on occasion or who, still worse, has to depend on a series of miracles. Leibniz says that his doctrine that each monad mirrors (perceives) the entire universe, though confusedly, while God perceives everything with complete clarity, gives sense to the theological claim that man was created in the image of God. In general, he argues that his universe, running completely smoothly according to deterministic laws that are maximally simple in relation to the immense variety of events, is much more beautiful and more worthy of God than would be the relatively chaotic universe conceived by his opponents.

There is another, more interesting, pattern of Leibnizian argument in which metaphysics and theology are interwoven. In a typical case it goes as follows. He first distinguishes what in effect are two kinds of partial orderings, that is, of such relations as "greater than" among the integers, "faster than" among moving objects, or "taller than" among people. For relations of the first kind a maximum is possible; for those of the second, it is not. The notion of a greatest integer, he says, is self-contradictory, as there is always a greater; and, likewise, it is impossible that there be a fastest-moving point on a rotating disk that has no boundary, since for any point p there will be another point p' that is farther from the center and hence moving faster. On the other hand, the notion of a tallest person is not self-contradictory, even if there happens not to be such an individual.

Now, the partial orderings that are connected with the fundamental properties of God, namely, the relations "know more than," "is more benevolent than," "is more powerful than," "is wiser than," are, all of them, relations of the first type. Some minds know more than others do, and this relation is clearly asymmetric and transitive, but, unlike the cases of "greater than" and "faster than," there is no inconsistency in the notion of a mind that knows the most (which, remarkably, Leibniz seems to equate with a mind that knows everything). Otherwise put, his claim is that it is in principle possible for some mind to know everything that is the case.

From this, he thinks, several important metaphysical principles follow. One such, as we have mentioned above, is the Identity of Indiscernibles. For if there were two individuals that were in principle indiscernible, it would no longer be possible for any mind to know everything true of either of them. Another is the principle of Sufficient Reason, for knowing implies knowing why; if something happened without there being a sufficient reason why it happened, even an all-knowing mind would not *know* that it happened.

In short, if it is possible for some mind to know everything about the world, the world has to be such that this is possible. (Of course, we recognize that this sort of reasoning is of dubious validity, because of the oblique contexts generated by "it is possible that" and "knows that"; but neither Leibniz nor most other philosophers who have argued along these lines seem to pay much attention to that.)

God helps Leibniz with his philosophy in still another way. He allows him to be a nominalist and yet to enjoy some of the theoretical advantages of realism. A nominalist believes that only concrete individuals exist, that there are no such things as abstract entities, whether numbers, geometric figures, sets, properties, concepts, propositions, or whatever. But at the same time he recognizes that there are many true statements that appear to be about such entities. To account for this, he has to find a way of reformulating such statements as statements that more clearly concern individuals only. To use Leibniz's favorite example: statements apparently concerning the abstract entity Heat are to be recast as statements involving, instead, the predicate "is hot," as applied to individual things.

Now, Leibniz's philosophy itself is full of talk about abstract entities, some of which are even original with him. There is the complete individual concept of Alexander, which involves everything that has ever happened, is happening, or will happen to him, and which even bears within it signs of everything that has ever happened, is happening, or will happen in the entire universe. So, as a nominalist, Leibniz has a lot of explaining to do. This is where God comes in. Leibniz emphasizes time and again that all of these individual concepts, and the rest of the "realm of ideas" are "ideas in the mind of God"; and he explains further than an idea, unlike a thought (which is an actual occurrence at a given time), is a disposition to have certain thoughts if certain conditions are met. In other words, to have an idea is to be disposed to think in a certain way.

Hence, the "reality" upon which statements like that about Alexander's concept are grounded is not a shadowy collection of abstract entities "subsisting" somewhere between Being and Nothing, but a particular though very special individual, God, with all his qualities, capacities, and dispositions. I think it clear enough that this is Leibniz's underlying view or attitude, even if he never states it as explicitly as I am doing now. He gives us very few indications of how specific cases are to be analyzed, but there can be little doubt, it seems to me, that in ascribing the aforementioned attributes to the complete individual concept of Alexander, he understands himself to be really talking about the state of God's mind when Alexander was created.

Those of us who have what might be called an "extensional" view of the world are inclined to postulate, behind every dispositional property, some nondispositional properties that are the ground of its application. The paradigmatic lump of sugar that is now soluble in water, even if it will never be dissolved, possesses this dispositional property by virtue of the nondispositional property of having a certain crystalline structure. Presumably God's capacity to create this or that kind of world is similarly based upon his knowledge, motives, and skills. And the same assumption would lead to the conclusion, I suppose, that a disposition of God or of anyone else to think in certain ways must be grounded in the nondispositional qualities of his mind.

It is not difficult to see how the same reductive strategy would apply to other statements about individual concepts and to statements about other abstract entities. In sum, Leibniz's belief in this very special individual, God, permits him to remain a nominalist while using the whole philosophical apparatus of concepts, propositions, ideas, possible worlds.

Doubts about the cognitive content of metaphysics in general, or of Leibniz's metaphysics in particular, need not prevent us from indulging in some meta-metaphysical speculation about the origin of these kinds of doctrine. The first thing that meets the eye is the remarkable similarity of structure, no matter how one is going to account for it, between the sentences of our language, on the one hand, and the elements of the realms postulated by the metaphysicians, on the other. Philosophers have often noticed this close relationship and have sometimes exploited it. It led Carnap, for instance, to his distinction of the material and formal modes, and to such suggestions as that the cognitive content of "pseudo object" sentences (for example, "A rose is a thing and not an event") could be expressed less metaphysically by sentences about language ("The word 'rose' is a noun and not a verb").

The isomorphism is especially striking in Leibniz. For him, the elements of the real world are individual substances with accidents. The simplest thoughts or propositions, correspondingly, consist of a subject concept joined to a predicate concept, and the simplest sentences consist of a subject expression joined by the copula to a predicate expression. (Incidentally, the copula, since it does not correspond to any individual or concept, is often thought to be dispensable, that is, replaceable by mere juxtaposition.) In the Leibnizian scheme, therefore, it appears that our subject-predicate language is admirably well suited to providing pictures of our thoughts, which in turn are pictures of the constituents of the world.

For example, when I tell you truthfully that Socrates is wise, what happens is that I utter a sentence 'A is B', where A and B are words or other linguistic expressions for concepts under which Socrates falls. In the real world there is the old man himself, with certain individual accidents that we may amalgamate under the heading "the wisdom of Socrates." The word "Socrates" expresses a complete individual concept under which our man Socrates and nobody else falls (or even could fall), and the word "wise" expresses a concept under which he also falls, this time by virtue of the aforementioned collection of individual accidents. So, in my assertoric utterance of the sentence "Socrates is wise," I am expressing the thought or proposition that Socrates is wise, that is, that the unique individual in the real world who comes under the concept expressed by the word "Socrates" comes also, by virtue of his accidents, under the concept expressed by "wise."

Of course, in all of this I do not succeed in conveying the full individuality of Socrates' wisdom; in effect I only inform you in that it lies within a certain range. But the range can be narrowed down, if desired, for our language offers a variety of further predicate expressions under which Socrates but not other wise people will fall by virtue of their particular brands of wisdom. We have seen that although the accidents of individuals are individual, things fall under various concepts by virtue of those accidents and hence, to the extent that they come under the same concepts, are thought of as similar. By the principle of the Identity of Indiscernibles we are assured that if individuals A and B are different, there is some concept under which one falls but not the other. In other words, it is in principle possible for a mind (by means of concepts, of course) to tell them apart; they cannot be completely similar.

At least two ways of accounting for this admirable isomorphism of language, thought, and the world present themselves. One is that somewhere back in the most remote history of the Indo-European languages our forebears, in their efforts to deal with the world of individual substances-with-accidents, were led by the structure of this world to develop ways of thought and speech reflecting that structure. For what could be more natural than to represent the existence of a fact or state of affairs by a picture, model, or some other moderate-sized, easily reproducible representation of the fact or state of affairs? On this hypothesis, the origin of the subject-predicate form of our simplest sentences, as well as that of the corresponding thoughts, is due to the fact that the world—"everything that is the case"—is made up of components that are structurally similar to the sentences or thoughts.

The other hypothesis is less flattering to metaphysics. It is that the causal connections are the other way around: what inclines us to say that the real world consists of substances-with-accidents is that our native language is one in which sentences have subjects and predicates. The metaphysician's insight into the most general features of Being qua Being is nothing more than a projection of the structure of language onto the world. The speaker of a language in which sentences do not have the subject-predicate form does not need to be pitied as having to work with a tool that is poorly adapted to its function; there is no reason whatever to suppose that the world fits our language in some way that it does not fit his.

This suggestion, that the basic outlines of traditional metaphysics, to which Leibniz adheres in the main, have no objective validity but are merely projections of certain grammatical features common to Indo-European languages, will, of course, remind the reader of the so-called Sapir-Whorf hypothesis of "linguistic relativity."[4] By considering the grammars of Semitic, Chinese, Tibetan, African, and American Indian languages, all of them fundamentally different from our own, Whorf and Sapir were led to "a new principle of relativity, which holds that all observers are not led by the same physical evidence to the same picture of the universe, unless their linguistic backgrounds are similar, or can in some way be calibrated."[5] The "unless" clause applies, of course, to our modern European languages. Here, Whorf explains, there is an apparent unanimity of major pattern; "but this unanimity exists only because these tongues are all Indo-European dialects cut to the same basic plan, being historically transmitted from what was long ago one speech community; because the modern dialects have long shared in building up a common culture; and because much of this culture, on the more intellectual side, is derived from the linguistic backgrounds of Latin and Greek." But speakers of languages with grammars radically different from ours cannot be expected to share our conceptualization of the world as consisting of objects that "have" properties and "stand in" relations to one another.

The whole matter is undeniably as puzzling and confusing as it is

---

[4] See, in particular, Whorf (1956), especially the last four papers, and Sapir (1949).
[5] Whorf (1956), 214.

apparently important to philosophy.[6] We are admonished that even in our attempts to consider the relation of our language and our world picture, we are still looking at things through our own language, as it were; we are in the position of a person who cannot remove his glasses and yet is trying to find out, by peering intently at the environment, to what extent his visual perception is distorted by the glasses. When Whorf tells us that a certain Nootka sentence, of which the English translation is "He invites people to a feast," has no subject or predicate,[7] we are strongly inclined to think that there *must* be a subject. If, as in Whorf's example, the element of the Nootka sentence that justifies the "he" in the translation is itself a Nootka sentence translatable as "He does" or "He acts," we try to save the subject-predicate structure by taking that element as subject anyway, arguing that there is no reason why one sentence should not be the subject of another. But are we doing anything more than insisting that if "He invites people to a feast" is true, there has got to be a state of affairs with a component that is denoted by "He" and that has an attribute expressed by "invites people to a feast"? So that if the Nootka sentence doesn't appear to have elements representing this component and its attribute, we should conclude only that we haven't analyzed it correctly? After all, we are told by the philosophers of language that the only way you can make a statement is to "identify" an object and then predicate something of it. Yet surely this point of view hints of provinciality and question begging.

It is indeed very difficult to know what moral should be drawn from the thought-provoking linguistic data put forward by Whorf and others. There is surely some philosophical significance, if only of an admonitory nature, in such facts as that the Nootka translations of "The boat is grounded on the beach" and "The boat is manned by picked men" not only fail to have the same grammatical structure but even do not—either of them—contain any unit corresponding to our word "boat,"[8] and in general that grammatically similar sentences of one language frequently have grammatically dissimilar translations in another. Whorf notes also that it is practically impossible to explain the use of basic metaphysical terms like "substance," "attribute," "event," "object," "relation," without what he calls "a circuitous return to the grammatical categories of the definer's language."[9] It must be granted that this is certainly true in Leibniz's metaphysics; in one of his explanations he even assigns grammatical cases to concepts.

Actually, we could cope fairly effectively with talk about substances and accidents, concepts, propositions, attributes, and the rest, if the projection of which I have been speaking were simple enough. But unfortunately the correspondence is far from being one-to-one. Presumably to take account of the obvious fact that even in the same language different sentences or other

---

[6] Cf., e.g., the discussion of it by a group of noted linguists, anthropologists, social psychologists, and philosophers, in Hoijer (1954).

[7] Whorf (1956), 242–43.

[8] Op. cit., p. 235.

[9] Op. cit., p. 215.

expressions may be synonymous, the metaphysics has had to be refined. So it turns out that different sentences of the same language may express the same proposition and different propositions may be made true by the same fact, with the corresponding arrangements, mutatis mutandis, for predicates, attributes, and accidents. What is worse, the different expressions need not even have the same structure. This is important, because it appears that the only practical way to determine the structure of a proposition, attribute, or other concept is to read it off somehow from that of a corresponding linguistic expression.

In earlier chapters we have seen how this problem stands in the way of deciding exactly what Leibniz means by several of his most important principles and doctrines. Thus, the Identity of Indiscernibles, interpreted as asserting that if A and B fall under the same concept (that is, are indiscernible in principle), then A is identical with B, becomes completely trivial if every predicate expresses a concept. For if A is different from B, A will fall under the concept expressed by "different from B', while B will not. As Russell and others have noticed,[10] to give this principle any content, we must somehow limit the predicates that express concepts (properties). The *salva veritate* criterion for identity is heir to the same difficulty, which in this case is aggravated by the fact that Leibniz himself sometimes applies the criterion to an example in which the predicates are of the suspect form.

What Leibniz says about relations, too, is incomprehensible if every predicate stands for a property. The claim that the relation of Loving between Paris and Helen "results" from the properties of Paris and Helen is practically empty if "loves Helen" expresses one of the properties of Paris. When Leibniz asserts that every relation requires "a fundament taken from the predicament of Quality,"[11] he plainly does not intend to accept "loves Helen" as expressing such a fundament; for he adds the explicating clause "or an *in*trinsic accidental denomination." "Lover of Helen," of course, would be an *ex*trinsic denomination of Paris.

It is therefore reasonably clear that, for Leibniz, not every predicate can express a concept (property), or, at least, that there must be a privileged class of predicates, which he never delineates satisfactorily, that represent the kinds of properties or qualities he considers fundamental.

Similar problems arise about the structure of a proposition, since that is not simply determined by the structures of the corresponding sentences. For example, does Leibniz mean to say that 'A is B' and 'AB is an entity' are the same proposition? If so, what are the subject and predicate of that proposition? What is the subject concept of the contingent truth "Every man is liable to sin" (bear in mind that the subject concept is supposed to contain the predicate concept)? Is it "Man" or "Every man," or are there in this case a plurality of subject concepts, those of every existent man?

The fact is, I fear, that in general Leibniz's definiteness of intention did

10   See chap. 7, p. 136.
11   C 9 (PM 134).

not reach to issues of this kind. I am confident that he could have coped with them satisfactorily if they had been brought to his attention, but for this my only support is faith in his genius.

Finally, I should like to include some thoughts about Leibniz's principle of Individuation, which, as I read him, he held from the beginning of his career to the end. The principle is "that every individual is individuated by its whole being." Of course the meaning of this is not crystal clear, but I have said that in the context of Leibniz's other doctrines it allows of at least two plausible interpretations, as asserting (1) that no two individuals have every property in common or (2) that every accident of every individual is unique to that individual.

Either way, Leibniz clearly holds that no attribute A of any individual X is so slight or insignificant that there could not be another individual that resembled X in every respect but A. This does not imply that there could be such another individual in the same possible world with the first. The features of Adam that determine him to be the first man may be only a part of his total makeup; hence, although there could be another person who resembled Adam in all those respects, that person could not exist in the same world with Adam. But it does imply that there could be another such individual, not the same one, in some possible world.

Here, of course, it must be assumed that all the features or properties under consideration are logically independent of one another. Perhaps that was what Leibniz was getting at when he made the complete concept of an individual consist of a kernel of mutually independent "simple" properties, from which all of the other properties would follow. If we do not make the assumption mentioned, we shall have Leibniz holding that some possible individual could resemble Adam in being rational and in being an animal without resembling him in being a rational animal. As we have seen earlier, however, Leibniz gives us no examples of simple properties, let alone a general criterion for deciding whether a given predicate stands for a property of that type.

Leibniz's principle is indeed a principle of Individuation, for to individuate something is to distinguish it from everything else, actual or possible, or to describe it by a description that not only *is not*, but *cannot be* satisfied by anything else. Now, consider some simple property P of, say, Julius Caesar. The question arises: Could Caesar have failed to have the property P? Or, in terms of possible worlds: Is there a possible world of which 'Caesar exists but is not P' is true? An affirmative answer to this is unacceptable, Leibniz would hold, because it would involve our identifying as Caesar a possible person whose properties differ from Caesar's as much as or more than do those of a possible person whom the Individuation principle distinguishes from him. To this argument an opponent might respond, I suppose, that it only shows that Leibniz's superessentialist view is already contained in his Individuation principle—and hence, so much the worse for the latter.

Let us therefore look again at his superessentialism in its own right. Could Caesar have failed to cross the Rubicon? Or, to take the strongest case: Could there have been an individual who failed to cross the Rubicon, but who was just like Caesar in all respects not implying or implied by that difference? (We leave open, for the moment, the question whether such an individual would *be* Caesar.) Leibniz's answer to this would certainly have been affirmative, and I see no reason to disagree. So let us suppose that in another possible world there is a concept of an individual who is just like Caesar except for what is involved in the cited difference. Now, is this individual Caesar?

We are urged not to think of this as a big problem, and not to treat it as though we were looking at a distant world through a telescope, trying to make out whether a certain indistinctly perceived individual in it is really our old friend Julius Caesar. Instead, we are to *stipulate* that it is he. "'Possible worlds' are *stipulated*, not *discovered* by powerful telescopes. There is no reason why we cannot *stipulate* that, in talking about what would have happened to Nixon in a certain counterfactual situation, we are talking about what would have happened to *him*."[12]

But hold on for a moment. If stipulating a possible world requires that the stipulated world be possible, in other words, that the counterfactual conditions involved be satisfiable, it may be harder to do this stipulating than it looks. We are interested in what would have happened if Caesar had not crossed the Rubicon, so we stipulate a possible world in which that is the case. But not just that. We assume that everything else in it is pretty much the same as in this world, except for such facts as are inconsistent with the hypothesis about Caesar's crossing. In particular, I suppose, we assume that the laws of biology and of physical science generally continue to hold.

These kinds of assumptions alone, as Leibniz pointed out, threaten to give us quite a mess, and matters become still more complicated when we assume in addition that, on the whole, the same individuals exist in the posited world as in ours. After all, the event called "Caesar's crossing of the Rubicon" was the result of myriad antecedent conditions and itself led to a limitless ramification of consequences. The great preponderance of these antecedents and consequences are completely beyond our ken, of course, though presumably knowable in principle. If we did know the whole story, however, we might even find that under the given conditions it was impossible that Caesar *not* cross the Rubicon; perhaps for the crossing not to happen there would have had to occur certain antecedent circumstances that in turn would imply, by the relevant physical and biological laws, that it would have to happen, after all.

In short, there is no guarantee whatever that our suppositions or "stipulations" are even consistent. An expressed counterfactual hypothesis will usually seem innocent enough by itself, but when the tacit ceteris paribus assumption is added, the matter becomes very complicated.

---

[12] Kripke (1972), 267.

It is interesting also to consider cases in which the counterfactual hypothesis about an individual involves a relatively drastic departure from that individual's actual state. What if Julius Caesar had had all the most prominent attributes of Moses? If we take these one at a time, the hypothesis again may appear harmless enough. We might think that Caesar could have had a beard, could have spoken Hebrew, and in general could have resembled Moses in each of many other such superficial respects. But when enough of the attributes are taken together, the balance tilts over to the other side, and we are inclined to say that any person with all *those* attributes would be Moses, not Caesar-in-Moses'-clothing.

Thus, the common intuition is that there is some limit, however indefinite, to how different an individual could be and still be the same individual. Small changes are conceivable; very large ones are not. Caesar could have been a bit taller, but he could not have been an inkstand.

In chapter 8 I have tried to construct an argument from Leibnizian principles to the Leibnizian conclusion that in this case the common intuition is incoherent.[13] From his view that there is a "continuum of forms" between anything and anything else—for example, between Caesar and an inkstand—it would seem to follow that if tiny changes are allowed as preserving cross-world identity, we have the unacceptable conclusion that anything could have been anything. Therefore, the notion that the attributes of an individual can be plausibly divided into two nonempty classes, the essential and the accidental, must be given up. Either all are accidental or all are essential; the first alternative is absurd; *ergo*, no individual could have lacked any attribute that he does in fact have.

I believe that Leibniz would have diagnosed his opponents' disagreement with this as resulting from a failure to think through the consequences of our most fundamental assumptions about what it is to be an individual. And the least that can be said for his own point of view, I think, is that it may have a salutary effect in warning us against being too casual in assuming that this or that feature of our world could be changed while everything else is left the same. One might even imagine that an increasing awareness of the dangers of such assumptions, rather than some shift in economic status or some regrettable effect of the aging process, is what explains why people tend to become more and more conservative as they grow older.

At the outset of this book I asked the reader's indulgence because, since in Leibniz's philosophy everything is connected with everything else, there is no "natural" place for the expositor to begin. Alas, for the same reason, there is also no natural place to end.

---

[13] Chap. 8, sec. 2.

Bibliography

Leibniz's immense *Nachlass* of manuscripts and letters is reasonably completely cataloged in Bodemann's two volumes, listed in section 1 below, under the abbreviations LBr and LH. I have cited unpublished manuscripts and letters, as is customary, by reference to these catalogs.

A bibliography of Leibniz's writings published before 1935 is E. Ravier, *Bibliographie des oeuvres de Leibniz* (Paris: Alcan, 1937); corrections and additions to this are given in P. Schrecker, "Une bibliographie de Leibniz" (*Revue philosophique de la France et de l'étranger* 63 [1938]: 324–46).

The huge secondary literature on Leibniz is covered, up to 1980, in Albert Heinekamp's new edition of the *Leibniz Bibliographie: Die Literatur über Leibniz* (Frankfurt: Klostermann, 1984). Also very helpful to scholars is Wilhelm Totok's *Leibniz Bibliographie*, vol. 14 of his *Handbuch der Geschichte der Philosophie* (Frankfurt: Klostermann, 1981, 297–374). This work, organized by topic, lists publications appearing in the years 1920–78.

Finally, an ongoing and complete bibliography of all publications concerning Leibniz, whether texts or secondary literature (including reviews), appears at the end of each volume of *Studia Leibnitiana*. For all these aids, students of Leibniz owe a huge debt of gratitude to the scholars of the Leibniz Archiv of the Niedersächsische Landesbibliothek, Hanover.

The following bibliography lists only items that are cited in this book or that have influenced my view of matters discussed therein. The first section comprises the works cited in the notes by abbreviation, in alphabetical order of the abbreviations; the second section includes general literature.

1. Texts, Translations, and Other Works Cited by Abbreviation

A   Leibniz, Gottfried Wilhelm. *Sämtliche Schriften und Briefe*. Herausgegeben von der Deutschen Akademie der Wissenschaften zu Berlin. Darmstadt, 1923 ff., Leipzig, 1938 ff., Berlin, 1950 ff. Cited by series, volume, and page.

Leibniz, Gottfried Wilhelm. *New Essays on Human Understanding*, Trans. and ed. (with notes) P. Remnant and J. Bennett. Cambridge, 1981. Because the pagination of this translation is identical with that of the Academy text (A.6.6), one citation serves for both.

A1   Leibniz, Gottfried Wilhelm. *Leibniz-Clarke Correspondence*, Trans. H. Alexander, Manchester, 1956.

B&C   Leibniz, Gottfried Wilhelm. *Hauptschriften zur Grundlegung der Philosophie*, Trans. A. Buchenau and E. Cassirer. 2 vols. Leipzig, 1906.

Burk   Burkhardt, Hans. *Logik und Semiotik in der Philosophie von Leibniz*, Munich, 1980.

C   Couturat, Louis, ed. *Opuscules et fragments inédits de Leibniz: Extraits des manuscrits de la bibliothèque royale de Hanovre*, Paris, 1903; Reprinted Hildesheim, 1961.

CL   Couturat, Louis. *La Logique de Leibniz*, Paris, 1901.

D   Leibniz, Gottfried Wilhelm. *Opera omnia, nunc primum collecta* . . . . Ed. Ludovicus Dutens. 6 vols. Geneva, 1768.

E   Leibniz, Gottfried Wilhelm. *Opera philosophica quae extant*. Ed. J. E. Erdmann, Berlin, 1840.

F   Leibniz, Gottfried Wilhelm. *Oeuvres de Leibniz*. Ed. A. Foucher de Careil. 2d ed. 7 vols. Paris, 1867 ff.

Fasz. 1   Leibniz, Gottfried Wilhelm. *Vorausedition zur Reihe VI—Philosophische Schriften—in der Ausgabe der Akademie der DDR*. Faszikel 1. Münster, 1982.

Fasz. 2   Leibniz, Gottfried Wilhelm. *Vorausedition zur Reihe VI—Philosophische Schriften—in der Ausgabe der Akademie der DDR*. Faszikel 2. Münster, 1983.

FC   Foucher de Careil, A., ed. *Nouvelles lettres et opuscules inédits de Leibniz*, Paris, 1857; Reprinted Hildesheim, 1971.

G   Leibniz, Gottfried Wilhelm. *Die philosophischen Schriften*. Ed. C. I. Gerhardt. 7 vols. Berlin, 1857–90; Reprinted Hildesheim, 1965.

GBr   Gerhardt, C. I. *Briefwechsel zwischen Leibniz und Christian Wolff*. Halle, 1860; Reprinted Hildesheim, 1963.

GM   Leibniz, Gottfried Wilhelm. *Mathematische Schriften*. Ed. C. I. Gerhardt. 7 vols. Halle, 1849–63; Reprinted Hildesheim, 1971.

Grua   Leibniz, Gottfried Wilhelm. *Textes inédits d'après de la bibliothèque provinciale de Hanovre*. Ed. G. Grua. 2 vols. Paris, 1948.

H   Leibniz, Gottfried Wilhelm. *Theodicy*. Trans. E. M. Huggard, London, 1952.

Jag   *Leibnitiana: Elementa philosophiae arcanae de summa rerum*. Ed. I. Jagodinski, Kazan, 1913.

Klopp   *Die Werke von Leibniz, erste Reihe: Historisch-politische und staatswissenschaftliche Schriften*. Ed. O. Klopp. 11 vols. Hanover, 1864–84.

L   Leibniz, Gottfried Wilhelm. *Philosophical Papers and Letters*. Trans. L. Loemker. 2d ed. Dordrecht, 1969.

LBr   Bodemann, E. *Der Briefwechsel des Gottfried Wilhelm Leibniz*, Hanover, 1889; Reprinted Hildesheim, 1966.

LH   Bodemann, E. *Die Leibniz-Handschriften der Königlichen öffentlichen Bibliothek zu Hannover*, Hanover, 1895; Reprinted Hildesheim, 1966.

M   Leibniz, Gottfried Wilhelm. *The Leibniz-Arnauld Correspondence*. Trans.
         H. T. Mason, Manchester, 1967.

NE   Leibniz, Gottfried Wilhelm. *New Essays Concerning Human Understand-
         ing*. Trans. A. G. Langley, Chicago, 1916.

P   Leibniz, Gottfried Wilhelm. *Logical Papers: A Selection*. Trans. G. H. R.
         Parkinson, Oxford, 1966.

PLR   Parkinson, G. H. R. *Logic and Reality in Leibniz' Metaphysics*, Oxford,
         1965.

PM   Leibniz, Gottfried Wilhelm. *Philosophical Writings*. Ed. and Trans. M.
         Morris and G. H. R. Parkinson, London, 1973.

R   Russell, B. A. W. *A Critical Exposition of the Philosophy of Leibniz*. Rev.
         ed. London, 1937.

S   Leibniz, Gottfried Wilhelm. *Fragmente zur Logik*. Trans. F. Schmidt,
         Berlin, 1960.

Saame   Leibniz, Gottfried Wilhelm. *Confessio Philosophi*. Critical edition with
         introduction, translation, and commentary by O. Saame, Frankfurt, 1967.

S&G   Smith, T. V., and M. Grene. *From Descartes to Kant: Readings in the Philo-
         sophy of the Renaissance and Enlightenment*, Chicago, 1933.

Schupp   Leibniz, Gottfried Wilhelm. *Generales inquisitiones de analysi notionum et
         veritatum*. Trans. and ed. (with commentary) by F. Schupp, Hamburg,
         1982.

W   Leibniz, Gottfried Wilhelm. *Selections*. Ed. P. Wiener, New York, 1951.

2. General

Abraham, W. "Monads and the Empirical World," *Studia Leibnitiana Supplementa*
    21 (1980): 183–99.
Adams, R. "Leibniz's Theories of Contingency." In *Leibniz: Critical and Interpretive
    Essays*, ed. M. Hooker, Minneapolis, 1982, 243–83.
Agostino, F. d'. "Leibniz on Compossibility and Relational Predicates," *Philosophical
    Quarterly* 26 (1976): 125–38. Reprinted in *Leibniz: Metaphysics and Philo-
    sophy of Science*, ed. R. Woolhouse, Oxford, 1981.
Angelelli, I. "On Identity and Interchangeability in Leibniz and Frege," *Notre Dame
    Journal of Formal Logic* 8 (1967): 94–100.
———. "On Individual Relations," *Studia Leibnitiana Supplementa* 21 (1980):
    200–212.
Arndt, H. "Die Entwicklungsstufen von Leibniz' Begriff einer Lingua Universalis," In
    Das Problem der Sprache, ed. H.-G. Gadamer, Munich, 1967, 71–79.
Baruzi, J. "Trois dialogues mystiques inédits de Leibniz," *Revue de métaphysique et de
    morale* 13 (1905): 1–38.
Black, M. "The Identity of Indiscernibles," *Mind* 61 (1952): 153–64.
Blumenfeld, D. "Leibniz's Modal Proof of the Possibility of God," *Studia Leibnitiana*
    4 (1972): 132–40.
———. "Leibniz's Proof of the Uniqueness of God," *Studia Leibnitiana* 6 (1974):
    262–71.
———. "Is the Best Possible World Possible?" *Philosophical Review* 84 (1975):
    163–77.
———. "On the Compossibility of the Divine Attributes," *Philosophical Studies* 34
    (1978): 91–103.

———. "Leibniz's Theory of the Striving Possibles," *Studia Leibnitiana* 5 (1973): 163–77; Reprinted in *Leibniz: Metaphysics and Philosophy of Science*, ed. R. Woolhouse, Oxford, 1981, 77–88.

———. "Superessentialism, Counterparts, and Freedom," In *Leibniz: Critical and Interpretive Essays*, ed. M. Hooker, Minneapolis, 1982, 103–23.

Boehner, P. *Medieval Logic*. Manchester, 1952.

Broad, C. "Leibniz's Predicate-in-Notion Principle and Some of Its Alleged Consequences," *Theoria* 15 (1949): 54–70.

———. *Leibniz: An Introduction*. London, 1975.

Burch, R. "Plantinga and Leibniz's Lapse." *Analysis* 39 (1979): 24–29.

Burkhardt, H. "Anmerkungen zur Logik, Ontologie, und Semantik bei Leibniz," *Studia Leibnitiana* 6 (1974): 49–68.

———. "Skizze der Leibnizschen Theorie der Prädikation," *Studia Leibnitiana Supplementa* 21 (1980): 83–93.

Cassirer, E. *Leibniz's System*. Marburg, 1902.

———. "Newton and Leibniz," *Philosophical Review* 52 (1943): 336–69.

Castaneda, H.-N. "Leibniz and Plato's *Phaedo* Theory of Relations and Predication," In *Leibniz: Critical and Interpretive Essays*, ed. M. Hooker, Minneapolis, 1982, 124–59.

Chauvin, S. *Lexicon Philosophicum*. 2d ed. Leeuwarden, 1713; Reprinted Düsseldorf, 1967.

Clatterbaugh, K. "Leibniz's Principle of the Identity of Indiscernibles," *Studia Leibnitiana* 3 (1971): 241–52.

———. *Leibniz's Doctrine of Individual Accidents. Studia Leibnitiana*, Sonderheft 4, Wiesbaden, 1973.

Couturat, L. "Sur la métaphysique de Leibniz," *Revue de métaphysique et de morale* 10 (1902): 1–25; English translation by R. Ryan in *Leibniz*, ed. H. Frankfurt, New York, 1972, 19–45.

Curley, E. "Did Leibniz state 'Leibniz' Law'?" *The Philosophical Review* 80 (1971): 497–501.

———. "The Root of Contingency," In *Leibniz*, ed. H. Frankfurt, New York, 1972, 69–97.

———. "Leibniz on Locke on Personal Identity," In *Leibniz: Critical and Interpretive Essays*, ed. M. Hooker, Minneapolis, 1982, 302–26.

Dascal, M. "About the Idea of a Generative Grammar in Leibniz," *Studia Leibnitiana* 3 (1971): 272–90.

———. "Language and Money: A Simile and its Meaning in 17th Century Philosophy of Language," *Studia Leibnitiana* 8 (1976): 187–218.

———. *La Sèmiologie de Leibniz*, Paris, 1978.

———. "Leibniz's Early Views on Definition," *Studia Leibnitiana Supplementa* 21 (1980): 33–50.

De Quincey, T. *Collected Writings*. 14 vols. Ed. D. Masson, London, 1897.

Descartes, R. *Oeuvres*, Ed. C. Adam and P. Tannery. 12 vols. Paris, 1897–1910.

Earman, J. "Perceptions and Relations in the Monadology," *Studia Leibnitiana* 9 (1977): 212–30.

———. "Was Leibniz a Relationist?" *Midwest Studies in Philosophy* 4 (1979): 263–76.

Echeverria, J. "L'Analyse géométrique de Grassmann et ses rapports avec la caractéristique géométrique de Leibniz," *Studia Leibnitiana* 11 (1979): 223–73.

Feldman, F. "Leibniz and Leibniz' Law," *Philosophical Review* 74 (1970): 510–22.

Fisch, M. "Peirce and Leibniz," *Journal of the History of Ideas* 33 (1972): 485–96.

Fischer, K. *Gottfried Wilhelm Leibniz: Leben, Werke und Lehre*. 5th ed. Heidelberg, 1920.

Fitch, G. "Analyticity and Necessity in Leibniz," *Journal of the History of Philosophy* 17 (1979): 29–42.

Frankfurt, H. ed. *Leibniz: A Collection of Critical Essays*. New York, 1972.

Frege, G. *Translations from the Philosophical Writings of Gottlob Frege*. Trans. P. Geach and M. Black. Oxford, 1952.

———. *Nachgelassene Schriften*. Ed. H. Hermes, F. Kambartel, and F. Kaulbach. Hamburg, 1969.

Freudenthal, H. "Leibniz und die Analysis Situs," In *Homenaje a Millas-Vallicrosa*, vol. 1, Barcelona, 1954. Reprinted in *Studia Leibnitiana* 4 (1972): 61–69.

Fried, D. "Necessity and Contingency in Leibniz," *Philosophical Review* 87 (1978): 575–84; Reprinted in *Leibniz: Metaphysics and Philosophy of Science*, ed. R. Woolhouse, Oxford, 1981, 55–63.

Furth, M. "Monadology," *Philosophical Review* 76 (1967): 169–200.

Gerhardt, C. *Die Entdeckung der Differentialrechnung durch Leibniz mit Benutzung der Leibnizischen Manuscripte auf der Königlichen Bibliothek zu Hannover dargestellt*. Halle, 1848.

Gerland, E. *Leibnizens nachgelassene Schriften physicalischen, mechanischen und technischen Inhalts*, Leipzig, 1906.

Graeven, H. "Leibnizens Bildnisse," *Abhandlungen der Königlich Preussischen Akademie der Wissenschaften*, 1916.

Grelling, K. "Identitas indiscernibilium," *Erkenntnis* 6 (1936): 252–59.

Guhrauer, G. *Gottfried Wilhelm Freiherr von Leibniz: Eine Biographie*. 2 vols. Breslau, 1846; Reprinted Hildesheim, 1966.

Hacking, I. "A Leibnizian Theory of Truth," In *Leibniz: Critical and Interpretive Essays*, ed. M. Hooker, Minneapolis, 1982, 185–95.

Hansch, M. *Godofredi Guilielmi Leibnitii Principia Philosophiae More Geometrico Demonstrata*. Frankfurt and Leipzig, 1728.

Hartmann, F., and M. Krüger, "Directiones ad rem medicam pertinentes: Ein Manuskript G. W. Leibnizens aus den Jahren 1671–72 über die Medicin," *Studia Leibnitiana* 8 (1976): 40–68.

Heimsoeth, H. *Die Methode der Erkenntnis bei Descartes und Leibniz*. Giessen, 1912.

Heinekamp, A. "Zu den Begriffen realitas, perfectio und bonum metaphysicum bei Leibniz," *Studia Leibnitiana Supplementa* 1 (1968): 207–22.

———. "Ars characteristica und natürliche Sprache bei Leibniz," *Tijdschrift voor Filosofie* 34 (1972): 446–88.

———. "Natürliche Sprache und Allgemeine Charakteristik bei Leibniz," *Studia Leibnitiana Supplementa* 15 (1975): 257–86.

———. "Über Leibniz's Logik und Metaphysik," *Studia Leibnitiana* 8 (1976): 265–87.

———. "Sprache und Wirklichkeit bei Leibniz," In *History of Linguistic Thought and Contemporary Linguistics*, Berlin, 1976, 518–70.

Hermes, H. "Ideen von Leibniz zur Grundlagenforschung: Die ars inveniendi und die ars iudicandi," *Studia Leibnitiana Supplementa* 3 (1969): 92–102.

Hintikka, J. "Leibniz on Plenitude, Relations, and the 'Reign of Law'," In *Leibniz*, ed. H. Frankfurt, New York, 1972, 155–90.

Hochstetter, E. "Zur Geschichte der Leibniz-Ausgabe," *Zeitschrift für philosophische Forschung* 20 (1966): 651–58.

Hofmann, J. *Leibniz in Paris: 1672–1676*. Cambridge, 1974.

Hoijer, H., ed. *Language and Culture*. Chicago, 1954.

Hooker, M., ed. *Leibniz: Critical and Interpretive Essays*. Minneapolis, 1982.

Huber, K. *Leibniz*. Munich, 1951.

Hunter, G. "Leibniz and the 'Super-Essentialist' Misunderstanding," *Studia Leibnitiana* 13 (1981): 123–32.

Ishiguro, H. *Leibniz's Philosophy of Logic and Language*. London, 1972.

———. "Contingent Truths and Possible Worlds," In *Leibniz: Metaphysics and Philosophy of Science*, ed. R. Woolhouse, Oxford, 1981, 64–76.

———. "Leibniz on Hypothetical Truths," In *Leibniz: Critical and Interpretive Essays*, ed. M. Hooker, Minneapolis, 1982, 90–102.

Jarrett, C. "Leibniz on Truth and Contingency," In *New Essays on Rationalism and Empiricism*, ed. C. Jarrett, J. King-Farlow, and F. J. Pelletier, Ontario, 1978, 83–100.

Jolley, N. "An Unpublished Leibniz MS on Metaphysics," *Studia Leibnitiana* 7 (1975): 161–89.

———. *Leibniz and Locke*. Oxford, 1984.

Joseph, H. *Lectures on the Philosophy of Leibniz*. Oxford, 1949.

Jourdain, P. "The Logical Work of Leibniz," *Monist* 26 (1916): 504–23.

Jungius, J. *Logica Hamburgensis*. Hamburg, 1638. Reprint, ed. R. W. Meyer, Hamburg, 1957.

Kabitz, W. "Leibniz und Berkeley," *Sitzungsberichte der Preussischen Akademie der Wissenschaften*, Phil. Hist. Klasse 24 (1932): 623–36.

Kalinowski, G. "Leibniz et les sémantiques des mondes possibles," In *Leibniz, Werk und Wirkung. Vorträge des IV. Internationalen Leibniz-Kongresses*, Hanover, 1983, 336–43.

Kangro, H. "Joachim Jungius und Gottfried Wilhelm Leibniz," *Studia Leibnitiana* 1 (1969): 175–207.

Kauppi, R. *Über die Leibnizsche Logik. Acta Philosophica Fennica*, Fasc. 12, Helsinki, 1960.

———. "Einige Bemerkungen zum principium identitatis indiscernibilium bei Leibniz," *Zeitschrift für philosophische Forschung* 20 (1966): 497–506.

———. "Substitutivity Salva Veritate in Leibniz and in Modern Logic," *Ratio* 10 (1968): 141–49.

———. "Die Idee der Logik in der Philosophie Leibnizens," *Studia Leibnitiana Supplementa* 3 (1969): 80–91.

Khamara, E. "Eternity and Omniscience," *Philosophical Quarterly* 24 (1974): 204–19.

———. "Leibniz and the Notion of Omnipotence," *Studia Leibnitiana Supplementa* 21 (1980): 240–46.

Khatchadourian, H. "Individuals and the Identity of Indiscernibles," *Studia Leibnitiana Supplementa* 3 (1969): 160–72.

Kneale, W. "Leibniz and the Picture Theory of Language," *Revue internationale de philosophie* 20 (1966): 204–15.

———. "Russell's Paradox and Some Others," *British Journal for the Philosophy of Science* 23 (1971): 321–38.

Kneale, W., and M. Kneale. *The Development of Logic*. Oxford, 1962.

Knecht, H. *La Logique chez Leibniz*. Lausanne, 1981.

Krause, W. "Ossa Leibnitii," *Abhandlungen der Königlich Preussischen Akademie der Wissenschaften*, 1902.

Kripke, S. "Naming and Necessity," In *Semantics of Natural Language*, ed. D. Davidson and G. Harman, 2d ed. Dordrecht, 1972, 253–355.

Krüger, L. *Rationalismus und Entwurf einer universellen Logik bei Leibniz*. Frankfurt, 1969.

———. "Probability in Leibniz: On the Internal Coherence of a Dual Concept," *Archiv für Geschichte der Philosophie* 63 (1981): 47–60.

Kulstad, M. "Leibniz's Conception of Expression," *Studia Leibnitiana* 9 (1977): 55–76.

———. "A Closer Look at Leibniz's Alleged Reduction of Relations," *Southern Journal of Philosophy* 18 (1980): 417–32.

———. "Some Difficulties in Leibniz's Definition of Perception," In *Leibniz: Critical and Interpretive Essays*, ed. M. Hooker, Minneapolis, 1982, 65–78.

Kulstad, M., ed. *Essays on the Philosophy of Leibniz*. Houston, 1977.

Lestienne, H., ed. *G. W. Leibniz: Discourse de métaphysique*. Paris, 1962.

Levin, M. "Leibniz's Concept of Point of View," *Studia Leibnitiana* 12 (1980): 221–28.

Lewis, D. "Counterpart Theory and Quantified Modal Logic," *Journal of Philosophy* 65 (1968): 113–26.

———. *Counterfactuals*. Oxford, 1973.

Lloyd, G. "Leibniz on Possible Individuals and Possible Worlds," *Australasian Journal of Philosophy* 56 (1978): 126–42.

Loemker, L. *Struggle for Synthesis: The 17th Century Background of Leibniz's Synthesis of Order and Freedom*. Cambridge, 1972.

Lorenz, K. "Die Begründung des principium identitatis indiscernibilium," *Studia Leibnitiana Supplementa* 3 (1969): 149–59.

Lotze, H. *Geschichte der Aesthetik in Deutschland*. Munich, 1868.

McCullough, L. "Leibniz and Traditional Philosophy," *Studia Leibnitiana* 10 (1978): 254–70.

Maher, P. "Leibniz and Contingency," *Studia Leibnitiana* 12 (1980): 236–42.

Mahnke, D. *Leibnizens Synthese von Universalmathematik und Individualmetaphysik*. Halle, 1925.

Martin, G. *Leibniz: Logic and Metaphysics*. Trans. K. Northcott and P. Lucas, Manchester, 1964.

———. *Leibniz: Logik und Metaphysik*, 2d ed. Köln, 1967.

Mates, B. "On the Verification of Statements about Ordinary Language," *Inquiry* 1 (1958): 161–72.

———. "Leibniz on Possible Worlds," In *Logic, Methodology and Philosophy of Science*, Vol. 3. Amsterdam, 1968, 507–29; Reprinted in *Leibniz*, ed. H. Frankfurt, New York, 1972, 335–64.

———. "Individuals and Modality in the Philosophy of Leibniz,'" *Studia Leibnitiana* 4 (1972): 81–118.

———. "Leibniz and the *Phaedo*," *Studia Leibnitiana Supplementa* 12 (1973): 135–48.

———. "The Lingua Philosophica," *Studia Leibnitiana*, Sonderheft 8 (1979): 59–66. [1979a].

———. "Identity and Predication in Plato," *Phronesis* 24 (1979): 211–29. [1979b]

———. "Nominalism and Evander's Sword," *Studia Leibnitiana Supplementa* 21 (1980): 213–25.

Mathieu, V. "Die drei Stufen des Weltbegriffes bei Leibniz," *Studia Leibnitiana* 1 (1969): 7–23.

Matson, W. *A History of Philosophy*. New York, 1968.

Meijering, T. "On Contingency in Leibniz's Philosophy," *Studia Leibnitiana* 10 (1978): 22–59.

Mittelstrass, J. "Die Begründung des principium rationis sufficientis," in *Studia Leibnitiana Supplementa* 3 (1969): 136–48.

———. "Monade und Begriff," *Studia Leibnitiana* 2 (1970): 171–200.

———. "Substance and Its Concept in Leibniz," *Studia Leibnitiana*, Sonderheft 9 (1981): 147–58.

Mollat, G. *Mittheilungen aus Leibnizens ungedruckten Schriften*. Leipzig, 1893.

Mondadori, F. "Reference, Essentialism, and Modality in Leibniz's Metaphysics," *Studia Leibnitiana* 5 (1973): 73–101.

———. "Leibniz and the Doctrine of Inter-World Identity," *Studia Leibnitiana* 7 (1975): 22–57.

———. "The Leibnizian 'Circle'," In *Essays on the Philosophy of Leibniz*, ed. M. Kulstad, Houston, 1977, 69–96.

———. "A Harmony of One's Own and Universal Harmony in Leibniz's Paris Writings," *Studia Leibnitiana Supplementa* 18 (1978).

———. "Solipsistic Perception in a World of Monads," In *Leibniz: Critical and Interpretive Essays*, ed. M. Hooker, Minneapolis, 1982, 21–44.

———. "Variations from World to World: 'Future' conditionals," In *Leibniz: Werk und Wirkung*, ed. G. W. Leibniz-Gesellschaft, Hanover, 1983, 500–507.

Mugnai, M. *Astrazione e realtà : Saggio su Leibniz*. Milan, 1976.

———. "Bemerkungen zu Leibniz' Theorie der Relationen," *Studia Leibnitiana* 10 (1978): 2–21.

———. "Intensionale Kontexte und 'Termini Reduplicativi' in der Grammatica Rationalis von Leibniz," *Studia Leibnitiana*, Sonderheft 8 (1979): 82–92.

Müller, K. "Gottfried Wilhelm Leibniz," In *Leibniz: Sein Leben, sein Wirken, seine Welt*, ed. W. Totok and C. Haase. Hanover, 1966, 1–64.

———. "Supra Ossa Leibnitii," In *Der Internationale Leibniz-Kongress in Hannover*, ed. R. Schneider and W. Totok, Hanover, 1968, 43–46.

———. "Bericht über die Arbeiten des Leibniz-Archivs der Niedersächsischen Landesbibliothek Hannover," *Studia Leibnitiana Supplementa* 3 (1969): 217–29.

Müller, K., and G. Krönert. *Leben und Werk von Gottfried Wilhelm Leibniz: Eine Chronik*, Frankfurt, 1969.

Naess, A. "Toward a Theory of Interpretation and Preciseness," In *Semantics and the Philosophy of Language*, ed. L. Linsky, Urbana, Ill. 1952, 248–69.

Nason, J. "Leibniz and the Logical Argument for Individual Substances," *Mind* 51 (1942): 201–22; Reprinted in *Leibniz: Metaphysics and Philosophy of Science*, ed. R. Woolhouse, Oxford, 1981, 11–29.

Nieraad, J. "Standpunktbewusstsein und Weltzusammenhang," *Studia Leibnitiana Supplementa* 8 (1970): 56–60.

Oberschelp, A. "Die Entwicklung der Leibnizschen Idee der unendlich-kleinen Grössen in der modernen Mathematik," *Studia Leibnitiana Supplementa* 2 (1969): 27–33.

O'Briant, W. "Leibniz's Preference for an Intensional Logic," *Notre Dame Journal of Symbolic Logic* 8 (1967): 254–56.

———. *General Investigations Concerning the Analysis of Concepts and Truths*, Trans. with commentary, Athens, Ga., 1968.

———. "Russell on Leibniz," *Studia Leibnitiana* 11 (1979): 159–222.

Ockham, W. *Philosophical Writings*, ed. and trans. P. Boehner, Edinburgh, 1957.

Ohnsorge, W. "Leibniz als Staatsbediensteter," In *Leibniz: Sein Leben, sein Wirken, seine Welt*, ed. W. Totok and C. Haase, Hanover, 1966, 173–95.

Parkinson, G. "Science and Metaphysics in the Leibniz-Newton Controversy," *Studia Leibnitiana Supplementa* 2 (1969): 79–112.

———. *Leibniz on Human Freedom*, Wiesbaden, 1970 (*Studia Leibnitiana*, Sonderheft 2).

———. "The 'Intellectualization of Appearances': Aspects of Leibniz's Theory of Sensation and Thought," in *Leibniz: Critical and Interpretive Essays*, ed. M. Hooker, Minneapolis, 1982, 3–20.

Patzig, G. "Leibniz, Frege und die sogenannte 'lingua characteristica universalis'," *Studia Leibnitiana Supplementa* 3 (1969): 103–9.

Plantinga, A. *The Nature of Necessity*. Oxford, 1974.

Popkin, R. "Leibniz and the French Sceptics," *Revue internationale de philosophie* 20 (1966): 228–48.

Poser, H. *Zur Theorie der Modalbegriffe bei G. W. Leibniz*. Wiesbaden, 1969 (*Studia Leibnitiana Supplementa* 6).

———. "Signum, notio und idea: Elemente der Leibnizschen Zeichentheorie," *Zeitschrift für Semiotik* 1 (1979): 309–24.

———. "Erfahrung und Essenze: Zur Stellung der Kontingenten Wahrheiten in Leibniz' Ars Characteristica," *Studia Leibnitiana*, Sonderheft 8 (1979): 67–81.

Quine, W. V. O. *Mathematical Logic*. Cambridge, 1947.

——. *Word and Object*. New York, 1960.

——. *From a Logical Point of View*, 2d ed. Cambridge, 1961.

Rescher, N. *The Philosophy of Leibniz*. Englewood Cliffs, N.J., 1967.

——. *Leibniz: An Introduction to His Philosophy*, Totowa, N.J., 1979.

——. *Leibniz's Metaphysics of Nature: A Group of Essays*. Dordrecht, 1981.

Riley, P. *The Political Writings of Leibniz*. Cambridge, 1972.

Robinet, A. "Du nouveau sur la correspondance Leibniz-des Bosses," *Studia Leibnitiana* 1 (1969): 83–103.

——. "Leibniz: Lecture du treatise de Berkeley," *Études de philosophie* (1983): 217–23.

Ross, G. "Logic and Ontology in Leibniz," *Studia Leibnitiana*, Sonderheft 9 (1981): 20–26.

——. *Leibniz*. Oxford, 1984.

Royse, J. "Leibniz and the Reducibility of Relations," *Studia Leibnitiana* 12 (1980): 179–204.

Russell, B. "Recent Work on the Philosophy of Leibniz," *Mind* 12 (1903); Reprinted in *Leibniz*, ed. H. Frankfurt, New York, 1972, 365–400.

——. *Our Knowledge of the External World*. London, 1926.

——. *A History of Western Philosophy*. New York, 1945.

——. *Human Knowledge*. New York, 1948.

——. *My Philosophical Development*, London, 1959.

Russell, L. "Possible Worlds in Leibniz," *Studia Leibnitiana* 1 (1969): 161–75.

Sapir, E. *Selected Writings*. Ed. D. Mandelbaum. Berkeley and Los Angeles, 1949.

Scheel, G. "Hannovers politisches, gesellschaftliches und geistiges Leben zur Leibnizzeit," In *Leibniz: Sein Leben, sein Wirken, seine Welt*, ed. W. Totok and C. Haase, Hanover, 1966, 83–116.

Scheffler, S. "Leibniz on Personal Identity and Moral Personality," *Studia Leibnitiana* 8 (1976): 219–40.

Schepers, H. "Zum Problem der kontingenz bei Leibniz: Die beste der möglichen Welten," In *Collegium Philosophicum*, Basel and Stuttgart, 1965, 326–50.

——. "Leibniz' Arbeiten zur Reformation der Kategorien," *Zeitschrift für philosophische Forschung* 20 (1966): 539–67.

——. "Begriffsanalyse und Kategorialsynthese von Logik und Metaphysik bei Leibniz," *Studia Leibnitiana Supplementa* 3 (1969): 34–49.

——. "Leibniz' Disputationen 'De Conditionibus': Ansätze zu einer juristischen Aussagenlogik," *Studia Leibnitiana Supplementa* 15 (1975): 1–17.

Schmidt, F. "Leibnizens rationale Grammatik," *Zeitschrift für philosophische Forschung* 9 (1955): 657–63.

——. "Die Entwicklung der Leibnizschen Logik," *Kantstudien* 52 (1960–61): 43–58.

——. "Die symbolisierten Elemente der Leibnizschen Logik," *Zeitschrift für philosophische Forschung* 20 (1966): 595–605.

——. "Zeichen, Wort und Wahrheit bei Leibniz," *Studia Leibnitiana Supplementa* 2 (1969): 190–208.

——. "Logik und Metaphysik bei Leibniz," *Studia Leibnitiana* 3 (1971): 85–98.

——. "Ganzes und Teil bei Leibniz," *Archiv für Geschichte der Philosophie* 53 (1971): 267–78.

Schneider, M. *Analysis und Synthese bei Leibniz*. Bonn, 1974.

——. "Das Problem der disparaten Sätze in Leibniz' Logik," *Studia Leibnitiana Supplementa* 21 (1980): 23–32.

Schneiders, W. "Deus subjectum: Zur Entwicklung der Leibnizschen Metaphysik," *Studia Leibnitiana Supplementa* 18 (1978): 21–31.

Scholz, H. "Leibniz," In *Mathesis Universalis*, Basel, 1961, 128–51.

Schopenhauer, A. *Die Welt als Wille und Vorstellung*, in A. Schopenhauer, *Sämtliche Werke*, 2d ed. Wiesbaden: Brockhaus, 1949, voł. 3.

Schröter, K. "Bericht über den Stand der Leibniz-Ausgabe der Deutschen Akademie der Wissenschaften zu Berlin," *Studia Leibnitiana Supplementa* 3 (1969): 217–29.

Schulz, D. "Die Funktionen analytischer Sätze in Leibniz' frühen Entwürfen zur Charakteristik," *Studia Leibnitiana* 2 (1970): 127–34.

Seager, W. "The Principle of Continuity and the Evaluation of Theories," *Dialogue* 20 (1981): 485–95.

Sinisi, V. "Leibniz's Law and the Antinomy of the Liar," *Philosophy and Phenomenological Research* 30 (1969): 279–89.

Sleigh, R. "Leibniz on Individual Substances," *Journal of Philosophy* 72 (1975): 685–87.

———. "Truth and Sufficient Reason in the Philosophy of Leibniz," In *Leibniz: Critical and Interpretive Essays*, ed. M. Hooker, Minneapolis, 1982, 209–42.

———. "Leibniz on the Two Great Principles of All Our Reasonings," *Midwest Studies in Philosophy* 8 (1983): 193–216.

Stein, L. *Leibniz in seinem Verhältnis zu Spinoza*. Berlin, 1888.

Steudel, J. "Leibniz fordert eine neue Medizin," *Studia Leibnitiana Supplementa* 2 (1969): 255–74.

Totok, W., and C. Haase, eds. *Leibniz: Sein Leben, sein Wirken, seine Welt*. Hanover, 1966.

Trendelenburg, A. "Leibniz de fato." In A. Trendelenburg, *Historische Beiträge zur Philosophie*, Vol. 2. Berlin, 1855, 188–91.

———. "Über Leibnizens Entwurf einer allgemeinen Charakteristik," In A. Trendelenburg, *Historische Beiträge zur Philosophie*, Vol. 3. Berlin, 1867, 1–47.

———. "Über das Element der Definition in Leibnizens Philosophie." In A. Trendelenburg, *Historische Beiträge zur Philosophie*, Vol. 3. Berlin, 1867, 48–62.

Utermöhlen, G. "Leibniz' Antwort auf Christian Thomasius' Frage 'Quid sit substantia?'," *Studia Leibnitiana* 11 (1979): 82–91.

———. "Leibniz im Briefwechsel mit Frauen," *Niedersächsisches Jahrbuch für Landesgeschichte* 52 (1980): 219–44.

Vendler, Z. "On the Possibility of Possible Worlds," *Canadian Journal of Philosophy* 5 (1975): 57–72.

Verburg, P. "The Idea of Linguistic System in Leibniz," In *History of Linguistic Thought and Contemporary Linguistics*, Berlin, 1976, 593–615.

Vlastos, G. "Reasons and Causes in the *Phaedo*," *The Philosophical Review* 78 (1969): 291–325; Reprinted with revisions in *Plato: A Collection of Critical Essays*, ed. G. Vlastos, Vol. 1, Notre Dame, Ind., 1978.

Weyl, H. "The Mathematical Way of Thinking." In *The World of Mathematics*, ed. J. R. Newman, New York, 1956, 1832–1849.

Whorf, B. *Language, Thought, and Reality*. Ed. J. B. Carroll. Cambridge, Mass., 1956.

Wiedeburg, P. "'Je ne vous dis rien sur les projets d'une Guerre Sainte, mais vous saurez qu'elles ont cessé d'estre à la mode depuis Saint Louis': Ein Beitrag zur Wertung des Consilium Aegyptiacum Leibnizens," *Studia Leibnitiana Supplementa* 14 (1969): 207–24.

Wilson, M. "On Leibniz's Explication of 'Necessary Truth'," *Studia Leibnitiana Supplementa* 3 (1969): 50–63.

———. "Possibility, Propensity, and Chance: Some Doubts about the Hacking Thesis," *Journal of Philosophy* 68 (1971): 610–17.

———. "Possible Gods," *Review of Metaphysics* 32 (1979): 717–33.

Windelband, W. *Geschichte der Philosophie*. Tübingen, 1935.
Wittgenstein, L. *Tractatus Logico-Philosophicus*. London, 1922.
Woolhouse, R., ed. *Leibniz: Metaphysics and Philosophy of Science*, Oxford, 1981.
Yost, R. *Leibniz and Philosophical Analysis*, Berkeley and Los Angeles, 1954.

Index